'Tremendous. Until the publicat   ...,...... .... vvuu, there
hadn't been an English language history of the GDR with which
to colour in that vanished country's past' Peter Hoskins, *Prospect*

'A masterpiece . . . Well-researched, well-written and profoundly
insightful, it explodes many of the lazy Western cliches
about East Germany' Andrew Roberts

'A gripping and nuanced history of the GDR from its beginnings
as a separate German socialist state against the wishes of Stalin
to its final rapprochement with its Western other against those
of Gorbachev. *Beyond the Wall* is a unique fresco of everyday
reality in East Germany. Elegantly moving between diplomatic
history, political economy and cultural analysis, it is an
essential read to understand not only the life and death
of the GDR but also the parts of it that still survive in
the emotions of its former citizens' Lea Ypi

'Superb, totally fascinating and compelling, Katja Hoyer's first
full history of East Germany's rise and fall is a work of revelatory
original research – and a gripping read with a brilliant
cast of characters' Simon Sebag Montefiore

'A fast-paced, vivid and engaging book. *Beyond the Wall* does
much to combat amnesia and Cold War prejudice, and
to normalize the GDR and the people who lived there'
Karen Leeder, *TLS*

'Enthralling, fascinating and very readable . . . An extraordinary
book' Peter Hitchens, *Mail on Sunday*

'What makes this meticulous book essential reading is not so
much its sense of what East Germans lost, as what we never
had. A history of the GDR that adds stability, contentment
and women's rights to the familiar picture of authoritarianism'
Stuart Jeffries, *Guardian*

'Absolutely fascinating' Andrew Marr, LBC

'Having begun her life behind the wall, Hoyer tells the story of the GDR with emotional intensity; but also with the detachment and balance of a professional historian who is determined to portray both the good and bad. And a very interesting story it is, too' Oliver Letwin, *The Tablet*

'A bold, deft history of the forty-one years of the German Democratic Republic. Hoyer is a historian with skin in the game' John Kampfner, *Literary Review*

'*Beyond the Wall* breaks away from Cold War stereotypes to depict "normal life" in the German Democratic Republic . . . unexpectedly resonant' Thomas Wieder, *Le Monde*

'Humane, deeply historically informed and compelling' Allan Mallinson, *Country Life*

'Hoyer tells the country's human story with a compelling eye for detail in a book that deftly unpicks the complexities and contradictions of the so-called People's State' Jeremy Cliffe, *New Statesman*

'There's been a swell of books about the former German Democratic Republic this year, but this chunky tome might be the best. Historian Hoyer blends large-scale political insights with engaging personal stories' *Independent*, Summer Books

'Katja Hoyer's monumentally successful history of the GDR is a call to restore the history of East Germany to the mainstream of German modern history . . . a feast of vignettes and anecdotes, it is a genuine pleasure to read' Roger Moorhouse, *Aspects of History*

'Through interviews and personal experience, Katja Hoyer brings a new understanding to a country that has now vanished . . . A fresh look at what life was like for average people in East Germany . . . intriguing and surprising' ABC Radio National

'Utterly brilliant. This gripping account of East Germany sheds new light on what for many of us remains an opaque chapter of history. Authoritative, lively and profoundly human, it is essential reading for anyone seeking to understand post-WW2 Europe' Julia Boyd

'A beyond-brilliant new picture of the rise and fall of the East German state. Katja Hoyer gives us not only pin-sharp historical analysis, but an up-close and personal view of both key characters and ordinary citizens whose lives charted some of the darkest hours of the Cold War. If you thought you knew the history of East Germany, think again' Julie Etchingham

'A fantastic, sparkling book, filled with insights not only about East Germany but about the Cold War, Europe and the forging of the 20th and 21st centuries' Peter Frankopan

'The joke has it that the duty of the last East German to escape from the country was to turn off the lights. In *Beyond the Wall* Katja Hoyer turns the light back on and gives us the best kind of history: frank, vivid, nuanced and filled with interesting people' Ivan Krastev

'A refreshing and eye-opening book on a country that is routinely reduced to cartoonish cliché. *Beyond the Wall* is a tribute to the ordinary East Germans who built themselves a society that – for a time – worked for them, a society carved out of a state founded in the horrors of Nazism and Stalinism' Owen Hatherley

'Katja Hoyer is becoming the authoritative voice in the English-speaking world for all things German' Dan Snow

'Katja Hoyer brilliantly shows that the history of East Germany was a significant chapter of German history, not just a footnote to it or a copy of the Soviet Union. To understand Germany today we have to grapple with the history and legacy of its all but dismissed East' Serhii Plokhy

ABOUT THE AUTHOR

Katja Hoyer is a German-British historian, journalist and the author of the widely acclaimed *Blood and Iron*. A visiting Research Fellow at King's College London and a Fellow of the Royal Historical Society, she is a columnist for the *Washington Post* and hosts the podcast *The New Germany* together with Oliver Moody. She was born in East Germany and is now based in the UK.

Beyond the Wall:

East Germany, 1949–1990

KATJA HOYER

PENGUIN BOOKS

PENGUIN BOOKS

UK | USA | Canada | Ireland | Australia
India | New Zealand | South Africa

Penguin Books is part of the Penguin Random House group of companies
whose addresses can be found at global.penguinrandomhouse.com.

First published by Allen Lane 2023
Published in Penguin Books 2024
003

Typeset by Jouve (UK) Milton Keynes
Printed and bound in Great Britain by Clays Ltd, Elcograf S.p.A.

A CIP catalogue record for this book is available from the British Library

The authorized representative in the EEA is Penguin Random House Ireland,
Morrison Chambers, 32 Nassau Street, Dublin D02 YH68

ISBN: 978-0-141-99934-0

In memory of Harry, the most faithful of companions, the most trusted of confidants, and always a calm refuge in hours of storm.

Contents

List of Illustrations

Free German Youth, 1973: Courtesy of ddrbildarchiv.de.

X World Festival of Youth and Students, 1973, East Berlin: Courtesy of Alamy.

Beginning of the summer holidays, Berlin 1972: Courtesy of ddrbildarchiv.de / Klaus Morgenstern.

Toys, 1982: Courtesy of ddrbildarchiv.de / Manfred Uhlenhut.

Palace of the Republic, 1976: Courtesy of akg-images / Straube.

Dresden's Socialist Reinvention, 1979: Courtesy of BEBUG mbH / Bild und Heimat, Berlin.

Kiosk, East Berlin, 1971: Courtesy of ddrbildarchiv.de / Klaus Fischer.

A man shovelling coal from the street to his basement in Halle, February 1990: Courtesy of IMAGO / Rainer Unkel.

Pioneers celebrating 25 years of Berlin Wall: Courtesy of Alamy.

Boy washing car, 1975: Courtesy of ddrbildarchiv.de / Manfred Uhlenhut.

Contract Worker from Mozambique, 1984: Courtesy of Das Bundesarchiv.

Couple in the Oderbruch region: Courtesy of OSTKREUZ / Harald Hauswald.

Cold War Europe in 1989

	Warsaw Pact
	Nato
	Non-aligned nations

FINLAND

Helsinki

SWEDEN

•Stockholm

ESTONIA

Baltic Sea

LATVIA

•Moscow

Copenhagen

LITHUANIA

SOVIET UNION

•Berlin

ERMANY

POLAND

Warsaw

•Prague

CZECHOSLOVAKIA

UKRAINE

TRIA

•Vienna

•Budapest

HUNGARY

Zagreb

ROMANIA

Black Sea

YUGOSLAVIA

Belgrade •

Bucharest •

BULGARIA

•Sofia

•Ankara

Tirana •

ALBANIA

T U R K E Y

L Y

GREECE

•Athens

| 0 | | 300 miles |
| 0 | | 500 km |

Federal Republic of Germany

German Democratic Republic

Baltic Sea

N

North Sea

Schleswig-Holstein

Hamburg

Mecklenburg

Bremen

Lower Saxony

Berlin

Brandenburg

Saxony-Anhalt

North Rhine-Westphalia

Hesse

Thuringia

Saxony

Rhineland-Palatinate

Saarland

Baden-Württemberg

Bavaria

Divided Germany split into Länder.

The GDR's division into five Länder was dissolved in 1952, but they will be used as place names throughout the book for clarity and consistency.

0   50 miles

0   100 km

Denmark

Baltic Sea

N

Rostock

Neubrandenburg

Schwerin

Federal
Republic of
Germany

Poland

West
Berlin

Berlin

Potsdam

Frankfurt

Magdeburg

Cottbus

Halle

Leipzig

Dresden

Erfurt

Gera

Karl-Marx-Stadt

Suhl

Czechoslovakia

0   40 miles

0   50 km

The GDR administrative districts from, 1952–90

The GDR

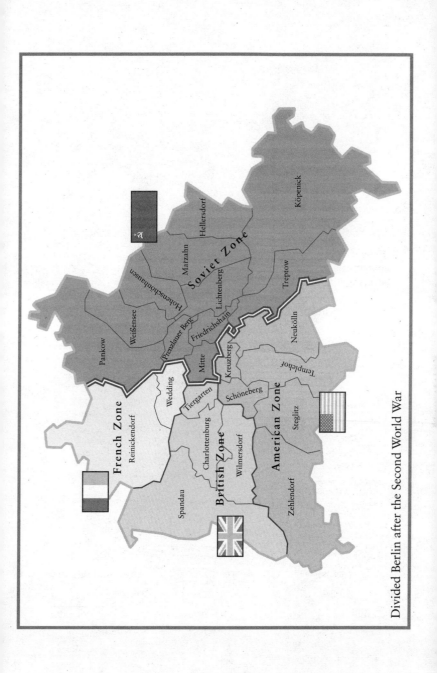

Divided Berlin after the Second World War

Preface

Halle, Saxony-Anhalt, 3 October 2021. A sixty-seven-year-old woman in a cream-coloured blazer and black trousers took to the stage. Perhaps the most powerful woman on earth, her image was instantly recognizable. Her trouser suits, blonde bob and matter-of-fact demeanour had become iconic. As she took her place between the flags of Germany and the European Union and adjusted the microphones on the lectern, many in the audience felt they were witnessing a historic moment. After sixteen years at the helm of Europe's largest democracy, the outgoing German Chancellor Angela Merkel had come to speak about national unity.

3 October is the closest thing Germany has to a national day. Known as German Unity Day, it marks the anniversary of the country's reunification in 1990 after forty-one years during which two separate German states existed: the Federal Republic of Germany (FRG) in the west and the German Democratic Republic (GDR) in the east. Thirty-one years to the day had passed since then, not enough time to bury the era of German division in the depths of history. On the contrary. Reunification, the outgoing Chancellor began her speech, was an event that 'most of us have experienced consciously and that has changed our lives'.[1]

1990 was a watershed moment not just for the nation but for Merkel personally. It marked the beginning of her steep rise to the pinnacle of German politics. In 1954, when she was only three months old, her father had moved the family from West to East Germany. Merkel would spend the first thirty-five years of her life east of the inner-German divide. They saw her grow from pastor's daughter to confident scientist and shaped her at least as much as the three decades since 1990.

Angela Merkel's long career at the top of German politics stands testament to the many successes of reunification. When the East German state that had been her home suddenly disintegrated and became part of the West German system it had opposed for so long, Merkel hit the ground running without looking back. Or at least without doing so in public. She understood that on paper her East German background was a political asset in a country that wanted to show it was now a united nation. But in reality that was true only so long as it remained her background rather than her identity. The establishment didn't want a constant reminder that the wall in East and West German minds would take longer to tear down than the physical one.

On the rare occasions when Merkel revealed details of her life in the GDR, this was met with hostility in the circles of power that are still largely dominated by former West Germans. When she said in 1991 that her doctoral dissertation in 1978 had required her to write an essay entitled 'What is the socialist way of life?' journalists moved heaven and earth to find the piece. 'Who knows what scandal they hoped to uncover,' Merkel later mused.[2] Such political work was part and parcel of university life in the GDR and seen as a chore by many, including Merkel herself, who received her only bad mark for this essay in an otherwise stellar set of academic achievements. As with many other aspects of life in the GDR, this episode too showed that 'it is obviously incredibly difficult to understand and make comprehensible how we lived back then', as Merkel remarked shortly before she became Chancellor in 2005.[3]

While Merkel had resigned herself to keeping a tight lid on her East German past, it remained a part of her she could not relinquish. In October 2021, with her political retirement in sight, she used the opportunity of her last German Unity Day in office to take issue with the way East German life stories like hers have been treated as skeletons in the national cupboard. A publication by the Konrad-Adenauer-Stiftung, a foundation close to Merkel's own political party, had praised her political adaptability in light of what they called the 'ballast of her East German biography'.[4] This unfortunate phrase clearly bothered the Chancellor. 'Ballast?' she bristled at this description of her early life. 'An unnecessary burden that can just be shrugged off?'[5] In this unusually personal public moment, she emphasized, she was not speaking as Chancellor but as 'a citizen from the East, as one of more than 16 million people who lived a life in the GDR and who experience such judgements again and again . . . as if this life before German reunification didn't really count . . . no matter what good and bad experiences one had'.[6]

Merkel's frustration with the way her early life in East Germany is still dismissed as irrelevant is shared by many of her fellow former GDR citizens. Surveys taken since 1990 have shown that the majority have continued to feel that they are treated as 'second-class citizens' in the reunified country. Two thirds continue to feel this way today.[7] Many have experienced explicit or implicit pressure to jettison their East German 'ballast' and seamlessly adjust to a culture that was new to them. Even Merkel, who adapted to the post-reunification world extremely successfully, climbing a steep political career ladder all the way to the top, was still reminded by the press that it occasionally 'shone through' that she was 'not a born Federal German and European'[8] – as if she was not a 'native', not an 'original' citizen of the country she had been elected to lead. After sixteen years in the highest political office of the land, this East German still had to prove her allegiance, disavowing what came before.

Just as individual East Germans are asked to minimize traces of their pre-1990 past, the nation as a whole seems supremely uncomfortable with the GDR as a chapter of its history. In many ways, the process of writing the GDR out of the national narrative began even before its final demise. In 1989, after the fall of the Berlin Wall, the former West German Chancellor Willy Brandt famously declared, 'Now what belongs together will grow together.' For many Germans, East and West, the division of their country, which had seemed a fact of life during the Cold War, now looked like an unnatural state of affairs, a product of the Second World War and perhaps a punishment for it. By 1990, had Germany not done enough to overcome this dark chapter of its past? Did it not deserve a fresh start without constant reminders of it? Francis Fukuyama's framing of the end of the Cold War as 'the end of history' seemed particularly apt for Germany. The nation wanted, indeed needed to see reunification as a happy ending to its tumultuous twentieth century. Acknowledging the continuing impact of Germany's decades of division as anything other than distant history destroys this comforting illusion. If the GDR is to be remembered at all, then it is as one of Germany's dictatorships – as remote, sinister and irredeemable as Nazism.

Drawing a line under both German states and seeing 1990 as a fresh start for all Germans was also out of the question. West Germans had grown too fond of the idea of 1945 as their 'zero hour', the point from which the tender shoots of democracy were growing out of the ashes of the Second World War. Whatever problems the infant Federal Republic may have had, the prosperity and stability it had produced were like a comfort blanket to a population that had known little but tumult since 1914. Here was a Germany to be proud of. West Germany was declared the continuity state and East Germany the anomaly. Reunification in 1990 therefore seemed a satisfying end to forced separation. And to many East Germans too it was just that. In 1989 and 1990, many voted for the dissolution of their country in both word and deed.

Consensual reunification does not mean that life in East Germany deserves to be forgotten or filed away as irrelevant history. The ups and downs of the GDR as a political, social and economic experiment have left a mark on its former citizens, who have brought these experiences with them – and not as mere 'ballast'. Millions of Germans alive today neither can nor want to deny that they once lived in the GDR. While the world that had shaped them fell with the Berlin Wall in 1989, their lives, experiences and memories were not razed with it. Yet the way much of the Western world saw it, the GDR had well and truly lost the Cold War on German soil, morally invalidating everything in it. When the German Democratic Republic vanished literally overnight on 3 October 1990, it lost the right to write its own history. Instead it had *become* history. And history is written by victors – East Germany's is no exception.

Much of the West is struggling to see even why anyone would choose to remember their lives behind the Iron Curtain. Winning the Cold War seemed to have proved alternative models of life wrong. Where Western consumerism and liberal values are remembered in full colour, the GDR is pictured as a grey, monotonous blur – a world without individuality, agency or meaning. In the Western imagination, East Germans wasted forty-one years in a walled-off Russian colony, controlled by the Ministry for State Security, better known as the Stasi. What is there worth remembering?

Writing off the GDR wholesale as a footnote in German history that is best forgotten is ahistorical. The East German state lasted for over forty years, longer than the First World War, the Weimar Republic and Nazi Germany combined. It was never the static land that time forgot between 1949 and 1989. Those decades saw immense change. Indeed, much of the GDR's trajectory was shaped by people and events whose formative years lay in the decades not just before the Wall was built in 1961 but before the country itself was founded in 1949. Germany had been in a near-constant state of upheaval since 1914 and the economic, political, social and psychological consequences of the tumultuous first half of the twentieth century did not suddenly disappear when the GDR was set up.

This book traces the roots of the German Democratic Republic beyond its foundation to provide context for the circumstances out of which the country was born in 1949. I outline the developments that followed through all four decades rather than treating them as a static whole. In the 1950s, the infant republic was almost entirely preoccupied with stabilizing its foundations politically and economically. It did so both with and over the heads of its citizens, resulting in a decade that was marked by a can-do spirit as well as violent outbreaks of discontent.

When the Berlin Wall was built in 1961, bringing the exodus of skilled labour to West Germany to a forced halt, the country seemed to settle. Ambitious building projects such as the reimagining of Alexanderplatz in Berlin with its iconic TV tower combined with the space craze and scientific breakthroughs to create a real sense of progress and national identity. Many East Germans were proud of their achievements as social mobility provided unprecedented opportunities for the working classes.

As the fruits of their labour created the highest living standards in the communist world in the 1970s, the GDR established itself on the world stage, becoming a member of the United Nations and being recognized by many countries around the world. East German products were exported as far as Britain and the United States. But the oil crises of the decade highlighted the GDR's inherent vulnerabilities and dependence on the Soviet Union (USSR). When Moscow reneged on its promised deliveries of oil and gas, East Germany could no longer uphold the living standards its people had been accustomed to without bankrupting itself in the process.

The ageing regime was beginning to lose touch and ran out of ideas. By the mid-1980s, the system had calcified, leaving it inflexible and brittle, in dire need of reform. When that wasn't forthcoming, the East German people themselves took the initiative to bring about change. Phases of opening to the West and drawing in on itself ebbed and flowed throughout each decade, and the experiences of East Germans, good and bad, were shaped by these complex tides of history.

The Stasi watched and often meddled with lives at every stage of the GDR's history, yet it did not render the East German people passive. Similarly, the state itself, while dependent on good will from Moscow, was never a passive Soviet satellite. East Germans lived and shaped a distinctly German experiment that spanned much of the second half of the twentieth century. Its political, economic, social and cultural idiosyncrasies deserve a history that treats it as more than a walled 'Stasiland' and gives it its proper place in German history.

Drawing on interviews, letters and records, this book makes room for a wide range of East German voices. Their life stories are integral to my account of the state they shaped and were shaped by. Interviewees for this book include politicians such as Egon Krenz, one of the last leaders of the GDR, and entertainers like pop singer Frank Schöbel. The majority consisted of those who made the state work: from teachers, accountants and factory workers to police officers and border guards. The result is a new history of the GDR that shows all facets of their vanished country – from high politics to everyday life.

The context of the Cold War created simplistic images of the Other on both sides of the Iron Curtain. The GDR painted an image of the West in broad and hostile brushstrokes while it in turn became a caricature of the monochrome world of communism that supposedly lay beyond the Wall. Over three decades have now passed since the disappearance of the GDR and a new generation of Germans has grown up without physical borders dividing them. They have never experienced the system competition of two Germanies nor the existence of two German armies pointing a terrifying arsenal of weapons at one another. As the Cold War and the intense hostility it bred drifts further into the past, we have new opportunities to study East Germany with emotional and political detachment.

Perhaps the wounds of separation, of identities lost and gained, were too raw to be examined during the immediate post-reunification era when it seemed preferable to allow them to scab over. Now, it is time to dare to take a new look at the GDR. Those who do so with open eyes will find a world full of colour, not one of black and white. There was oppression and brutality, yes, and there was opportunity and belonging. Most East German communities experienced all of this. There were tears and anger, and there was laughter and pride. The citizens of the GDR lived, loved, worked and grew old. They went on holidays, made jokes about their politicians and raised their children. Their story deserves a place in the German narrative. It's time to take a serious look at the other Germany, beyond the Wall.

1. Trapped between Hitler and Stalin (1918–1945)

Siberia will freeze your big mouth shut!

German Communists

Sverdlovsk, Siberia, 16 August 1937. Twenty-four-year-old Berliner Erwin Jöris was pushed into a small cell. The darkness stank of sweat, excrement and fear. Of the fifty-eight other political prisoners who already languished there only a handful wearily turned their gaunt faces to the door to eye up the newcomer. Erwin looked around for somewhere to sit, but there was no space on the cramped floor. So he stood in the only place he could, by the latrine – a large barrel with a lid. He stood for hours, then days, then weeks. His feet swelled up, his mouth went dry and his throat burned with every rasping swallow. One day, he collapsed, clutching his chest with weak hands as he was dragged off to the sick bay. There a doctor looked him up and down, concluded that he was only feigning illness and sent him back into the cell.

The food rations in Sverdlovsk prison were not enough to sustain even a fit young man like Erwin Jöris. Once a day, a piece of 'Stalin Cake' was dished out – stale bread with a ladle of coffee. When Erwin collapsed again, nobody paid him any attention. In his delirium, he heard the prison door open. A soldier shouted a name into the cell, somebody answered, 'Here!' 'You've got ten years. Come. With your belongings.' The prisoners around him began to talk of trials and of 'waves of arrests'. One said, 'These tribunals only flick through your file briefly. If they have slept well, it could be your lucky day and you get five years. If they are drunk: twenty-five years.'

Every time the door opened, silence fell among the prisoners. Who would it be this time?[1]

Erwin Jöris was one of many German communists who had emigrated to Soviet Russia in the 1930s. Since communism and socialism had grown out of their obscure intellectual roots in the mid-nineteenth century, they had become mass movements in Germany, fuelled by industrialization and urbanization. While German far-left politicians and activists had been used to the deployment of varying degrees of state violence against their ideology, the ascent of Adolf Hitler was a new milestone. Erwin and his comrades were forced to flee from the Nazi regime in Germany, which began to crack down hard on the left once Hitler became Chancellor on 30 January 1933. They sought refuge in the Soviet Union. With its political and ideological roots in the October Revolution of 1917, it was the first and only realization of the political utopia they had dreamt of as they toiled and starved through the years of hardship that had followed the First World War. There, they would show their gratitude by doing all in their power to help build a better world. According to the historian Peter Erler, roughly 8,000 adult German political émigrés lived in Russia by the middle of the decade.[2] Apart from politically active communists, this included workers, actors, musicians, artists, architects, scientists, teachers, authors and many more individuals bound together by their disillusionment with everything that had gone wrong in their fatherland since 1914.

Born on the eastern outskirts of Berlin in 1912, Erwin Jöris belonged to a generation of young socialists that had cut their teeth (figuratively and literally) on the streets of German cities rather than in the trenches of the First World War. He was still a young boy when his father helped push Kaiser Wilhelm II, the last German monarch, into exile during the German Revolution of November 1918. His childhood was marked by the blood-soaked tales of the Spartacist Uprising in January 1919 and by the poverty and hunger his family experienced during hyperinflation in 1923.

The anger, squalor and violence of the working class neighbourhoods around him formed the backdrop to Erwin's upbringing.

Capitalism had failed the working classes for whom there had been little but misery during his lifetime. It was no wonder that by 1928, at the age of sixteen, he decided that there must be another way for his generation. Erwin joined the Young Communist League of Germany (KJVD), the youth wing of the German Communist Party (KPD). They organized marches, trained their recruits in street fighting, writing and distributing propaganda leaflets, and published a newspaper called *Die Arbeit* (Labour). This was supposed to prepare their teenage recruits to continue their parents' class struggle. Between 35,000 and 50,000 young Germans joined the KJVD and fought for what they hoped would be a better Germany.

Erwin Jöris and his comrades ran into serious trouble after Adolf Hitler had been made Chancellor on 30 January 1933. When an arson attack on the German parliament, the Reichstag, happened barely a month later, on 27 February 1933, the Nazis claimed that the culprit was one Marinus van der Lubbe, a young Dutch communist who admitted the deed under torture. Hitler convinced the eighty-five-year-old and increasingly frail German President, Paul von Hindenburg, to grant him emergency powers to squash the communist revolution the Dutchman had supposedly tried to incite. An increasingly feeble-minded Hindenburg agreed and used the emergency powers that Article 48 of the constitution afforded the German President to sign the infamous Reichstag Fire Decree. The legislation suspended civil liberties and allowed Hitler's men to arrest opponents at will and without charge or trial. This in turn amounted to a death sentence for many German communists.

In Prussia, around 10,000 communists were incarcerated within a fortnight after the fire. Among them was Erwin Jöris, who was sentenced to protective custody and interned in one of the earliest concentration camps, KZ Sonnenburg, which was opened on 3 April 1933 near Kostrzyn in what is now Poland. Youngsters like Erwin were small fry to the Nazis. They were after the leaders of the KPD who might yet deny them success in passing legislation through the Reichstag, which they needed to do in order to dismantle democracy under a legal guise. Communist deputies still held 100 of the 584 seats since the last election in November 1932. After the fire, a merciless manhunt ensued on each and every one of them.

Only a few days after the fire, on 3 March 1933, the Nazis arrested the KPD leader Ernst Thälmann, nicknamed 'Teddy'. On the same day, a Prussian commission had lifted legal restrictions off the Gestapo, the newly established secret police. This practically allowed them free range in terms of policing methods and punishments. Thälmann would be the first victim of a ruthless secret police force let off the leash. He was repeatedly mistreated as the authorities tried to gather information for his trial. On several occasions, he was dragged from his cell in Moabit prison into the Gestapo headquarters in the Prinz-Albrecht-Straße in Berlin. There he received the worst kind of punishment that a lawless security apparatus was capable of. On 8 January 1934 four of his teeth were knocked out and he was beaten bloody with a sjambok, a rhino-hide whip that would later be associated with the apartheid regime in South Africa where it was widely used by police forces. Thälmann would eventually be murdered in KZ Buchenwald in 1944.

In order to escape Hitler's thugs, many German communists fled abroad. Some continued to be politically active and built resistance cells in Prague and Paris with the help of the Communist International (Comintern), an organization promoting world communism directed by the Soviet Union. Many former KPD members moved straight to Moscow where they offered their services to the communist state. They took their spouses and children with them and began to build new communities in a place they had idealized over the course of their struggles in the 1920s and early 1930s. It would be in Moscow rather than Berlin where ideas for communism on German soil began to germinate.

Life in Paradise

Moscow, late October 1936. Wladimir Leonhard was beginning to get used to life in the Russian capital. The teenager had moved there in the summer of 1935 with his mother Susanne Leonhard, a German communist writer. The two were close, bound by their shared political outlook for which they had both been forced into exile. Susanne had even named her only son after her great idol, Vladimir Ilyich Ulyanov, better known as Lenin. It had always been just the two of them for as long as the boy could remember. His mother had divorced his father Rudolf Leonhard in 1919 after only one year of marriage and moved from Berlin to Vienna where she worked in the Soviet embassy and fell in love with the ambassador himself, Mieczysław Broński. As their marriage too was dissolved after only a short time, the couple went their separate ways. Mother and son retained the name of Susanne's first husband and moved back to Berlin where she worked as a journalist and devoted all her time to communist activism. Like so many of their comrades, they had had to flee from the Nazi regime and emigrated to Russia.

In Moscow, the single mother had been unable to find suitable accommodation for herself and fourteen-year-old Wladimir, and so the boy was put up in the Kinderheim Nr. 6, an orphanage that became famous for housing the children of mainly Austrian communists who had been killed or gone underground. The teenager enjoyed the privileged life the home afforded him but was always glad to see his mother, who had taken residence as a lodger in a shabby flat in a different part of Moscow.

When they met up on an afternoon in late October 1936, Wladimir was enjoying himself as he always did when he saw his mother. She bought him sweets at his favourite shop, Vostochnye Slastosty (Eastern Sweets). He told her that he was worried about some technical drawings he had to finish as homework, and she promised she would help him. When they said their goodbyes, Wladimir rushed off in a hurry as he had more work to do. His mother stood in the street and waved. When the boy returned the next day to see his mother, she was not there. She had been arrested and would be dragged off to the Vorkuta gulag, a work camp nearly 2,000 kilometres north-east of Moscow, where around a quarter of a million prisoners were to die over the next two decades.

His mother's arrest came as a complete shock to Wladimir. Like thousands of their fellow Germans, the Leonhards felt they had all to gain from emigrating to the USSR. Not only would they escape the devastating Nazi sweeps that had put so many of their friends and colleagues into concentration camps and prisons, but they would also get a chance to help build a better world. With the Russian Revolution in 1917, the first real communist experiment had begun. German socialists and communists had hoped in vain for the revolution that their compatriot Karl Marx had prophesied in the middle of the previous century. Even the First World War had failed to be the moment of truth for their fatherland. Yet the idea of a world revolution as salvation for the working classes had never lost its pull for many of the poorest labourers. The endless violent street battles, the precarious work that never seemed to generate enough money and the chaos and hardship of the 1920s were endured in the belief that Marx was right. The revolution would come.

In the post-war years of the 1920s and early 1930s, millions of disillusioned, hungry and tired workers toiled in Germany's industrial cities. They were ignored by a wealthy urban elite so preoccupied by their own desire for mind-numbing entertainment that they paid little heed to the invalids in the street, the twitching wrecks of the shell-shocked and the war stories of those with injured pride and broken dreams. German workers in turn became bitter and hard. They saw their meagre savings wiped out, while their jobs were insecure at best and often completely gone after the Great Depression began in the wake of the Wall Street Crash of 1929. They saw their often conservative values trampled and belittled by those who embraced the growing Americanization of German culture. What seemed exciting, new and adventurous to the urban middle classes appeared frivolous and amoral to those who neither had the time nor the money to indulge in the new culture.

Many German workers needed purpose and a sense of belonging. Communist meetings, the social activities provided by workers' associations and even the violent street clashes with the nationalist veteran groups called the *Freikorps* and later Hitler's SA thugs provided much-needed escapism in a world that seemed to hold no future for them. In this context, a 1925 brochure called *What Did 58 German Workers See in Russia?* became instrumental in creating a paradisiacal image of the Soviet Union. It was inspired by the communist Hermann Remmele, who had led a group of his comrades on a grand tour of sorts through Russia. The pamphlet was based on their reports and boasted of 'female workers who proudly talked of their equal treatment'[3] and of wages that were '33 per cent higher' if one takes into account that workers lived rent-free and had excellent healthcare. All of this must have made the Soviet Union seem like the promised land to the unemployed and the destitute as well as to idealist intellectuals. Having experienced the First World War and its appalling consequences, older German communists wanted to believe there was a better alternative and saw the Soviet Union as a beacon of hope, especially after the waves of arrests in Berlin in 1933.

For most German political refugees their time in Moscow began as a great adventure. 'Are there Germans here in Moscow?'[4] asked the teenage Wladimir Leonhard when he arrived at Moscow station with his mother and was driven to 5 Granovsky Street where an acquaintance had agreed to put them up for a few days. To his surprise there were thousands of Germans in the neighbourhood. There was a diverse group of exiles who had all hoped to find a fairer society in the capital city of the first 'actually existing socialism' ('real existierender Sozialismus'), as the bulky German phrase had it. There were many workers and politicians, as one would expect, and also actors, artists and Bauhaus architects who had made names for themselves in the vibrant urban atmosphere of Weimar Germany and were despised by the Nazis for their left-leaning ideology. Among the émigrés were many Jews, for whom life in Germany had become even more dangerous since 1933.

Most of the high-profile German communist exiles were quartered in the Hotel Lux in Moscow. Its guest list read like a who's who of world communism. Among its most famous residents were Ho Chi Minh, Johannes R. Becher (a writer who would make a name for himself in the GDR), the Hungarian Imre Nagy, who would be executed as a result of his role in the Hungarian Uprising of 1956, and Clara Zetkin, one of Germany's earliest communists and women's rights activists who died in Moscow and whose urn was carried to its resting place by none other than Joseph Stalin himself. In 1933, the Hotel Lux had 300 rooms laid out to house a total of 600 guests. While initially there had been high praise for it from visitors who had travelled there for conferences of the Communist International from 1921, the building had since had two more levels added and was still bursting at the seams after the mass exodus from Germany in the mid-1930s. Post-1933, sources speak of broken door hinges and rats more often than of elaborate banquets and silk curtains.

The German Bauhaus architects, like other Hotel Lux guests, were attracted by the idea of building a new world – quite literally in their case. Their left-wing leanings had already jarred with German conservatism during the Weimar years and many were ready to start a new life in the Soviet Union well before the Nazis seized power in Berlin. The most prolific group of exiled German architects was the so-called Brigade Meyer, an eclectic mix of men and women, students and staff of the Bauhaus School in Dessau. They had followed the Swiss architect Hannes Meyer, who had moved to the Soviet Union from Dessau, where he had been a master architect at the school. In 1930, he took up a post in Moscow, where he lectured on architecture and attracted a circle of German followers.

The German Bauhaus enclave very quickly became disillusioned with their work in Russia. Initially welcomed as elite visionaries, they were increasingly hemmed in by Soviet bureaucracy, the lack of building materials and frustratingly low quality standards. The cracks in their new buildings reflected those in their relationship with the Soviets around them. Those they worked with regarded their privileged position with envy; those in the upper political ranks began to view the foreigners with suspicion. Meyer himself eventually had enough and moved back to Switzerland – convenient for him as he had a refuge, unlike his German followers who were now trapped between Hitler and Stalin.

Margarete Mengel, a Jewish-German communist who had been Meyer's secretary, partner and mother of his son Johannes, could not get a visa for Switzerland and had to stay. She was arrested and shot on 20 August 1938. Johannes was only eleven years old when his mother was murdered and ended up in a home for criminal youths. He was still a teenager when he was deported to the Ural region as a forced labourer, working in mines. Johannes did not find out what happened to his mother until 1993 and then decided to move to Germany, aged sixty-seven.[5]

Other people in Meyer's group did not fare much better. Philipp Tolziner, a Munich-born Jewish architect, was arrested in 1938 and sentenced to ten years in a gulag near Solikamsk. Under torture, he confessed to having been a German spy and gave up the names of two further colleagues who he mistakenly thought had left the country.

Stalin's German Operation

NKVD Order 00439 by N. Yezhov, 25 July 1937.

Through recent material produced by agents and through investigation it has been proved that the German General Staff and the Gestapo organized widespread spying and espionage in the most important and especially in defensive industries and that for this purpose they are using the German nationals that now live there . . . In order to suppress this activity of German reconnaissance completely, I ORDER:

From 29 July of this year the arrest of all German nationals who work in military factories or in factories which produce defence goods or goods for the railway system or have been dismissed from any of these sectors.[6]

This order was issued under the name of Nikolay Yezhov, head of the USSR's Ministry of the Interior (NKVD), but it is missing his handwritten signature and is known to have originated directly from Stalin himself. By 1937, the dictator had become convinced that the Nazis' sharp rhetoric against the Soviet Union would soon convert into a real invasion. As early as 1926, when Hitler had argued in the second volume of his book *Mein Kampf* that 'in Russian Bolshevism we must see the attempt undertaken by the Jews in the twentieth century to achieve world domination',[7] he had portrayed the fight between Germany and its Russian foe as a struggle for survival between mutually exclusive civilizations. By the middle of the 1930s, Hitler's flagrant breaches of the Treaty of Versailles in his rearmament programme were being paraded in public while much of the West looked on and congratulated him. To Stalin, a Nazi invasion was a question of 'when', not 'if', and he was convinced that the USSR would stand alone when it happened.

Naturally prone to paranoia, Stalin turned 'the bureaucratic institutions of the Soviet Union into extensions of his inner personality', according to political psychologist Raymond Birt.[8] Among the many characteristics of a paranoid personality which Birt sees in Stalin, there is a tendency to play the victim and a need to 'prove that persecution is real'.[9] Stalin began to see Hitler's agents everywhere, busy preparing the imminent attack. He had let German architects build his new cities. German politicians seemed to be infiltrating the Comintern, something Stalin had long been suspicious of as the German contingent made up one fifth of its members and had still failed to prevent the Nazi takeover in their home country. German men and women worked in mines and ammunition factories. German schools and children's homes trained new recruits right under his nose. In short, there were Germans everywhere and if they conspired to help their compatriots at home, they could do some serious damage.

Stalin's fear had been simmering since 1933 and by 1936 it had reached fever pitch. Hitler's fifth column needed to be eradicated. Completely. Stalin's suspicions went way beyond the recent German exiles. Anyone who spoke German, had German citizenship, was ethnically German or had no citizenship but some connection to

Germany was targeted. He was talking about tens of thousands of people.

NKVD Order 00439 started the so-called German Operation in which a total of 55,005 people would be arrested. Of those, 41,898 would be shot and 13,107 receive long sentences.[10] This also included three quarters of all the political émigrés. No matter how favoured they had once been by the Soviet regime, nobody was safe as entire families, blocks, streets and factories were wiped out. More members of the KPD's executive committee died at Stalin's hands than at Hitler's.

Hermann Remmele, the leader of the group that penned the propaganda brochure *What Did 58 German Workers See in Russia?*, was to endure a fate that would stand in for many German communists. Once a darling of the Soviet political elite (Grigory Zinoviev had called him 'the best and most precious asset of the German party . . . the gold of the proletariat'), he was arrested in Russia in May 1937 on charges of spying and sabotage. Two years later, he was sentenced to death and shot on the same day, 7 March 1939. His son Helmuth died on his way to a gulag in Siberia and his wife Anna would succumb to health problems caused by a horrific spell in Moscow's Butyrka prison.[11] Such family tragedies would repeat themselves thousands of times as Stalin's communist utopia turned out to be a dystopian hell.

In a bitter twist of fate, those who had been incarcerated by the Nazis in early concentration camps in 1933 made it to the top of the list of suspicious individuals. In the eyes of Stalin and his henchmen, anyone who had escaped Hitler's clutches must have given the Nazis something in return. Perhaps a promise to infiltrate the Soviet Union, get a job in a munitions factory and begin to organize systematic sabotage to prepare a German invasion.

When Erwin Jöris was arrested in his workplace in Siberia in 1937, the authorities quickly found out that he had somehow escaped a Nazi concentration camp. Now he was working in one of Stalin's industrial centres. After four months in Sverdlovsk prison, Siberia, Erwin was transferred to Lubyanka prison in Moscow. The handsome neo-baroque building with its distinctive yellow brick facade had been built at the turn of the century on the site that had once housed the headquarters of Catherine the Great's secret police. Now Stalin's infamous security chief Nikolay Yezhov directed the Great Purge from his office on the third floor. Like many of his fellow German exiles, Erwin had been oblivious to the scale and nature of the purges and thereby to the grave danger to himself.

The German Operation formed only a fraction of the terror. Since Stalin's personal paranoia had become state policy, whole factories, streets and communities were emptied. Millions of people were arrested between 1936 and 1938, usually charged with 'counter-revolutionary' activities. The total number of deaths during the Great Terror is estimated to be around a million. Executions at Lubyanka prison, where Erwin was held, were carried out in a purpose-built chamber in the basement, or at a nearby courthouse on Nikolskaya Street which was later dubbed the 'shooting house' by many Moscow exiles. Lubyanka is still in use now – as a prison and as the headquarters for the KGB's successor organization, the FSB (Federal Security Service of the Russian Federation).

The prison cells at Lubyanka had no windows. There is still an argument as to whether prisoners were located in the basement of the building or in the windowless upper floor as they were taken there blindfolded and deliberately disoriented with sleep deprivation. What we do know from the testimonies of those that survived was that men and women were held at Lubyanka without trial and tortured until they confessed to having been members of a fascist or Trotskyist conspiracy. Some were humiliated by being shackled naked to the cold floors, while guards insulted and beat them. Others were shot, hanged or committed suicide. Those that survived were sent to gulags in the east. Gallows humour had it that Lubyanka was the tallest building in the capital – you could see Siberia from its basement.

The NKVD had an easier solution for the prisoner Erwin Jöris. As a German national, he was sentenced to deportation. This happened to many German communists in exile as it fulfilled the twin roles of appeasing Hitler in the build-up to the Molotov–Ribbentrop Pact by denying his enemies safe sanctuary and eliminating suspicious foreign elements without dirtying Soviet hands. The NKVD knew they were delivering their former comrades straight into the arms of Heinrich Himmler's security apparatus. In April 1938, Erwin was put on a train. A Gestapo officer was already waiting for the troublesome communist before he had even reached the Polish border. Upon arrival in Berlin, he was transferred to Moabit prison, the very same in which KPD leader Ernst Thälmann had languished while the Gestapo questioned and tortured him.

Even high-profile figures such as Willi Budich, a German communist of the old guard who had been a member of socialist parties since 1910, were unable to escape the accusations that they had somehow made a pact with the Nazis to be released from incarceration. His story is another harrowing tale of a German communist who had escaped Hitler only to be targeted by Stalin.[12] Budich had spent a lifetime fighting for his communist ideals. When his future wife, a Russian law student called Luba Gerbilskaya, first met him at the World Congress of the Comintern in December 1922, he already bore the mental and physical scars of his struggle. She would later remember that 'he looked older than his thirty-two years . . . This was due to the hard and dangerous life of this revolutionary and heroic communist, but in his eyes shone humour and a warm heart.'[13] Budich had been a KPD Reichstag deputy when the Nazis came to power in 1933. In 1932, he had already proved that he would fight tooth and nail to keep the 'brown pest' at bay. In a violent brawl with Nazi thugs in the debating chamber itself, his kneecap had been bashed into a pulp with a chair. He would never regain the use of his leg. After the Reichstag Fire in 1933, the SA hunted him down and interned him at Columbia concentration camp in Berlin where they tortured him half to death. When he was released, it was with broken legs and severely impaired vision and hearing. His wife, who had fled to Moscow with their two young daughters Irina and Marianne-Leonie, organized for him to be transferred there as well. Yet decades of ideological struggle and a crippled body to show for it would not be enough. He had somehow evaded prolonged imprisonment in Nazi camps and this made him suspicious. In September 1936, Budich was arrested for being a member of the 'Wollenberg-Hoelz-Organization' – a fictitious group invented by the NKVD to enable them to charge seventy German communists with being members of a 'counter-revolutionary, terrorist, Trotskyist conspiracy'.[14] Budich was tried in March 1938 and shot on the same day. He would only be rehabilitated posthumously in 1956, three years after Stalin's death.

The idea of German spies played right into the irrational fear of a counter-revolution stoked by Western agents in the USSR. It was a powerful seed of suspicion that found fertile soil in minds brutalized by years of violence. Life had been cheap on the bloody battlefields of the Eastern Front in the First World War. Yet it had been even cheaper during the years of the Russian Civil War from 1917 to 1922, when a staggering 8–10 million people died. In the decade that followed Lenin's death in 1924, the power struggle from which Stalin emerged victorious and the subsequent modernization programme would demand countless more victims in grain requisitions, famines, industrial accidents, gruelling work conditions and further political repression. Stalin lost no sleep over the arrest and murder of tens of thousands of Germans.

Meanwhile, the enormous wave of arrests in 1937 caused panic among the ranks of the exiled communists. Proving you were unswervingly loyal to Stalin was no longer the exclusive domain of careerists and ideological extremists. It had become a matter of life and death. The only way to prove that you were not a 'fascist coated in red' was to denounce those that supposedly were just that. When Stalin suddenly lost his temper in February 1937 and burst out that 'everyone in the Communist International works for the enemy',[15] the German delegation panicked. This led to a frenzy of denunciations. Grete Wilde, a German communist who had been in the KPD since 1921, shortly after its launch, held a job in the Comintern's cadre department in Moscow when these events unfolded. Without hesitation, she produced over twenty pages of denunciations against fellow German communists. They covered the biographies of forty-four of her colleagues and claimed they were 'Trotskyists and other hostile elements among the ranks of the KPD'.[16] Yet even this unspeakable betrayal could not save her. The NKVD was convinced that she was shielding the true culprits. Grete herself was arrested on 5 October 1937 and deported to Karaganda labour camp in Kazakhstan where she is thought to have died in 1944. Such patterns of suspicion, denouncements and betrayal left deep scars on those German communists who survived them, scars they would take back to their home country after the war.

Communist Children

Moscow, 1937. The waves of arrests during the Great Terror left a large group of German children abandoned or orphaned. If deemed old enough to hold political opinions, they too were sometimes deported. Often they ended up in orphanages or were given new names and put into homes for criminal youths. Even the children of the communist elite, who had previously led privileged lives, began to feel the terror that held the capital in its grip.

Most of the children of the German communist expat community attended the Karl-Liebknecht-Schule, a German-speaking institution in Moscow. Founded in 1924, it was run by German intellectuals who had built the 'school of their dreams'[17] in the land of socialism as they felt this had become increasingly difficult to do in Germany. Here they would raise a new generation of idealists. Left-leaning German teachers were attracted by this idea and moved to Moscow to teach. The school was a bubble that shielded its pupils from the Russian world around them and it continued to do so for a surprisingly long time. But this bubble too would burst when the Great Terror became all-encompassing. Wladimir Leonhard described it in his memoirs:

> *Beginning in March 1937, one teacher after another was arrested. The first one was our German teacher, Gerschinski, a German communist who had himself been taught at the Karl-Marx-Schule in Berlin as a pupil and then emigrated to the Soviet Union in 1933. There followed the history and geography teacher, Lüschen, also an alumnus of the Karl-Marx-Schule. Eventually our maths and chemistry teacher, Kaufmann, too was arrested. . . . The teachers who were left were not only completely overworked but also scared for their lives. Every one of them knew that it could be his turn tomorrow. They lost all confidence and were often hardly able to finish a lesson, which of course we as pupils noticed.*[18]

There was little resistance from the German children and teenagers as the adults in their lives began to vanish one by one. They had been taught to endure suffering. The ideology imprinted on them said that factionalism is the worst enemy of the world revolution and internal doubters and dissidents must be silenced and carved out of the movement before their cancerous lies split the unity of communism and allowed its enemies to defeat it.[19] Leonhard describes how a ten-year-old girl in his children's home in Moscow reacted to the arrest and deportation of her father. As they sat together in a group in the evening, her words betrayed her desperate desire to uphold the pillars of her world and explain why Stalin had taken her father:

> *I believe these things are best explained with an example. Imagine one of us has an apple, which is very precious to him, as it is his only one. In this apple there is a rotten, or perhaps even poisonous bit. If you want to save the apple, you will have to cut out this poisonous or rotten bit to save the rest. As you cut it out, perhaps so as not to poison yourself, you might cut out more than you need to, so that there is definitely only healthy matter left. Perhaps this is what these purges are about.*[20]

The Karl-Liebknecht-Schule produced a cadre of child communists who had never known a different ideology. Their parents were without fail part of the hardcore of the German communist group and had decided to bring them to Soviet Russia just as Stalinism had begun to transform the country. In their school, all of their teachers were of a similar mould and perhaps even more so once the purges began. It made ideological sense to these children that their parents should be sacrificed.

Those among the German communist children who were older, like Wladimir, also understood that they were barred from their fatherland. It was a terrible situation that had a deep psychological impact. As the pupils of the Karl-Liebknecht-Schule were young enough to fall through Stalin's murderous sieve, many graduates would later form the core of those who returned to Germany after the Second World War to help build socialism in their country. Wolfgang Leonhard, as Wladimir later called himself, could therefore claim with some justification in an interview in 1997 that 'the history of the GDR probably began in the Karl-Liebknecht-Schule'.[21]

Self-Censorship

Soviet Union, 1938–1939. Like the ten-year-old girl in Wladimir Leonhard's children's home, many adult German communists too had been able to convince themselves that the purges might be necessary. An even more powerful and enduring idea was that 'wise father Stalin' did not know anything about the excessive violence his underlings committed in his name. Helmut Damerius, a German communist who was arrested under false accusations as part of the German Operation on 17 March 1938, is a typical example. He had gone through hell, first at Lubyanka prison in Moscow and then at Solikamsk gulag where he spent his sentence of seven years' hard labour. During this time he wrote a total of seventeen letters to Stalin. He would later explain that he did so because 'I was full of hope to find justice in this way. I would write to Stalin, all would be explained and justice would be restored. In the meantime, I would behave like a communist and work hard for the good of Soviet power.'[22] His letters never received an answer.

This powerful idea also gripped Hedwig Remmele, the daughter of Hermann and Anna Remmele. Despite the fact that her father, brother and husband had all been murdered by the NKVD while she had been ordered to stay in Siberia with her daughters long after the war had finished, she still clung to the notion that Stalin would help. She too kept writing letters to the authorities in the hope that they would allow her to return to Germany from her exile in Siberia where she had been moved after her parents had been arrested. She was still there when she heard of Stalin's death in 1953. Upon receiving the news, she suffered a nervous breakdown. In her mind, her last hope to be released had evaporated. She would eventually return to Germany in 1956, twenty years after she had left.

For those who survived the Great Purges of 1936–1938 and who were not completely disillusioned with Soviet-style communism, a new test of loyalty to Stalin lay in store: the Molotov–Ribbentrop Pact. When on the night between 23 and 24 August 1939 Hitler's Germany and Stalin's USSR signed a nonaggression treaty, it changed everything for German communists in the Soviet Union. As horrifying as the purges had been, those who wanted a psychological and ideological way to deal with them found one. No matter how many comrades died at the hands of the NKVD, it was all for a greater good: to defeat 'Hitlerism' and fascism at home. The antifascist agenda which the KPD in Moscow still trumpeted was the single-most powerful tool in their ideological repertoire. The Hitler–Stalin pact destroyed this illusion.

Still, the KPD leadership in exile led by Wilhelm Pieck and Walter Ulbricht were willing to bend their propaganda to fit around the unlikely agreement of friend and foe. They immediately promoted a new narrative: the war that was about to begin was provoked by the imperialist nations of France and England. The Soviet Union supported the 'peaceful' ambitions of Germany. The communist resistance cells in London, Paris and Prague were naturally outraged that they were now being asked to accept Hitler's government. Kurt Hager, a German communist in exile in Britain, wrote under the pseudonym Felix Albin that 'We German anti-fascists will under no circumstances give up the fight against the Nazi regime.'[23]

Even in Moscow itself, the KPD had a tough time convincing the remnants of the communist enclave, now terrified and fatigued after two years of brutal purges. Walter Ulbricht was ordered to present ideas as to how this could be achieved to the executive committee of the party, the politburo, on 9 September 1939, mere days after the German attack on Poland. Ulbricht's notes for the session give an interesting insight into just how much argumentative creativity was required: 'The pact of the Soviet Union with Germany supports the international working class as it forces German fascism under the heel of the Soviet Union, thereby contradicting its lies about the Soviet Union.'[24] This was the line to be taken. The use of such words as 'fascist' and 'Hitlerite' was banned from KPD material; the party offices elsewhere were to be closed, particularly the one in Paris which had proved to be too independent from the Comintern puppeteers in Moscow.

After the purges, KPD internal cleansing and the ludicrous ideological U-turn following the Hitler–Stalin pact, the inner circle of the communist enclave in Moscow had boiled down to a fanatical core. This small group was to show unquestioning obedience to Stalin and cut all ties to their former German comrades. At the heart of this select clique sat Walter Ulbricht and Wilhelm Pieck, who would later be tasked to build socialism in Germany in Stalin's image.

Leaders

Neither Pieck nor Ulbricht were marked out for leadership through a particularly charismatic personality or oratory skill. Both had shown unconditional loyalty to Moscow since the revolution in 1917 and could count on protection and support from the Soviet Union as far as anyone could. Wilhelm Pieck was a communist of the old order. Born in 1876, he had joined the Social Democratic Party

(SPD) in 1895 and found a natural ideological home in its radical left wing. He spent much of the First World War in prison as he continued to work with the leaders of opposition to the war – Karl Liebknecht and Rosa Luxemburg. When the KPD was created in the winter of 1918/19, he was one of its founding members and immediately pushed for voluntary subjugation to Moscow. He even met Lenin personally, in autumn 1921, to receive instructions at a meeting of the leadership of the Comintern. With such a long track record of ideological purity and loyalty to Soviet Russia, Pieck made it through the purges in Moscow unscathed. His friendly, open face betrayed his ruthless mind. Nobody could rely on reputation alone to see them through Stalin's wave of terror, and so Pieck busied himself denouncing former comrades and aiding the cleansing of his party to reassure the regime in Moscow of his continued service. He stood ready to help his adopted motherland when Hitler invaded it in June 1941 and Operation Barbarossa began.

Pieck's comrade Walter Ulbricht also shows that it was not charisma or leadership qualities but rather obedience and usefulness that decided the careers – and survival – of German communists in the 1930s and 1940s. A plain-looking, stocky man, around 1.65 metres tall, Ulbricht spoke with the provincial accent of his native Saxony, sounding slightly comical to his predominantly urban audiences. His voice had an unusually high pitch and did not carry well when addressing large crowds of people. His writing too was full of empty phrases and repetition – not exactly the stuff that inspires revolutions. As a KPD deputy in the Reichstag, his rhetorical duels with the Nazis' propaganda chief in Berlin, Joseph Goebbels, highlighted Ulbricht's lack of eloquence in a particularly stark manner. Nevertheless, their verbal stand-offs often provoked violent clashes between their respective supporters. So too, when the two ideologues spoke at the Saalbau in Berlin-Friedrichshain on 22 January 1931 in front of 4,000 people – the result was a mass brawl with 100 injured. But the heat always came from the situation itself rather than Ulbricht's words. The stiff apparatchik was no match for the verbal fireworks of Joseph Goebbels. After one of their debates in the Reichstag, Goebbels wrote in his diary on 6 February 1931: 'Little intermezzo with the KPD man Ulbricht, who rants against me – in front of an empty house – and then my hour has come . . . I am in top form. Talk for a whole hour in front of a packed house . . . riotous success and the whole house saw it like that. Everyone loved it.'[25]

Born in 1893, Ulbricht was also from an older generation of German communists, if nearly twenty years younger than Pieck. He joined the SPD in 1912 and spent the First World War fighting in Poland, Serbia and Belgium. He was among the founders of the KPD in 1919 and travelled to Russia in the early 1920s where he heard Lenin speak, which left a lifelong impression on him. Like Pieck, Ulbricht also spent the Nazi years in exile – first in Paris, then in Moscow, where he too proved his unswerving loyalty to Stalin. Ulbricht's behaviour during the purges was marked by moral ambivalence. On the one hand, he wrote letters to Georgi Dimitrov, the head of the Comintern, and Lavrentiy Beria, Stalin's notorious security chief, on behalf of the German émigrés who had suffered under Soviet oppression. On 28 February 1941, for example, he pleaded on behalf of German women whose husbands had been arrested or murdered.[26] On the other hand, Ulbricht also went out of his way to write denunciations about former comrades to ingratiate himself with Stalin's terror regime. For instance, he denounced a Frau Baumert for anti-Soviet propaganda on the basis that the woman had said that some Czech immigrants regretted their move to the USSR given that they had never had it so bad as now.[27] Ulbricht proved over the years in Moscow that he had no firm moral compass and no other aim than to serve Soviet Russia. His loyalty could be depended upon.

When Hitler attacked the Soviet Union on 22 June 1941, Ulbricht and Pieck changed the propaganda output of the KPD yet again. Literally overnight, they returned to the old slogans of the 'merciless fight against Hitlerite fascism' and the remaining communist leaders fell into line. It was Ulbricht's task to 'educate' the German people about the evils of national socialism and lift the spell that

Hitler had cast over his countrymen. He would be responsible for planning and delivering German-language radio broadcasts via Radio Moscow while also directing a re-education programme for the German prisoners of war that the Soviet Union began to capture and hold in camps.

In his first radio broadcast, on 26 June 1941, he appealed to his compatriots: 'The working people of Germany and the Soviet people must create the preconditions for lasting peace and for real friendship between both peoples through the common struggle for the fall of the fascist warmongers.'[28] It had little effect. Not only were German radios, the so-called *Volksempfänger* (People's Receivers), mass produced by the Nazis and designed so that the reception of foreign radio stations required altering the devices but also the signal itself was weak and unreliable.

Besides, Ulbricht had left his fatherland in 1933 and had not experienced Nazism for long. His time as an exile in Moscow had put him out of sync with his fellow Germans. Many had enthusiastically signed up to Nazi ideology, but even those who had not were often won over by some of Hitler's actions: job creation schemes, the Strength through Joy programme that made holidays affordable, or rearmament and early successes in the war. Ulbricht was utterly perplexed when his KPD delegation tried to speak to all 1,500 German prisoners of war at the transitional camp of Temnikov in October 1941 but received a hostile response. His report complained that 'ten years of living and thinking in two different systems had eradicated all common ground between people'.[29]

The ultimate sign of Ulbricht's detachment from the German men who fought the bloody fight in the East for their Führer came at Stalingrad. By the winter of 1942/43 the German 6th Army was stuck there, cut off from supplies and surrounded by enemy troops. Soldiers were freezing to death without proper winter equipment. They were starving, and the atmosphere oscillated between bleak depression and determination to hold out. Attempting to win the desperate men over to the communist cause, Ulbricht blared his high-pitched, wooden voice into the freezing ears of his compatriots. Giant speakers had been rolled right to the front lines, at risk of life and limb as they were within reach of German fire. Ulbricht wanted to tell his miserable compatriots that their fight was futile. They must give up and join the resistance against Hitler. Ulbricht's report from 18 December 1942 shows how this went down: 'We speak to the soldiers of the 371st division. At the first announcement we are greeted with ten heavy mines.'[30] One of Stalin's commissioners of the Communist Party of the Soviet Union, who had been assigned to Stalingrad, sceptically supervised the proceedings. His name was Nikita Khrushchev and this was his first meeting with the KPD leaders. Summing up the results of their dangerous attempts to persuade *Wehrmacht* soldiers to give up, he chuckled at supper: 'Well, Comrade Ulbricht, it doesn't look as if you have earned your dinner tonight. No Germans have surrendered.'[31]

German communists in Moscow may have had limited success in helping Stalin win the war, but after the war, they stood on the right side of history, ready to return to their fatherland as victors.

Survivors

Stalin's purges were so far-reaching that only one quarter of German exiles in Russia survived them. Of the nine German members of the politburo of the KPD who had gone into exile in the Soviet Union only two were still alive at the end of the war: Wilhelm Pieck and Walter Ulbricht.

As it was so unlikely that a German communist who had moved to Russia in the 1930s was still alive by 1945, it is worth asking what those who were had in common. It was possible to survive exile in the Soviet Union for only three reasons. The most likely was that they had completely subordinated themselves to Stalin and proved without a shadow of a doubt that they had forsaken their dubious German colleagues and indeed their country. In this way, people such as Fritz Erpenbeck were allowed to return to Germany in 1945 to rebuild the country.[32] Erpenbeck had realized in the nick of time that the purges would cost most German communists their lives and promptly renounced his German citizenship in December 1936 before the NKVD Order 00439 gave deadly formality to the policy of eradication of foreign spies. He then made himself useful to the Soviets by churning out their propaganda in various media outlets as a journalist.

A second way to escape Stalin's henchmen was to have been young enough during the time of the purges so as not to be perceived as a serious threat. While many German teenagers were also dragged off to remote work camps or simply vanished forever under different names, a fair proportion of children were transferred to Russian schools or workplaces where they quickly assimilated. By the time the Great Terror began to fizzle out, they had shown that their lifelong indoctrination had borne fruit. They had become true communists, perhaps even true Russians. Most accepted or learned to suppress what happened in the Soviet Union as they returned to Germany after 1945.

The third way to survive the Great Terror of 1936–1939 was sheer luck. Erwin Jöris is one such example – he never bowed and he was old enough to be targeted by both Hitler and Stalin, repeatedly. His story of survival truly is remarkable. Of the communists sent back to Germany like him, some were executed by the Nazis (especially those who had long been on the Gestapo's list as troublemakers) while some died in concentration camps. Many were considered 'cured' of their political aberration after their horrific experiences in Soviet prisons and were unceremoniously integrated into the *Wehrmacht*. This is what happened to Erwin. Yet again, he was lucky as he survived not only the bitter fighting on the Eastern Front from 1941 to 1945, where he was deployed, but also Soviet captivity into which he had been taken in the last moments of the war, at the Battle of Berlin.

When Erwin was finally free to go and returned to Germany in September 1945, he quickly found that he was not welcome in the territories occupied by the Red Army. He began to talk about what had happened to him in Stalin's workers' paradise. What's more, he was brave enough to name individuals he had worked with in Sverdlovsk before he was arrested and who had denounced many of their colleagues in an attempt to save their own skins. This rubbed a lot of people up the wrong way. People who now held a political monopoly in the eastern part of occupied Germany, and who were favoured by their Stalinist overlords, did not need Erwin Jöris running around to tell everyone what they had been up to in Moscow while their fellow Germans fought, starved and suffered during the war.

The same experiences were shared by political prisoners who returned from gulags. Anna Remmele, the widow of the murdered KPD politician Hermann Remmele, who had herself languished in one of Stalin's dungeons, attempted to return to Germany after the war. Walter Ulbricht had been a close family friend in the 1920s and so the desperate widow turned to him repeatedly. Yet he now completely ignored her and refused her frequent requests to return home. She died a broken woman in 1947 – on the same foreign soil where her husband and her son had been brutally murdered while her daughter and grandchildren were still stuck in Siberia.

Unlike Anna Remmele, Erwin Jöris had made it back into his fatherland and refused to be silenced. His insistence to make it known to the world what had happened in Moscow earned him renewed repression. On 19 December 1949, the Soviet secret police arrested him and interned him in the brutal NKVD prison in Berlin-Hohenschönhausen. It had been hastily set up after the war in a compound formerly used as an industrial-sized soup kitchen. The storage facilities where inmates were housed were underground much like the prisons in Moscow. Prisoners felt so isolated and the droning of the industrial fans was so overwhelming, the place was quickly dubbed the 'U-boat' (submarine). Erwin languished in one of the sixty damp, windowless cells without heating. He had a bucket for a toilet and faced an array of torture methods designed to break him. In the 'U-boat', prisoners were mellowed with spells of solitary confinement in KGB-style water cells. These were a little larger than a telephone booth, so that the prisoner had no choice but to stand. They were sealed so that, with the help of a raised doorstep, they could hold a few centimetres of water on the floor, often ice-cold and ankle-deep. Prisoners were deprived of sleep, flogged, made to stand for hours, beaten up or isolated until they became apathetic and agreed to whatever their captors wanted to hear.

But Erwin had been through worse. He had become a hard man who could withstand suffering of an incredible magnitude. After a year in the 'U-boat', he had still not yielded. Eventually, he was put in front of a Soviet military tribunal which sentenced him to twenty-five years of hard labour in a gulag. He endured this too and was released early, in 1955. Upon his return to East Berlin, he immediately fled to Cologne where he lived until his death in 2013 at the age of 101.

Until the end of his long life, Erwin Jöris never forgot his exchange with the Soviet judge who sentenced him in 1949. When the latter told him that he faced twenty-five years in a Soviet gulag, a punishment that might as well have been a death sentence, he sneered, 'Siberia will freeze your big mouth shut!' Erwin coolly retorted, 'And yours.'

Zero Hour?

As the Second World War neared its end, it became clear that the enormity of the crimes committed by the Nazi regime made it impossible to hand power back to the German people immediately after defeat. In contrast to the Imperial regime during the First World War, the Nazi system had been all-encompassing, tainting every aspect of life in Germany and raising complicated questions of culpability. Political and moral defeat left no institutions upon which authority could be bestowed. While the Allies agreed that unconditional surrender followed by occupation was the only acceptable solution, rifts between the Soviets and their Western wartime partners over the future of Germany were also increasingly laid bare. At the Yalta Conference in February 1945, Stalin had still tried to convince Winston Churchill and Franklin Delano Roosevelt of the efficacy of breaking Germany into smaller segments so as to render the country unable of ever posing a threat to European peace again. This idea was dismissed by the Western Allies, who feared Soviet domination on a continent devastated by war.

By way of compromise, the victors agreed to build a decentralized, demilitarized and denazified Germany together. The country and its capital would temporarily be split into four zones of occupation for administrative purposes. Stalin seemed to have accepted this solution and initially displayed no real interest in establishing a Soviet puppet state on German land. His priorities were to obtain reparations because his country desperately needed them, and because he needed to be certain that Germany would be too weak to turn into a threat again. A neutral and demilitarized Germany which could serve as a granary and steel mill to the Soviet Union seemed an acceptable solution. The historian Sergey Radchenko, who has studied the Soviet archival records of this period extensively, has argued that Stalin's inner circle were pushing in this direction, most notably Lavrentiy Beria, the much-feared NKVD chief, and Foreign Minister Vyacheslav Molotov, who were both far more vocal about the issue than Stalin himself.[33]

As each occupying power was expected to run the part of Germany it had been allocated, Stalin looked to the remaining German communists in Moscow for convenient and loyal support in rebuilding the economy, politics and even cultural life in his zone. Given Stalin's apparent lack of interest, it is tempting to ponder whether it would have been possible for a democratic system to rise from the ruins of East Germany which the Soviet Union occupied at the end of the war. The violent birth trauma of German communism inflicted by both Hitler and Stalin might have kindled a desire in the remaining exiles to see this as a chance to build a peaceful kind of socialism – a better system than the one in the Soviet Union and a better Germany than those that had come before. Stalin himself did not appear to have stood in the way of this to begin with. He had publicly doubted the feasibility of the Soviet system in the German context and was extremely reluctant to be pinned down on the specifics of Soviet policy and his plans for post-war Germany. Much of the detail appeared to have been hammered out by the KPD leadership itself rather than by Stalin's men.[34] So was there a missed chance at the end of the war for the German exiles to build the Germany many dreamt of? The answer has to be no for a number of reasons.

Stalin may not have set specific policies and he was certainly keen to avoid the sharp propagandistic rhetoric in Germany that had been used in the Soviet Union (words such as 'socialism', 'revolution' and 'dictatorship of the proletariat'[35] were to be avoided in German propaganda as it was feared that this would be met with hostility from the population), but he did set the broad agenda. There was never any doubt that 'anti-fascism', the nationalization of key industries and the redistribution of land were to be key policies, and no German communist would have been able to choose a path for the Soviet Zone of Occupation that strayed too far from these set parameters.

In addition, while Stalin was alive, his deep-seated mistrust of the Western Allies played out with the same pathological paranoia which had converted into the Great Terror internally. For Germany, this meant that a unified country under joint leadership with the other victorious nations was out of the question. As much as Stalin at times seemed to have wanted to rid himself of the responsibility that came with running a country that was culturally, linguistically and historically alien to him, he could not let go if it meant losing the geostrategic advantage it held as a buffer zone and bargaining chip. Germany was also indispensable for the resources it supplied to a country brought to its knees by a genocidal war.

Most importantly, however, Stalin's stranglehold had distilled the German communist diaspora down to its most ruthless and pro-Soviet core. The KPD leadership in Moscow from which Stalin chose the men who would build socialism in Germany had survived the Great Terror not by chance but through their abdication of morality.

When in February 1944, the politburo of the KPD received orders to begin planning for a post-war order in Germany, it fell to those men who had proved loyal to Stalin above all else to do the job: Walter Ulbricht and Wilhelm Pieck.[36] While they were largely left to their own devices by Stalin, they were closely watched by the Comintern boss, Georgi Dimitrov, a Bulgarian communist who had gained Stalin's trust when he decided to defend himself against the Nazis who accused him in 1933 of having played a key role in the Reichstag Fire. Following his calm and powerful rhetoric with which he humiliated the Nazis in their own show trial, admirers across the world had said, 'There is only one brave man in Germany, and he is a Bulgarian.'

Dimitrov's surveillance was largely unnecessary. Anton Ackermann, another obedient servant of the Soviet regime who had run the propaganda outlet 'Free Germany' for them and received the Order of the Red Star in 1945 as a reward, was responsible for economic planning.[37] He spoke for all his colleagues in the planning committee, when he told students of the Communist Party in a lecture in 1944: 'There is nothing more holy to us than the interests of the Soviet Union. It is and remains our true fatherland.'[38] With 70 per cent of the KPD membership of 1933 eradicated, the bulk of the German communists had evaporated. What remained was the ideological sediment, a group of Sovietized ideologues who sought to create a replica of what they had found in Russia in the country they had once called home.

It is hard to see another, more democratic alternative for German socialism to the regime that would emerge after the Second World War. The very founding principles of the KPD were rooted in Soviet ideology. The quasi-religious adoration of the Russian model led to a process of self-censorship among the German communists and to one of selection of the most obedient and least imaginative individuals. Theirs was an evolution that began with bullying, scheming and exclusions in Germany in the 1920s and culminated in murderous denunciations under the umbrella of Stalin's terror in 1937. Genuine idealists and dreamers such as Erwin Jöris were either murdered, imprisoned, exiled or otherwise silenced. Those who survived Stalin's purges through sheer luck, determination or by merit of their youth quickly realized that they were not to be part of the Soviet-style utopia that Stalin's favourites sought to build in post-war Germany. They were silenced yet again and often over a great number of years. Many fled to the West, some decided to keep their mouths shut. The contribution that the Soviet Union and the Second World War made to the building of socialism in Germany was what made it possible in the first place, but only within a set framework, and one which only allowed the most Sovietized individuals a say. Stalin may not have shown a keen interest in modelling the Soviet Zone of Occupation in his own image, but the Germans he had allowed to live and return there did.

1945 is often collectively remembered in Germany as Zero Hour – or *Stunde Null*. Germans liked to think of it as a fresh start after the bitter years of war. Weighed down by guilt, humiliation and material hardship, they gave in to the illusion that total defeat provided a blank canvas on which to create a better Germany. But for those who found themselves in the Soviet Zone of Occupation, and thereby either by choice or by accident under Stalin's heel, the canvas had never been blank. It had always been red and embossed with a hammer and sickle.

2.   Risen from Ruins (1945–1949)

Liberation? Strange word.

The Price of Defeat

Potsdam, Brandenburg, 27 April 1945. In the early hours of the morning thirty-one-year-old Dorothea Günther and her neighbours were huddled together in the basement of their block of flats. Dorothea had been a slender, fashionable young woman with wavy hair and a penchant for elegant clothes. Now she was sitting between heaps of coal, steeling herself for the arrival of the Soviets. For days, artillery fire had terrorized the residents of her house, destroying the few remaining bridges and roads out of Potsdam. Trapped, the frightened civilians awaited their fate while their Führer was planning his suicide 30 kilometres north-east, in his bunker under the Chancellery in Berlin. At 11 a.m., Red Army soldiers hammered on the door. The tenants were lined up at gunpoint and patted down for valuables. Dorothea noted that the hands that searched her were full of gold rings. A particularly large amber crystal adorned the index finger on the trigger of the weapon that was pointed at her chest.

When the search was over, Dorothea left the house to find fabric for clothes. Spring was well under way, but without electricity, gas or water, the threat of disease was ever present. At least she could try to stay warm and clean. Her husband Martin also needed fresh underpants and urged her to go. As she was heavily pregnant, the couple agreed that it would be safer for her to walk past the columns of Soviet soldiers. Men who were found wandering the streets were usually arrested and sometimes shot on the spot. But rumour had it that pregnant women were considered untouchable by the Red Army. All the other women in the community were terrified of being dragged off by drunken men eager for revenge. Many girls blackened their faces with soot and wore dirty rags to look older and less attractive. When Dorothea received a tip from her sister-in-law, Elfriede, that the Karstadt department store in town was being looted, she decided to take a chance. Two younger women from the neighbourhood tagged along, hoping to be safe in the company of an expectant mother.

The trio found the shop doors wide open and walked in, quickly grabbing the items they had come for. Dorothea was particularly pleased to see that there was even some wool left, which she could use to make warm clothes for her baby. Looking around for a pair of underpants for her husband, she suddenly heard the by-then infamous phrase, 'Komm, Frau!' growled in a harsh Russian accent. She turned and saw to her dismay that her two companions were being dragged off by soldiers. The women screamed and pleaded, 'Help us, Frau Günther! They can't do anything to you.' Hoping that that was true, Dorothea allowed herself to be taken as well and was manhandled up a spiral staircase towards an area where the soldiers had their temporary accommodation. The women panicked and clung on to the handrail, screaming and shouting. One of the men drew a gun and pointed it at Dorothea who stammered in broken Russian that she was pregnant, but to no avail. Her desperate thought at that moment was that Martin would surely prefer a raped wife to a dead one, so she let go and allowed herself to be shoved up the stairs. Drawn by the commotion, an officer came running up and demanded to know what was going on. Dorothea pointed at her swollen belly, and begged for mercy for her unborn child. In a rush to get back to his duties, the officer indicated with a downward flick of his thumb to let the pregnant woman go. The other two were dragged upstairs.

When Dorothea Günther recalled all of this in 2010,[1] she did so with the peculiar mix of detachment and bitterness that is typical of her generation. Taken together, the fates of the men and women

who awaited the end of the war in April and May 1945 surrounded by artillery bombs, robbery, theft, rape and murder form
an indelible picture of helplessness, defeat and despair. Dorothea
remembered vividly how her father lost all hope as he predicted a
future that would bring only 'subjugation under Bolshevism' and
the 'downfall of the German people'. However, she also remembered that during those days her neighbourhood was actually
moulded into the 'people's community that the Nazis had propa-
gated for years'. People cooked together on an improvised fire pit.
They queued behind one another for hours at the wells to get
water. They exchanged valuable pieces of advice for survival. In
the ruins of Germany, the embers of defiance glimmered amid the
ashes of despair.

Many women found it hard to see a silver lining in the dark clouds
that hung over them in the spring of 1945. Soviet soldiers arrived in
the West exhausted, traumatized and raging. Hitler had waged a
brutal war on the Eastern Front, which caused well over 20 million
Soviet deaths. The Führer had explicitly ordered his generals to con-
duct a *Vernichtungskrieg*, a war of ethnic annihilation free of the
conventions of regular warfare. He left the military leadership in no
doubt as to the monstrous scale and nature of the conflict they were
to win for him. On 30 March 1941, he impressed on them that in the
impending invasion of the Soviet Union 'we have to move away
from the idea of soldierly camaraderie. . . . We do not fight this war
to preserve the enemy.'[2]

German soldiers wreaked havoc in the East and the horrific
crimes committed on the civilian populations remained largely
unpunished as the *Wehrmacht* pillaged, raped, torched and slaugh-
tered their way towards Moscow. Stalin's men opposed Hitler's
murderous military machine through sheer numbers and will-
power. Red Army soldiers who, in the face of malnutrition,
hypothermia and seemingly insurmountable odds, even thought
about giving up risked being shot on Stalin's order. Around 150,000
Soviet soldiers died at the hands of their own officers. The rest
fought on, and when the tides of war had finally changed, it was

time for them to exact their terrible revenge. They were egged on by their commanders and Soviet propagandists, such as the popular writer Ilya Ehrenburg whose infamous pamphlets asserted that 'The Germans are not humans' and incited soldiers to take revenge on every one of them, not sparing women or children.

And so it was that long columns of drunken, brutalized men descended on eastern Germany in the last stages of the Second World War. Fuelled by their own alcohol rations or, when those were in short supply, even by dangerous industrial chemicals which were looted from remaining stock or factories, an orgy of violence ensued on an unprecedented scale. It is estimated that 2 million German women were raped by Soviet soldiers – around 100,000 in Berlin alone – often several times in gang rapes or over the days and weeks of the final Red Army advance on Berlin. The cold statistics obscure the true horror of these crimes and the psychological scars they would inflict on the women themselves as well as on East German society as a whole.

Some of the most harrowing accounts come from the memoirs of Marta Hillers, who was thirty-three years old at the end of the war. A journalist originally from Krefeld in western Germany, she was a well-educated woman who had studied in Paris and spoke French and even a little bit of Russian. She had moved to Berlin in 1934 to work as a freelance writer for several newspapers and magazines. Her descriptions of the cruel acts of rape committed by the victors include her own and are written with a cold detachment that is chilling to the core. In two weeks at the end of April 1945, she had seen and experienced the whole 'catalogue' of rape, as she put it. There were 'gentle' types who patted women on the back afterwards and helped them up on their feet again. There were those who craved female company and wanted to play cards in between. Some seemed to enjoy the terror of their victims, as Marta experienced herself:

The one shoving me is an older man with grey stubble, reeking of alcohol and horses. He carefully closes the door behind him and, not finding any

key, slides the wing chair against the door. He seems to not even see his prey,
so that when he strikes she is all the more startled as he knocks her onto the
bedstead. Eyes closed, teeth clenched.[3]

Published anonymously, Marta's collection of diary entries was first translated into other languages as *A Woman in Berlin*. A German version in 1959 was so reviled that it was withdrawn and Marta never wanted it published again in her home country while she was alive. It was only in 2003, after her death, that a new edition was released in Germany and her identity revealed. It was as much the graphic detail that Germans were not ready to hear as it was the unashamed pragmatism of the young woman who endured this fate. Speaking a bit of Russian, Marta was able to seek out protection from the very men who had abused her. She found herself a 'wolf to keep the wolves at bay', as she put it, and entered a relationship of sorts with a high-ranking Russian officer. 'I am very proud that I have actually managed to tame one of the wolves, probably the strongest of the pack.' This was something few in Germany could bear to hear for decades to come – on either side of the Iron Curtain. In West Germany, Marta's apparent amorality offended the sensibilities of the time. In the East her descriptions disrupted the concept of Soviet 'liberation'.

All over the eastern areas of Germany that lay in the path of the Red Army's advance, many people experienced their first encounters with Soviets as a brutal conquest. Renate Demuth, only eight years old in 1945, remembered years later how the soldiers entered her family home in Olbersdorf, Saxony. Her father had died in a prisoner of war camp, only a few kilometres from what was to become the new German border to Poland and Czechoslovakia. Her mother was alone in the house with her, her brother Lothar, still a toddler, and her older sister Friedl, aged eighteen, when the soldiers hammered on the door. Renate's little fingers clenched around the folds of her mother's skirt as the men searched each room for valuables – and female prey. Her teenage sister lay in bed when one of them barged into her room. Bleary-eyed, he stared at

Friedl's face. She was ill and had a nasty rash with open sores on her cheeks. The soldier took one look at her, turned away in disgust and decided to inflict vengeance on the neighbours instead. A few days later, a high-ranking officer set up a command post in a requisitioned farmhouse behind the Demuths' home. Renate remembered her relief: 'He told us that his windows were always open and that we should shout if his men should try it on again. Then we had some peace.'⁴ Her family too had found a wolf to keep the pack at bay.

Some girls and women gained a different impression of their occupiers. Brigitte Fritschen was born in 1944, in Waldenburg near Breslau (now Wrocław in western Poland), and was still a baby as the war drew to a close. Nonetheless, the events that were to unfold as the town was ransacked by the advancing Red Army would leave a lasting mark on her life. There were only women and old men left in the street where she lived with her mother and grandparents. Some of the women were pregnant, many had small children. Brigitte's mother too tried to survive without her husband as he had been captured on the Eastern Front. She had heard horror stories about rape from villages further to the East. Worse, she had been told about how the Soviets would slit the throats of any German child they could find. Her blood ran cold as she thought of her little Brigitte. In their desperation, the women in the neighbourhood gathered all of their children in one room and guarded the door with their lives. Brigitte was one of the youngest of the dozen or so children in this 'nursery', as the women began to call it. Day and night the mothers sat in front of the door and waited in fear. When the Soviets finally arrived, their guard proved futile. A young soldier barged his way past them with his rifle and entered the room. Brigitte's mother froze in terror as the door slammed shut between her and her baby daughter.

There was silence. The women held their breath and listened. Would the man cut the children's throats? Some couldn't endure the tension any longer and cried for help. But who might have come? There were only Red Army soldiers in the streets outside. Behind the door, in the nursery, it was still dead silent. Finally, the women could not stand it any longer, and they opened the door. The young man had not cut a single throat. Instead, he knelt in front of the little beds and was sobbing bitterly. He cried and cried. The women stared as his tears continued to flow.

> *Eventually, my mother carefully tapped him on the shoulder. He had his arm around one of the babies. He turned around and tried to explain, using gestures and expressions. He said the word 'Haus' and then again and again 'Mama – Mama – Mama' and then the German word for 'tree'.*[5]

In his despair to be understood, the young soldier showed a rope and a noose with his hands. Germans had hanged his mother. He had also had a little sister – he mumbled the English word 'sister – sister' – who had been the same age as the little girl he now held in his arms. The Germans had hanged her too.[6]

In East German collective memory, the Russians' fondness for children stands in stark contrast to the contempt they showed their mothers. Renate Demuth remembered how soldiers stole her mother's only mode of transport, a bicycle ('even though those arseholes didn't know how to ride it and made a right hash of it'[7]). But she also recalled that the soldiers would always give her food and treats when they could: 'My brother Lothar and I were always sent [to them] – "as children they won't hurt you," everyone said. So big pockets were sewn on to our clothes in which we could hamster the vanilla sugar or potatoes they gave us.'[8]

Overall, the brutality of the Soviet occupiers was the impression that stayed with a society mainly made up of women, children and older people. The terror of the spring and summer of 1945 would resonate through East German memory for decades. However, as men returned to their homes and craved a new beginning, silence fell over the experiences of millions of German women. Indeed, many women themselves looked down on those who attempted to speak up about what had happened. They saw it as a shameful and humiliating experience that was best forgotten. This silencing was supported by the political elites of the GDR who were keen to promote Soviet Russia as a brother state, the saviour who had liberated the German people from the yoke of Nazism.

'Liberation' would always remain a bitter and hollow word to those German women and girls who paid for it with their bodies and minds. The Berlin journalist Ursula von Kardorff summed up the situation in her diary: 'So this is defeat. Naively, we always imagined it differently, or actually not at all. Anything, anything had to be better than Hitler. But liberation? Strange word.'[9]

Stalin's Task Force

Calau, Brandenburg, 30 April 1945. Three days after Dorothea Günther's ordeal at Karstadt, a chartered American Douglas plane from Moscow landed 80 kilometres east of Frankfurt an der Oder, which today forms the border between Germany and Poland. It carried ten men, who had been carefully selected from the most loyal inner circles of the German communist community in Moscow. A list of their names, finalized three days before departure, bears last-minute, handwritten annotations by Wilhelm Pieck.[10] He had scribbled the destination (Berlin) and the date of departure (30/4) and added another group by hand, which would, however, never be deployed. The impression of ad-hoc planning conveyed by the pencil scratchings is also confirmed by Wladimir Leonhard, who was to become the youngest member of this group, twenty-four years old at the time. He noted in his 1955 memoirs that he was simply held back at the end of an editorial meeting of the radio station 'Free Germany' for which he had read propaganda texts since 1943. That was in mid-April, and the editor-in-chief Anton Ackermann casually told him, 'Congratulations, you will join the first group to return to Germany.'[11]

Two weeks later, Wladimir looked out of the window of a west-bound plane, anticipating the return to the city of his childhood, Berlin. Around him sat nine other men contemplating their homecoming to a country that had changed beyond recognition since they had left it over a decade earlier. The leader was Walter Ulbricht, by now one of Stalin's most trusted men in Moscow. He lent his name to the 'Gruppe Ulbricht', as the posse came to be called. While it is unknown exactly how these men were selected and by whom, they reflected all the different skills the Soviets felt they needed in Berlin to rebuild an 'anti-fascist' Germany. There were expert propagandists such as Karl Maron and Fritz Erpenbeck who had worked for newspapers and radio. There were pedantic bureaucrats with organizational skills such as Richard Gyptner and Otto Winzer. There were likeable, genuine, down-to-earth working class types such as Hans Mahle and Gustav Gundelach. Walter Köppe was probably chosen for being an authentic Berliner. He originated from the capital and still spoke with the broad, undiluted accent of his urban home. Completing the picture were Wladimir Leonhard as a representative of the new generation who had undergone a full communist education, practically from birth, and Ulbricht as the unwavering, pro-Soviet leader. The group was a microcosm of the remnants of the communist enclave in Moscow.

At approximately 3.30 p.m. on 30 April 1945, the same afternoon as the German exiles from Moscow arrived at the Polish-German border, Adolf Hitler shot himself in a private room in his bunker around 95 kilometres to the west. Blazing artillery fire still rained down daily on Berlin. Instead of the thousand-year Reich he had promised, he left behind razed cities and destroyed lives. That evening, at 10.40 p.m., the red Soviet flag would be hoisted on the roof of the Reichstag building.

The Gruppe Ulbricht marvelled at the destruction, misery and despair they saw from the back of the truck that carried them to Marshal Zhukov's headquarters, 30 kilometres east of Berlin. When the capital finally fell on 2 May, they were immediately deployed. While ordinary men, women and children like the Günthers, Marta Hillers or Renate Demuth were trying to survive and rebuild their lives, Ulbricht and his fellow German communists had been charged with the task to identify and extinguish any remnants of fascism in order to lay the human foundations for a new kind of Germany.

Part of Ulbricht's brief was to establish trust in the Soviet administration. This was not an easy task. The ideologues, who had spent the entire war in exile, had little understanding of the day-to-day struggle of the people for whom they purported to be building this new state. In turn, they were viewed with suspicion, as Stalin's lackeys who had turned their back on the fatherland, betraying the men and women who had toiled and died for it. Now they had returned triumphant, shoulder to shoulder with the drunken horde of foreign invaders who danced on the streets as they murdered, raped and plundered their way into the heart of a defeated nation. The hostile atmosphere was inflamed further by the absence of food, fuel and other essentials. While some Germans found meaning and hope in the idea of rebuilding and renewing, many did not want to do so under Stalin's boot.

As these future political leaders were keen to establish positive relationships with the public, they downplayed their Russian connections as much as possible. Ulbricht, for example, personally asked Wladimir Leonhard to change his first name to the more German-sounding 'Wolfgang'. Otto Winzer was still travelling under his pseudonym 'Lorenz' to avoid identification. Pieck's entire annotated list of members is labelled 'Top Secret!' and the very existence of the Gruppe Ulbricht would be denied for a decade after it was formed.

Ulbricht's men were not free to act as they pleased. Even before their departure from Moscow, the Bulgarian Comintern boss Georgi Dimitrov had summoned Wilhelm Pieck to relay a message from Stalin himself: 'those departing are not at the beck and call of the KPD, but receive directions from the Red Army'.[12] Once in Germany, Ulbricht had to report to the Soviet occupation authorities almost every night – be that to discuss the re-establishment of culture and entertainment in Berlin or to consult on seemingly trivial matters such as approval for his leaflets encouraging Berliners to make use of 'every spot of land'[13] to grow food. At the same time,

Ulbricht's talent for organization and his unblemished record of loyalty to the Soviets quickly gained him the trust of the Soviet authorities in Germany. He was pleased to report back to Pieck who was still in Moscow in May 1945: 'It has already got to a point where, when there are complicated questions, the commanding officers call us to ask for a specialist who can help with questions of organization when it comes to the re-establishment of administrative systems.'[14] Nonetheless, Stalin would personally summon his German delegation eleven times to his office at the Kremlin between June 1945 and April 1952 and he had two private meetings with his German stalwart[15] – more a sign of his inherent mistrust than a real interest in the political future of his occupation zone.

If anything, Stalin seems to have been keen to curtail the ideological zeal of the German communists. Historians are still arguing about what his exact plans for post-war Germany were. What is clear is that his initial instructions for Ulbricht worked towards a solution for the whole of Germany, not just the areas he occupied. This did not mean the setting-up of a system in the Soviet image. Dimitrov, who attended one of Stalin's meetings with Ulbricht on 7 June 1945, recorded in his diary that Stalin 'suggested to definitely explain [to Ulbricht's fellow Germans] that the introduction of the Soviet system in Germany is wrong; what is necessary is the installation of an anti-fascist, democratic, parliamentary regime'.[16] While this sentiment may not have originated out of a love for Western-style politics, it was clear that in the early summer of 1945, Stalin was still keen to collaborate with his capitalist allies. The establishment of a separate East German state was not the original plan.

In Germany, Ulbricht obediently relayed Stalin's message to his group and sent them into the capital to enact their mission. Wolfgang Leonhard remembered that Ulbricht instructed them to build anti-fascist administrations in all twenty districts of Berlin. Then Ulbricht uttered the sentence that would become inextricably linked with East German politics. Summing up the mission to rebuild a government in Berlin, Ulbricht told his disciples, 'It has to look democratic, but we must have everything in our hands.'[17]

Restless Germans

Berlin, May 1945. The physician Dr Otto Müllereisert clambered through heaps of rubble on the way to his hospital. The place was running short of everything – bandages, morphine, medicine. But he was determined to do what he could for the desperate patients in his crowded waiting room. At least he was still needed. He still had purpose. On his way, he spotted something odd in the window of a shop, which had been looted and stood open without a door or glass. Two human-shaped figures lay there, wrapped in paper 'like Egyptian mummies'.[18] Curious, the doctor asked for one of the figures to be unwrapped. He baulked when the paper was peeled away and a naked, male body emerged. Otto's heart sank. 'Where have these dead bodies come from?' he asked and was escorted down a dark, half-buried set of steps into an air raid shelter. When he opened the heavy door, he was hit by the stench and sight of twenty people, all wrapped in blankets on the stone floor. Some were breathing heavily, others seemed barely conscious. Typhus. Without another glance, Otto slammed the door shut. He turned and looked directly into the tired eyes of the man who had led him down into this 'fever hell'. 'We have to seal off this basement completely. Guard the entrance at all times,' he told the man. The answer still rang in the doctor's ears as he hurried away: 'But my wife is down there, what am I supposed . . .' There was nothing he could do.

Allied bombing, artillery fire and house to house fighting had reduced German cities to ashes from which the ruins of broken houses protruded. The situation in the countryside was often better than in the cities, but villages that lay in the way of enemy advances were also ravaged. Müncheberg, a small mediaeval town about half-way between Berlin and the new Polish border, for example, was left with only 15 per cent of its former housing stock. Cities such as Dresden and Berlin were unrecognizable. The capital alone was buried under 55 million cubic metres of rubble – described by contemporary sources as enough to form a wall, 5 metres tall and 30

metres wide and stretching from Berlin to Cologne.[19] Dresden and
Berlin have burned themselves into collective memory as the worst
examples of war-ravaged cities, but there are many others. Rostock,
for instance, a large German port on the Baltic coast, suffered damage to 85 per cent of its housing stock due to British and American
bombing. Overall it is estimated that 20 million Germans were
made homeless by the Second World War as nearly half of the
country's housing was destroyed.

As food, water and electricity supplies had broken down, injured,
hungry and sick Germans crawled out of their ruined homes, scurrying past Red Army soldiers to the nearest water pump or to find
anything edible. Timber from collapsed buildings was retrieved as
firewood; parks and green spaces deforested – first without, then
with Allied consent. Berlin resident Erika Reinicke, then eleven
years old, remembered how her family treated themselves to a theatre visit at Christmas in 1945. They went to see Franz Lehár's romantic
operetta *The Land of Smiles*. The entrance fee was one coal briquette
per person so that the room might be heated.[20]

The people who Walter Ulbricht encountered upon his return in
1945 were not the same people he had left behind in 1933. There
were 16 million inhabitants in the Soviet Zone of Occupation at the
end of 1945, around a million more than there had been before the
war. This may seem surprising given that a total of 10 million Germans had been captured as prisoners of war and well over 5 million
had fallen on all fronts. Many of the former were being gradually
released from 1945 onwards but the 3 million or so captured on the
Eastern Front were often held in work camps for much longer,
sometimes years. Many perished in terrible conditions, never to
return. But their numbers were made up by the influx of German
refugees from the east. The victorious Allies had agreed that it was
necessary for the preservation of peace in Europe to expel ethnic
Germans from the lands east of the River Oder, from areas that
became part of Poland, Czechoslovakia, Hungary, Yugoslavia, Romania and the Soviet Union. While they stipulated that this was to be
done 'in an orderly and humane manner', the reality experienced by

those who fled or were expelled was very different. Met by the fervent hatred of Red Army soldiers and the civilian population which had suffered terrible hardship and atrocities at German hands during the war, the refugees were subjected to wanton acts of cruelty, rape and murder. Their journey would often take years as they travelled on foot, in long columns dragging their remaining belongings behind them on overloaded wooden carts.

Sternberg, Western Poland, February 1945. Ilse Hentschel was eight years old when Russian soldiers drove her family out from her home town of Sternberg (now Torzym in western Poland). Her father had been drafted into the *Wehrmacht* as a driver and was still in Soviet captivity in 1945, so Ilse and her two older sisters Christel (fifteen) and Gisela (ten) set off together with her mother and grandmother. Not knowing where to go, they simply joined one of the endless columns of other desperate families moving westwards along the Bundesstraße 1, which ran all the way to Berlin. Ilse still remembers how the family observed the countless bodies of civilians and soldiers strewn by the roadside with a sense of impending doom. Every member of their little group caught typhoid fever. For the rest of her life Ilse would be grateful for the sugar that some softhearted Soviet soldiers had given the sisters so that their mother could make the unripe apples they found along the way edible by cooking them, making a kind of sweet mush. Ilse believed that this saved her life. Her grandmother was beyond saving. She died when a wound in her leg began to fester. Her little granddaughter helped with grim determination as the family 'wrapped her in a blanket, put her on the cart and dragged her to the nearest cemetery where we buried her'.[21] Like so many others, Ilse's family slowly migrated westwards, seeking shelter in burnt-out farmhouses, squeezing on to overcrowded trains, sleeping rough at the stations as one never knew when the next train might arrive. She would eventually begin her new life near Potsdam, south-west of Berlin. Her fate was shared by millions. By 1950, one quarter of the East German population would consist of these displaced Germans from the east.

Ravaged by defeat, starvation, homelessness, grief and the victors' violent retribution, the people in the Soviet Zone were restless and desperate. Their frustration seemed likely to boil over into civil unrest. They had nothing more to lose, which made them volatile and hard to control without a functioning security apparatus. Nazi governmental structures had collapsed and the free-for-all on the burgeoning black markets did little to rebuild societal norms and structures. Expelled and brutalized by the Red Army, they were also unlikely to accept a narrative of liberation and place their trust in the foreign occupiers. Walter Ulbricht and his men seemed to have been given an impossible brief when they were asked to restore order and begin to build trust and stability.

The Reign of Deputies

Berlin, 2 May 1945. Wolfgang Leonhard and the other members of the Gruppe Ulbricht looked out of the windows of their cars as their column made its way westwards from the Soviet headquarters in Bruchmühle through the Berlin suburb of Friedrichsfelde into the centre of the once-proud capital of the Third Reich. The city of Wolfgang's childhood had vanished and he was met with post-apocalyptic scenes that put him in mind of Dante's Inferno.

Fire, ruins, lost and hungry people scurrying around in torn rags. Dazed German soldiers who seem to have lost all comprehension of what was going on. Singing, cheering and often drunk Red Army soldiers. Groups of women clearing up the rubble under the supervision of the Red Army. Long columns of people patiently waiting at the pumps to fill a bucket of water. Everyone looked terribly tired, hungry, worn and torn.[22]

The Gruppe Ulbricht had their work cut out.

The first task for the Moscow exiles was to create a system of local governance in the Soviet Zone of Occupation and they threw themselves into their work with great enthusiasm and energy.

When they arrived in Berlin with the brief to find suitable candidates to fill the positions of mayors, councillors and other public offices, they were simply told to stick to 'anti-fascist' men and women. This proved easier than the group had anticipated as the Nazi regime had left meticulous records of politicians and office holders during the Weimar Republic who were dismissed from their positions during the Hitler years. Ulbricht was keenly aware that he could not merely fill all the vacant roles with communists. That would never do if he wanted to create a stable system that would enjoy the support of the people. He directed his task force to apply the following system: 'Each district council must be led by a mayor and two deputies (with the first deputy also taking responsibility for matters of personnel) and have departments for food distribution, economy, social matters, healthcare, traffic, work deployment, education, finance, church matters etc.'[23] Crucially, he stressed that it was important that the political composition of these leadership teams reflected the local context:

> We have no use for communists as mayors, except perhaps in Wedding or Friedrichshain [both traditional communist strongholds]. The mayors in working class districts should usually be Social Democrats. In middle-class areas – Zehlendorf, Wilmersdorf, Charlottenburg etc. – we have to place a bourgeois man at the top, someone who was once in the Catholic Centre Party, the Democratic Party or the German People's Party. Even better if he is a physician; but he must be an anti-fascist and someone we can work with.[24]

While Ulbricht was happy for anyone with 'anti-fascist' credentials to fill the slots in the political front rows of local administration, he was also keen to ensure that decision-making capacity was handed to those who agreed with his vision for Germany. The real power over policy and personnel would not lie with the mayors themselves but with their deputies – carefully chosen for their willingness to help Ulbricht build socialism on German soil.

Ulbricht's system of deputies was implemented everywhere in

the Soviet Zone. His group and three others like it, also sourced from the German communist diaspora in Moscow, busied themselves raking through police records, lists of concentration camp inmates and active politicians from the Weimar years. They found people like Erich Zeigner, a fifty-nine-year-old former SPD politician, who was installed as the mayor of Leipzig on 16 July 1945. He had been a lifelong Social Democrat and languished in the concentration camps of Sachsenhausen and Buchenwald for it. He was also a respectable and well-spoken man from a middle class background with a university degree in law and economics and a PhD. He would remain the mayor of Leipzig and worked in tandem with the Soviet occupiers and their German helpers until his death in 1949. Not all appointments, however, worked as smoothly as this. When Otto Baer was appointed as Magdeburg's mayor, the SPD man and trade unionist seemed a good choice. He too had been incarcerated by the Nazis and later constantly harassed by them with curfews and house searches. But Baer quickly proved to be his own man and ran into conflict with the Soviets which earned him his dismissal and a ten-week spell in an NKVD prison. On the whole, however, the reign of deputies fulfilled Ulbricht's brief to a tee: it looked democratic but all was in communist hands.

Peoples' Friendship

Berlin-Friedrichstadt, 8 May 1945. The war was over. The *Wehrmacht* had surrendered and ordered the cessation of all hostilities. The Gruppe Ulbricht had already been hard at work for nearly a week when a man arrived from Moscow who had originally been assigned to their task force but then retracted at the last minute. The Soviets had feared that his Jewish background might earn him the hostility of the Nazified German public which they wanted to win over. But the man was useful and so he was sent to Berlin after all, only a week later than his comrades. Rudolf Herrnstadt spent VE Day rummaging through the sorry remains of the Mosse-Haus in Berlin's newspaper district, Friedrichstadt. Once the home of many of the capital's liberal newspapers such as the *Berliner Tageblatt*, the building with its grand futurist facade had been the tallest secular structure in Berlin. Now it lay in ruins, burnt out and littered with human bodies. Unperturbed by the sweet, heavy stench of decay, the communist journalist combed the sea of rubble for a printing press and typewriters.

Herrnstadt was a single-minded man; he always had been. His father, a well-to-do lawyer and solicitor in the Upper Silesian city of Gleiwitz (now Gliwice in southern Poland), had expected his son to follow in his footsteps, but young Rudolf had other plans. He wanted to be a writer and dropped out of university. Having no income, his father made him work in a local paper factory, but after two years he rebelled again and moved to Berlin against the express wishes of his parents. There he began to work his way up from poorly paid freelance journalism to a fixed position as a foreign correspondent in Prague, Warsaw and Moscow. Despite his bourgeois upbringing, he requested to join the KPD in the 1920s, and the party eventually admitted him after initial hesitation given his social background. Years later, when he edited the newspaper of the National Committee for a Free Germany in Moscow, he would still amuse his working class colleagues with his stiff, old-fashioned language, particularly the fact that he addressed his subordinates with 'Sie', the formal form of 'you'.

The talented propagandist had a crucial role to play in the build-up of governmental structures in the Soviet Zone. He saw it as his duty to establish a popular newspaper for his compatriots that would be a vital tool in their re-education. Having spent the war in Russia, he had grown to love its language, people and culture. He had neither time nor patience for the stories of rape and plunder he was hearing from the people who had allowed Hitler to attack the Soviet Union and commit horrific crimes there. His Jewish background made this hostility all the more personal and he was shocked at the self-pity displayed by Berliners.

When Herrnstadt eventually found a printing press in the district of Kreuzberg, he wasted no time in starting the work of re-education. On 22 May 1945, only a fortnight after his return to Germany, the very first edition of his newspaper was printed with a circulation of 100,000 copies: the *Berliner Zeitung* was born. Its first ever headline would become famous: 'Berlin lives again!' Herrnstadt soon became frustrated when his mix of pro-Soviet propaganda and information had little effect on the attitude of the German people towards their Soviet liberators. People read his paper in their droves, but what they were after was useful information – changes in food distribution, new rules and regulations, missing friends and relatives that might have reappeared. It would take years for the trauma of 1945 to fade into distant memory. Under the immediate impression of war, his readers continued to display much hostility towards the Soviets – a far cry from the 'peoples' friendship' Herrnstadt was trying to propagate.

In order to confront the issue head-on, Herrnstadt penned a much-discussed article in November 1948, entitled 'About the "Russians" and about us'. It was an eloquent rant about what he would say to someone who argued that his brother-in-law was just 'peacefully standing by the roadside when [the Russians] whacked him on the head and stole his bike'.[25] The author admitted that the war had 'brutalized, yes in some cases brutalized people' but he avoided any direct reference to rape. Instead he argued indignantly that Germans must understand that to the Soviets they were bystanders to a terrible regime that had ravaged their motherland. Surely it made sense that the brother-in-law, who may well have stood by the roadside innocently, was a bitter enemy in the eyes of the victims of a war launched by his fellow Germans. But it did not make sense to everybody. Over the next few weeks, the newspaper's office was flooded with angry letters.

Rudolf Herrnstadt's inability to understand or connect with the German public was typical of the returning Moscow exiles. Still keen to hide their connection to the Soviet occupiers, the Gruppe Ulbricht and others who were sent back had no idea what it was like to be on the wrong side of history. They felt they had the moral high ground.

A Brand-New Government

As Walter Ulbricht and his team were looking for candidates with which to fill the deputy system, the Soviet Military Administration in Germany (SMAD) began its work on 9 June 1945. Its main purpose was to govern the eastern portion of occupied Germany in tandem with the American, British and French zones in the West. This meant restoring infrastructure, food and water supplies, policing and life in general without jeopardizing the unity of the country. Eventually, the administration of Germany had to be handed back to its own people, but first thoroughly denazified governmental structures were to be established.

Initially, the Soviets were much more willing to place trust in the German people than their Western counterparts. In the second issue of Rudolf Herrnstadt's *Berliner Zeitung*, a framed quote by Joseph Stalin himself seemed to promise swift reconciliation: 'The Hitlers come and go, but the German people, the German state remain.'[26] Stalin's attitude towards Germans was highly ambivalent. The murderous paranoia and persecution that were the hallmark of the purge years clashed with his fascination for German culture, literature and art. Now that the war was over and Germans no longer posed a threat to him or his people, Stalin was ready to believe that the German people had fallen under Hitler's spell and were not inherently warlike (as the Americans initially assumed). The Soviet Zone was therefore quick to place power back into German hands. Only one day after the SMAD had begun its work, the formation of political parties and trade unions was permitted in SMAD Order No. 2. The next day, the German communist party, the KPD, was refounded with the Moscow exiles at its heart. Wilhelm Pieck returned from the USSR on 1 July 1945 to become its chairman.

The formation of the KPD on 11 June 1945 did not mean that the Soviet Zone had been strapped on an unstoppable historical conveyer belt to secession. Valentin Falin, a Soviet diplomat and Germany expert who was to serve as ambassador to West Germany in the 1970s, remembered that the meetings between Ulbricht and Stalin in the summer of 1945 always had German unity at their core. Stalin stressed again and again that 'Germany must be preserved as a unified state. No split, no experiments which might jeopardize the social order in Germany. The task is to bring to a completion the bourgeois-democratic revolution of 1848.'[27] Falin's comments must be taken with a pinch of salt – as a Soviet diplomat during the Cold War, he had every incentive to play down Stalin's role in the division of Germany. But the fact is that other political parties and organizations were allowed to form in the Soviet Zone three months before the Western Allies did the same. The Social Democratic Party, the Christian Democratic Union (CDU) and the Liberal Democratic Party of Germany (LDPD) were founded in June and July, followed by the Free German Trade Union Federation (FDGB) on 13 July 1945. So-called Antifa Committees spontaneously formed everywhere across the Soviet Zone. They were made up of a wild mix of individuals, among them socialists, communists, liberals, Christians and other opponents of Nazism. Former bystanders and even Nazi Party members also sometimes joined in the hope that this would keep them out of trouble now that the tides of history had turned against them.

In the north German port town of Greifswald, liberals, democrats, pastors, communists, socialists and many others who had been opposed to the Nazi regime came together even before the end of the war and merged into a formal Antifa Committee afterwards. The little Hanseatic town contained 60,000 people at this point (twice as many as had lived there in 1933), half of whom were ethnic Germans who had fled from Eastern Europe. The need for functioning local administration was urgent and the Soviet commander allowed the committee to set up shop in the town hall, a beautiful thirteenth-century brick building, fittingly bright red in colour. From there the committee began to build up structures to try to alleviate the terrible humanitarian situation – the lack of food, water and shelter for the refugees had led to rampant outbreaks of diseases such as typhoid fever but also to crime and a general

breakdown of law and order. While they worked under the watch-
ful eye of the Soviets, the committee independently declared that
it wanted to 'destroy fascism in the city and in the countryside
through the education of the population about the causes and
course of the war'.[28]

In theory, this pluralistic political landscape was set up to facili-
tate a functioning democracy. There was genuine enthusiasm from
groups all across eastern Germany who saw a chance to redeem
themselves and their country by building a better Germany and
helping to extinguish the embers of fascism, which still glowed red
hot in 1945. Wolfgang Leonhard was touched by all of this. So many
of his compatriots seemed to roll up their sleeves to rebuild, physically and politically. 'It was a wonderful thing,' he gushed, 'every
anti-fascist understood that he must not do his own thing but communists, social democrats, leftists, liberals – all together!'[29]

The Great Purges – Part II

Greifswald, Mecklenburg, 28 May 1945. It was the middle of the
night when an NKVD officer knocked on Hans Lachmund's door.
When Hans opened it, he was immediately arrested without charge.
He was a central member of the Antifa Committee and in the previous weeks he had worked feverishly with his friends and colleagues
from their newly established offices in Greifswald's town hall to
establish functioning administrative structures. Hans had been a
lifelong passionate democrat. Politically active in the Weimar years,
he then joined underground resistance organizations to oppose the
Nazis. On 8 May 1945, when the war was finally over, he was made
a central member of the new Greifswald city council – with the full
consent of the Soviets who thought the middle class image of the
lawyer would be a useful asset. When the NKVD turned up to
arrest him in the dead of night, it came as a complete shock to him.
No explanation was given and Hans would spend the next three
years in political internment camps.

At first, he was kept at Camp No. 9 in Fünfeichen, near Neu-brandenburg. Previously known as Stalag II A, it was a prisoner of war camp in which thousands of the *Wehrmacht*'s enemy soldiers had died (6,000 of the Red Army alone). Now it was for politically suspicious Germans. Hans was surrounded by former Nazi Party members, as well as countless teenagers who had been members of the Hitler Youth. In the autumn of 1945, he was transferred to Special Camp 2 at Buchenwald, near Weimar. They had barely cleared up the remains of those who died there at the hands of the Nazis – in April thousands of Weimar residents were forced to visit the camp and view the piles of bodies – when the new political prisoners were moved in three months later. There would be 6,000 of them by the end of 1945.

While the political set-up in the Soviet Zone initially looked democratic, just as Ulbricht had briefed his group, a process of forceful political streamlining was already under way as the Soviets and their German helpers began to look into the background of those comprising the anti-fascist committees. An atmosphere of paranoia swept through the ranks of the Moscow exiles, echoing the terrifying years of Stalin's Great Purges. Could they really trust this mayor? Was that counsellor really a communist? Did they know that the Antifa Committee in this town is not in reality a covert fascist reorganization? When Wolfgang Leonhard told Walter Ulbricht with youthful enthusiasm that spontaneous antifa groups had sprung up everywhere, his boss's response bordered on hysteria. 'We have to dissolve these units immediately!' Ulbricht demanded. After all, he explained, there was no telling whether these cells contained secret Nazis who were masquerading as anti-fascists.

The mass incarceration of political enemies in NKVD Special Camps (or Spezlags) would continue until they were finally dissolved in 1950. Initially introduced by NKVD Order 00315 on 18 April 1945 with the aim to 'cleanse the hinterland of hostile elements while Red Army troops were fighting', the remit of incarcerations was gradually widened. Hans Lachmund was apprehended in Greif-swald on the basis of some previous links to freemasonry which had been discovered. Between 1945 and 1950, a total of ten Special Camps were set up. The official NKVD figures speak of 157,837 prisoners in total, of whom 756 were shot outright by the Soviets' own admission. It is estimated that 35 per cent of those incarcerated in the camps died of the atrocious conditions there.[30]

The wave of arrests was the most obvious marker that the supposedly democratic and pluralistic set-up in the Soviet Zone was being eroded as soon as it had been established. Thousands of enthusiastic opponents of the Nazi regime, particularly in 'Red Berlin', as Jospeh Goebbels had so often sneeringly called the city, had genuinely wanted to work with the Soviets to build a better Germany. They looked forward to getting involved after years of oppression by the Nazis. Now any political activism, indeed putting your head above the parapet at all, became dangerous. And so many East Germans turned in on themselves. They wanted nothing to do with the Soviets or their German enforcers.

Workers of the Soviet Zone Unite!

Berlin-Mitte, 21 May 1946. Walter Ulbricht and Wilhelm Pieck sat left and right of the SPD leader Otto Grotewohl in the front row of the benches that had been put up on the stage of the grand Admiralspalast on Berlin's Friedrichstraße in the city centre. Miraculously, the building had survived the bombing, artillery fire and street fighting of the previous months intact. The impressive structure had once housed luxurious amusement venues such as Roman-style baths, an ice skating rink and a bowling alley before it was converted to a full-scale theatre with 2,200 seats in 1930. Joseph Goebbels did not think much of the expressionist style it had been decorated in and had the grand hall changed again to the classicist design that it still features today.

It seemed odd for Ulbricht to summon the representatives of the two working class parties, SPD and KPD, to such a pompous, bourgeois place, but he needed to impress them. Both camps had severe reservations about what was about to happen: the merger of social democracy and communism into one Socialist Unity Party, the SED. Otto Grotewohl looked content as he sat between Ulbricht and Pieck; he smiled and clapped in all the right places. But he too had initially been sceptical about the union. A book printer by trade, Grotewohl had built a political career in the SPD in the Weimar Republic when he occupied several positions from Reichstag deputy to cabinet member. He never reneged on his principles once Hitler had ascended to power and carried on working for the underground resistance movement, which earned him several prison spells and constant harassment from the Gestapo. He had been in Germany all those years and never ceased to fight.

Unlike Ulbricht and Pieck, Grotewohl had watched the Soviets march into Berlin bringing yet more misery to the population. Like many of the socialists and communists who had remained in Germany, he was more than a little suspicious when the German exiles returned from Moscow and assumed to take over. However, Egon Bahr, a fellow SPD man, and Jacob Kaiser, then leader of the Christian Democratic Union, would later both swear that Grotewohl experienced a miraculous transformation after he had been summoned to a meeting at the SMAD headquarters in Karlshorst 'from which he returned a changed man'.[31] We will never know what exactly happened in Karlshorst but Grotewohl was now onside. Many other SPD members remained a problem. When the party's Berlin cells of the Western sectors held a vote on whether they wanted an immediate merger with the KPD, 80 per cent of them voted against the idea and so the SMAD quickly banned any such votes in their sector.

Ulbricht was keen to ensure that the event at the Admiralspalast on 21 August 1946 would stir the hearts of those hardened socialists who had all endured their fair share of suffering. The representatives of their respective parties were seated under giant banners with the faces of Karl Marx, Friedrich Engels and August Bebel, the iconic nineteenth-century founding fathers of socialism. This was to remind the 507 KPD delegates and 548 SPD members present of their common working class roots, a time long before ideological divisions splintered the movement in the First World War. Together, as the SPD, they had become the largest political party in the Reichstag in 1912 before the war, but the bitter infighting that followed tore the movement apart. The wounds remained so raw through the Weimar years that the two factions could not even bring themselves to unite against Hitler, a situation with calamitous consequences, not least for the delegates themselves.

Ulbricht reminded everyone of this painful legacy of division when he said, 'From today, there will be no more Social Democrats and no more Communists. From today, there will only be Socialists.' His remarks were met with roaring applause. Pieck and Grotewohl symbolically shook hands, leading to more applause. Together they would chair the newly formed SED party, an organization that would dictate East German politics for over four decades.

Junker Land in Peasant Hands

Ballenstedt, Saxony-Anhalt, 31 August 1945. Joachim Ernst, Duke of Anhalt, was confused when armed and uniformed Russian men appeared at his residence, Ballenstedt Castle. The baroque building situated in the mountainous Harz region of Saxony-Anhalt had been the seat of the mediaeval House of Ascania for centuries. When the duke opened the door to the Russians, he was not particularly worried. His anti-fascist record was good. The forty-four-year-old had been a vocal opponent of Nazi rule and spent three months in Dachau concentration camp in the winter of 1944. He welcomed the liberation from Nazi tyranny. His heart sank when he noticed that the Russians wore blue trousers and caps with a cornflower blue top and maroon band underneath (the colour of which fittingly translates from Russian as 'nettle'). These were no ordinary Red Army soldiers. They were NKVD officers. They arrested the duke without charge and dragged him to the 'Red Ox' in Halle, an infamous prison, so named because of the distinctive red colour of its brick facade.

Joachim Ernst tried to explain that he had been opposed to the Nazi regime and would pose no danger to a democratic Germany. But to the communists this meant nothing. In their eyes, all German aristocrats, indeed anyone of wealth, had blood on their hands; they had all financed Hitler's rise to power. The Duke of Anhalt was eventually transferred to NKVD Special Camp 2 at Buchenwald, where he began to starve and eventually contracted hunger typhus. He died there at the age of forty-six.

Many aristocrats, particularly the former 'Junkers', as the Prussian landed gentry were called, suffered such fates. For once there was unity in purpose between the SPD and the KPD: both wanted far-reaching social reform and both harboured a deep-seated resentment towards the nobility. Land reforms were a rather uncontentious issue between them. Supported by the Soviets who pointed to their own brutal history of land redistribution in the wake of the First World War as an example, they set to work under the slogan 'Junker land in peasant hands'.

On 29 August 1945, the 'Democratic Bloc' formed of the representatives of all the new parties decided that any private land above 100 hectares, an area equivalent to 140 football pitches, would be seized without compensation. Joachim Ernst von Anhalt's 20,000 hectares were well above this limit and seized when he was arrested. His youngest son, Eduard Prinz von Anhalt, is still fighting to regain his family's property and castle today. They were not the only family who lost their land. A grand total of 3.3 million hectares were confiscated, equivalent to 35 per cent of the Soviet Zone's agricultural land; in Mecklenburg in the north it was 54 per cent. Alongside the land, affected families lost their houses, facilities, personal belongings, even clothes, as they were expelled from their homes overnight. As if that was not enough, they were also forbidden from settling in their home districts, as a visible sign that the former class enemy had been banished.

It was as if class structures could be exorcised from German society by physically dispersing the landed gentry. Two thirds of the land were then redistributed in tiny segments of around 20 hectares to so-called new peasants while the last third remained in state hands. The inexperience of the 'new peasants' combined with the fact that the land segments were far too small for profitable farming and the lack of adequate farming machinery meant that food production took an immediate hit. The East German agricultural sector would suffer the consequences of this for decades to come.

Pillage and Plunder

Berlin, 22 October 1946. Helmut Breuninger woke up in the small hours of the morning. Someone was knocking on the door. When he opened it, he was greeted by two Red Army officers and an armed soldier. One of the officers told him, 'By order of the Soviet Military Administration, you must work in your subject for five years in the Soviet Union . . . You will take your wife and your child. You may take as many of your belongings as you like. Start packing.'[32] Helmut hastily nailed some wood together in his garden to make crates, which the family then stuffed with the things they wanted to take. A few hours later, lorries appeared outside the house and soldiers loaded them with the young family and their belongings. When they reached the station, two trains were already waiting, steam billowing from their chimneys. The Breuningers' belongings filled one of the freight wagons while the family was seated together in the passenger compartment. They stared out of the windows as the rubble of the city gradually turned into the flat fields of Brandenburg. Where the journey might end, they did not know.

Helmut was a thirty-five-year-old physicist, originally from Germering, a small town just outside the Bavarian capital of Munich. Like many scientists he had worked for the German armament industry and lost his job when Hitler lost the war. He was grateful when he found work at Askania Works in Berlin, a company specializing in precision mechanics and optics, where the Soviets had restarted production. There, he helped develop autopilot systems for aeroplanes. The expertise of German scientists and engineers in rocket science, armament and aviation technology was highly sought-after by all the victors of the Second World War. They had agreed at the Potsdam Conference in July and August 1945 that forced labour of key personnel was acceptable and that individual staff could be asked to relocate abroad – the latter, however, was not to happen without their consent.

Initially the SMAD followed these guidelines and scientists across their zone worked in the reopened labs and factories. However, Moscow became increasingly concerned about the security implications of German scientists being entrusted with sensitive information about the Soviet Union's military projects. After all, they were free to roam, including into the Western Zones. There was nothing to stop American or British personnel from speaking to east German scientists or even entering the sites, especially in Berlin. So a decision was made to remove thousands of specialists from the Soviet Zone of Occupation. As this was unlikely to be met with unanimous enthusiasm, it had to happen in one fell swoop.

Operation Osoaviakhim was a coordinated round-up of key workers all across the Soviet Zone. On the night of 22 October 1946, over 2,000 German physicists, chemists, engineers and scientists woke up to knocks on their door and were asked to pack immediately. Many said later that they were treated humanely. To their bemusement some were told they could take any woman they liked – their wife or their mistress. Often they could take as many of their personal effects as they wanted, including furniture or cars. Irmgard Gröttrup, wife of the rocket scientist Helmut Gröttrup who had worked on the V2 project under Wernher von Braun, told the Soviets that she must take two cows, so that their children would always have enough milk. Her wish was granted. But for all that the Soviets bent over backwards to accommodate the family's requests, Frau Gröttrup also noted that there was a force behind their kindness. In her memoirs, she wrote that as she began to pack her family's belongings, 'simply to be free for a moment, I tried to get out through the back door. Impossible! The barrel of a gun, a broad face: "Nyet." '[33]

The Gröttrup family and their two cows arrived in Moscow on 28 October 1946. They and seventy-three other specialists were then transferred to the island of Gorodomlya in the Seliger Lake north-west of Moscow. There they lived in a golden cage. Karl Breuninger, who was two years old when he and his parents were transferred to the Soviet Union, remembers that 'the Germans were better paid than the Russians'.[34] Soon they began to befriend the locals. Clemens Pingel, whose father had been a colleague of Breuninger's at Askania and was also abducted, described how 'the Russians would ask our parents: are you Nazis? As the answer was no, they drank vodka together.'[35] Most of these scientists were released from their duty in the 1950s and were astonished to find that they were asked which Germany they would like to return to. Some chose to return to Austria.

Apart from this huge loss in scientific expertise, the Soviet Zone in Germany also began to lag behind its Western counterparts in other economic areas. At Yalta, Stalin had insisted on vast reparations to be paid by Germany, of which he reckoned the Soviet Union deserved 50 per cent. The Soviet Union had exhausted itself in the horrific battle of attrition on the Eastern Front. Reparations were not just fair punishment to Stalin but an economic necessity if his people were to avoid a repeat of the terrible scenes of civil war that followed the First World War. However, British and American interests lay in rebuilding Germany, as they feared that with much of France in ruins, Soviet domination over the continent would otherwise become all but inevitable. The spectre of the Treaty of Versailles still haunted Western minds. A fixed reparations sum such as the £6.6 billion that pushed the Weimar economy permanently to the brink was to be avoided at all costs. A compromise was reached whereby each power was allowed to take reparations from their own zone of occupation. In addition the Soviets would receive

10 per cent extra from the West as they had lost out on the Ruhr region, the beating heart of Germany's powerful industry.

Stalin enforced the reparations agreement with full force in his zone. This began on a personal level with individuals tearing bicycles out of German hands – an image that would stick in many German minds for decades. Wristwatches were particularly popular with Soviet soldiers, who could often be heard shouting 'Uri! Uri!' (the German for watch is Uhr) as they entered the houses of the vanquished. The iconic photograph of the Red Flag being hoisted on the roof of the Reichstag had to be altered as one of the soldiers on it visibly had two watches on his wrist, a clear indicator of the widespread looting and not exactly the stuff of history textbooks. In people's houses, soldiers swiped everything that could be transported back home such as jewellery, radios and sewing machines. Bigger items such as furniture or washing machines were packed up and sent back on endless columns of trains to the Soviet Union. Mostly, these private loots were alcohol-fuelled rampages involving as much destruction as theft. What the soldiers could not carry or did not understand was often riddled with bullets, chucked out of windows or smashed to pieces. The journalist Marta Hillers describes the scene of one of the many lootings of the basement of her house in Berlin: 'Absolute chaos below: wooden partitions battered down, locks torn off, trunks split open and trampled . . . Left and right the neighbours rummage about by flickering candlelight. Shrill cries and wailing. Eider down whirls through the air, the place reeks of spilled wine and excrement.'[36]

All of this was legitimized by Nikolai Berzarin's decree of May 1945. The Soviet first commander of occupied Berlin had given his consent to months of private pillage. The brash officer, who would die in an alcohol-fuelled joy ride on a motorcycle in Berlin-Friedrichsfelde, was not impartial to a bit of looting himself. Public information posters were put up ordering Germans to surrender their items on pain of death. Local collection points were set up where those items that had not yet been stolen could be surrendered.

On a more systematic level, German museums, art galleries and private houses were robbed of countless pieces of art. Among the priceless collections was the Eberswalde Hoard, the largest prehistoric gold treasure ever found on German soil. Like thousands of other items, it was secretly stashed away in the Pushkin Museum in Moscow, never to see the light of day again. Often accomplished with crowbars, the dismantling of German industry in the Soviet Zone was as crude as it was comprehensive. Machinery, raw materials, test tubes, chemicals, optical lenses, whole laboratories were packed up in boxes and shipped east. Train tracks were dismantled, cabling ripped out of the ground and from walls. In total, this robbed the Soviet Zone of Occupation of one third of its industrial base.

Alongside the systematic hollowing out of industry, science and culture, the gradual nationalization of the economy was the other hallmark of Stalin's zone. It made it clear from the beginning that things were done very differently in the East compared to the Western Zones. As early as July 1945, a central bank was set up. This provided the necessary financial structure so that the nationalization of heavy industry could begin in September 1945 – without compensation for the previous owners. From June 1946, this was extended to smaller companies with 200 of them merged into twenty-five large, Soviet Stock Companies. In order to control this now large-scale economic project, the SED set up its own German Economic Commission, placing the management of goods, services and raw materials not only in state hands, but explicitly into the party's. By April 1948, it was the turn of even more small private enterprises to be merged into public companies, called VEBs. The end result was that 60 per cent of the economy in the Soviet Zone was already state owned by 1948, a year before the establishment of the two German states.

Whether deliberate or not, economic policy in the East had cemented the split from its Western Zones. Even if the conflict between the Soviet Union and the Western Allies had not come to a head in Berlin in 1948 and 1949, it is difficult to see how two such radically different economies might have worked within a common political framework. While the West was beginning to rebuild and enter into a constructive partnership with their Anglo-American occupiers, the East was subject to plunder and nationalization. The result was that the GDR and the FRG were built on two diametrically opposed economic foundations in 1949.

Road to Division

Berlin, 8 May 1948. On the day of the third anniversary of the end of the Second World War in Europe, Major General Sergei Ivanovich Tiulpanov gave a speech to the SED elites. A bear of a man with a bald head and broad, round features, he had proved to be his own man rather than Stalin's puppet in Berlin. In his position as director of propaganda for the SMAD, he had forged close links with the German communists in Berlin, particularly Walter Ulbricht. Now, he felt, it was time for action, time to create an East German state in the Bolshevik image. Stalin's continued hesitancy and insistence that a whole-German policy should be pursued fell on Tiulpanov's deaf ears. He told the SED that from now on there will be a new course, 'one that takes the division of Germany as a done deal and . . . aims at the establishment of a system in the image of the People's Democracies [i.e. the USSR]; we work in the full expectation of forming a sovereign state.'[37]

Ulbricht was delighted. He had long come to the conclusion that a separate East German socialist state was to be preferred over a neutral one for the whole of Germany. Even Grotewohl, the ex-SPD man, was disillusioned in January 1948, when he told his comrades at a party meeting, 'There is no doubt in my mind that Germany will be torn apart into two zones.'[38] But many of his colleagues were shocked. Tiulpanov tried to allay their doubts with the argument that an ideological 'conquest of the whole of Germany'[39] was only possible from the secure power-political base of the Soviet Zone of Occupation. Extension into the West was to be fought as a class struggle and over a long time if need be.

There has been much debate about Stalin's involvement in the shift in policy on the ground in Berlin. From 1947, many in the SMAD and even more in Ulbricht's inner circle of power worked towards a separate East German state. They had visibly begun to establish institutions and structures accordingly. The matter will never be fully resolved, but Tiulpanov's going rogue in Berlin annoyed Stalin so much that he had many of his family members in the Soviet Union arrested under spy charges in order to force his propaganda man in Germany to return to Moscow. Ulbricht too was repeatedly summoned to explain himself. Nevertheless, both men were allowed to continue their careers.

Meanwhile, the Cold War had begun to unfold on the world stage. The most spectacular manifestation of the increasing tensions between the erstwhile allies was undoubtedly the Berlin Blockade. Pumping $1.5 billion into the Western Zone under the European Recovery Program, better known as the Marshall Plan, the US authorities needed to ensure that these vast funds would not just trickle into the quicksands of inflation. Therefore they introduced a new currency, the Deutsche Mark (DM), in the US and British zone as the two had been merged in 1947, and in the French one, which joined soon after. Stalin could neither accept the flow of Marshall Aid itself nor its physical manifestation, the new banknotes, into his zone. The currency was stabilized by a fixed exchange rate of DM4.2 to $1, which tied it directly to the US economy. As Berlin was in the middle of the Soviet Zone, its Western sectors were economically interlinked with it. The introduction of a new Western currency and attendant economic programmes there would invariably leak elements of capitalism into the nationalized economy of the East.

Inge Schmidt, a twenty-year-old bookkeeper from Köpenick, a south-eastern district of Berlin which now lay in the Soviet sector, worked for an independent chemical engineer in the Kolonnen-straße in Schöneberg in the American sector, just down the road from Tempelhof Airfield. She would always remember the additional hours of work the currency reform caused her as she carefully allocated the prescribed salary ratio for those who worked for Ing

Chem F Hempel GmbH but lived in the Soviet Zone. Like her, they would receive 10 per cent of their salary in the new West German marks and 90 per cent in the hastily rolled-out East German marks. Meticulously converting each employee's payments while marking the percentages in green and red ink, Inge was part of the Soviets' failing efforts to block the spread of the Western economic system through an inner-Berlin door that was still wide open.[40] Stalin decided to slam that door shut while he still could.

On 24 June 1948, the Soviets blocked all land and water traffic to and from West Berlin. They also stopped any delivery of food, water, fuel and other supplies from their own zone of the city to the others. One of the most dramatic hostage crises in history had begun – the first real Cold War showdown with over 2 million lives at stake in West Berlin. The Western Allies parried Stalin's move with a spectacular airlift, flying a total of 277,804 supply planes into the German capital – at its busiest, on 16 April 1949, an Allied plane landed in Berlin every minute. But German division could no longer be averted. The half-hearted attempt of the SED to create a constitution for the whole of Germany, which it ratified in Berlin-Mitte in October 1948, was nothing more than showboating. The division of Germany would be hugely unpopular with its people but it was now the preferred outcome for decision makers both East and West. Naturally, all sides were keen to blame the other as the splitter.

Stalin himself was still reluctant to accept the reality on the ground. Unhappy with the SED's agitation for an East German state, he ordered Ulbricht, Pieck and Grotewohl to Moscow on 12 December 1948. He chided them for being brash, comparing them to the 'teutons of old who fought the Romans naked but took heavy losses'. What was needed was a 'cautious policy', he told them.[41] If that was not clear enough, he explicitly forbade them from proclaiming a 'People's Democracy' in his zone. Only if the creation of a West German state could no longer be averted were they to plan for an East German one.

Events in the West eventually solved the conflicts in the East. On

8 May 1949, exactly four years after the German capitulation, the Parliamentary Council of the Western Zones approved the new constitution which had been drafted since the previous September. With its proclamation on 23 May, the Federal Republic of Germany was born. Now Stalin's hands were tied. On 27 September he met an SED delegation in Moscow – Ulbricht, Pieck and Grotewohl had waited ten nail-biting days to see him. Resigned, Stalin consented to the foundation of a German Democratic Republic. The trio returned to Germany with the news and began to talk the Christian Democrats and the Liberals into giving their consent. Not only that, they also agreed to postpone elections to 1950. A mixture of intimidation and promises of glittering political careers secured the consent of the two parties. Seeing how easily the democratic parties gave way to the establishment of a dictatorship of the proletariat, the SED propagandist Gerhart Eisler bragged that 'Once we form a government, we will never give it up again, neither through elections nor any other methods.' Ulbricht is said to have replied smugly, 'Not everyone has understood that yet.'[42]

The German Democratic Republic was founded on 7 October 1949. Wilhelm Pieck became its President, Otto Grotewohl its Minister President. Ulbricht, the man who had tirelessly worked towards this moment, took on the seemingly humble role of one of Grotewohl's three deputies. He had implemented his system of deputies even here. Grotewohl and Pieck represented the union of social democrats and communists, lending the new government an air of legitimacy, while real power lay with Ulbricht and everyone knew it.

The question of whether or not this post-war German division was inevitable has been hotly debated over the years. It was hugely unpopular with the German public, both East and West, and both sides were quick to blame the other. The East pointed to the introduction of a new currency and the rollout of Marshall Aid as violations of the Potsdam Agreement, which had stipulated that such decisions needed to be made by all four Allies. Stalin had not even been invited to the London conferences where such matters were discussed. The West pointed to the Sovietization of the economy in Stalin's zone and the Berlin Blockade as the ultimate act of aggression.

In truth the decision for or against the foundation of two separate states was never in German hands. Not yet eighty years old as a unified nation state, Germany had forfeited its right to self-determination given the devastation it had wreaked in two world wars. Total collapse in 1945 had placed it at the mercy of its occupiers who were more concerned with their own condition than that of the country they had defeated. Germany, and Berlin specifically, had become the focal point of increasingly volatile international tensions between Soviet Russia and the West. It was here that the border between those two power blocs ran and any breach of it was increasingly likely to spill over into outright war. It was in the interest of both sides to cement that dividing line, even brick it up and fortify it, as was to happen twelve years later. Hitler envisioned Germany as the axis around which the world evolved. His vision had come true after all, albeit not in the way that he had intended. The two Germanies and the split capital were now the centre of a power struggle that would engulf the whole world for decades. The GDR, Stalin's unwanted child, was the westernmost outpost of his Soviet Empire whether he liked it or not.

3.   Birth Pangs (1949–1952)

We will one day live as we work today.

The GDR Is Born

It is easy to forget that the birth of the German Democratic Republic on 7 October 1949 did not create a neat counterpart to the Federal Republic of Germany in the West. We like to see the world in diametric opposites, and this is no different when it comes to the division of Germany: capitalist and communist, East and West. This creates the illusion of a country split down the middle with two halves that are mirror images of each other. In reality, the Soviet Zone of Occupation had been one of four segments, not two. Taken on its own and made into a state, it was a lot smaller than its Western neighbour which amalgamated three zones.

In 1949, the GDR had 18.4 million inhabitants to the FRG's 50.4 million. In Berlin, the Eastern sector had roughly half the population of the Western one (1.2 million and 2.1 million, respectively). Socially, the two Germanies were different as well. The FRG had been allocated most of the Catholic regions and suddenly found itself with a 50/50 ratio of Catholics and Protestants, while in the East there were 15 per cent Catholics and over 80 per cent Protestants. German refugees from Eastern Europe often arrived and stayed in the East where they made up a staggering quarter of the population while accounting for 16.5 per cent of people in the West. The Western Allies gave economic aid while the Soviets took reparations; the East was largely agrarian while the West had the industrial heartlands; the FRG had to create a new capital in Bonn while the GDR could stick with Berlin; the West had been formed half a year before the East. The list of differences could go on.

The German cake had not been cut into even pieces by the Allies at Yalta. But there the GDR was: a brand-new Germany with a socialist government that vowed to build a better society out of the ruins of the old. Many of its citizens were all too happy to roll up their sleeves to make it come true against the odds. Now all that the new country needed was a head of state.

The President

Berlin-Mitte, 11 October 1949. Margot Feist was a little nervous as she waited with a congratulatory bunch of flowers in her hand. Wilhelm Pieck was about to finish his speech any minute now. The charismatic twenty-two-year-old had been chosen to be the first to congratulate the freshly elected first President of the German Democratic Republic on behalf of the Provisional People's Chamber that had confirmed him in this role. To this end they had all assembled in the festive hall of Hermann Göring's former Air Ministry. The colossal structure was the largest of its kind in Berlin and had been purpose-built to accommodate over 2,000 rooms. Ironically, the very place from which Göring's staff had organized their deadly bombing campaigns on the cities of Europe remained almost unscathed when much of Berlin was destroyed by Anglo-American air raids. But such matters lay in the past as the assembled deputies opened a new chapter of German history.

As the youngest deputy of the People's Chamber, Margot Feist was a rising star in the Free German Youth (FDJ), the socialist mass organization founded in 1946 for young people between the ages of fourteen and twenty-five. Margot wore her bright blue uniform with pride, the yellow emblem of a rising sun gleaming on her chest and arm. She knew her mother would have been pleased to see her at this moment. Both her parents, Gotthard, a shoemaker, and Helene, a worker in a mattress factory, were fiercely proud of their working class heritage and had been active members of the KPD in the 1920s and 1930s. When Hitler came to power, they organized underground resistance, and their flat in Halle became one of only three illegal communist information hubs in Germany for the flow of communication from the exiled KPD leadership in Prague. Gotthard Feist spent years in the concentration camps of Lichtenburg and Buchenwald as well as in Halle's prison for his convictions, and his daughter inherited his fanatical belief in the fight for the communist world revolution. When her mother Helene suddenly died in 1940, Margot was only thirteen years old.

Nine years later, a wide-eyed Margot Feist watched the seventy-three-year-old chairman of the SED give his inauguration speech. Wilhelm Pieck finished by inviting his listeners to join in as he praised the foundation values of the newly formed state: 'national unity, democracy, economic, political and cultural prosperity, friendship with the Soviet Union and all other peace-loving peoples'[1] – 'HURRAH! HURRAH! HURRAH!' bellowed Margot with everyone else in the hall. There was roaring applause as the beaming young woman shook Pieck's hand.

The day drew to a close with a mass spectacle that could have rivalled Albert Speer's coordinated torch processions during the Nazi era. Over 200,000 youths had followed the call of the FDJ leadership to Berlin and gathered on the vast Bebelplatz. While the huge square in front of the Humboldt University had recently been named in honour of the founder of the SPD, August Bebel, it was also here where the masses had gathered sixteen years earlier to burn tens of thousands of books. But to the FDJ, other layers of history were more important. As the orange glow from their torches lit up the adjacent Unter den Linden boulevard, they were reminded that this was where the early communists had fought their battles; where Rosa Luxemburg and Karl Liebknecht, the founders of the KPD, had joined in the German Revolution of November 1918 that had forced the abdication of the last German Kaiser, Wilhelm II. Now it was the turn of the excited boys and girls gathered there in 1949 to make history. They carried placards with the famous 1946 photograph of Grotewohl's handshake with Pieck when they had merged their parties and created the SED. And they carried images of Stalin.

For all his initial reluctance, the Soviet dictator now openly supported the creation of the German Democratic Republic. In his congratulatory telegram he declared, 'The experiences of the last war have shown that it was the German and the Soviet people who have made the biggest sacrifices in this war ... If both of these peoples can show the determination to fight for peace with the same mobilization of force with which they fought the war, then peace in Europe can be considered a certainty.'[2] Once again, Stalin's words reflected the odd admiration he held for Germany. Only four years after the end of an existential war inflicted on his people by Germans, he was painting a picture of equal 'sacrifice' and 'potential'. Blessed by Stalin and heralded by its youth, the GDR made its first political steps.

The Constitution

The first constitution of the GDR became effective on 7 October 1949. Article 1 asserted that 'Germany is an indivisible, democratic republic', and this was not just an empty phrase. The entire legal framework of East Germany was designed so that, once this became possible, it could easily merge again with West Germany's which used similar language. At the same time the constitution of the Federal Republic, the *Grundgesetz* or Basic Law, which in essence is still Germany's constitution today, was labelled 'provisional' in 1949. Neither of the two German governments was willing to cement the divisions on paper yet.

In theory the set-up of the German Democratic Republic had several things in common with its Western counterpart. It too was initially designed as a federal system, in accord with the agreements regarding the decentralization of German politics made by the Allies at the Yalta and Potsdam conferences. East Germany was

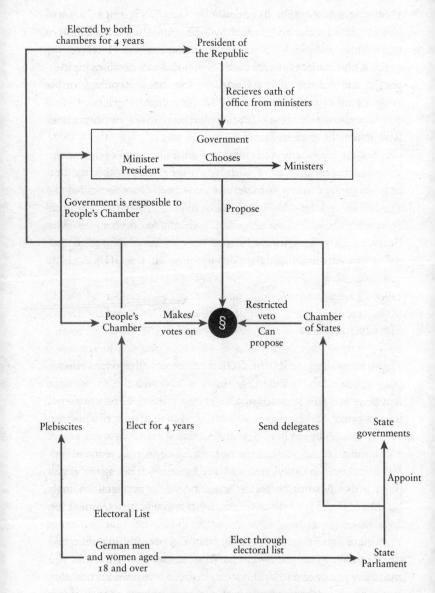

The Constitution of the GDR in 1949

divided into five *Länder*: Brandenburg, Saxony, Thuringia, Saxony-Anhalt and Mecklenburg, which will be used as place designations throughout the book for clarity and consistency. However, the socialist leadership was fundamentally opposed to federalism for ideological and political reasons, and the five *Länder* would soon be replaced by fourteen *Bezirke* or districts, which largely served an administrative role, implementing decisions made by the central government in East Berlin.

Similarly, the bicameral structure of East Germany's government mirrored that of the West. There was a lower chamber called the *Volkskammer* or People's Chamber and an upper chamber called the *Länderkammer*. While the latter was effectively a council of the regional representatives akin to the *Bundesrat*, which Germany maintains to this day, the People's Chamber was a parliament filled with elected representatives of the people. This looked democratic, just as Ulbricht had intended. All the permitted parties continued to exist. Alongside the Liberal Democrats (LDPD) and the Christian Democrats (CDU), there were the National Democratic Party (NDPD) and the Democratic Farmers' Party (DBD). On paper, the GDR continued to be a multi-party system, right to the very end. In practice, however, the members and supporters of the other parties were severely pressed to tow the line of the ruling SED. They also each had a fixed, allocated seat share in the People's Chamber and during elections people merely filled the seats by approving a set list of candidates. The upper chamber of the *Länderkammer* was abolished altogether in 1958 – a logical conclusion of the abolition of the *Länder* themselves, if six years delayed.

The role of the President was largely ceremonial, again in tandem with this role in West Germany. Wilhelm Pieck willingly became a figurehead for a political course steered by Ulbricht. By 1960, when Pieck died, reunification had slid out of view. The Berlin Wall would be built the following year as a physical manifestation of the insurmountable divide between the two Germanies. This made any pretence of a future merger of the constitutions unnecessary. The role of the President served no more purpose and so it died with its first and only occupant. It was replaced with a Council of State, the *Staatsrat*, the chair of which was the SED leader Walter Ulbricht himself. In this role, he delegated tasks to an array of ministers with whom he also discussed policy and made decisions. They would meet as the Council of Ministers, the *Ministerrat*, and pass on their work for the People's Chamber to ratify.

While the constitution of the GDR may have looked similar to that of the FRG on paper, its practical implementation was significantly different. All decision-making flowed from the ruling SED party whose influence could not be altered through elections.

The Party Is Always Right

Sie hat uns Alles gegeben.	She gave us what she had,
Sonne und Wind. Und sie geizte nie.	The sun and wind. She always gave.
Wo sie war, war das Leben.	For the life she gives, we're glad.
Was wir sind, sind wir durch sie.	All that we are, she has made.
Sie hat uns niemals verlassen.	She has never deserted us
Fror auch die Welt, uns war warm.	When the world was cold, we were warm.
Uns schützt die Mutter der Massen.	Shielded by the mother of the masses.
Uns trägt ihr mächtiger Arm.	Carried in her strong arm.
[Refrain:]	[Chorus:]
Die Partei,	The Party,
Die Partei, die hat immer recht.	The Party, she is always right.
Und, Genossen, es bleibe dabei.	And, Comrades, thus it will always be.
Denn wer kämpft	He who fights
Für das Recht, der hat immer recht	For what's right, will always be right.
Gegen Lüge und Ausbeuterei.	Against vile lies and foul tyranny.

Wer das Leben beleidigt,	He who to life is unkind,
Ist dumm oder schlecht.	Is thick or a blight.
Wer die Menschheit verteidigt,	He who defends mankind,
Hat immer recht.	Is always right.
So, aus leninschem Geist,	Made in Lenin's ideal,
Wächst von Stalin geschweißt,	Forged in Stalin's steel,
Die Partei, die Partei, die Partei!	The Party, the Party, the Party!
Sie hat uns niemals geschmeichelt.	She never raised in us false hope.
Sank uns im Kampfe auch mal der Mut,	When courage in battle seemed to fail,
Hat sie uns leis nur gestreichelt:	She touched us gently and spoke:
Zagt nicht – und gleich war uns gut.	Forward – and all was soon well.
Zählt denn auch Schmerz und Beschwerde,	Does it matter if we feel pain,
Wenn uns das Gute gelingt?	If we do good and succeed?
Wenn man den Ärmsten der Erde	If for the poorest we can gain
Freiheit und Frieden erzwingt!	The right to live in peace and free.
Die Partei . . . [Refrain]	The Party . . . [Chorus]
Sie hat uns Alles gegeben.	She gave us what she had,
Ziegel zum Bau und den großen Plan.	Bricks to rebuild and the great plan.
Sie sprach: Meistert das Leben!	She said: Use the life you have!
Vorwärts, Genossen, packt an!	Forward, Comrades, you can!
Hetzen Hyänen zum Kriege –	When hyenas howl for war –
Bricht euer Bau ihre Macht!	Your work will break them!
Zimmert das Haus und die Wiege!	Build houses and cradles for all!
Bauleute, seid auf der Wacht!	Builders, watch out for them!
Die Partei . . . [Refrain]	The Party . . . [Chorus]

'Lied der Partei' (Song of the Party), also known as 'Die Partei hat immer recht' (The Party is Always Right). Lyrics and music by Louis Fürnberg, 1949.

The SED party invariably dominated all aspects of policy within the East German constitution. Its chairman occupied a role that combined representative and political leadership of the country. It automatically held the highest number of seats in parliament and ministers were chosen carefully according to political compliance with the SED's wishes. Proponents of the GDR system have claimed that, while this is true, the SED itself was structured in a democratic way which allowed change from within. The party was built like a pyramid: there was the General Secretary at the top, leading the inner circle of power, called the politburo. Then followed the Central Committee, which included experts in specialized fields, who were in turn elected by the Party Congress at the bottom of the hierarchy. The Congress would meet every five years and delegates were sent there from local branches in factories and workplaces. In theory, it was possible for a worker to be elected as the SED representative for their factory. On behalf of their colleagues, they could then elect the experts in the Central Committee who had influence over policy decisions.

In practice, however, a GDR citizen would have found it very hard to get heard at every turn if their views did not meet with the approval of the party leadership. The word *Kaderpolitik* (cadre policy) was openly used by the SED to describe their tight hold over political appointments. Cadres were trained, raised and monitored, ideally from youth, before they were gradually trusted with high office. The instruments of government were mere administrative tools, implementing the policies directed by the SED rather than make and shape their own. This was not a secret either. The SED's directive of 17 October 1949 concerning the running of government ordered that 'Laws and bills of importance, materials used in the process of law making, any suggestions for laws and regulations must be shown to the politburo or its secretariat for approval before they are passed by the People's Chamber or the government.'[3] What this meant was that each and every aspect of the legislative process would be controlled by the SED. The People's Chamber never had a draft law put in front of them that had not been discussed, scrutinized and approved by the upper echelons of the SED first. Despite its pseudo-pluralistic set-up, the German Democratic Republic never lived up to its name.

Right from the beginning, the SED steered a course straight towards politicization and control of public discourse. Article 6 of the constitution declared that 'Incitement to boycott of democratic institutions and organizations . . . is a crime' – which allowed the SED to crack down on political opponents. The article was used to justify the entire catalogue of punishments from fines and brief spells in prison to the death penalty. A particularly high-profile case was that of Georg-Siegfried Schmutzler, a CDU member and ordained Lutheran pastor. In his role as student pastor at Leipzig from 1954 to 1957, he continued to voice sharp criticism of the SED authorities and their ever-tightening political apparatus. He was arrested on 5 April 1957 on charges of 'incitement to boycott'. The courts used this as the legal basis for his five-year prison sentence at Torgau in Saxony.

The case was the focus of a media spectacle in both Germanies. The West selected passages to showcase political persecution in the East despite cracking down on opponents to their own system, including an outright ban of the KPD in 1956. The East tried to show how subversive Schmutzler's actions had supposedly been when what his words amounted to was protected under the last sentence of the very same Article 6 that got him arrested in the first place: 'Exercising one's democratic rights in line with the constitution is not incitement to boycott.' Pressure from the church communities on the regime intensified and so Schmutzler was released from prison early, in 1961, and resumed his activities as a pastor in Dresden before becoming a lecturer at the Theological Seminary in Leipzig. In the 1980s he moved to West Berlin where he died in 2003. Cases like his prove that even the first constitution, which looked democratic, provided only an illusion of civil rights and basic freedoms.

Consolidation of Power

Berlin-Prenzlauer Berg, 25 July 1950. Walter Ulbricht was letting the thunderous applause of his comrades wash over him. He had celebrated his fifty-seventh birthday a few days earlier and now stood on the stage of the Werner-Seelenbinder-Halle, a venue in the north-east of Berlin. It had only just been converted from its previous function as a cattle market on the grounds of an abattoir. Ulbricht tried to speak over the continuous roar emanating from his SED colleagues, but his brittle voice could not cut through the noise. The party's newspaper *Neues Deutschland* would gush later that day that 'the cheering and clapping built up further and would not end'. He had just been elected as General Secretary of the SED, a position that made him, in the eyes of his biographer Mario Frank, 'the mightiest German of his time'.[4]

Ulbricht had suddenly stepped into the limelight. Now that the state was beginning to consolidate itself, there was no more need for the real leader to lurk in the shadows of his own deputy system. Those in the inner circle were in the know. Pieck noted that there had never been 'any doubt that Walter Ulbricht would be General Secretary. This was obvious from everything in the previous practice of the Party.'[5] But the plain-looking man from Saxony surprised many external observers when he emerged from the shadows. Fritz Schenk, a twenty-year-old member of the SED in 1950, 'only noticed Ulbricht after he had become General Secretary and appeared more and more during important Party or public events; other than that, Pieck and Grotewohl were the representatives who spoke for the SED. Ulbricht only appeared on the scene when the system gradually calcified.'[6]

Ulbricht's new title of General Secretary was, along with the other structural changes within the SED, modelled on the Communist Party of the Soviet Union. He had obtained permission from Stalin earlier in the year to begin to emulate Soviet structures in the GDR so long as it was not on too big a scale. The Soviet leader was still reluctant to give up on the idea of a neutral, unified Germany and was unwilling to jeopardize this option just to accommodate Ulbricht's pleading. But the fervent German Stalinist pressed on with his Soviet-style reforms which systematically minimized the democratic elements of the GDR's constitution and of the SED's internal procedures.

A Soviet-style nomenklatura was built up within the politburo of the SED from 1950, which decided upon vital appointments within the party itself as well as within all levels of governmental structures. This required the careful 'checking' of candidates for each office and monitoring of their activities and attitudes following appointment. The SED began this process with a wholescale 'cleansing' of their own backyard. On 24 July 1950, one day before Ulbricht's appointment as General Secretary, Wilhelm Pieck warned that 'the revolutionary vigilance in the Party's ranks must be in every way increased so that the bourgeois-nationalist elements and all other enemies of the Proletariat and agents of imperialism, under whatever flag they may sail, can be uncovered and eradicated'.[7] According to a SMAD directive, around 10 per cent of the membership of the SED needed to be 'eradicated' in this way. Ulbricht's regime was so keen to prove the GDR's credentials to Stalin that it exceeded expectations. Between December 1950 and December 1951, the number of SED members and candidates fell from 1.6 million to 1.2 million[8] – 25 per cent had been 'eradicated'.

The paranoia with which the leadership searched for subversion and enemy activity in its own ranks bears eerie parallels to the Great Purges, which Pieck, Ulbricht and the other surviving Moscow exiles had experienced in the 1930s. In December 1950, Ulbricht sent a letter to all SED members warning them that 'since 1945 elements hostile to the Party have joined us to hide their dirty business behind their membership cards or to build their careers for selfish reasons'.[9] The message was clear: any Western leanings, any social democratic attitudes on display and you were on your way out. This was particularly hard for the former SPD members who had been coerced into the merger with the KPD only four years earlier.

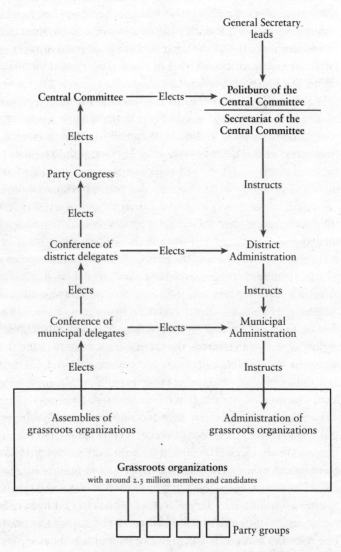

General Secretary leads

Central Committee —— Elects —— **Politburo of the Central Committee**

Secretariat of the Central Committee

Elects

Party Congress

Elects

Conference of district delegates —— Elects —— District Administration

Elects

Conference of municipal delegates —— Elects —— Municipal Administration

Elects

Instructs

Instructs

Instructs

Assemblies of grassroots organizations

Administration of grassroots organizations

Grassroots organizations
with around 2.3 million members and candidates

Party groups

Structure of the Socialist Unity Party (SED)

Another group that came under blanket suspicion during this time were SED members who had survived the Nazi regime by emigrating westwards, to France, Britain or the USA. Even being a core member of the SED's inner circle of power was not enough to allay the irrational fear that such a past now created in Ulbricht's mind. Paul Merker, a fellow Saxon who had been a KPD member since 1920 and was a member of the newly created politburo in 1950, suddenly found himself accused of being a 'French Agent'. When the Second World War broke out, he had used his position in the secretariat of the KPD in Paris to encourage exiled German communists to register with the French authorities. His intention had been to legalize their status and to ensure they could be deployed in resistance. But once France was occupied, the paper trail left by German communists made it easy to hunt them down, which cost many of them their freedom or even their lives.

In the summer of 1950, Merker's actions in Western exile were enough for him to be swept away by paranoia whipped up by show trials elsewhere in the Eastern Bloc. László Rajk, a Hungarian communist politician, had been executed the previous autumn after having been declared a 'Titoist spy' and an 'imperialist agent' by the show trials set up by Hungary's new leader Mátyás Rákosi. The post-war split of Yugoslavia under its leader Tito from Stalin's power bloc in Eastern Europe had created palpable angst in Moscow, the ripples of which would reverberate through Eastern Europe and shake the GDR. The tension had reached boiling point when the American communist Noel Field was arrested in Prague in 1949. During the war, Field had become a spy for the NKVD and built up a network across Europe to help communists escape the Nazis. As such, he had come into contact with thousands of them, including Paul Merker. Under torture, Field claimed to have built up an underground network of 'imperialist spies' in Eastern Europe. His 'confession' led to show trials and arrests everywhere, including the GDR.

Ulbricht had not only developed very sensitive antennae for Stalin's violent outbreaks of paranoia during the time of the Great

Purges, but he was also keen to prove to his idol that East Germany was a dependable friend to Soviet Russia. This was the perfect opportunity to show the dictator that his 'unwanted child'[10] was in fact a great addition to the family of Soviet states. Paul Merker was found to be a 'French spy' and excluded from the SED on 22 August 1950. His subsequent arrest was only prevented by Wilhelm Pieck's intervention on his behalf. Many others were not so fortunate. Leo Bauer, who had also worked for Field's network during the war before joining the KPD in Hesse in the American Zone, had decided to become a member of the SED in East Berlin instead. In 1949, he was appointed editor-in-chief of Deutschlandsender, a radio channel from which he greeted his East German listeners with Bach and Mozart every morning – 'just right for the workers' breakfast time'. His jovial and independent character quickly clashed with Ulbricht's dour nature, and in 1950, he too found himself sucked into the maelstrom of the Noel Field Affair. He was arrested on 23 August and then tortured by both German and Soviet interrogators.[11] He broke down and incriminated himself as well as friends and colleagues. In 1952, a Soviet tribunal sentenced him to death for being an 'American spy' and he sat in his cell awaiting his execution when Stalin died in 1953.

The gradual de-Stalinization that followed meant that many political death sentences were converted into prison sentences and this included Bauer's. He received twenty-five years of hard labour in Siberia instead, which would also have been akin to a death sentence had not the agreement that West German Chancellor Konrad Adenauer made with the USSR over the repatriation of German prisoners saved him in 1955. Bauer spent the rest of his life in West Germany where he became active in the SPD and advised Willy Brandt when the latter became the first Social Democrat post-war Chancellor. He died in 1969 of long-term health problems caused by his incarceration in Russia.

The ideological purges did not stop within the SED itself. The other parties of the 'Democratic Bloc' were also targeted. The CDU stood by helplessly as 900 of their members were arrested.

Seemingly non-political offices such as directorships of the new state-run VEBs, the trade unions or scientific institutes were purged and replaced with ideologically reliable candidates. At local level, Ulbricht's substitute system was phased out and key positions were now filled with communists. By 1955, the nomenklatura system controlled appointments for around 7,000 positions.[12] The SED's hold over German politics had been well and truly consolidated.

Elections and Voting

The first elections in the GDR took place during this period of feverish paranoia on 15 October 1950. The system that was devised then became a precedent for all future elections until 1990. The seats of the *Volkskammer*, the GDR's parliament, were pre-allocated to the different political parties and groupings in fixed proportions on which the elections had no bearing whatsoever:

Party/Group	Explanation	Number of Seats
SED	Socialist Unity Party	110
CDU	Christian Democrats	67
LDPD	Liberal Democrats	66
DBD	Democratic Farmers' Party	33
NDPD	National Democrats	35
FDGB	Free German Trade Union Federation	49
FDJ	Free German Youth	25
DFD	Democratic Women's Association	20
KB	Cultural Association	24
Others		37

Seat allocation in the GDR People's Chamber after the election in 1950.

The function of the vote was not to increase the share of the favoured political party but to fill the seats with candidates. The system is based on the doctrine of 'democratic centralism'. The idea is often associated with Lenin, who explored it in his influential 1902 pamphlet *What is to be done?* He argued that within a political party all offices must be elected from the ground up while all directives given by the elected upper echelons must be obeyed at the bottom. This is how a democratic hierarchy without factions is supposed to be achieved. The line of decision-making went up and down in a straight line without the sideways diversions of a pluralist system.

This communist logic sees a multi-party system as one that serves to perpetuate the reign of those in power as it promotes factionalism among the population. When you vote for a political party, rather than an individual, the odds are stacked in favour of those with the biggest funding and the best campaigning infrastructure. Established parties dominate thought and can exclude individuals who lack the power, connections or money to form their own party and succeed with it. The party system acts as a break or buffer between the people and government, which had indeed reassured many a nineteenth-century sceptic that democracy did not have to mean mob rule. It is also why many people in Western democracies today feel that their voice is not heard and that they have no way to break through despite free and secret elections.

Replacing a multi-party parliament with a council of directly elected individuals is, at least in theory, not in itself undemocratic.

The idea was that a factory could send an elected representative, as could a university, or a women's organization. These delegates would then meet in a central council – or 'Soviet' in Russian – to decide on policy matters, elect an executive and so on. So far so democratic. The reason why so many of the manifestations of this theory have turned out to be nothing more than puppet parliaments who rubber stamp legislation for those who wield real power is that it is open to manipulation. In the case of the GDR's council, the *Volkskammer*, the list of candidates was completely fixed. The voting process worked as follows:

GDR citizens entered their local polling office and were given a set list with the names of the candidates for their constituency. To express their consent with this list, they folded the piece of paper and put it in the ballot box. It was possible to do this in secret, such as behind a curtain or in a voting booth, but this was publicly discouraged. There was only one way to express discontent with the set list: crossing out the names of all the candidates. Votes were then simply counted as a percentage of those who had given their consent to the set list.

The result of this farcical procedure was that all of the elections before the fall of the Berlin Wall seemed to show near-complete agreement with the composition of the *Volkskammer*. The 1950 election, for example, produced a result of 99.7 per cent approval for the list on offer. Pressure to attend elections was nonetheless enormous. The turnout in 1950 was recorded as 98 per cent. This process was ridiculed by many GDR citizens who dubbed it 'paper folding'.

And yet, despite the coercion, purges, rigged elections and public pressure, 'the particular, hard-line form of communism which developed in the GDR in the 1950s was not inevitable',[13] as historian Mary Fulbrook has pointed out. There remained serious opposition to many of Ulbricht's measures including from within the upper echelons of the SED. German communists, social democrats and liberals had suffered too much under the yoke of the Nazis to hand power to another dictatorship under Walter Ulbricht. They found means to express their discontent as did ordinary people, be that through open protest, art forms or leaving the country, in ways that were often effective enough to bring about change.

The Free German Youth

East Berlin, 15 August 1951. An army of 50,000 young men and women stood ready to cross the sector boundary from East to West Berlin. Robert Bialek, leader of the delegation from Saxony, had gathered his 10,000-strong contingent in Treptower Park, just southeast of the city centre on the banks of the River Spree. Normally, the large green space with its river views, giant Soviet war memorial and pruned terraces was a relaxing, quiet place that contrasted sharply with the chaos of the ruined city around it. But on this day, it was a sea of 10,000 blue shirts.

Twenty-six-year-old Robert was a characterful young man who had opposed the Nazis in his home town of Breslau and now wanted to help shape a better society. Wolfgang Leonhard knew him well since they had attended the same course at the SED's Party Academy Karl Marx together in 1947. Wolfgang was impressed by Robert's 'honest nature' which bordered on the kind of 'naive openness' that could make one vulnerable in the rough political world of the 1950s. His 'thirst for action' and 'ability to communicate his opinions exceptionally effectively' had placed him on a steep career trajectory.[14]

On 15 August 1951, Robert had his doubts that what they were about to do was right. He felt uneasy when the FDJ's leader Erich Honecker rushed up and breathlessly ordered him to take the left flank and follow the units that had already marched on West Berlin. As an afterthought Honecker added that it might be wise to position the girls in the middle for protection as serious clashes were to be expected. As he ran off again, he shouted over his shoulder, 'I trust you to bring everyone back!' Robert did not feel good about this. As they marched on to the boundary that marked the divide between East and West Berlin, between communism and capitalism, the stakes could not have been higher.

The first World Festival of Youth and Students on German soil, for which the blue-shirted youngsters had gathered, had the motto 'For Peace and Friendship – Against Nuclear Weapons'. The shock over the destructive power of nuclear technology, as witnessed during the American bombings of Hiroshima and Nagasaki in August 1945, still reverberated around the world when the Soviets carried out their first successful test of a nuclear device four years later. The possibility that the horrors of the Second World War in Europe, still so vivid, would pale in comparison with a nuclear conflict was on the minds of many of Robert's compatriots as he marched his young troops ever closer to the centre of Berlin. Just before they got there, they encountered some of their boys running the other way. Their uniforms were torn, some were limping, some had bloodied faces. One shouted, 'Robert, don't go there, they will beat you all into a pulp. We went in there and they bashed us back out. Many of us are injured.'[15]

Robert was still hesitating, unsure what to do, when Honecker reappeared to tell him to abandon the march and send everyone back. The 'Peace March' on West Berlin was cancelled. The whole botched campaign had been Erich Honecker's attempt to bolster his own reputation and that of his new mass youth movement. It back-fired spectacularly. The SED leadership was furious and rightly criticized Honecker's march on West Berlin as a dangerous act of bravado. His political career was only saved by the fact that Hans Jendretzky, the head of the SED in Berlin, made the mistake of including Walter Ulbricht himself in his criticism of Honecker. Relieved, Honecker remarked to a colleague, 'That was lucky – with that I was off the hook . . . Walter now felt personally attacked and lambasted Jendretzky who went quiet as a mouse.'[16]

It is easy to see why Honecker felt the need to prove himself and his organization with such a reckless act. The World Festival of Youth and Students in 1951 was only the third of its kind since the event had been introduced in 1947 to further the cause of inter-nationalism among the communist countries and sympathetic organizations in the West. Honecker was proud to have secured the festival for East Berlin as the host city so shortly after the war. Around 61,000 guests attended to watch the 26,000 participants from 104 countries. It was a great opportunity for the GDR to prove its value to Moscow and the world, and Honecker was right at the centre of it all. Unfortunately for him, the organization of the event was a disaster. There was not enough accommodation in the war-ravaged city for the international guests; food supplies were inadequate; and the FDJ had not yet built up the numbers needed to run such a large-scale event. So Honecker had to recruit 'Friends of the Youth' to help out – with the involuntarily comical result that there were elderly pensioners running around in the blue uniforms of the Free German Youth. Even the spectacular opening ceremony with its huge placards of Stalin on parade could not take away from the embarrassment caused by the chaos in Berlin.

Worst of all for Honecker was that the sector boundaries to West Berlin were still fully open, allowing the tens of thousands of young socialists to cross over freely. West Berlin shops put on a glittering display of the fruits of capitalism. Mayor Fritz Reuter also made the most of it, giving out free food and inviting the communist young-sters to political events. Hans Modrow, who would later become one of the last communist leaders of the GDR, remembered that some of his comrades even took souvenir photos with the free bananas.[17] Furious, Honecker had responded, 'Reuter has invited us. Fine, we will come. But not as he imagined.'[18] That Honecker's ego was so dented by his botched Youth Festival that he allowed himself to be provoked into humiliating action is probably because he was one of the youngest and least experienced members of the polit-buro. At the end of the war, he had only been thirty-two years old and had spent the previous ten years in prison as the Nazis had arrested him in 1935. He had had very little time to develop political resilience or learn the ropes of organization in the way that Ulbricht and the other Moscow exiles had. He was an outsider and very con-scious of it.

Honecker was also somewhat of a cultural outsider. Born in 1912 in Neunkirchen, in the Saarland by the French border, he still spoke with the soft accent of his home region. Combined with his natural inclination to mumble and a voice that had a tendency to break into a higher pitch than he wanted, this often made him difficult to understand. Over the years, he audibly began to imitate Walter Ulbricht's Saxony accent and made an effort to speak more clearly. But Honecker's speech would always remain a source of amuse-ment to his critics, anti-fascist credentials or not.

Honecker has often been accused of having exaggerated the humble conditions in which he grew up. He was the son of a miner and had five siblings. The family may not have starved – they had their own land, including a bit of livestock (a cow, some goats and chickens and sometimes a pig) – but to claim that Honecker lied about his working class credentials, as some historians have, goes too far. The milieu in which he was born and raised was thoroughly dominated by radical socialism. At the age of ten, young Erich was sent to a communist children's group together with some of his siblings and he joined the Young Communist League of Germany (KJVD) in 1928 at just sixteen years old (incidentally, just as Erwin Jöris, who was also born in 1912, did in Berlin at the same time) even though the organization had only 200 members at the time.

Honecker was ambitious from an early age. Battling through the countless preparation seminars and youth development courses that were necessary to apply for a stint at Moscow's International Lenin School, he impressed key people with his drive and work ethic. He was awarded a place and spent a year in the Russian capital from August 1930 to August 1931. The training and ideological schooling he received there would leave a long-lasting impact on him – he was not quite eighteen years old when a train whisked him off to the 'Land of Lenin'. Staying at the Hotel Lux, like so many foreign communists before and after him, he 'felt right at home' as he would later put it.[19] He was trained in communist ideology and practices such as 'self-criticism', a process whereby an individual publicly reflects on his or her ideological failings or mistakes. This has sometimes been compared to confession in religious contexts, but was often used during purges to humiliate and punish victims publicly by forcing them to admit to supposed shortcomings. Pupils at the Lenin School were also subjected to a gruelling work schedule which included some time at Stalin's new industrial showpiece, Magnitogorsk in the Ural Mountains. Honecker came back a changed man – his time in Russia had hardened him, both ideologically and physically. As it turned out, both helped him survive the long years of captivity at the hands of the Nazis. In 1933, he was still able to launch resistance against Hitler's regime from his home region, the Saarland, as it was not yet part of Germany. But when it was reincorporated into Germany following a referendum in 1935, Honecker first fled to France and then travelled to Berlin illegally with a printing press in order to continue his resistance from the capital. It was there that he was arrested in December 1935 and sentenced to a ten-year prison spell for treasonous activities.

Released from Brandenburg-Görden prison after the SS guards had fled, at the end of April 1945, Honecker was keen to rejoin the communist movement and made his way to Berlin on foot. He moved in with his girlfriend Charlotte Schanuel, a female prison guard nine years his senior. The two had begun an illicit relationship when he was still incarcerated and she had provided him with information from the outside. Together they listened to BBC radio broadcasts about Allied bombings and she had even helped him escape at one point, but he was unable to find safe refuge in the last chaotic weeks of the war in Berlin and returned to the prison after a few days. The couple married in 1946, and Charlotte died a few months later of a brain tumour. Honecker would never mention this first marriage in public.

Based at his girlfriend's house from 4 May 1945, Honecker had no idea where to start. He had no knowledge of the Gruppe Ulbricht and his pre-war contacts were of little use after ten years of imprisonment. He had no idea who had survived the war and who had not and was oblivious to the events in Moscow. On 10 May, as he made his way through the pathways carved into the piles of rubble in Berlin, he was spotted by Hans Mahle, who recognized the gaunt figure of his comrade Erich despite the fact that he was still wearing prison clothes. 'Mahle', whose actual name was Mahlmann, was an amiable man, only one year older than Honecker. Both had been aspiring members of the KJVD in the early 1930s. He was also one of the ten men of the Gruppe Ulbricht and knew how useful Honecker could be to their mission.

Mahle took Honecker straight to a requisitioned flat at Prinzenallee 80, which served as the Gruppe Ulbricht's HQ in Berlin. There, Ulbricht personally asked him what his plans were. Honecker mumbled something about wanting to return to the Saar region to rebuild the communist group there. But this was a naive plan – the region would fall to the French very soon, as Ulbricht well knew, and he was not going to waste an ideologically trained communist who had just proved to be a principled man to the core in ten years of political imprisonment. He convinced Honecker to stay and join the Central Committee of the KPD. Nearly twenty years apart in age, the two men were to develop a mentor–student relationship over the next fifteen years. The carpenter and the roofer were both from working class backgrounds and often found themselves at odds with the middle class intellectualism of some of their colleagues. Both found it difficult to develop real friendships with those around them. Both were ruthless pragmatists rather than ideological purists.

Honecker's first task was to build up a mass youth group. He had experience with the structure of communist youth organizations from his time in the KJVD between 1928 and 1933. He had also observed the rise of the Hitler Youth as a far more attractive and effective means of channelling youth rebellion into political fervour. Both Ulbricht and Honecker had come to the conclusion that the communists had simply been outdone by the Nazis when it came to youth engagement and they were not going to make the same mistake again. The new incarnation would not just be a small organization of hand-selected recruits for future leadership positions in the party. It would be a broad church with the potential to engage all young people. This would also have the benefit of providing a basis to justify to the Soviet occupiers why there should only be one youth group rather than allowing the churches and other parties to form their own.

Initially, Honecker had a tough time convincing the SMAD of the benefits of having a centralized youth organization. The Soviets were happy to legalize the formation of local groups but were sceptical about a central committee that would control them from Berlin. They would only grant this if Honecker's new youth organization matched the 'anti-fascist' front idea at governmental level, if it was pluralist and included bourgeois and church elements and not just communists. After arduous negotiations, Honecker won over the Catholic cathedral vicar Robert Lange and the Protestant youth pastor Oswald Hanisch as well as three SPD representatives. They joined the three KPD men to set up the new organization. He suggested the politically neutral name 'Free German Youth' and took his proposal to the SMAD in February 1946. On 7 March, it was official: the FDJ was born. Its distinctive blue shirts with the bright yellow rising sun would accompany the GDR's history until the very end.

The FDJ unashamedly offered those young Germans who had felt at home in the Hitler Youth a chance to rehabilitate themselves. Boys and girls could join if they were between fourteen and twenty-five. This meant that its membership in 1950 was born between 1925 and 1936 – they were Hitler's children, under ten years old when he came to power and shaped by his world view. The Nazi regime had been unique in its attention to young people and genuinely captured the imagination of many children and teenagers. Psychologically, the young had lost all reference points in their lives when the Third Reich collapsed. Many had rebelled against their parents to join Hitler's ranks. Now the FDJ provided a new, yet familiar, framework for them. Those among them who had previously held positions of rank in the Hitler Youth would not be judged or excluded from leadership positions in the FDJ, and so many flocked to Honecker. They found familiar routines such as marching, torch processions and mass gatherings, all of which allowed them to gradually grow into the new ideology. It worked. Upon official legalization of its final format by the SMAD, the FDJ already had 400,000 members. The only world they had ever known fell apart alongside Hitler's promises. Now their zealous belief in the Führer could be redirected on to Stalin with surprising ease.

When the Soviet dictator sent a telegram to congratulate the FDJ for its first ever 'Convention of the German Youth' in June 1950 to which half a million youngsters had flocked, the FDJ leadership was delighted despite the fact that Stalin's message had conveyed the lack of enthusiasm he still felt for all things GDR. It was decidedly mundane: 'I thank the participants of the German youth convention, those freedom fighters, for their greetings. I wish the German youth, the builders of a unified, democratic and peaceful Germany, new successes with this important work.'[20] If anything, this was meant to serve as a reminder that the German communists were supposed to work towards unification rather than build their own structures. But the FDJ was blown away by its hero's words. They printed a special edition of their newspaper *Junge Welt* (Young World) with Stalin's image on the front page and sent an astonishing 800,000 copies of it into German cities, towns and villages. They also put up 300,000 posters and 100,000 placard newspapers for good measure.[21]

Such enthusiastic engagement was part of the organization's allure. What's more, this appeal also worked in West Germany, despite attempts by Konrad Adenauer's government to clamp down on the movement. The 1950 'Convention of the German Youth' in East Berlin was also attended by 27,000 Western members of the FDJ. When 10,000 of them decided to return home to the West in a coordinated march across the border, they were demonstrably held back by West German border guards to make a point: if you like socialism so much, why don't you stay? The youths camped by the Herrnburg/Lübeck border for two days before they were let back into West Germany. There, they continued to demonstrate against the rearmament policy of the Adenauer government and its attempts to integrate Germany into Western alliances. They sailed to the island of Helgoland in February 1951, for example, to demonstrate against British bombing tests there. When they prepared an unofficial poll of the West German population about their attitudes towards rearmament, the Chancellor had had enough. On 26 June 1951, he banned the FDJ in West Germany, making it and all its symbols illegal.

When the West German youngsters rebelled against the ban of the FDJ and were joined by Christian youth organizations for a demonstration in Essen on 11 May 1952, things got out of hand. The protesters threw stones; the police opened fire on the masses. They severely injured two people and shot a twenty-one-year-old FDJ member from Munich, Philipp Müller, who bled to death. These terrible scenes would cause an uproar in the East German FDJ where Honecker swore 'revenge for Müller through the downfall of the treacherous Adenauer clique'.[22] The GDR named many streets and schools after Müller. The FDJ and Honecker claimed the moral high ground, for now.

Erich Mielke and the Birth of the Stasi

East Berlin, 22 March 1950. Kurt Müller, the deputy leader of the KPD in West Germany, arrived at the office of the Central Committee in East Berlin. His East German comrade Hans Rosenberg had invited him to the GDR telling him that he was needed. When he arrived in Berlin, he was not met by his contact but by Walter Ulbricht himself. After a brief exchange, he was bluntly told that he was under arrest and dragged off to the remand prison of the newly formed Ministry for State Security, better known as the Stasi.

Kurt Müller was one of the first prisoners at the four-storey brick building at Albrechtstraße 26. It had only just been renovated and reopened a few days before his arrival. Its thirty-five individual cells were guarded by a small group of new recruits whom the deputy leader of the Stasi, Erich Mielke, had personally sworn in.[23] What had been Müller's crime? He had seemed successful in rebuilding the KPD in the West and was not only its deputy leader but had also been elected into the *Bundestag* as a communist member of parliament. Yet when the Stasi had interrogated his 'kidnapper' Hans Rosenberg, he had replied that Müller had always had 'diverting opinions' and that 'his character was not very good'. Furthermore, he had been part of the Neumann–Remmele group in the exile years in the Soviet Union.[24] Both Neumann and Remmele were arrested and executed during Stalin's Great Purges. The GDR was keen to prove to Stalin that its new security apparatus would work in tandem with that of the 'Big Brother' to the East. While Stalin's paranoia and wrath over Tito's independence in Yugoslavia raged through Eastern Europe, Ulbricht and his underlings were looking to emulate this. The fact that Müller had also been involved with funds provided by the American Noel Field made him the perfect candidate for the first Soviet-style show trial. Mielke himself questioned his famous prisoner repeatedly:

> *Mielke: Did you know you had been a member of a Trotskyist*
>   *organization?*
> *Müller: That is not true . . . But I did join Neumann before 1932.*
> *Mielke: When?*
> *Müller: From 1931 to 1932.*
> *Mielke: When did you make contact with Neumann?*
> *Müller: At the beginning of 1931 through Remmele.*
> *Mielke: When exactly?*
> *Müller: When I was chairman of the ZKJV [Central Communist Youth*
>   *Organization].*
> *Mielke: When did you make contact with Neumann?*
> *Müller: Through Remmele.*
> *Mielke: When did you make contact with Remmele?*
> *Müller: When I was chairman of the ZKJV.*
> *Mielke: What was Remmele's theory?*
> *Müller: Hit the fascists where you can.*
> *Mielke: When did you make contact with Neumann?*
> *Müller: At the beginning of 1931.*[25]

And so the tortuous circle of questions went on and on. Mielke would always interrogate at night, starting at 10 p.m. and ending between 4 and 6 a.m. While this was going on, the prisoner had to stand for the whole time. In the morning he was not allowed to sleep after 6 a.m. There were periods of about eight to ten days where he was not allowed to sleep at all and interrogations would take place twice a day from 11 a.m. to 4.30 p.m. and then again from 10 p.m. to 6 a.m. Mielke was trying to soften his prisoner for the great public showdown of the German purges: his own show trial.

But the newly established Stasi had not yet earned Stalin's respect. Kurt Müller was transferred to the Soviet NKVD in August 1950.

The Soviets locked him into the notorious 'U-Boat', the prison in Berlin-Hohenschönhausen, where Erwin Jöris had also been incarcerated. There Müller was held in a tiny, narrow cell. Then he was transferred to a water cell with no windows and no furniture; the floor was permanently flooded with 2 centimetres of water. Müller also spent some time in the infamous Cell No. 60 which was about as big as a broom cupboard and had a wooden plank fixed to each side of the wall, which only left a tiny gap in the middle. It was designed so that there was not enough space to comfortably stand, walk or lie down. Above his head, an industrial fan roared day and night without break. After nearly three years of torturous imprisonment, Müller was sentenced by the Soviets to twenty-five years of hard labour and deported to Siberia. He would be released in 1955 as part of Konrad Adenauer's deal with the post-Stalinist USSR to release German prisoners back to their home country. He was still not broken. Kicked out of the KPD, he joined the SPD in West Germany and wrote a letter to Otto Grotewohl detailing the conditions of his interrogation at the hands of Erich Mielke and the NKVD and demanding that those responsible be punished.[26] He never received a reply.

Erich Mielke's ruthless and psychologically erosive methods had been honed during long and thorough training in Moscow. In contrast to Ulbricht and Pieck, Mielke never tried to hide his connection to the Soviet Union. He even called his staff 'Chekists' in allusion to the Soviet secret police whose methods provided the inspiration for his own in the GDR.

Born in 1907 in the working class district of 'Red' Wedding in Berlin, Erich Mielke grew up in a world of dreary tenements, populated by hardline socialists and communists. His father Emil, a woodworker, was radicalized during the First World War, which 'damaged him' as his son would later describe it. Emil had fought on the Russian front and, upon return, joined the newly founded KPD. Erich Mielke turned out to be an intelligent and ambitious young man. He worked hard to be accepted into the local selective school. Despite all its ambitions for social mobility, the Weimar Republic never managed to raise the proportion of working class students in grammar schools above 7 per cent, yet they were the only route to university. The young Erich Mielke became radicalized by the poverty that was inflicted upon the people around him after the Wall Street Crash in 1929. As Wedding began to vote for the KPD in huge numbers (40.6 per cent in 1929), many regions of the rest of Germany began to look to the Nazis for solutions. It was time for action as far as Mielke was concerned. In 1931, at the age of twenty-four, he joined the paramilitary wing of the KPD, the *Parteiselbstschutz* (Self-Protection Squad of the Party).

The atmosphere in Berlin had reached fever pitch in 1930. At demonstrations and strikes both policemen and communists were regularly injured or even killed. The radicalized left vowed to avenge each murdered worker by killing two policemen. On 9 August 1931, Erich Mielke and some accomplices targeted one of Berlin's most prolific officers, Captain Paul Anlauf. The forty-nine-year-old had been in charge of policing many of the communist events and shown merciless determination to crack down on communist activity. For this, he was nicknamed 'Schweinebacke' (Pig Face) in left-wing circles. On that day, the police were on high alert as the troubles in Berlin seemed to get more heated by the day. Anlauf and two colleagues, Sergeant Richard Willig and Captain Franz Lenck, patrolled the Bülowplatz in Berlin-Mitte. The large square was framed by the Volksbühne theatre, the famous cinema Babylon and the KPD headquarters. Shortly after 8 p.m. shots rang through the air. Paul Anlauf had been hit through the head from behind and died instantly. Franz Lenck had been shot through the lung and staggered into the foyer of the Babylon where he collapsed and succumbed to his wound. Richard Willig was hit in the arm and the stomach but survived. Mielke would never admit to the murders directly and we still do not know whether it was he who pulled the trigger. What is certain, however, is that he was there on the night. He had been involved in the planning and was happy to carry out the 'Bülowplatz Job' as he would later call it. There can be no doubt that he had the training, mindset and cold-bloodedness for it.

A huge bounty was placed on the heads of Mielke and the other suspected police killers. The 23,000-mark reward showed how serious the government considered the matter – a worker earned around 150 marks a month. Mielke and his partners-in-crime had to flee to Moscow. There, he received thorough training at the Comintern's Military School and at the Lenin School where he was taught by the likes of Ulbricht, Pieck and Dimitrov. His timetable consisted of ideology, combat, counter-intelligence, street fighting, surveillance, interrogation and many other skills he would later deploy. Mielke witnessed first-hand Stalin's increasing paranoia and the speed with which the arrests and executions around him gathered pace. He would later write that he 'took part in the trials against the traitors and enemies of the Soviet Union'.[27] Many of his closest associates were arrested and murdered, such as Hans Kippenberger, who is named as his referee on three documents from his time in Moscow.

Mielke himself got out of Russia just in the nick of time. He was deployed to Spain to help the communists in the Civil War from 1936 to 1939. This meant that he sat out the worst excesses of Stalin's purges on the Iberian peninsula, which was not only the westernmost tip of Europe and as far away from Stalin as was possible, but also out of Hitler's reach. However, in March 1939, the KPD in exile summoned Mielke to Brussels and gave him new tasks in Belgium and then France. As the Nazis expanded their reach westwards, life as an illegal communist, who was still wanted for the two police murders of 1931, became very dangerous. Mielke attempted to flee to Mexico aided by his comrade Wilhelm Kreikemeyer who was trying to organize the necessary papers and secured him 1,000 francs from Noel Field's communist help fund. Neither worked and Mielke was arrested in 1943. He worked as a forced labourer under a false identity to avoid being tried for the police killings. At the end of the war, he immediately returned to Berlin, which he reached on 14 June 1945.

Mielke would never admit to his attempted escape to Mexico or the funds received from Noel Field. Having been in exile in the West, rather than the Soviet Union, put him at the centre of the SED's waves of self-cleansing. Any association with the deadly maelstrom of the Noel Field Affair would have ended his career and possibly his life. The only witness to these events was his former colleague Willi Kreikemeyer, who was himself arrested in 1950 under suspicion of being an American spy. Mielke questioned his old associate personally, following which Kreikemeyer was excluded from the SED. On 31 August he was found dead in his cell. Whether he was murdered by Mielke or whether he killed himself out of despair is still uncertain. But the only stain on Mielke's communist CV had been extinguished with Kreikemeyer's life.

Mielke had clearly lost nothing of his ruthlessness and fervour during the war. Five years before Kreikemeyer's mysterious demise, immediately upon his arrival in Berlin in 1945, Mielke had reported to the KPD leadership of whom he knew many from his time in Moscow and from the Weimar years. Due to his extensive training in security and policing skills, Mielke was an ideal candidate to help build the new police forces in Berlin. He showed significant skill and intelligence, which allowed him to rise to a position in the Central Committee of the party where he coordinated the police and justice sectors from December 1945. He worked closely with Walter Ulbricht as he sensed that this was where all power gravitated. Wilhelm Zaisser, who had been his senior commanding officer in Spain, and would be his boss at the Stasi, remarked, 'Given the speed with which Erich climbs up Walter's backside, you won't even see the tips of his boots!'[28]

Apart from his police work, Mielke was also trusted with the build-up of the forerunner of the Ministry of the Interior, an area where it fell to him to find trustworthy communists and root out social democrats, liberals and other undesirable elements. There would be no deputy system at the core of the future civil service under Ulbricht. Mielke also worked on denazification and the establishment of a new 'political police', the *Kommissariat 5*. Both meant that Mielke played a central role in the waves of arrests of the post-war years where former concentration camps and Nazi prisons were repurposed to hold former Nazis but also scores of 'bourgeois' elements who had run foul of the increasingly paranoid regime under Ulbricht.

By May 1949, Mielke's *Kommissariat 5* already counted 800 members. This would be the core from which the Ministry for State Security was founded in February 1950. It must have stung that Wilhelm Zaisser became its first head while Mielke became his deputy. But unlike Mielke, Zaisser had returned to Moscow after the Spanish Civil War was lost and worked there throughout the war. He was a man Stalin knew and trusted. Mielke would bide his time. For now, he was content to work behind the scenes to build and extend the Stasi, selecting, recruiting and training staff and growing the organization to his own liking, while Zaisser did the political work and kept the connection to Ulbricht. It was Mielke, not Zaisser, who had the prison in the Albrechtstraße set up in the style of NKVD cells. And it was Mielke who had Kurt Müller dragged from West Germany, caused the death of Willi Kreikemeyer and spent night after night personally interrogating his prisoners with methods learned in Moscow.

While the Stasi was a small organization in February 1950, when it started off with 1,100 members, in Mielke's hands it would soon grow to one of the largest and most complex police organizations the world had ever seen. Historian Mary Fulbrook was right to argue that 'the insecurity of the East German regime both informed and exacerbated the inculcation of a friend/foe mentality'.[29] The GDR was unique among the Eastern Bloc nations in that its very existence was never ensured. Ulbricht, Mielke and those working with them did not only have to defend their state against the West but also against Stalin, who would still have rather seen it integrated into a unified, neutral Germany. They felt they had to prove that their state was a pure, trustworthy and 'uncorrupted' outpost of the Soviet Empire. This became even more urgent once Adenauer's FRG began to integrate itself into the West definitively through rearmament and NATO membership in 1955.

Meanwhile, the GDR regime was frightened of its own people. The comparison to West Germany was always there. GDR citizens had relatives in the West. They listened to the radio and saw what was going on. They had memories of high living standards before the war. Their restlessness and demands made the regime nervous. Ulbricht was acutely aware that he was a member of a small clique that formed a hardline Muscovite island populated by the like-minded survivors of the purges in the USSR and East Germany. Surrounded by enemies, Ulbricht craved the 'Shield and Sword' that Mielke's Stasi promised to be to him and the SED. And Mielke was all too willing to make himself and his organization utterly indispensable.

Good Will

Given that most of the men and women who were involved in the governmental and party structures of the newly established GDR had suffered horrendous political persecution during the Hitler years, one might have expected more resistance to the lack of democratic process within the new constitution. Here was a chance to build the better Germany many had dreamt of; why was there not more anger at the corruption of this ideal? Paradoxically, the answer lies precisely in the experiences of fascism and war, which had led many Germans to value stability and unity over pluralistic discussion. This was true East and West. Germans were exhausted and the majority wanted little to do with politics. Since 1914, there had been little respite from ideology, war, economic turmoil and rapid political change. A middle-aged German in 1949 had seen the whole spectrum of political systems in their lifetime, but none of the offerings had shown a functioning democracy. Where was a love for voting, citizens' rights and a pluralistic society meant to come from? What the German public wanted was not an array of parties on a voting slip every four years but food on the table, a restored roof over their heads and a future without war and economic disaster.

The difference between East and West was that the West delivered these things immediately while the East did not. Konrad Adenauer, the first Chancellor of the FRG, was re-elected with results that modern politicians can only dream of: in 1953 and again in 1957, when his party received an astonishing 50.2 per cent of the vote despite a system of proportional representation which usually leads to coalition governments. This enabled him to run the country without forming a coalition for the only time in its history since 1949. All of this under Adenauer's famous slogan: 'Keine Experimente' – No Experiments.

East Germans too wanted no experiments in the 1950s. They wanted peace, secure jobs, food and an opportunity to rebuild their disrupted lives. The result was a tendency to accept compromise and avoid conflict which affected even politicians whose instincts were naturally opposed to the idea of a dictatorship of the proletariat, such as Carl Klußmann, a founding member of the Liberal Democratic Party. He declared in an interview for the regional newspaper *Volksstimme* (People's Voice) in June 1957 that 'it is on every person in the German Democratic Republic to pledge himself to this state'. He blamed Adenauer's firm integration of the Federal Republic of Germany into the West as the main obstacle to reunification and the Soviets supported this argument. It was therefore possible for a liberal politician to find a meaningful place within the SED's dictatorship. Like Klußmann, many others believed that the GDR needed to hold out until the reunification of their fatherland as a neutral and peaceful country could be achieved. In the meantime, things needed to be rebuilt, the economy strengthened and people's lives improved. This was not the time for political idealism and principles. Despite his personal differences with the SED course, Klußmann died in 1957 as their ally. His gravestone reads: 'Until his last hour, this friend of our party knew no respite from his political duty to party and state.'[30]

The appeal of a genuinely anti-fascist, socialist Germany so shortly after the demise of the Nazi regime should not be underestimated. People such as the writer Bertolt Brecht chose to move to the East as the West began to reintegrate former Nazis into politics, public life and policing. Many individuals, like Erich Honecker, had spent years in prisons and concentration camps suffering for their political beliefs and holding out for a time when things would change. Now, for the first time in German history, they saw a chance to build the socialist, classless and just society they dreamt of. If that came with an initial phase of repression, then that was only to be expected. Marxist doctrine, which many of those who now found themselves in political roles had been schooled in, held that the dictatorship of the proletariat was a necessary stage in the transition from capitalism to socialism. While the ruling elites were still clinging on to their privileges and power, the working classes needed to hold the reins tightly. The post-war years seemed to provide the perfect historical context for this as former Nazis and their sympathizers needed to be removed from politics and society first before things could open up. In the early 1950s, many intellectuals were still willing to accept this dogma.

While the new East German state could certainly not lean on the widespread support and compliance of its citizens in the way that the Nazi regime had been able to, it was not immediately met with widespread resistance either.

Economic Catch-Up

Ketschendorf, Brandenburg, 1951. Regina Faustmann was fairly happy with how things had turned out. The sixteen-year-old girl had gone through a lot in her young life. Her father had died in 1945, leaving his wife to look after their three children just as the Red Army was advancing. Her mother spoke a little Russian so she was recruited to do the laundry for the victorious soldiers in exchange for food. As the Soviets knew she had three children to feed, they were always generous, and the young family never had to go hungry, nor were they harmed in any way. When she was old enough, Regina began an apprenticeship as a chemical lab technician at the local DEKA works, a tyre manufacturer that had opened in her home town in 1940 and immediately resumed work after the war. It was not what she had dreamt of doing with her life – she had wanted to become a seamstress like many in her family before her – but things did not work out that way. Besides, she had stable work with which she was able to help support the family, and then there was also a handsome young tyre maker called Günther who had entered her life. With him she began to frequent the new theatres, dance clubs and cinemas that sprung up everywhere. The Soviets and their German comrades had agreed that a rich cultural scene had to be built up immediately for morale, but also because the Soviets simply loved entertainment in all its forms.

Regina and Günther had both joined the newly established FDJ. As a Catholic, Regina felt included in the wide range of activities on offer, which she undertook alongside her Protestant and non-religious peers. There were social activities and music but also serious work to help rebuild Germany such as scrap-metal collection. It felt good to be part of a collective effort. The only thing that annoyed her sometimes was that the Soviets had a habit of turning up at the tyre factory unannounced and confiscating the goods that had just been manufactured, which messed up production schedules, targets and the coordination of the manufacturing process.[31]

Regina Faustmann's example is typical of a young generation of Germans who were enthusiastic about rolling up their sleeves and playing their part in rebuilding their country. There was much to do. Cities still lay in ruins – Regina's own home town of Fürstenwalde had lost its bridge over the River Spree which would not be properly rebuilt until 1959. Industry and agriculture had been exhausted by Hitler's megalomania. And a new Germany needed new buildings and architecture.

The twenty-year-old Reinhold Limberg came up with a song to capture this spirit in 1947. During the war, he had been deployed in the German navy as an underage helper through the Hitler Youth. He was taken prisoner and, once released from Soviet captivity, he returned to his father's farm in Mecklenburg in the north. It was during the tough labour there that he had an idea for a song to capture what he and many other young Germans, disenchanted with their previous fascination for Hitler, were feeling:

Jugend erwach, erhebe dich jetzt,	Oh, youth awake, arise anew,
Die grausame Zeit hat ein End!	The terrible time has an end!
Und die Sonne schickt wieder	And the sun sends again
Die Strahlen hernieder	The rays down to us men
Vom blauen Himmelsgezelt.	From the blue blue sky up above.
Die Lerche schickt frohe Lieder ins Tal,	And the lark sends cheerful songs into the valley,
Das Bächlein ermuntert uns all.	The small stream brings us all joy,
Und der Bauer bestellt	And the farmer's field
Wieder Acker und Feld,	Will produce a new yield
Bald blüht es all überall.	Soon everything flowers anew.
[Refrain:]	[Chorus:]
Bau auf, bau auf,	Build up, build up,
Bau auf, bau auf,	Build up, build up,
Freie Deutsche Jugend, bau auf!	Free German Youth, build up!
Für eine bessere Zukunft richten wir die Heimat auf!	For a better future, we're Building our country up!
Allüberall der Hammer ertönt,	Everywhere the hammer strikes,
Die werkende Hand zu uns spricht:	The working hand speaks to us:
Deutsche Jugend, pack an,	German youth, help too,
Brich dir selber die Bahn,	This job is on you,
Für Frieden, Freiheit und Recht!	For peace, freedom and justice!
Kein Zwang und kein Drill,	No pressure, no drill,
Der eigene Will'	Just your own free will

Erfülle dein Leben fortan.	Fulfil your own life henceforth.
Blicke frei in das Licht,	Look straight at the light,
Das dir niemals gebricht.	So you never lose sight.
Deutsche Jugend, steh deinen Mann!	German Youth, steadfast go forth.

'Jugend erwach!' (Youth Awake!). Lyrics and music by Reinhold Limberg, 1947.

Written in typical socialist style, directly addressing its listeners, the song has rightly been categorized as propaganda. But to dismiss it as the work of the SED to which the German youth was involuntarily subjected is wrong. Many East Germans who were young during this period describe the pride with which they began to build a new economy for themselves and many sang this song with genuine enthusiasm.

For all the can-do spirit of its young people, the GDR was already losing the game of catch-up before the two German opponents had even begun to play. The problem was not work ethic, and not even the central planning aspect of the GDR's young economy (after all, most Western countries still fixed prices, wages and rations for years to come). It was the immense burden the young state carried on its shoulders – a load so heavy that it persists in eastern Germany today, despite the fact that for over thirty years it has been part of a European and global power, the fourth largest economy in the world.

The part of Germany that was allocated to the Soviet Union as its zone of occupation was not only much smaller in size and population than the Western Zones, but it also lay in an area of few natural resources. For energy, for example, the GDR was almost entirely dependent on lignite, also known as brown coal. This soft, combustible material forms when peat is compressed over time. It lies relatively close to the surface so it is cheap to source, but at a huge cost to the environment. Not only does its mining leave unsightly craters behind that would turn entire East German regions into desolate moonscapes, but its energy content is comparatively low, creating a lot of pollution when burned for electricity, heat or steam power. The GDR was in desperate need of energy. Help from the Soviet Union was never reliably forthcoming. A gargantuan effort was undertaken to make the GDR self-sufficient, largely based on lignite. It would continue to provide 70 per cent of all energy, which meant that by 1970, the GDR ended up being the world's largest lignite producer, sourcing more than Soviet Russia and West Germany together. There was very little else and other raw materials such as black coal, copper and iron ore were all in short supply too.

The lack of iron ore in the East also meant that Germany had never developed much of an ironworks industry in the region. Germany's industrial heartlands of the Ruhr lay in the far west. However, the Soviets were desperate for reparations and keen to make use of the expertise and high productivity of their captive German comrades. To this end, an entire new town was created out of nowhere, in the far east of Brandenburg, by the Polish border: Eisenhüttenstadt (Ironworks City). It was a model socialist city with newly built housing blocks for the workers and their families alongside recreational and green spaces.

The Soviet Union's rapacious young nuclear industry was also demanding that its new brother states help with the supply of uranium. It sent exploration teams out and found deposits of the precious material in Thuringia and in the Ore Mountains of Saxony. The sites were immediately guarded by NKVD troops and mining began at first with forced labour, then with coerced labour consisting of men like Ernst Wicht. In the autumn of 1948, the youngster had only just finished his training as a gardener and moved to the Thuringian capital of Erfurt where he enjoyed the fact that 'life was getting back to normal'. Suddenly, he was told to appear at the job distribution office. There two men tried to convince him to begin work as a miner to source 'peace ore' as they called the uranium that was needed for nuclear weapons. 'I gave them all sorts of excuses but was told that they could force me anyway with a work deployment duty,' Ernst remembered.[32]

Half a year later, he was marched past armed Soviet guards to the entrance of the uranium mine of Wismut to receive his four-hour training course. The work was exhausting and dangerous. For hours on end he worked with a jackhammer without protection. At lunchtime, he and his colleagues sat on wooden crates which contained the uranium ore they had sourced, not knowing anything of its destructive radiation. Occasionally someone would joke that if Ernst wanted to have children one day he had better not sit on the peace ore for too long. Ernst worked alongside other people who had been coerced to join as well as locals who had already voluntarily worked there for a couple of years. There were also forced labourers, mostly former Nazi Party members. Ernst quickly began to see the positives: he and his family received much higher food rations and wages than regular workers elsewhere. The rigid shift system created close bonds between the workmates, and the planned economy with its reward system for reaching or surpassing targets sparked a competitive streak in many who took pride and sometimes even boyish glee in staying another hour or two to hit a certain figure. But Ernst also witnessed countless work accidents caused by insufficient training or care. In the end, he had to leave this job when he developed tuberculosis and was hospitalized.

Despite everything, he would later look back on his time in 'Wild Wismut' with a sense of melancholy: 'It is difficult to stop doing something that perhaps you have not grown to love but to accept. It had become familiar and my family could live off it very well.'[33] Wismut was later jointly owned by the GDR and the Soviet Union with a 50/50 split and would go on to make East Germany the fourth largest producer of uranium in the world. But to begin with, all its exploits were the Soviet Union's and the terrible ecological and human costs all East Germany's.

This pattern was repeated elsewhere. Private looting and theft aside, the Soviets had officially taken reparations and compensation for occupation costs in excess of $15 billion out of the GDR by 1953.[34] This encompassed the wholesale dismantling of entire factories and other fixed assets as well as the sourcing of useful raw materials. Lead piping was ripped from walls, iron climbing frames stolen from playgrounds and entire train lines deconstructed and relaid in the Soviet Union. The GDR might have recovered from this eventually had it not been for the crippling scale of the ongoing reparations that were literally taken from German assembly lines. What Regina Faustmann reported for her tyre factory played out across the manufacturing sector in the GDR. Red Army soldiers would turn up, often unannounced, and confiscate what the factory had just produced, with devastating effects on economic planning, supply lines and worker morale. In total, 60 per cent[35] of ongoing East German production was taken out of the young state's efforts to get on its feet between 1945 and 1953. Yet its people battled on. As early as 1950, the production levels of 1938 had been reached again despite the fact that the GDR had paid three times as much in reparations as its Western counterpart.[36]

East Germany's ambitious social restructuring also had severe economic consequences. The reallocation of huge areas of land from aristocratic owners, who had experience, knowledge and the equipment to farm effectively and the ancient social structures in their villages to support their industry, into tiny segments that were given to 'new farmers' was economically disastrous. As late as 1959, the politburo was still being informed that fruit production had taken a hit of 38 per cent and vegetables 33 per cent compared to what the sector should have yielded that year[37] (although this was exacerbated through long droughts). Economically catastrophic, this land redistribution intended to break up the ancient aristocratic structures that in the eyes of many had contributed to much of Germany's social tension over the decades. In addition, a quarter of the East German population consisted of refugees from Eastern Europe, largely farmers who had lost everything. To give them a slice of land carved out of the great estates of a former Prussian Junker seemed fair to many even if it made little sense economically and came without compensation for the previous owners.

The same applies to denazification. Where West Germany had openly welcomed former Nazis back into the civil service, teaching, culture and even the police, the GDR made anti-fascism its foundational dogma. While there were many important exceptions, particularly in the armed forces and in the insufficient attention given to the thorough investigation of the Holocaust, on the whole denazification in the East was deeper and had an impact on the economy. Teachers, civil servants, politicians and even engineers and policemen were removed from their positions and replaced with inexperienced but ideologically less problematic individuals. This debilitating loss of expertise, alongside the large-scale relocation to the Soviet Union of specialist personnel such as scientists, meant that the young economy simply lacked the key personnel to succeed.

Despite the best efforts of East Germans keen to rebuild and to prove that a better Germany was possible, the GDR stood no chance to build a functioning economy in the early 1950s. Combined with the long hardships suffered during the war, and for older Germans the memory of the economic disasters of the Weimar Republic and the First World War, this was utterly demoralizing. While Adenauer swept his West Germans away with an 'economic miracle' that brought consumerism and enjoyment back into people's lives, all that Ulbricht had to offer was an economic cataclysm. The backbreaking work his people were subjected to could only be endured so long under his promise that 'We will one day live as we work today.' It wasn't good enough.

The Stalin Note

Cheine, Saxony-Anhalt, 29 May 1952. Anneliese Fleischer, a fourteen-year-old girl, was sent home from school. When she arrived, a lorry was parked outside and the family's belongings were loaded onto it. Nobody knew what was going on. Her father, with his leg in a cast from a recent accident, stood by helplessly as her mother asked her to help carry furniture and boxes from the kitchen, sitting room and bedroom to the lorry. Where would they be taken? Anneliese heard somebody say something about Siberia. Eventually, the family were told they were being resettled to an area further away from the border with West Germany. Their home in Cheine lay only a few kilometres from Lower Saxony, West Germany.[38] Between May 1952 and the building of the Berlin Wall in 1961, a total of 11,000 people were forcefully resettled away from the inner-German border. Dubbed 'Aktion Ungeziefer' (Operation Vermin), the entire plan was kept top secret. Residents were not told what was happening; their new neighbours were suspicious. It was implied that those forcefully moved had done something to deserve it, a story perpetuated to this day.[39]

In reality, Operation Vermin was a symptom of the panic in the upper echelons of power. Ulbricht, and more importantly Stalin himself, had become convinced that West Germany was fully committing to becoming the easternmost outpost of American military influence in Europe. They were not entirely wrong. The Korean War, which had begun in 1950 and was still raging – unwinnable despite huge US efforts – alongside the proclamation of the communist People's Republic of China in 1949 and the first successful Soviet tests of nuclear weaponry had triggered a lot of fear in Washington. It culminated in the feverish search for communist conspirators during the era of McCarthyism in the early 1950s. As a result, US President Harry S. Truman put enormous pressure on the receptive West German Chancellor Adenauer to begin the serious build-up of armed forces in his country and integrate it into the anti-communist defence bloc of NATO, which had been set up in 1949. Adenauer knew he needed European consent for this, particularly from his highly sceptical French neighbours. A brilliant negotiator, as charismatic as he was authoritative, Adenauer sat down with the French and began to persuade them of the efficacy of closer West European cooperation. An autonomous Germany with its own military would naturally have to be firmly anchored into Western structures, such as NATO or the European Defence Community, but if it was, it could be a cost-effective and trustworthy ally.

Now it was Stalin's time to panic. He was ready to pay almost any price to avoid a remilitarized German state in the heart of Europe. On 10 March 1952, he sent the so-called Stalin Note to the representatives of the Western Allies in Germany. It offered the reunification of Germany as a neutral state. This is often brushed aside as a mere propaganda move, but as the West German historian Wilfried Loth has convincingly shown, there are numerous documents that indicate that Stalin was serious.[40] The note offered a number of significant concessions, notably Germany would be allowed to build 'its own national armed forces (land, air and sea) which are necessary for the defence of the country'.[41] Reparations and denazification would be considered complete, so that '[n]o kind of limitations are imposed on Germany as to the development of its peaceful economy'.[42] The country could potentially be admitted into the newly formed United Nations. Even 'free all-German elections' were to happen, as an additional note from 9 April confirmed.[43] The only obligations on Germany were that it had to accept 'the borders established by the provisions of the Potsdam Conference', i.e. the loss of its former territory in Eastern Europe, and that it must not 'enter into any kind of coalition or military alliance directed against any power which took part with its armed forces in the war against Germany.'[44] The latter was to fulfil two functions. It would stop a unified Germany from entering an alliance against Soviet Russia, i.e. NATO, and it was designed to reassure the French that a unified neighbour would not be a threat to them again. Loth argues that this shows Stalin no longer angled for a Germany in the socialist image (if indeed he ever had done), but that he was content with one that 'satisfied Soviet security demands'.[45]

Some in the GDR leadership too were happy with a neutral unified Germany, such as Rudolf Herrnstadt, the editor of the party newspaper, who had returned to Berlin shortly after Ulbricht and was now part of the Central Committee of the SED. He bluntly told his colleagues in the inner circle of power, 'Some of us would do well to . . . free themselves of the undialectical assumption that the unified, democratic Germany that is coming will simply be a larger copy of the current German Democratic Republic.'[46] But this view was to alienate him from the all-powerful Ulbricht and he would be excluded from the SED in 1954. The General Secretary and his supporters were palpably relieved when Adenauer's government turned down the offer of a neutral Germany and instead began to cement West Germany's position in the Western alliance under American leadership.[47]

That this was not the outcome Stalin had wanted becomes obvious in his response to the signing of the so-called Germany Treaty by the FRG and the former Western Allies, the US, Britain and France, on 26 May 1952. This recognized the FRG as a sovereign state and paved the way to NATO membership. Stalin panicked. His successor Khrushchev would later speak of a 'war psychosis' that gripped Moscow and remembered how 'we believed that America would invade the Soviet Union and we would go to war. Stalin trembled at this prospect. How he quivered! He was afraid of war. He knew we were weaker than the United States.'[48] Stalin's paranoia was back. He would have happily sold the German communists down the river if it meant avoiding another war.

Meanwhile, Ulbricht saw the matter settled when Adenauer shot down the Stalin Note. He pressed ahead with an open agenda of 'building socialism' at the Second Party Conference on 9 July 1952. Stalin had reluctantly agreed to this but it is telling that his written consent only arrived a day before the conference while SED protocols of 3 July already show that there was talk of the build-up of socialism as the new 'strategic aim' of the SED.[49] However, Stalin still refused to allow Ulbricht to change the national flag, which was exactly the same as that of West Germany – the black-red-gold tricolour of the liberal 1848 revolutions. It would only be embossed with the GDR's emblem in 1959, six years after Stalin's death: a hammer for the working classes, a compass for the middle classes and a ring of rye for the peasantry.

The new *Aufbau des Sozialismus* (Building Socialism) programme included economic measures such as the collectivization of agriculture in so-called Agricultural Production Cooperatives (LPGs) and of crafts in equivalent Production Cooperatives for Trades (PGHs). Importantly, it allowed Ulbricht and Pieck to push for the build-up of the GDR's armed forces. Angered by the West's refusal to accept a neutral Germany, Stalin gave a directive to the SED in April 1952 in Moscow to 'build a People's Army – without palaver – the pacifist period is over'. They were also told to secure 'that dangerous border'.[50] The upshot of this was that Operation Vermin would remove children like Anneliese Fleischer and their families from their homes to clear a 5-kilometre-deep control zone in which only trusted individuals could live. Everyone who wanted to go there had to have a good reason. The border itself became a 10-metre-wide fortification, which armed guards would patrol with orders to shoot. It was created to keep West Germans out of the GDR as Stalin's fear of invasion spilled over on to his German comrades. Later it would serve to keep 16 million East Germans in.

The question as to whether there was a real chance of German unification in March 1952 has often been dismissed out of hand with attempts to portray Stalin as the disingenuous party. The documents paint a different picture. It was Stalin who would have liked to have seen a unified Germany, even if this came at the huge cost of lost reparations and territorial influence. But it is also too easy to put all the blame on Adenauer and his refusal to accept Stalin's offer, as Kurt Schumacher, the leader of the SPD in West Germany, did when he accused Adenauer of sacrificing German unity on the altar of Western integration and remilitarization. Had West Germany accepted the offer and demanded to see free elections as promised by Stalin, it is very unlikely that Ulbricht and Pieck would have allowed this. There are indications that Otto Grotewohl, Rudolf Herrnstadt and others within the SED leadership were happy to compromise their socialist ideals for German unification, but Ulbricht and Pieck had expressed their concern for months over the lack of cooperation from a well-fed, depoliticized and fairly content West German public to participate in demonstrations they had tried to instigate. It is likely that negotiations over what form 'free elections' were to take would have failed. Ultimately, the prospects of German unification in 1952 were undermined by Germans, not by Stalin, just like the GDR became increasingly a German project rather than a Soviet one.

4. Building Socialism (1952–1961)

What is this GDR?

1953 – Make or Break

Leipzig, Saxony, December 1952. Heinz Just was frustrated. Day in and day out, the seventeen-year-old boy dragged himself to his dead-end job at the metal factory in Leipzig, one of the new state-owned VEBs. He had trained to be a metalworker and looked forward to starting at the VEB Fräsmaschinenwerk, but when he reported for work on his first day in September 1950, he was told that metalworkers were not needed; he would operate machines instead. The teenager grumbled about having to swap the satisfaction of the trade he had learned in his apprenticeship for the mind-numbing and backbreaking task he had been given, but it was no good. He was told to get on with it, and it would only be temporary anyway. Two years later, Heinz was still operating three machines simultaneously in a shift system that included night work and irregular hours. When he received his tax summary in December 1952, he stared at the figures in grim resignation: in the four months since September, he had earned 1,000 marks before tax. That worked out as 250 marks a month – just above minimum wage but well below the average income of around 400 marks. This was not enough to move out of his parents' house; not enough even to get a girlfriend as he would later remember with some bitterness.[1]

By 1952, the GDR authorities were fighting an uphill battle trying to get the economy going and they did so on the backs of workers such as Heinz Just who worked relentlessly and often under hazardous conditions to fulfil the targets of the GDR's first five-year plan, which had begun in 1951. The enormous economic burden under which the country was suffocating from birth had been made even heavier since 1950. Around 20 per cent of the harvest was affected by a potato beetle blight, which the government claimed had been deliberately dropped from American planes as a form of biological warfare. Ilse Hentschel in Brandenburg remembers how school closed repeatedly in the summer so that pupils could roam the fields to collect the 'Amikäfer' (Yankee beetles) in jam jars and shoeboxes which the public had donated.[2] Production targets in agriculture had already taken a huge hit due to the haphazard land redistribution and collectivization efforts – now the beetles threatened to eat East Germans out of house and home. Production targets became impossible to meet.

In addition, neither the beefing-up of the inner-German border nor the build-up of a standing army to a target of 300,000 men from April 1952 had been factored in when the five-year plan was first conceived. As the GDR's armed forces doubled in size from 55,000 soldiers at the beginning of 1952 to 113,000 by mid-1953, they began to eat up vast amounts of resources that the sickly little economy did not have – 11 per cent of state expenditure went into the military. Today Germany is struggling to spend even the 2 per cent it is obliged to under NATO guidelines. Meanwhile, other important sectors such as education and health were kept at 8 per cent and 6 per cent, respectively.[3] When he announced the plan in July 1950, Ulbricht had still bragged that his 'progressive Germany would, once the war damage was eliminated, supersede the imperialist Germany in terms of living standards'.[4] By the beginning of 1953, he was asking his people to be frugal. Food remained rationed until 1958 while the West German economy had abolished rationing in 1950. Hermann Matern, one of the Moscow exiles who had returned to Germany just one day after Ulbricht with another group (Gruppe Ackermann) and by 1952 had risen to prominence in the Central Committee of the SED, was perfectly blunt about the situation. He told his comrades as early as July 1952, 'The weaponry for our armed forces must be the best, technologically and in terms of effectiveness. But we have to be honest. This will cost money – and worse: resources . . . Our economy will have to bear this load, our working people.'[5] The party was asking for a huge sacrifice from the East German public so it could meet Soviet demands as well as its own.

Not everyone grinned and bore it as stoically as Heinz Just. In particular, those with skills that were highly sought-after in the post-war context, such as engineers, tradespeople and skilled builders, did not always agree that they should sacrifice their living standards for some remote higher purpose. They could earn good money in West Germany where they would be welcomed with open arms. While the GDR authorities were busy fortifying the inner-German border, Berlin – still an occupied city run jointly by the Allies – had open sector borders which could be passed freely. It was easy and legal to travel to East Berlin, walk into West Berlin and then board a train to the FRG. In the first six months of 1953 alone, 330,000 people would leave the GDR, and their skill and labour were desperately missed. Brigitte Fritschen, then only nine years old, remembered how angry her mother was that the local doctors in Pirna, Saxony, had moved away, leaving the population without adequate medical care. Among those who had left were also 37,000 farmers, many of whom had had their land confiscated without compensation so they had nothing to lose.[6]

The panic, now spreading through the politburo like wildfire, created an impending sense of doom with disastrous consequences. The political 'cleansing' of the party now spilled over into wider society as subversion was suspected to lurk at every corner. The situation was truly dire for East Germany at the beginning of 1953 and it was in the middle of this chaos that Joseph Stalin died.

Leipzig, Saxony, 5 March 1953. Everyone would later remember where they were and what they did when they heard the news. When the twenty-five-year-old chemistry student Hubert Marusch learned of Stalin's death, he was struck by a sense that something monumental had happened. It was not that he had been particularly emotionally invested in the dictator as many of his contemporaries seemed to be, but Stalin had always been there. Despite the fact that Hubert had chosen to pursue a scientific career, he had to complete the obligatory 'Social Science' unit at university like all his fellow students. While it was not graded, one still had to pass and Hubert chose to write about Stalin's pamphlet *The National Question*, singing the praises of the Georgian's 'great and wise work'.[7] He had always enjoyed the annual festivities for Stalin's birthday at the great hall of the Capitol cinema in Leipzig that coincided with the beginning of the Christmas holidays and family reunions.

Hubert recalled that newspapers wrote that 'the world is holding its breath' and that improvised eulogies were held everywhere. He himself attended one in the darkened lecture theatre of his chemical institute, which had been draped in black bands for the occasion. There, 'with a tearful voice, a comrade gave a eulogy about the greatest scholar and politician of all times'.[8] On the day of Stalin's funeral, a giant statue was put up in Leipzig, in front of the ruins of the New Theatre, which had been destroyed in an air raid in 1943 and was soon to be replaced with a new opera house. On 9 March, the workers of the city marched past it in a funeral procession, laying wreaths as Hubert looked on from a bus on the way to his next lecture.

For Walter Ulbricht it was a deeply personal loss. No other person in his life had a comparable impact on the leader of the GDR. While their relationship was by no means reciprocal, Ulbricht saw – or wanted to see – something of himself in the Soviet despot. Both men were comparatively short (around 1.65 metres), both had physical defects which their enemies always sought to exploit: Stalin's left arm was crippled from an accident at the age of twelve while Ulbricht had health issues with his larynx, which caused the reedy, high-pitched voice he was often ridiculed for. Ulbricht himself maintained that this was due to a severe bacterial infection at the age of eighteen but rumours of throat cancer never quite abated in the corridors of power. Neither of the two were great orators. Stalin's Georgian accent sounded just as provincial to Russian ears as Ulbricht's Saxon drawl did to German ones. Their characters were similar too in many ways. Both were ruthless loners, enjoyed comparatively spartan lifestyles, had remarkable recollection of detail and a great talent for organization. Perhaps the most chilling similarity was the desire for absolute power – both reigned with a single-minded determination that saw political opponents eliminated and paranoia that suspected the shadows of enemies lurking in every corner. But both men followed a course of realpolitik with an ideological flexibility that allowed for even extreme U-turns if they served to preserve their power.[9] Still, they had an asymmetrical relationship – Stalin the leader of world communism, Ulbricht the humble disciple.

The politburo too was shocked. Kurt Hager, a member of the Central Committee, described later that Stalin's 'death filled me with deep pain. I stood at the window of my office at the Karl-Liebknecht-Haus and fought down the tears. Stalin had been a part of our lives.'[10] Ulbricht would go even further and write in the Monday edition of the *Neues Deutschland* newspaper: 'The greatest human of our era has passed away. But his work lives on and will guide the way for progressive mankind for centuries to come.' Stalin's works were immediately reprinted in special editions, a Stalin Museum was being planned and the newly created industrial town of Eisenhüttenstadt was renamed Stalinstadt in the dead man's honour.

Stalin's death hit the reeling GDR right at its lowest point. The enthusiasm of the founding years was beginning to give way to widespread discontent with the economic situation. The ideological optimism, particularly among the young, had in part been pinned on Stalin's personality cult. Like Lenin before him, the Soviet dictator had exuded an irresistible pull on those who were susceptible to it. His victorious leadership during the Second World War had followed the seemingly miraculous transformation of his country into an industrial giant that could even withstand the onslaught of Hitler's forces. That all of this came at a huge human cost did not dissuade the young socialists who craved an idol. If anything, it put the hardships endured during and after the war into perspective and gave them purpose.

Ulbricht was no match for his idol. In fact, his attempts to emulate Stalin's charisma were positively comical. For his upcoming sixtieth birthday on 30 June 1953, he had commissioned the DEFA, the state-owned film company founded in 1946, to make a seventy-four-minute documentary about his life. Entitled 'Master Builder of Socialism', it shows Ulbricht as the wise and omniscient father of the nation who would lead his people to a better future. Following glorified footage of Ulbricht and the young GDR, all underlaid by dramatically composed music, the film ends with the words: 'Comrade Walter Ulbricht is the creator of our plans, the man with a sharp eye and a quick decision, the friend of life and youth, the General Secretary of the Party of the Working People.'

Lavrentiy Beria, Stalin's much-feared NKVD chief and one of the men to step into the power vacuum after his death, looked at Ulbricht's clumsy propaganda efforts with disdain: 'I have never seen a bigger idiot in my life,'[11] he commented in the spring. The Soviets quickly made the film disappear and it would only resurface again in 1997. Ulbricht did not have the means to galvanize his people in crisis through his personality; he would have to face off the GDR's most existential crisis with violence.

17 June Uprising

Jena, Thuringia, 17 June 1953. Gerlinde Böhnisch-Metzmacher, a seventeen-year-old schoolgirl, walked through the historic Bachstraße in the centre of one of Germany's oldest university cities. Wading ankle-deep through the paper that angry protesters had thrown out of the windows of the FDGB-Haus, the local headquarters of the state-controlled trade union organization, she allowed herself to be pulled along by the throngs of people moving in the direction of the Holzmarkt, the old city centre.

The crowd's ire was aimed at the SED district administration.

When Gerlinde arrived, she saw how people had already broken into local offices and were throwing 'beautiful old typewriters' out on to the square, alongside a flurry of paper and files. Listening to loud chants of 'Down with the work quotas!' and 'We want free elections!', she suddenly spotted a human shape dangling from a lamp-post. Squinting at it in the distance, she could make out the insignia of the East German police. The teenager's first thought was: 'Oh God, they hanged a policeman!' but she would later find out that what she actually saw were the trousers, coat and hat of a police officer who had been stripped of his 'Russenuniform' by angry protesters and made to depart the scene in his underpants. Christa Schleevoigt, another teenage girl at the Holzmarkt, was repeatedly embraced by elderly men and women in their seventies. In tears, they told her, 'You young people will see it happen! It will finally get better!'[12]

Scenes like this played out all across East Germany on 17 June 1953. What began with spontaneous strikes of East Berlin workers at the Stalinallee the day before spread rapidly via RIAS (Radio in the American Sector of Berlin) and was replicated quickly all across the country.

Over three years into its existence and despite Walter Ulbricht's boasts of economic superiority to the West, East Germany was struggling to provide the daily essentials for its people. The SED regime's response to the financial crisis was to make East Germans work harder for less money. The funds for reparations and rearmament just had to be found whether the people were willing – and able – to carry this heavy load or not. Boasting that the 'reins had to be held firmly', Walter Ulbricht ordered the scaling up of state oppression. By May 1953, 66,000 people languished in East German prisons, twice as many as the year before, and a huge figure compared to West Germany's 40,000.[13] The General Secretary's revival of the 'class struggle', officially announced in the summer of 1952 as part of the state's 'building socialism' programme, had escalated into a struggle against the population, including the working classes. Prices for food and essentials were constantly raised while state subsidies were cut to try to plug the deepening holes of a bankrupt economy. The party was rapidly losing the support of its core: by 1953 only 38 per cent of SED members came from a working class background.[14]

Ulbricht overstepped the mark when he raised work quotas yet again by 10 per cent in May 1953, asking people to work even harder for less money while shelves in shops remained empty. Over 120,000 people had already left the GDR to seek their fortunes in West Germany and among them were now more and more members of the working classes who fled the dictatorship of the proletariat that purported to act in their interest. Among them was Gerhard Rudat, a nineteen-year-old tool manufacturer from Dittelsdorf, at the border tripoint of Germany, Poland and Czechoslovakia. He had arrived there in October 1947 with what was left of his family after an arduous two-and-a-half-year journey from his home town of Fuchsberg, East Prussia. The son of refugees had to rejoin school in the fifth grade at the age of fourteen as his education had been disrupted by war and expulsion. He was proud to have learned a proper trade after graduating from school, first as a motor mechanic at the Phänomen Works in Zittau, the nearest town, then as a tool manufacturer, a higher-level course for which he had been recommended because of his excellent work. Young, talented and enthusiastic workers like Gerhard should have formed the core of Ulbricht's new 'workers' and peasants' state' but by 1953 they had reached their limit. Worn out, angry and disillusioned, many turned their back on his state. Gerhard and his girlfriend too packed their bags and made their way to Berlin. From there, they crossed over the open boundaries into the Western sectors on 15 June 1953, one day before the unrest on the Stalinallee marked the beginning of the uprising. From West Berlin, they took a train to West Germany proper. As tens of thousands of East Germans did the same and joined the throng of homecoming prisoners of war and the remaining refugees from Eastern Europe, the FRG was quickly overwhelmed by the tide of people. Local administrations held newcomers in camps, sometimes in abysmal conditions. Gerhard and his girlfriend ended up in one such camp in Bochum, a mining and steel city in North Rhine-Westphalia in the far west of Germany. There he had to sweep the streets and cut grass as the GDR certificates he had worked so hard for meant nothing. Gerhard was too ambitious to give up the skill and recognition he had earned back in Zittau. When the relationship with his girlfriend broke down, he 'had had enough'.[15] He returned home in 1954.

Most of those who left the GDR never returned and the state began to haemorrhage its talent and skill. Internally too, despair and anger began to spill over into strike action and demonstrations. Reports of attacks on local SED officials and on people and buildings associated with the Soviet occupiers now arrived regularly in Berlin and Moscow. The SED leadership was summoned to the Kremlin at the beginning of June. There, they were told to drop the 'forced build-up of socialism in the GDR' as the 'development of the GDR could not be separated from the question of reunification of East and West Germany into one German state'. Ulbricht and Grotewohl were also told that they would do well to remember that the notion that the Soviet Union 'only pursued the question of German reunification for propagandistic aims is a huge mistake'. Instead, 'the unification of Germany and its transformation into a peaceful and democratic state' would be the aim as 'a split Germany in the centre of Europe would mean nothing but the forced remilitarization of West Germany [and] open preparation for a new war'.[16]

After Stalin's death in March, a triumvirate had emerged in Moscow, which consisted of Nikita Khrushchev, Georgy Malenkov and Lavrentiy Beria. The trio immediately embarked on a new course: de-Stalinization and more peaceful relations with the West as the Soviet Union was still reeling from the economic and social costs of the war. All three contemplated German unification as it had the potential to lead to a de-escalation of conflict in Europe, reducing both the costs and the attention the situation permanently required. Beria in particular is said to have hoped that East Germany could be traded in, in exchange for large-scale financial support from the

United States. In this context, he had made a series of derogatory remarks about the GDR leadership who presided over a country that was 'not even a real state'.

It seemed as though Ulbricht's days were numbered. His bene-factor in Moscow had died, there was mounting opposition within the SED leadership, particularly from his Stasi chief Wilhelm Zais-ser and his newspaper man Rudolf Herrnstadt, and not least from East Germans themselves. Alluding to Ulbricht's distinctive beard, Pieck's voluminous figure and Grotewohl's spectacles, some pro-testers on the streets began to chant, 'Spitzbart, Bauch und Brille sind nicht des Volkes Wille!' – 'Goatee, belly and glasses are not the will of the masses!' It looked as though both Ulbricht and his young socialist state were going to be sacrificed so that peace in Germany and Europe could be secured.

Having received orders from Moscow to do so, the SED leader-ship announced a 'New Course' on 9 June 1953 and even admitted that 'a number of mistakes' had been made. The collectivization of agriculture was put on hold, the focus on heavy industry over con-sumer items was to be shifted and – on strict Soviet insistence – civil rights would be strengthened. Even the word 'socialist' was scrapped from SED parlance and Ulbricht's self-glorifying film banished to the darkest corner of the archives. Crucially, however, the govern-ment did not take back the increased work quotas, and nothing changed for the aggrieved workers. In real terms the new work demands meant that workers in some fields lost around a third of their income.

Enough was enough. Of all the places in the GDR, it was the Stalinallee in Berlin where the protests began on 16 June 1953. At Block 40, builders stopped working and began to march down Ulbricht's socialist boulevard towards the newly dubbed House of Ministries, Goering's old Air Ministry where the GDR had been founded. They stood there in their work boots, the dirt and sweat of their labour still on their faces; many held their tools in their hands or slung over their shoulders. There could not have been a more fit-ting snapshot of what had become of Ulbricht's dictatorship of the proletariat. The angry crowd chanted, 'Das hat alles keinen Zweck, der Spitzbart muss weg!' – 'No point in reform until Goatee is gone!' They demanded to speak to Ulbricht who was now also being urged by his Minister of Industry, Fritz Selbmann, to talk to the workers. Still utterly tone-deaf to the situation, Ulbricht responded, 'But it's raining, that will disperse them.'[17] It did not. Like wildfire the words 'General Strike' made the rounds. It was whispered, shouted, written and broadcast into every corner of the state. Many had heard the news via the West Berlin radio station RIAS but even East German state TV could hardly avoid talking about the outbreaks of unrest that had taken place in Berlin. In the evening, Otto Grotewohl finally announced that the increase in work quotas was to be retracted and even Ulbricht offered 'serious dialogue'. But it was too little too late.

The atmosphere was tense. Buses and trains stopped operating to try to prevent mass gatherings and travel to Berlin where the workers had put the message about that they would meet at 7 a.m. at Strausberger Platz, a large public square from which they would march down the Stalinallee to Alexanderplatz. In the end, unrest broke out everywhere. Willy Brandt, who was to become the mayor of West Berlin four years later, watched on as 12,000 workers from the steelworks in Hennigsdorf, north-west of Berlin, marched through his city: 'Some wore their wooden work shoes, some were bare-chested with their protective goggles pushed up on their foreheads, many carried fire pokers, others tools.'[18] The middle classes were now also being swept up by the tides of anger. They joined the workers in over 250 cities and towns everywhere in the GDR. The whole country was on its feet.

In many places, the marches and demonstrations spilled over into violence as the protesters freed prisoners and attacked the hopelessly undersized security forces. They told policemen to throw away their 'Russian' uniforms and join in, forcing them to strip and humiliating them. A gang of youths climbed the Brandenburg Gate and tore down the Red Flag which still flew there. They burnt it, accompanied by loud jeers. Party offices were raided across the country. What had begun as an expression of the frustrations of the working classes was descending into complete chaos accompanied by arson, looting and vandalism.

The GDR government had lost control of the situation. It is estimated that the number of people who had joined the riots in Berlin exceeded 100,000 while in Halle and Leipzig 60,000 and 40,000 turned out respectively – a total of a million people is said to have taken part across the country.[19] The police were outnumbered and forced to hide in heavily barricaded headquarters if they still could. Nobody knew where Ulbricht was. Rumours spread: Ulbricht had been deposed; Pieck had poisoned himself; Western police would come to help.

The Soviets had seen enough. At 1 p.m., they declared a state of emergency in 167 of the 217 boroughs of the GDR. The state of alert in Moscow is reflected in the fact that the Chief of the General Staff Vasily Sokolovsky flew to Berlin himself to take control. The son of Belarusian peasants was a battle-hardened commander who had led the fighting on the Eastern Front during the Second World War, defending Moscow against the Nazis and winning the largest tank battle in history at Kursk. Now his skill and ruthlessness were deployed against the people of East Germany.

'After one and a half days an adventure was ended which had turned the democratic sector of Berlin into a tinderbox which could have set the world on fire.'[20] This was how the SED propagandist Karl-Eduard von Schnitzler described the pitiless crushing of the uprising through Soviet force. Lacking clear leadership and aims, the protesters stood no chance at all against the tanks and troops that were now let loose on them. Most of the men and women who had just joined in went home while those who remained on the street became more violent and resistant. They were particularly hostile in the hotbeds of Berlin, Magdeburg, Halle and Leipzig. Around 15,000 people were arrested of whom 2,500 were convicted, with some receiving very long prison sentences.[21] The total number of deaths is still highly disputed but most historians now assume that at least fifty-five protesters were killed with at least twenty executed for their part in the uprising. The killings included twenty-six-year-old metalworker Alfred Diener from Jena. The previous day, he had stood shoulder to shoulder with other citizens of the city such as the schoolgirls Gerlinde and Christa. On 18 June 1953, he was taken to nearby Weimar, tried and executed.

The protests petered out quickly but the atmosphere in East Germany remained tense as everyone waited to see whether there would be a backlash. Restrictions remained in place. The seventeen-year-old Regina Faustmann, pregnant from her boyfriend Günther whom she had met at the tyre factory where she worked as a chemical lab technician, was looking forward to their wedding on 26 June 1953, a mere nine days after the uprising. But the restrictions for public gatherings had not yet been lifted. She would not have been able to have a wedding – the bride and groom, Catholic minister and witnesses alone would have exceeded the three people that were allowed to congregate. Regina's family pleaded with the local authorities and received a special permission for the wedding to be held with around forty people – they were even allowed to ring the church bells. A People's Police officer paid a visit to ensure that the wedding party had not suddenly turned into an agitated political mob.[22]

In the months after the uprising a further 6,000 people would be arrested and this included SED leaders who had shown reluctance during the events. Some had even openly switched sides and made remarks such as 'We are not members of the SED but of the SPD' as a report from a party office near Leipzig complained.[23] Questions were asked about the efficiency of the GDR's security apparatus that would now be tightened.

It was ultimately one of the great ironies of German history that Ulbricht's neglect of the wishes of his people, accompanied by a staggering degree of arrogance and stubbornness, secured not only his own political survival but also that of his state. The Soviets had told Ulbricht in no uncertain terms that he needed to stop his propagation of the class war, including the persecution of the churches, collectivization of agriculture and political harassment of liberals and social democrats. In exchange, he would receive economic help and a reduction of the reparations load. A similar directive was also given out to the other Eastern European states after Stalin's death. Had Ulbricht followed this instruction in letter and spirit, it might well have calmed down the situation in East Germany and the Soviets might have replaced him. It was the virulence of the uprising and Ulbricht's response to it afterwards which meant that Khrushchev stuck with the devil he knew in Germany, especially as he was involved in his own brutal power struggle against Beria at home. The latter had been the most vocal proponent of liberalization in the satellite states and the East German uprising was an ideal opportunity to accuse him of destabilizing errors that amounted to treason. Malenkov, Molotov and Khrushchev joined forces against him. On 26 June 1953 the former NKVD chief, once so feared and dangerous, was arrested. On 23 December he was sentenced to death and immediately executed by a shot through the forehead. Subsequently, both Ulbricht and Khrushchev were keen to entangle political opponents with Beria's fall and it suited them both to come to an arrangement. They each consolidated their hold over politics through carrot-and-stick methods.

The next few years forced Ulbricht to take responsibility for the situation that had led to the uprising at least in part and make concessions that would ultimately lead to the restructuring of government as well as to the partial economic, cultural and social opening of the GDR. But he would also tighten the screws on political opponents and dissidents, building up the police, the army and the Stasi.

A New Course

Barvikha Sanatorium, Soviet Union, July 1954. Walter Ulbricht needed a break. He arrived at the purpose-built medical complex near Moscow to recover from a lengthy spell of bad health. Four weeks away from the problems in Berlin were supposed to relieve some of the mental and physical strain of the last few years. Bar-vikha had been completed in 1935 as a luxurious retreat for ailing politicians from the Soviet Union and allied countries. It was here that the Bulgarian Comintern chief Georgi Dimitrov died in 1949 after his health had suddenly deteriorated. Over the years, the sana-torium has seen many famous visitors, among them Aleksey Tolstoy, Boris Yeltsin and Hugo Chávez.

When Ulbricht arrived, he joined the ailing President of the GDR, Wilhelm Pieck, who was then seventy-seven years old and recovering from his second stroke, which he had suffered in July 1953, just after the uprising. Ulbricht himself had also endured severe health complications since then. The sixty-year-old had already spent two weeks in a hospital in Germany in May 1954 and had struggled to recover fully. It was time to take a break even though this would have been very difficult for a man whom many described as a workaholic. His second wife Lotte travelled with him to Bar-vikha. Ten years younger than her husband, she had begun a relationship with him in Moscow in 1938 after her first husband had been arrested by the NKVD during Stalin's Great Purges. The cou-ple lived together in Moscow and continued to do so when they returned to Germany at the end of the war. As their own relation-ship had remained childless, they adopted a two-year-old girl called Maria Pestunowa from an orphanage in Leipzig. Now called Beate Ulbricht, she was the daughter of an enslaved Ukrainian labourer who had died in an air raid. Beate had a difficult relationship with her adoptive parents from the outset. By most accounts, Ulbricht was a loving father who played with his daughter and read her bed-time stories when she was little.[24] But he was also too preoccupied with work to really address the psychological and social difficulties the girl faced. While her parents travelled to Barvikha Sanatorium in the summer of 1954, she stayed in Berlin attending the newly dubbed Wilhelm Pieck School where she was bullied and beaten up by her peers on a regular basis.

While many historians have argued that the Ulbricht regime had re-established its grip over the people a year after the uprising, it is unlikely that Ulbricht himself saw it like that. In the summer of 1954, the two most powerful men in the GDR sat in a health resort, nearly 2,000 kilometres from their capital, attempting to recover from severe mental and physical strain. The shock of 1953 and its aftermath had taken their toll.

Ulbricht's first response to the 1953 uprising had been two-fold: reassure the public that their concerns had been heard; and deal with the internal opponents that had been revealed during this moment of crisis. As the SED had already announced the 'New Course' shortly before the uprising, it was now time to show that they meant it. They eased travel restrictions to West Germany, rowed back on their repression of church life and temporarily halted the collectivization of agriculture. Importantly, the hated work quotas were reduced back to their original levels before the 10 per cent rise. In order to appease the angry population further, they introduced rapid and far-reaching changes to improve living standards. The writer Erich Loest, an SED member at the time, remembered that 'announcements of new laws and decisions were made daily: . . . increase of the minimum amount for old-age pensions from 65 to 75 marks . . . increase in new housing, more repairs for existing flats . . . 40 million marks extra for old people's homes and kindergartens.'[25] To some extent, this seems to have worked. While 184,000 people still left the GDR in 1954, this compares favourably to the 331,000 that did so in 1953.[26] Many farmers returned to their land as they no longer feared that they might have to hand it over to the state without compensation. Suddenly, the shelves were full of groceries and consumer products that many East Germans had not seen in such quantities since the beginning of the war.

What had changed? Why was the GDR suddenly able to afford their citizens better living conditions? The economy was still burdened by the same problems that had led to the crisis in the first place, but with Stalin dead and Beria arrested, their ideas of a reunified, neutral Germany became tainted. Being associated with such ideas meant being associated with fallen leaders. Most Soviet politicians, Khrushchev included, were keen to avoid this potentially deadly trap and distanced themselves openly from the legacy of the two men. With regard to Germany, this meant pursuing a policy of two states by supporting the GDR. The first thing to do was to lift the economic stranglehold of reparations which had nearly choked the young state to death. The remaining debt of $2.5 billion was written off and the last thirty-three industrial conglomerates released back into German hands.[27] Scientists were released from the USSR, though those who had worked on sensitive projects had to promise that they would return to the GDR and not West Germany. This affected the Gröttrups, for example, who had lived on Gorodomlya island since 1946 so that Helmut Gröttrup could work on the Soviet rocket programme. They returned in November 1953 but managed to leave East Germany via Berlin with the help of British and American intelligence services. Most of the scientists returned to the GDR and helped rebuild the economy.

In addition, the Soviets granted a loan of 485 million rubles alongside food subsidies.[28] 'Three thousand wagons in one week, loaded with butter, cooking fat, oil and tinned fish,'[29] remembered Loest. Gerd Vanselow, at the time a thirteen-year-old schoolboy who lived near Schwerin in the northern state of Mecklenburg, recalls what a difference this made compared to the early 1950s. 'I still can't stand the sight of turnips,' he joked later, 'we had nothing else after the war. There was no meat at all. We resorted to putting up mouse traps in which we put seeds to catch sparrows. But by the mid-1950s things got much better. I really can't complain. We had everything we needed and I never had to go hungry again.'[30]

With the population now comparatively appeased, and assured that he could count on support from Moscow again, Ulbricht turned his attention towards opponents in his own party. Just before and during the uprising itself, the General Secretary of the SED had come under sharp criticism from within the Central Committee itself. Elli Schmidt, the forty-five-year-old head of the Democratic Women's League, told Ulbricht in no uncertain terms whose fault she thought the 1953 uprising was: 'It was the entire spirit which collapsed in our party, the rush, the dishonesty, the evasion of the people and their concerns, the threats and the boasting – this is what got us here in the first place. And this, dear Walter, is mostly your fault, and you don't want to admit that without all of that, there would not have been a 17th June.'[31] Like her allies, the journalist Rudolf Herrnstadt and the Stasi chief Wilhelm Zaisser, Schmidt had voted to oust Ulbricht during a night meeting on 7 July 1953. Despite this bravery, none of Ulbricht's opponents had the killer instinct to finish off their leader who was reeling without Soviet support. Once Beria had been pushed from power in Moscow on 26 June, however, Ulbricht was able to establish a connection: like Beria, his enemies had supposedly all been part of a defeatist plot to sell out socialist ideas in exchange for capitalist money. Herrnstadt, Zaisser and Schmidt had all been in Moscow during the worst years of Stalin's purges and the fear of entanglement with fallen Soviet leaders ran deep. All three buckled at the thought of being accused of 'factionalism'. Ulbricht was able to remove them from the Central Committee on 26 July 1953, exactly a month after Beria's fall. By the spring of 1954, they had all been excluded even from the party itself.

Ulbricht may have been able to survive politically but not without having his wings clipped severely. He was forced to accept 'the greatest responsibility for these mistakes' and admit that he had made individual decisions himself rather than following the collective principle of the party. The secretariat of the Central Committee, the hub of Ulbricht's power, was reduced from eleven to six members, and he did not get to pick the replacement for Zaisser as head of the Stasi. Ernst Wollweber was chosen, sidelining Erich Mielke once more. Furthermore, Ulbricht's title of 'General Secretary' was changed to 'First Secretary of the Central Committee' to put emphasis on the *primus inter pares* principle which he had hitherto treated with contempt.

The public humiliation piled on top of the strain of the power struggle within the Central Committee and his troubled private life had a significant impact on Ulbricht's health. But when he returned from Barvikha Sanatorium, he had gathered new strength and new confidence. It was time to abandon the 'New Course' and steer things back to socialism. Ulbricht openly declared, 'We never had any intentions to embark on such a wrong course and we will never embark on it.'[32]

Militarization

The events of 17 June 1953 had shown that Ulbricht's infant republic was vulnerable. The First Secretary had spent the day of the uprising in the Soviet military headquarters at Karlshorst, hiding from the chaos outside and watching anxiously as Soviet tanks and troops restored order. He had lost control over his people and his country, and it frightened him. Beria had sneered, 'What is this GDR? It's not even a proper state. It only exists because of Soviet troops, even if we call it the "German Democratic Republic".'[33] It was true. The Stalin Note of 1952 had also shown that the GDR was little more than a geopolitical pawn to Moscow, to be played, even sacrificed, as required. Ulbricht was determined to change that. In order to come up with an explanation for the mass uprising that not only deflected responsibility but could serve as justification for the swift build-up of a comprehensive security apparatus at all levels, the workers' uprising of June 1953 was declared an 'attempted fascist coup', instigated and coordinated by Western agents in Germany.

The Cold War expert Christian F. Ostermann, who specializes in US policy towards East and West Germany, argues that there is some truth to the idea. While the uprising itself was a spontaneous event born out of the frustration over workload and pay, it was also stoked by the West. President Eisenhower did not sanction direct military action to help overthrow the GDR regime, but the West Berlin radio station RIAS broadcast logistical information to help coordinate action across Germany on 16 and 17 June. West German agents, aided by American intelligence, also planned and undertook further action in the aftermath to destabilize the political situation in the GDR following the uprising.[34] While Western historians have traditionally not paid much heed to this idea, Ostermann's work with archival evidence from the SED files as well as recently declassified material from US governmental archives shows a different picture: 'the Eisenhower administration, while surprised by the uprising, quickly recognized the opportunity for "rollback" and devised a psychological warfare plan with the aim of further destabilizing the situation in East Germany'.[35]

Supported by their American allies, West Germany saw the events of 17 June as an opportunity to encourage further unrest. Only five days after the uprising, the Senate in West Berlin renamed the Charlottenburger Chaussee 'Straße des 17. Juni' – this is a 3.5-kilometre-long boulevard that runs the width of West Berlin and ends at the Brandenburg Gate where the Eastern sector began. Barely two weeks later, the West German government declared 17 June an annual public holiday for the whole country. Historians are still exploring the impact of Western intervention, but what is certain is that Ulbricht and his allies believed their republic was under siege. As a result, they sought to build up a far-reaching security system that would protect the GDR against internal and external enemies.

The scale of this undertaking is astonishing and easily puts the GDR among the most efficient and ruthless police states that have ever existed. The country's nervous leadership was keen to instil a defensive spirit into each and every institution, which in turn led to the widespread militarization of society. Local crisis management groups were set up immediately after 17 June 1953. They consisted of SED representatives, state officials, members of the different police branches and the Stasi. They would lead the response to any internal threats and coordinate on the ground while a central 'Commission for Security Questions' provided the umbrella organization for them and came up with an overall strategy. In 1960, this would morph into the National Defence Council, the GDR's highest security body. The structures were set up to identify, target and root out any form of dissent before it could lead to a large-scale uprising.

To this end, other organizations were militarized and politicized as well. Set up in the Soviet Zone of Occupation straight after the end of the Second World War, the *Volkspolizei*, or People's Police, usually referred to as *VoPo*, became a highly centralized internal security force. Its members swore 'to be loyal to my socialist fatherland' and fulfilled a dual role of law enforcement and day-to-day surveillance. But the ambitions for it quickly clashed with economic realities. It would eventually reach staff levels of only 80,000, which is low compared to the 333,000 police officers in Germany today. In fact, Karl Maron, a member of the Gruppe Ulbricht who had become the head of the *VoPo* at the age of forty-seven in 1950, made constant and vocal complaints to Ulbricht about the underresourcing of his forces. In 1953, he told the leader that one third of officers who had undergone firearms training had not been able to fire a single shot during their course due to a shortage of ammunition and weapons. Ulbricht was unimpressed. He had no money to build up the police properly and told Maron to cut 20,000 officers while creating a volunteer force to aid the police. Accordingly, this Voluntary Auxiliary of the People's Police grew from only 27,000 in 1952 to 160,000 by 1960. These helpers had no uniforms, simply a red armband to denote that they supported the *VoPo*. They could be deployed in almost any supporting role from 'educational activities in residential areas, factories and collectivized farms' to general policing. Ulbricht's neglect of the People's Police in favour of other elements of the security apparatus was obvious. By 1959, the force was still lacking 29 per cent of the firearms it had been promised, and staff turnover was still high at around 14–17 per cent annually. But the reliance on civilian volunteers that came with this underresourcing paradoxically allowed state influence to seep into much deeper layers of the GDR's communities than a conventional force might have achieved.

In order to instil a sense of military readiness as well as foster the 'class consciousness' that Ulbricht felt was still lacking in the German proletariat, a paramilitary organization was also set up in 1953, the *Kampfgruppen der Arbeiterklasse* (KG), Combat Groups of the

Working Class. These were open to male and female workers, who would receive military training in uniform during their spare time as well as in dedicated time periods for which they would be excused from their work. The minimum age was twenty-five, and party membership was not required, although 60 per cent of members would later hold it. By the mid-1960s, membership had swollen to 180,000 and it would rise to over 200,000 by the end of the 1980s. Historians have often claimed that the popularity of the KGs was largely due to the promise of a 100-mark pension boost for membership, but that is not the only explanation why hundreds of thousands of GDR citizens spent their weekends rolling through mud and practising military drill formations. As widespread as the uprising had been in 1953, it had also shocked many people up and down the country. The young socialist republic had opened up new opportunities to the masses. Tens of thousands of young people from working class backgrounds had been encouraged to study, promoted to leadership positions and received scholarships. A significant proportion of this social demographic saw in Ulbricht's regime the first incarnation of a Germany that fought for them. The Nazis had always struggled to win over the working classes and Weimar had seemed a system run by middle class social democrats, which talked the talk but achieved little in practice to address the lack of social mobility. There were many workers who suddenly had opportunities, economic security and recognition. They saw in the 1953 uprising a threat to their new status so they wanted to do their part to support the new regime. Some 5,000 KG members even helped defend the construction of the Berlin Wall in 1961.[36] Still, it is also safe to assume that the thrill of firearms training, the allure of uniforms and the promise of a sense of camaraderie and adventure played their part in attracting many into membership of the KG.

Other voluntary security organizations included Voluntary Auxiliary of the Border Police, established in 1958, inspectors of farming collectives, trade union officials, supervisors within the FDJ and many more roles in individual clubs, factories and associations. This entire apparatus worked alongside the Stasi, police and military and involved a staggering 750,000 people in total.[37] The historian Jake Holliday, who specializes in both East and West German remilitarization after the Second World War, speaks of 'a bewildering multitude of security organizations with overlapping purposes'.[38] In addition, the army-style drills and marching of the FDJ, combative language used in the education system and the constant presence of uniforms on the streets gave life in the GDR a distinctly military feel.

Following West Germany's remilitarization from 1952, Stalin had instructed Ulbricht to build up armed forces in East Germany from April of the same year. Willi Stoph, the Minister of the Interior, was tasked to set this up. The thirty-eight-year-old had been involved in the KPD before Hitler's rise to power but served in the *Wehrmacht* for the entirety of the war, where he became an officer and was awarded the Iron Cross, Second Class. And yet he somehow managed to be classed as a 'Victim of Fascism' and rose quickly within the SED. His military expertise was useful as few of the other party functionaries had any. On 1 July 1952, Stoph had ordered the establishment of the *Kasernierte Volkspolizei* (KVP), the Barracked People's Police. As the name suggests, they differed from the *VoPo* in that they were put up in barracks and received military training. Their uniform, first dark blue, then khaki, was modelled on that of the Red Army. During the 1953 uprising, they had already numbered tens of thousands, but only 8,200 were deployed and none of them had received permission to shoot, a fact that highlighted that it was Soviet intervention that had propped up Ulbricht's regime, not his own troops. But this was about to change. Both Ulbricht and Khrushchev wanted to pull Soviet intervention out of the GDR as far as possible. From August 1953, the KVP was slowly transformed into a military force with officer schools set up to train its first set of new leaders. In October 1955, Willi Stoph ordered it to be boosted to around 150,000 men in total. Following the formation of the West German army, the *Bundeswehr*, in November 1955 and its immediate integration into the anti-communist military alliance of NATO, the

KVP became the *Nationale Volksarmee* (NVA), National People's Army, on 18 January 1956. Ten days later, it joined NATO's communist counterpiece, the Warsaw Treaty Organization, often referred to as the 'Warsaw Pact'.

With its official foundation, the NVA also received new uniforms. Out went the Soviet-style khakis, in came *Wehrmacht*-like greys. The fact that NVA soldiers looked disturbingly like their *Wehrmacht* forebears has often been commented upon but is largely misunderstood. Willi Stoph, a former soldier, understood the mindset of potential recruits better than many of his comrades at the time. The two obvious comparisons that he was keen to avoid were the *Bundeswehr*, who initially wore the US-style uniforms of their Western sponsors, and the Red Army, whose look had been the inspiration for the uniforms of the Barracked People's Police. Stoph was quick to sneer at the West German army, who, as he put it, had been 'dressed up in their capitalist costumes'. But he also understood that looking East was not an option. The 1953 uprising had shown just how deep-seated the resentment towards the Soviet occupiers had become in parts of the population – it was often the 'Russian' uniforms of the *VoPo* and the Red Flags on buildings that attracted the ire of the protesters. In addition, German women and children had not forgotten the terror of their 'liberation'. Most important perhaps was the anti-Soviet sentiment among the bulk of German men, who were now asked to join a volunteer army – in contrast to the conscript armies of both West Germany and the other Warsaw Treaty nations. Around 200,000 of the potential recruits had languished in Soviet special camps in the post-war years; millions had only just returned from Soviet captivity, broken and resentful. Furthermore, the behaviour of the stationed Red Army soldiers, while reined in after the initial excesses of the spring of 1945, remained a subject of contempt for many German civilians. While they kept a tight lid on public discussion of such matters, the GDR authorities collated statistics on crimes committed by Soviet soldiers, who suffered from bad pay and terrible living conditions compared to their German counterparts in the NVA. As late as the

1970s and 1980s, they still clocked up 27,000 offences, an average of over five a day. Among these offences were 705 reported incidents of rape, which amounted to around one a week.[39] Both Ulbricht and Stoph understood that the NVA could not model itself on a force with such a bad reputation in a country that had still harboured considerable pride in its military tradition, despite two lost world wars.

So the NVA uniforms had to be distinctly German. The only thing that was visibly new when compared to the *Wehrmacht* kit was the flat steel helmet. The model that was chosen had been in the latest stages of development from 1943, but the war had ended before it could be fully rolled out. The magazine *Neue Berliner Illustrierte* proudly described the new shape as follows: 'the members of the National People's Army of the GDR are better protected with the new steel helmet which is made from first-class material and in an over-flattened shape. It was modelled on the earlier German *Stahlhelm* under consideration of the latest research and allows a maximum amount of visibility and mobility.'[40] Many young men joined up and the force numbered over 100,000 in the 1950s before conscription was introduced in 1962.

The threat from external and internal enemies was an ever-present spectre in the GDR. The little state and its people had a permanent mindset of beleaguerment, which was partially justified but also bolstered by Ulbricht's personal paranoia. However, the extensive security network allowed many East Germans a voluntary opportunity to take a stake in the defence of their new country and wove a tight fabric of belonging and community around those who wanted it. This was the most divisive characteristic of the GDR: a threat to those who resented the permanent state of alert and politicization of life; an opportunity for others who craved meaning and belonging in contrast to what they perceived to be the empty consumerism of the West. Still, the vast majority of GDR citizens continued to live their daily lives unperturbed by these developments. They nodded politely at the *VoPo* patrolling their street, sent their children to pioneer holiday camps and smiled proudly at their sons' new uniforms.

De-Stalinization

Kremlin, Moscow, 25 February 1956. It was shortly after midnight when Nikita Khrushchev finally began to fill the tense silence in the Great Hall of the Kremlin. The 20th Congress of the Communist Party of the Soviet Union had officially ended the previous day, but selected delegates were asked to stay for a final session that very night. Special passes were issued to the chosen party members who would be allowed to attend this 'closed session'. Anybody else, including foreign journalists and the leaders of affiliated political parties from other countries, were excluded. The few hundred invited guests were filled with intense anticipation when Khrushchev began to speak. Over the course of the next few hours, he delivered a blistering attack on his former ally and leader Joseph Stalin. He revealed that Lenin's testament had been critical about Stalin; that Stalin had betrayed the 'collective principles' of leadership and seized power for himself; that the 'Man of Steel' had become a victim of his own personality cult, which had made him paranoid and susceptible to the influence of that 'rabid enemy of our party', Lavrentiy Beria.

When Khrushchev began to disclose the scale of Stalin's purges and dramatically pointed to the 100 or so former party members whom he had released from prison camps and invited to join the secret session, it was too much to bear for some of the stunned members in the audience. Several men had to leave the hall as they felt faint and ill from what they had heard. Others just sat in stunned silence as Khrushchev continued to list Stalin's crimes, relentlessly chipping away at a Soviet demi-God. While the audience had been ordered to maintain strict silence about what they had heard, the shock ran too deep. The Kremlin's corridors hummed with excited chatter and hushed reactions that ranged from confusion and outrage to jubilation and relief. Stalin's icon had been well and truly smashed.

The blast of Khrushchev's explosive speech reached Walter Ulbricht earlier than most. He was in bed in his accommodation in Moscow when a Soviet comrade woke him up at around 3 a.m. The sleepy SED leadership congregated and were told what Khrushchev was at that point still relaying to his party in the Great Hall. Nobody said a word. The shaken German delegation went back to their rooms to ponder the implications of what they had just learned. By breakfast time, Ulbricht had pulled himself together, and told the party's reporter Karl Schirdewan to 'feel free to say that Stalin is no longer a classic [of Marxism]'.[41] Ever the pragmatist, Stalin's German disciple only needed a few hours to come to terms with the sudden dissolution of his hero.

Upon his return to Germany, Ulbricht immediately set about distancing himself from the now dangerous vortex that was Stalin's legacy. It had already swallowed up Beria and other once-powerful individuals. Writing in the SED newspaper *Neues Deutschland* a week after Khrushchev's secret speech, he confirmed for all and sundry what he had told his comrades at breakfast in Moscow: 'Stalin cannot be counted as a classic of Marxism.' Naturally, his colleagues in the politburo saw this as the screeching U-turn that it was. Where Ulbricht had previously praised Stalin as a 'brilliant general', he suddenly claimed the *Vozhd* had not prepared the Soviet Union well enough for the war against Hitler. The man who had once been a 'genius' had apparently not listened to the military experts around him enough. He even began to attack the brutal and hasty collectivization process in the USSR, which had cost countless people their lives, and repeated Khrushchev's argument that this was due to Stalin's personality cult and lack of a collective approach to decision-making.

It did not take much for Ulbricht's enemies to see the parallels between Stalin and his biggest German fan. In the GDR too they had a man who had tried to establish a personality cult through propaganda films and postage stamps. Here too they had collectivized too quickly, imprisoned thousands of innocent people and been subject to the whims of a single leader. Ulbricht had no choice but to pre-empt the inevitable backlash. He initiated a temporary 'thaw' in the Cold War by imitating Khrushchev's reforms. Both men had to be extremely careful not to be associated with the wrongdoings of a man whom they had served for so long. In the GDR, this meant that Ulbricht rehabilitated some of his former enemies who had been expelled in the wake of his power struggle after the 1953 uprising. Elli Schmidt, for example, who had asked such uncomfortable questions of her comrade Walter, was suddenly readmitted into the fold of the SED; so too were older enemies such as Paul Merker, who had been arrested as a 'French spy' by the Stasi in 1950 when the feverish search for internal enemies had first escalated. By October 1956, around 21,000 people had been released from prison.

Relics of the old Stalinist cult disappeared unceremoniously. The industrial town of Stalinstadt became Eisenhüttenstadt once again. The Stalinallee in Berlin, where the workers had first begun their protest on 16 June 1953, became the Karl-Marx-Allee, and the memorial to the dictator which had crowned it vanished overnight.

But this did little to silence Ulbricht's enemies. Criticism was loud and direct this time. 'Why aren't we on a reform course like the USSR?' demanded someone in the politburo. 'Don't we have a personality cult in the SED too?' asked another member rhetorically. Ulbricht's impulsive response showed that this was beginning to hit very raw nerves. Without pointing at anyone in particular, he exploded, 'I will have everyone arrested.'[42] The only trouble was that Ernst Wollweber, the head of the Stasi and in charge of political arrests, was not his man. He had been appointed at Soviet behest after the 1953 uprising. During the war, Wollweber had worked as a terrorist with direct orders from Moscow, and had very little contact with the KPD in exile. This made him something of an enigma to Ulbricht and meant that he had direct connections to the Kremlin. Almost everyone else in the politburo sat in his or her seat because of Ulbricht's links to Stalin, but not Wollweber, the man who would have to agree if Ulbricht was to arrest anyone, let alone 'everyone'.

By the autumn of 1956, the majority of the politburo were loudly demanding a 'third way' between Stalin's hardcore communism and Western-style capitalism. One opposition group around the publisher Walter Janka and the philosopher Wolfgang Harich demanded 'to remain within the framework of Marxism-Leninism. But we want to move away from Stalinism.'[43] Ulbricht was cornered when, unexpectedly, the Hungarian Uprising came to the rescue.

The popular Hungarian leader Imre Nagy tried to find a 'third way' for his country too, with more independence from Moscow. But he went too far when, on 1 November 1956, he demanded that Hungary leave the Warsaw Pact. This was tantamount to breaking out of the Soviet Empire, and the loss of prestige as well as economic and military power might have lost Moscow the Cold War there and then. Three days later, 6,000 Soviet tanks rolled into the country in order to re-establish communist rule where it was not wanted. The efforts of the Hungarians to oppose this were mercilessly crushed, with 30,000 people killed and Nagy himself captured and executed. The thaw was well and truly over. Now all Ulbricht had to do was to step on the right side of history. Despite the fact that Wollweber had been ill and was in hospital when the situation in Eastern Europe began to escalate, Ulbricht claimed he had stood by and gathered no intelligence on the matter. Simultaneously, he accused Janka and Harich of instigating sectionalism and had both men arrested. They received long prison sentences. Wollweber was forced to retire while other opponents were quietly removed from their positions and given insignificant jobs. Another critic of Ulbricht's, Gerhart Ziller, who had clashed with the First Secretary over economic questions, came under such mental strain that he took his own life in December 1957.

As ever, Ulbricht was ruthless and thorough in the cleansing of the circles of power. Implicating all of his political enemies with the idea of instigating a dangerous 'third way' of the Hungarian variety, he purged the party down to regional and local levels. In the 1957 election 60 per cent of the regional candidates of 1952 did not resume their posts. At local level, the number went up to 71 per cent.[44] Ulbricht had once again remained in the saddle, against the odds.

Building Socialism – Resumed

Cottbus, Brandenburg, 1960. The nineteen-year-old Gero Vanselow decided to follow in his father's footsteps and join the air force. His mother had told him stories about 'Papa', whose tragic death in 1945, when his plane was shot down by friendly fire over Germany, had served to create a golden glow around the still image on the mantelpiece. Now it was time for Gero to become the man they had both lost. When he turned up at the recruitment office and said that he wanted to become a pilot, Gero was told that his biography was not acceptable for this role. He had a distant aunt and uncle in Cologne. Gero had never met these Western relatives but this fact did not make his 'cadre-political baggage', as he would later jokingly call it, any lighter. Unperturbed, the young man asked if he could join in a ground role instead as this would afford him no opportunity to fly over the inner-German border. He was accepted and immediately impressed with his affable manner and technical skill. He quickly rose through the ranks and was sent to Leipzig to complete an engineering degree in communications technology which allowed him to access officer ranks. The little refugee boy from Stolp in Pommern (now Słupsk, Poland), who was raised by a single working mother and caught sparrows in his mouse trap after the war so the family had something to eat, would one day be an *Oberstleutnant* (lieutenant colonel) of the NVA.[45]

Like Gero, many East Germans began to find new opportunities for themselves in the GDR as its first ten tumultuous years had come and gone. Most people knew little of the vicious power struggle that played out in the political corridors in Berlin, and fewer would have cared if they had. The late 1950s were marked by a sense of consolidation. The dust was settling on the German division as each of the two states was coming to terms with itself. There had been a brief rekindling of hostilities in Berlin after Khrushchev, buoyed by having sent the first satellite, Sputnik, into space in 1957, demanded that Berlin be demilitarized and foreign occupation troops withdrawn. This demand may have ruined Eisenhower's Thanksgiving festivities in the Southern US state of Georgia in November 1958, but the conflict was resolved quickly. Most historians now think that rather than making a serious demand, Khrushchev was merely testing Western resolve. He is supposed to have called Berlin 'the testicles of the West: every time I want to make the West scream, I squeeze on Berlin'. The move was as much aimed at the world as it was at Moscow, where he had finally won the murderous battle for political power that had played out after Stalin's death. But this also had a stabilizing effect on the GDR, which now enjoyed confident Soviet backing for all to see.

Like Khrushchev, Ulbricht too had sidelined or silenced most of his political enemies and embarked once again on his programme of 'building socialism'. This brought back renewed collectivization and nationalization efforts. By 1961, 90 per cent of agricultural production came from the 'socialist sector', meaning collectivized or state-owned farms. In retail too, only 10 per cent of the sector remained in private hands, and the figure for private industry sat at 4 per cent of the market.[46] However, these figures are (deliberately) misleading. They hide the fact that a new system of semi-nationalization had been introduced whereby previous private owners remained in charge of running their business while the state stepped in as the creditor. This was a compromise many could live with as it meant lower personal financial risk to the former owners, while a degree of independence was retained. However, those who left the country were still mostly former landowners, industrialists, business owners, middle class tradespeople and intellectuals.

Political stabilization also brought a degree of social and economic calm. The year 1959 saw the lowest numbers of citizens leaving the GDR since its foundation a decade earlier. Living standards began to rise as the average monthly income had nearly doubled between 1950 and 1960.[47] The housing situation was still tense, but many people accepted that the cities especially had seen such devastation that it would take a while until decent flats and houses would be available in their place of choice.

Christine Nagel, who was in her late teens by the end of the 1950s (one year younger than Gero who joined the NVA at this point), would have liked to move to Dresden with her boyfriend when he returned from basic training in the army in 1959. But she was told by the local authorities that this was impossible. The Saxon city had been so heavily bombed during the war that it took nearly ten years to clear the rubble before any work to rebuild could even begin in earnest. Christine accepted that those who had remained in the ruined city and committed to its rebuilding were the first ones to receive adequate housing as it slowly became available from the mid-1950s. When the young couple got married in 1961, they planned to move to Wismar or Rostock by the Baltic Sea where 'they needed people to help rebuild and housing was readily available'. But then Christine became pregnant and worried that her parents, who lived in Dresden, would not be able to help with childcare. So they applied for a flat again. This time, married and expecting a child, they had moved right up the priority ladder and were eligible for a 36-square-metre flat on the third floor of a new block in Louisenstraße in Dresden's *Äußere Neustadt* (Outer New Town), just outside of where the old city walls had been. The little flat only had two bedrooms, each a tiny box, just large enough to fit a bed and a cupboard. There was also a small kitchen-corner and a small lounge. This contained the only source of heating, a stove, the coal for which had to be carried up from the cellar. There was no fridge and in the summer milk could only be cooled with large ice blocks which a man sold from the back of a horse-drawn cart in the street below. There was no bathroom and no running water, only a tap in the central hall, which all residents shared.

In this basic flat Christine lived for eight years with her husband and young daughter. She had 'never been happier in her life'. All her neighbours had small children. They washed their laundry together at the communal tap as their children rode their scooters up and down the large corridor. Christine would drop her daughter at her neighbours' so she could do some shopping or go out. The whole street met at the nearby public bath house to chat and relax. Christine counted herself lucky to have so much support. She was only twenty years old and knew little about childcare or household chores. The family outings down to the banks of the River Elbe may seem humble but they count among Christine's fondest memories. Despite the socialist economic system, ambition was also rewarded so that employees were encouraged to work hard. Christine remembers how little spare time there was as she was keen to accumulate more and more hours for the Workers' Building Society programme. This allowed people who could show that they had spent 500 or more hours 'building up' (for example, clearing rubble in Dresden) and made regular contributions to the fund to apply for better housing. By 1969, Christine had managed to do this and the family was offered a new flat. 'I thought I was dreaming!' she remembered later. The place was twice as big as their old one and had its own bathroom.[48]

Life stories like Christine's are commonplace among workers who began to find their feet, and perhaps even more importantly, their place in society, in the late 1950s and early 1960s. There were programmes to promote workers into higher positions if they showed skill and a good work ethic. Many were the first in their family to be sent to university or college to upgrade their status from skilled worker to engineer. Women too could now combine family life and career and were indeed encouraged to do so. Christine struggled to find a place for her young daughter at first as the childcare system was still being established and single mothers received preference over married ones. But from the age of three her daughter was entitled to a place in the local kindergarten which allowed Christine to return to work full time.

Historians have often dismissed this as a cynical move by the GDR government to utilize the entire workforce as it struggled to recruit enough labour in the earlier years. This is not only to underestimate the drive towards gender equality as an inherent feature of socialist ideology but also insulting to the women concerned. They took pride in their new roles and in being equal partners to the men they worked with. Nobody would have told the teenage Regina Faustmann in 1950 that she only began her apprenticeship as a chemical lab technician because the government encouraged her to do so. She took pride in her work – just like her male colleagues – and was pleased that she was able to continue to pursue this career when she had children. East German women had a social life outside the family home where they went out for a beer with their workmates in the evenings and felt part of wider society in a way that would take much longer to develop in West Germany. While in the GDR just over half of all women worked by 1955 and this rate would rise to two thirds by 1970,[49] in the FRG only a third of women were in employment in 1950 and only 27.5 per cent were working in 1970.[50]

As the 1950s drew to a close, life in the GDR had begun to settle down. Of course the economic problems had not disappeared. The pre-existing problems had been inflamed further by the West German Hallstein Doctrine in 1955, the FRG's foreign policy stance that it would not establish diplomatic and economic relations with any country which chose to recognize the GDR as a sovereign state. Given the size of the West German economy compared to the East, few countries dared to pay the economic price for snubbing Bonn's express wish. A trade embargo in anything but name, it forced the GDR into economic and diplomatic isolation and complete reliance on Soviet good will for imports and exports as the Hallstein Doctrine would not be lifted until 1970. The result was that products such as coffee, soap or chocolate were still hard to come by. Nonetheless, the last ration coupons disappeared in 1959 and the majority of the population had come to terms with the country they lived in.

Overtaking without Catching Up

Zerbst, Saxony-Anhalt, 27 January 1960. A 'fit and healthy' twenty-year-old man was interviewed by Lieutenant Weber, head of the local Stasi branch in Zerbst, a small town halfway between Magdeburg and Wittenberg. The place was a shell of its former self. It had once been the proud residence of Anhalt-Zerbst, a Holy Roman principality, run by the House of Ascania. Where there had once been mediaeval splendour, there was now rubble and a few new buildings. Thanks to a military air base, which Hitler had had built there in 1935 as part of his plans to establish a powerful *Luftwaffe*, Zerbst was targeted by American air raids. Over 200 tonnes of incendiary bombs were dropped on the little town, destroying 80 per cent of it and nearly all of the old town centre. Like many locals, the young man in front of Lieutenant Weber was full of anger at the 'capitalist-imperialist' forces that had supposedly led to Hitler's regime and the terrible war it had wreaked. According to Weber's notes, he was 'keen and immediately offered his services to the Guards Regiment of the MfS [Ministry for State Security]'.[51]

The interviewee was Hagen Koch, who had been brought up as a fervent socialist by his father, now a teacher but originally a professional soldier who had served for sixteen years by the time his career ended with the Second World War. Hagen was only five years old then and lived in abject poverty like many of the other children around him. When he entered school, most of his teachers were new recruits, just like his father, trained for their role as standard bearers in a socialist Germany. They impressed on him that Hitler alone could not have fought this war. Instead war was an inevitability in capitalist societies which unavoidably embraced aggression and imperialism as the insatiable demands of their greed-based economies pushed for more resources and new markets. Hagen soaked it all up, wide-eyed and idealistic. He would help build a better Germany and protect it from its enemies. This enthusiasm quickly marked him out. After he left school and finished an apprenticeship in technical drawing, he was approached by the Stasi. At the age of nineteen, in 1959, he was told that war was once more looming and he 'would fight, in the Ministry for State Security, in the first line of defence for peace in our small country, the GDR'.[52] The teenager did not have to be asked twice. In the ardent belief that he was doing the right thing, he joined the Guards Regiment of the Stasi, its paramilitary division. It would later be called the Felix Dzerzhinsky Guards Regiment, in honour of 'Iron Felix', the Bolshevik revolutionary who had founded the Cheka, Soviet Russia's secret police force. Its main task was to protect official buildings and events. With his skills as a technical drawer, Hagen would go on to help determine the exact location of the Berlin Wall, and protect it while it was being built.

Paradoxically, it was tension created by the government that gave young men like Hagen Koch the idea that their young state needed defending, not civil unrest. East Germans were just beginning to settle into their new post-war lives. Like a raw wound that was only just starting to scab over, the lives of the citizens of the GDR began to heal. But it was a slow and fragile process. Brick by brick, new housing emerged, but it was basic and there was still not enough of it. Workers were proud to have acquired new qualifications and to join the many social and professional organizations available, but they still earned little and worked long hours. Childcare systems were in place but often still miles away from home. Cultural outlets like theatres, concert halls and cinemas sprung up everywhere and were hugely popular and Elvis found many fans among the East German youth. This was a symptom of the same dizzy craving for distraction that had marked the immediate post-war years. The people of the GDR were beginning to heal from the political, economic, social and psychological consequences of the war, but they had yet to fully recover. Ulbricht, never a man of the people, misjudged the situation completely.

To Ulbricht, the fragile calm seemed like solid contentment – the perfect time to resume his contentious 'building socialism' campaign. At a political level, this meant consolidating the First Secretary's own position. When the GDR's first President, Wilhelm Pieck, died in office on 7 September 1960 at the age of eighty-four, Ulbricht was prepared. Pieck had long suffered from severe health issues, in part due to being grossly obese. When he rested with Ulbricht at the Barvikha Sanatorium near Moscow, following the strain of the 1953 uprising, Pieck was already recovering from his second stroke, which left him with 'mild paralysis on the right, a slight drooping of the corner of the mouth, wheezing or snoring, slowed down pulse, tone of the limb musculature lowered' according to the medical notes.[53] This joined other long-term issues such as liver cirrhosis. His death came as no surprise. Ulbricht had his old comrade cremated and the ashes interred with great ceremony at the Memorial to the Socialists in Friedrichsfelde Central Cemetery, an honorary resting place for 'those who fought for the socialist idea', set up in 1951. Commemorative postage stamps were issued. Pieck's birthplace of Guben by the River Neiße, which since 1945 straddled the German-Polish border, was renamed Wilhelm-Pieck-Stadt in 1961. The man had not even been buried when Ulbricht, five days after his death, moved to abolish the role of President, making himself the pinnacle of the GDR's political pyramid.

'Building socialism' also entailed social reform. But Ulbricht's hectic pace sought to create a new utopian people's community so quickly that even the most apolitical family would have found it invasive. In July 1958, he passed a bizarre set of 'Ten Commandments':[54]

1. Thou shalt always work towards the international solidarity of the proletariat and of all working people as well as for the inseparable bond of all socialist countries.
2. Thou shalt love thy country and always stand ready to use everything in your might and all your skill for the defence of the power of the workers and peasants.
3. Thou shalt help to abolish the exploitation of the people by the people.
4. Thou shalt do good deeds for socialism, for socialism leads to a better life for all working people.
5. Thou shalt contribute to the build-up of socialism in the spirit of mutual help and comradely collaboration, respect the collective and heed its critique.
6. Thou shalt protect the people's property and multiply it.
7. Thou shalt always strive for higher achievements, be frugal and consolidate the socialist work ethic.
8. Thou shalt raise your children in the spirit of peace and socialism to become well-rounded, confident and physically strong people.

9. Thou shalt live a clean and decent life and respect your family.
10. Thou shalt practise solidarity with the other peoples who fight for national liberty and defend their national independence.

The religious connotations of this biblical set of moral and social rules were deliberate. Ulbricht was not merely setting out a series of guidelines but he was also prescribing a new lifestyle to his compatriots. He set out in detail the values they should pursue and how they should develop themselves both spiritually and physically. To this end, he deployed the education system, the Free German Youth and a range of cultural institutions. A conference of like-minded writers in the city of Bitterfeld declared in April 1959 that it wanted all divisions between culture and work lifted. They wanted coal miners to write, poets to work shifts in a steel mill, libraries to be introduced in factories, and theatres to produce plays that were accessible to everyone but fulfilled a moral purpose too. The FDJ's newspaper *Junge Welt* declared that Western music was simplistic and deliberately seductive to keep the masses sedated and stupid. Referring to Elvis Presley specifically, it declared, 'His "songs" are like his face: daft, stupid and brutal.' In January 1958, the GDR government decided that 60 per cent of the music played in dance clubs had to be either produced in the GDR or in fellow socialist countries. In the coming decades, many a drunken teenager would giggle tipsily at the uniformed man who turned up at their party around midnight to ask if the correct ratio of capitalist and communist music had been adhered to. While there were amusing sides like this to Ulbricht's invasive restructuring of social life in the GDR, and the majority of people simply grumbled and joked their way through this, it was too much for many writers, artists and actors who now began to turn their back on the GDR en masse to seek creative freedom in West Germany.

Of all the new changes, Ulbricht's sharp economic U-turn was perhaps the most painful to bear. At the 5th Congress of the SED in

1958, he had declared that he intended to develop the GDR's economy 'within just a few years so that it proves once and for all the superiority of the socialist system of the GDR as compared to the imperialist forces of the Bonn state'.[55] This became the mantra for the seven-year plan from 1959 – 'Overtaking and Catching Up', later changed to 'Overtaking without Catching Up' – to prove that the GDR was not merely trying to imitate hollow Western consumerism but was creating a meaningful life full of beautiful products and wholesome pleasures.

However, by the GDR authorities' own admission, the little state's economy still lagged around 30 per cent behind that of its bigger neighbour. Absolutely everything had to be thrown at the effort to outdo West Germany in GDP per capita, consumer products, food availability and so on. Meanwhile, Khrushchev was still demanding deliveries of goods and resources straight from the assembly lines of many East German factories. This may not have been on the post-war scale any more but still posed a considerable impediment to the GDR's recovery. Distribution problems added to a perceived crisis as the central planning struggled to get products where they were needed. Collectivization was also pushed again. The voluntary programme from which many farmers had benefited in the wake of the 1953 uprising as they received state subsidies and were allowed to continue to run their own farms was now abandoned and farmers were forced to join collectives, the Agricultural Production Cooperatives, whether they wanted to or not. This led to many of them packing their bags and leaving the country. They had lost everything and felt they might as well start again from scratch in a state that would allow them to run their own agricultural businesses. The same process also affected skilled workers and tradespeople. Small businesses and individual tradespeople were forced into state-owned conglomerates, which meant they lost all sense of ownership over their work and made less money than they did as individuals. They too often joined the throng westwards.

By 1961, the GDR had already lost 1.3 million people and there was no end in sight. Annual figures seemed to head towards the 300,000 mark, which they had previously already crossed in the crisis years of 1955 and 1957. It was mostly intellectuals, professionals, skilled workers and those who had owned large farms who sought to benefit from a new life in West Germany. Many young people who had just enjoyed one of the excellent new apprenticeships or university courses also left as they stood to earn more money, achieve a higher social status or have a greater range of consumer products available to them. According to statistics taken by West German authorities who processed the arriving East Germans, six out of seven 'refugees' between 1952 and 1961 had left in the hope that this would raise their living standard. Only 14.2 per cent left because they feared 'a threat to life or limb or to their personal freedom'.[56]

The dip in numbers in 1958 had shown that many of these professionals might have been persuaded to remain had Ulbricht not pressed ahead with his uncompromising push to 'build socialism'. As it was, the steady brain drain deprived the GDR's economy of a range of skilled professionals. This created further anxieties and anger in those who stayed. Entire regions were left without doctors and nurses. Engineers and architects were missing to rebuild collapsed bridges and bombed-out housing. The absence of key workers in steel mills and coal mining caused disruptions to whole chains of industry. The lack of experienced farmers meant food shortages. The likes of Brigitte Fritschen, a teacher now, Gero Vanselow, who had just joined the air force, or Hagen Koch, who had just joined the Stasi's Guards Regiment, were angry. They felt deserted and accused those who left of being greedy while they worked long hours to build a fairer society. This anger in turn was intensely felt by those who considered emigration, often giving them the last push to leave. Ulbricht had to do something or these social, economic and political tensions would tear his republic apart.

How the Elite Lived

Wandlitz, Brandenburg, spring 1958. A group of officious-looking men in suits got out of their cars at the small state-owned forest between the pleasant settlement of Wandlitz and the mediaeval town of Bernau. Under the suspicious gaze of the bemused locals they began surveying the land. They were on a top-secret mission to investigate the area's suitability for a closed residential area where the SED officials could live with their families. Following the tumultuous events of the Hungarian Uprising in 1956, in which some communist officials had been killed by the angry masses, Ulbricht felt that the current living arrangements of GDR politicians were no longer safe. Key members of the politburo lived within a few hundred metres of each other in requisitioned houses in the leafy area around the Majakowskiring, an oval street in the Pankow district in the north of Berlin. Walter and Lotte Ulbricht occupied number 28, which was next door to Wilhelm Pieck in 29. The Honeckers resided in number 14, next to the kindergarten of the GDR government in number 13. The journalist and editor of the SED newspaper *Neues Deutschland*, Rudolf Herrnstadt, lived on the same street before he fell from grace, as did the poet and Culture Minister Johannes R. Becher. Schönhausen Palace, a baroque, yellow-fronted manor house in landscaped gardens, which served as Pieck's official residence where he could welcome important foreign officials such as Ho Chi Minh and Khrushchev, was also only 350 metres away. When the Soviets had requisitioned the area in 1945, they secured it with fences and walls. Everything the VIPs needed lay within. 'Pankow', as it simply became known after the district it was in, had become a self-sufficient enclave, accordingly nicknamed 'Gorodok' (Little Town) by the Soviets.

But it was too close for comfort to the city centre as far as Ulbricht was concerned. A single wall would not keep an irate army of malcontented workers at bay, as Hungary had shown. The shock of East Germany's own uprising in 1953 also still ran deep. A settlement outside of Berlin could be secured properly and it would also give the health-conscious Ulbricht plenty of space for exercise. The First Secretary began each working morning with ten minutes of aerobics before breakfast and complemented this with long walks with his wife Lotte. As he moved out of Berlin, he would also come to enjoy rowing on the nearby lakes in the summer and ice skating on them in the winter. When the surveyors came back from Wandlitz and reported that a suitable area had been found that not only met Ulbricht's personal needs but also provided an adequate environment for twenty-three politicians and their families, the matter was decided.

The *Waldsiedlung* (Forest Settlement) was built between the summers of 1958 and 1960 on 60 hectares. Situated around 35 kilometres north of the city centre, it was an ideal location; far enough outside the capital to be safe and idyllic with its lakes, streams and shady woodlands, but also within half an hour's drive of the government buildings in Berlin. The Soviet ambassador's summer residence at the nearby Liepnitzsee was in easy reach. The settlement had its own health clinic, clubhouse, shop and hair salon. It had a private lake shore with a little boathouse, a swimming pool and its own cinema. The SED functionaries lived in the inner circle of the Waldsiedlung in unnamed streets where the houses were simply numbered from 1 to 23. Ulbricht himself took residence in number 7; the Honeckers moved into number 11. Erich Mielke, Stasi chief since 1957 when Ernst Wollweber had fallen from grace, lived in number 14. Beyond this inner ring was an outer one where staff lived. There was also a bakery, a petrol station and a butcher.

By contrast to the political leaders of other nations – both East and West – the GDR's elite lived in humble surroundings. Their houses were airy and spacious when compared to the two-bedroom flats afforded to young families up and down the country, but they were far from extravagant or luxurious. All twenty-three houses were grey, functional blocks with tiled roofs that looked not unlike the early prefab buildings raised to house the masses in GDR cities. The Ulbrichts received the largest house, which had ten rooms but was still very spartan in style. The ground floor had a large room in which the SED leader could receive guests, a dining room and a private lounge. Visitors often said the reception rooms felt sterile and bland. On the first floor, there was a study for Walter Ulbricht, another (slightly larger) one for his wife, a bathroom, a massage room with wall bars for Ulbricht's exercise and a little surgery where he would receive treatment from his private doctor, Arno Linke.[57] There was even a bunker for the families of the politburo members. The plan was that they would shelter there in the event of a nuclear attack while the politicians would continue to run what was left of the country from the government bunker in Berlin.

The SED bosses had everything they needed in Wandlitz. They were picked up in the morning by private cars, chauffeured to Berlin and returned in the evenings. Security arrangements were tight. Six hundred and fifty men and women worked and lived in the settlement. Their lives were carefully monitored and they had undergone rigorous background checks before they were employed. All personnel at Wandlitz joined the Stasi, from the drivers to the technicians. The inner ring around the twenty-three houses of the politicians was fortified with a 2-metre-high concrete wall, which was lit up at night. The outer ring was fenced with signs that said 'Wildlife Research Area' to keep the settlement a secret. There were no signs along the A11 motorway, which was only 3 kilometres away so that the politicians and their families could swiftly be evacuated if an attack was imminent. The Waldsiedlung never appeared on any map of the area. It was guarded by 200 soldiers in thirty-three guard posts, around the clock, every day.

Instead of finding happiness in the pleasant, if somewhat petit-bourgeois, surroundings, the politburo members found themselves in a golden cage. Margot Honecker would later repeatedly refer to the Waldsiedlung as 'The Ghetto' (as did many ordinary East Germans when the existence of the place began to trickle through the fog of rumours). She complained that it afforded her no privacy; every step, every word, every decision was carefully monitored. She was assigned a 'shadow' for security reasons and would later go out of her way to acquire a driving licence and a Wartburg car so she could flee the stuffy surroundings at times and shake off her shadow.[58]

The isolation of the SED elites behind a shroud of secrecy and high concrete walls also led to resentment, ridicule and suspicion among parts of the population. There were rumours that 'those up there' lived in splendour in their 'luxurious ghetto'. People talked of golden bathroom fittings and fantastical villas while everyone else had to make do with rudimentary housing and coffee substitute. It did not take much to confirm Ulbricht's image as a cold and wooden apparatchik but Wandlitz did exactly that.

The concept behind Ulbricht's Waldsiedlung was both a symptom and a cause of a widening gulf between the regime and its people. It was a symptom because Ulbricht never managed to shake off the suspicions he harboured against his own people. The psychological impact of a life lived in a Germany where communists were the enemy and were incarcerated or worse was immense. This was not something that Hitler had introduced. Ulbricht had been hunted by the government of Wilhelm II and then the Weimar authorities before the Nazis drove the anti-communist persecution to unprecedented heights. He had spent time in prison; many of his comrades had been murdered by Germans. It is hardly surprising that upon his return in 1945, he suspected that at the very least residual hatred towards 'the reds' lingered. In addition, much of his time in Moscow was overshadowed by fear as the vast majority of those who arrived with him in the 1930s fell victim to the Stalinist purges. Ulbricht's entire life had been one of permanent tension and watchfulness, and this was not going to change now that he was in his sixties.

But the isolation at the Waldsiedlung was also a cause for the rift between regime and people, and it set up a pattern that would outlast Ulbricht's reign. Asked by a new colleague in May 1984 whether walling in the political class was really the right thing to do, Erich Honecker mumbled, 'Well, this is how Walter [Ulbricht] set it up. Perhaps we should mull it over again and have another think whether it should stay this way.'[59] Elite politicians of other states also live in political and social bubbles for security reasons, but Ulbricht's Waldsiedlung was extreme. It completely removed those who made life-or-death decisions from the people who were affected by them; and this in a state where everything was centrally planned and organized, from the books that people were allowed to write and read to the type of fruit that could be imported. This division not only led to bad decision-making and a complete lack of feedback from the people when combined with the lack of free media and individual enterprise, but it also created mutual resentment and suspicion. 'Those up there' and 'the people' lived very different lives and began to suspect the worst of each other.

A Decade of Missed Chances

The story of the GDR's first decade as a brand-new social, economic and political experiment on German soil was one of missed chances. Contrary to many later depictions, the overwhelming sentiment of the East German population was not one of immediate resentment towards Ulbricht's regime and envy of Adenauer's but of relief and even enthusiasm. The majority of people who lived through the 1950s in the GDR remember the years of war, persecution in Eastern Europe, bombing, rape, chaos and captivity as horrific experiences which strongly contrasted with the sense of new beginning of the late 1940s and early 1950s.

Workers in particular did not mind so much that their flats were small and that they had a limited choice on the shelves of grocery shops – they had not been able to afford much before the war as they had often lived in cramped tenement housing or rural poverty. In the 1950s, they had a chance to begin new careers as teachers, skilled workers or in the armed forces. They were respected by the state, even became its focal point, rather than being treated as a nuisance, to be placated at best, suppressed at worst. Young people happily swapped the brown shirts of the Hitler Youth for the blue ones of the FDJ, where they found both familiarity in ritual and new excitement in the change of morality and values. There was purpose and satisfaction in clearing up and rebuilding, and people craved the sense of collective effort that the socialist system offered them after the gruelling last years of the war.

But East Germany's fate did not lie in the hands of its people as the 1953 uprising readily demonstrated. Both East and West Germany were part of a global political power game in which they were mere pawns to start with, played and sacrificed as needed by the Soviets and the Americans. Both Ulbricht and Adenauer proved to have their own (often unbending) convictions but neither had much room for manoeuvre and neither was willing to move from a stance that bound their Germany tightly to the power bloc they deemed to be the morally superior one. This made both leaders suspicious and tightened their respective stance to a point of no return, even if there had been the political will in Washington or Moscow for moderation.

Ulbricht had two further issues to deal with compared to Adenauer. One is the memory of terror in Moscow during the Great Purges, which compounded his lifelong experience of persecution and illegality. Adenauer had also lived dangerously during the Nazi years but had a long political career and a sense of rootedness in Cologne that bore no resemblance to Ulbricht's hectic biography. Fear for his own life and the survival of his state never took on the feverish frenzy of the SED elite's paranoia. The other issue specific to the East was the suffocating weight of its economic burden. It is accepted by most historians that the post-war years in both Germanies were marked by the apolitical mood of the 'ohne mich' (count me out) generation. But Adenauer had Marshall Aid, Germany's industrial heartlands and the lack of reparations payments on his side, granting him and his economic minister Ludwig Erhard the opportunity to create an 'economic miracle'. This placated people and gave West Germans the prosperity, safety and consumerism they craved after the war. By contrast, the East German economy never stood a chance to get going in the early 1950s. Historians have been quick to point to the planned economy as the root of failure but the impact of the economic system is impossible to measure when the basics are missing – from natural resources, energy and industry to a stable currency. Adenauer had even been able to prop up the West German mark against the dollar at a fixed rate.

Nonetheless, a charismatic leader with a finger on the pulse of his people could have done things differently. Walter Ulbricht certainly played a part in creating a situation which many middle class Germans in particular found unbearable. The brief lull in the emigration figures in 1958, when Ulbricht had been forced to slow the pace of his collectivization and nationalization programmes, indicate that there was willingness, even from the middle classes, to tolerate lower living standards within reason. There were many in the politburo who argued for moderation – Herrnstadt, Schmidt and Wollweber for example. But Ulbricht systematically sidelined dissenting voices and created a Stalinist regime that tolerated no discussion.

However, it is questionable if an open border between the two Germanies would ever have been feasible. Let's imagine for a moment that Ulbricht had set up a moderate, social democratic system with strong state intervention on a social, economic and cultural level as some reformers in the SED demanded. Workers might have supported this as it afforded them new opportunities and greatly improved social mobility. However, once trained and skilled, after years of study, they would still have entered a classless society where their status may have afforded them prestige but few luxuries. The GDR subsidized rents, set up comprehensive and affordable childcare and began to build flats. But a trained engineer would always be able to earn more money in the West, buy a larger house there and afford things that others could not. A classless society, by definition, prevents above-average lifestyles. Those that stand to lose out from this will always be the middle and upper classes, irrespective of whether there is censorship and oppression or freedom and moderation. The fact that another Germany lay just a short drive or, in Berlin, just a short walk away would have greatly appealed to skilled workers, professionals, intellectuals and others with above-average incomes. This would have led to a brain drain perhaps not quite as drastic, but in the long run just as devastating to the GDR's strangulated economy.

It is a fact that the Berlin Wall that was about to be built would go on to bring misery to countless individuals. It would separate families and friends. It would lock people in and it would lock people out. But all sides – Adenauer and Ulbricht, Kennedy and Khrushchev – understood that the path towards it had been set in motion a decade earlier.

5. Brick by Brick (1961–1965)

Nobody has any intention of building a wall!

The Berlin Wall

House of Ministries, East Berlin, 15 June 1961. 'First Secretary, does the formation of a neutral Berlin, in your opinion, mean that there will be a border at the Brandenburg Gate?' Veteran journalist Annamarie Doherr, West Berlin correspondent for the *Frankfurter Rundschau*, let the effect of her words settle. Over 300 journalists had assembled in the Great Hall of the House of Ministries. All eyes were on Walter Ulbricht at whom the question had been directed. For weeks the First Secretary of the German Democratic Republic had lobbied Nikita Khrushchev to find a solution for the 'Berlin problem'. Three million East Germans had turned their back on his 'workers' and peasants' state', 80 per cent of them via Berlin. The GDR had lost 7,500 doctors, 1,200 dentists, one third of its academics and hundreds of thousands of skilled workers, many of whom had recently been trained at great cost.[1] What could Ulbricht possibly say to Doherr and her readers, to everyone in the room and to his own people? That he needed East Germans to stay whether they liked it or not? And then there were the security implications of this open gap in the border. Berlin had become a city of spies. Around 500,000 people crossed the border every day from both directions and there was no telling who was friend or foe among them. Berlin's status as an occupied city, jointly governed by powers locked in ideological conflict, became increasingly unsustainable as trust broke down and the Cold War reached new heights of hostility. On 4 June 1961, Khrushchev demanded that Berlin be made a neutral city and all foreign armed forces withdrawn from it. Moscow regarded West Berlin as a splinter in the heart of socialist Eastern Europe and a security risk due to the open border. At the same time, the West understood that withdrawal from their sectors of Berlin exposed them to a takeover. The stalemate of this Berlin Crisis made Ulbricht's long-standing ambition to close the last open passage between East and West palatable to Washington, Moscow and Bonn.

The clumsy words that Ulbricht finally found in answer to Doherr's question would go down in history as one of the most tragicomical lies ever told. In his high-pitched voice, he told the assembled journalists, 'I understand your question to mean that there are people in West Germany who wish to see us mobilize the workers of the capital of the GDR to build a wall, yes? Errr . . . I have no knowledge of any such intention . . . Nobody has any intention of building a wall!' Work on this wall that nobody wanted to build began just a few metres away and barely two months later, on 13 August 1961.

Berlin-Mitte, 13 August 1961. When Gerda Langosch woke up in her flat at Kieler Straße 3, she had no idea what had taken place outside her home overnight. The twenty-eight-year-old had lived in this street all her life; she was born in her parents' flat in number 18 and had only moved out in 1957 when she got married. Now she was five months pregnant and looked forward to starting a family with her husband. The area around the Kieler Straße had once been one of Berlin's poorer working class districts, full of tenement blocks with multiple small flats. But aerial bombing and artillery fire had razed almost all of the twenty houses in Gerda's street to the ground. Only two badly damaged buildings still stood, number 18 and number 3. The somewhat random way that Berlin was carved out into four occupation zones meant that Gerda now lived in the Soviet sector of Mitte even though she felt much closer to the neighbouring working class district of Wedding, which belonged to the French sector. That is where she had attended school, where most of her

Unter-den-Linden, Berlin, 3 June 1945.

Rebuilding Berlin.

A brand new city. Eisenhüttenstadt in the 1960s.

Orbitaplast – biggest producer of plastics, 1964.

Kühlungsborn beach, Baltic Sea, July 1956.

Freyburg gravel pit, 1960.

Village Fair in Thuringia, around 1965.

Mothers, Berlin, June 1964.

Labour Day, 1963.

On the train, 1960s.

Children greeting cosmonaut Valentina Tereshkova, 1963.

Elvis Presley fans, East Berlin, 1960.

Walter Ulbricht, 1960.

Erich Honecker, 1985.

friends lived and where she had gone to church. Nevertheless, the thought of leaving Kieler Straße, giving up her home and immediate proximity to her parents, never occurred to her.

On the morning of 13 August 1961, Gerda and her husband heard the shocking news on the radio: the SED had erected an 'anti-fascist protection wall' between the Western occupied sectors of Berlin and its own Eastern one. Their street bordered directly on the Berlin-Spandau Ship Canal to the west and north, and the Boyenstraße to the east, both of which formed the border to the other sectors. They would be surrounded by this 'anti-fascist protection wall' on three sides. When the young couple realized this, they rushed out of the house, curious to see if anything was visibly different. The canal looked just as ever, nothing had changed, but it was a fairly wide waterway that had acted as a natural district boundary since 1945. From Gerda's parents' house they would be able to see on to the Boyenstraße. When they arrived there, Gerda's mother told them that she had looked out of her kitchen window while making breakfast and was baffled at what she saw: 'Spanish riders', defensive wooden barriers with barbed wire, had been put up all along the street. Only then did she switch on the radio to find out what had happened. Gerda's husband wondered if it was still possible to pass, and wandered off into the Western sector in between the still sparsely distributed Spanish riders on the Boyenstraße. Nobody asked him any questions and it occurred to him that this was his last chance to stay in the West. But he turned around, walked through the primitive early border defences again and rejoined his pregnant wife for a life in the East.[2]

While Gerda and her family had been fast asleep, at 1 a.m. a coordinated process had begun which quickly closed the 170-kilometre-long border between East and West Berlin and between West Berlin and the rest of the GDR. It was a hastily constructed combination of concrete, barbed wire, Spanish riders and still only lightly guarded waterways serving as dividers. Border police were ordered to heighten and strengthen the existing vehicle barriers between the Soviet sector and the others while keeping order. Night after night there were 'incidents' at the wall as frightened, desperate and angry citizens on both sides demanded to know what was going on.

Ulbricht was well aware of the negative press his wall was going to generate, and was keen to create an illusion of it as a collective and popular effort for the security of the GDR. Rather than just deploying NVA soldiers and border units, the regime also drew on the KGs, the paramilitary volunteer Combat Groups of the Working Class set up in the wake of the 1953 uprising. Now numbering well over 100,000 men and women, they seemed a force large enough to secure the immediate border to West Berlin. As they were civilians, any accidental or deliberate crossing into the West was less likely to be regarded as an act of war. They were ideally placed to guard the border on the Western side.

The Spanish riders outside Gerda Langosch's house were put up by KG troops some time in the early hours of the morning. Erich Honecker, who had been charged with the task of preparing and executing the border closures, wrote in his official memoirs that he 'had suggested deploying the political and military fighting power of the working class, meaning the workers of socialist companies in the uniforms of the Combat Groups at the border directly. Together with units of the People's Police they were to secure the immediate border to West Berlin.'[3] The military units of the NVA and the Stasi's Guards Regiment formed the second tier of defence, to be deployed to support the KGs and People's Police where necessary. The Red Army was only to be used in an absolute emergency, namely in the event of NATO intervention. This shows how edgy the regime had become. It was keen to avoid conflict with the West and the building of the Berlin Wall was part of this plan, but could not rule out that things might escalate into outright war on 13 August 1961. There was no way of knowing how Bonn or Washington would respond. Berlin had been at the centre of Cold War tension for well over a decade now, and both sides were supremely conscious of the potential escalation even a small incident there could cause. As ordinary people rushed to the emerging wall on both sides of the city, all it took was a nervous guard to pull the trigger or for tensions between the armed units of East and West to spill over into an exchange of fire. The Cuban Missile Crisis a year later showed just how close the world stood on the brink of nuclear warfare. In the heated context of the early 1960s, the building of the Berlin Wall might well have provided the spark that turned the Cold War into a hot one. And both Ulbricht and Honecker knew it.

An enormous responsibility lay on the shoulders of the civilians in the Combat Groups who were asked to support the building of the wall. Yet, many of the 8,000 or so who would be deployed in total were as enthusiastic as was to be expected from a voluntary militia force. One comrade by the name of Helmut Egerland returned from holiday early as he had heard the news on the radio and wanted to help. Another, Walter Schindler, a local group leader, described the experience of his unit:

> *Those days were a real baptism of fire for us. They were tough. Sometimes, during the early days, we had to sleep on bare tables and chairs, worked through twelve-hour shifts and more, then had a two-hour break before the alarm called us again. It poured down with rain and it was cold. But where volunteers were needed, the entire unit reported . . . But never did such difficulties harm our morale. Quite to the contrary: with every deployment our camaraderie grew as did our willingness to fight and our class consciousness.*[4]

Not all of the KGs proved to be this keen. Due to a combination of insufficient on-call systems and patchy communication as well as genuine fear or opposition to the partition of Berlin, only 65.5 per cent of the Combat Groups' expected strength could actually be mobilized in August 1961.[5] Some 2,100 KGs, People's Police, border guards and soldiers also used the proximity to the border and their ability to stroll into the Western sectors of Berlin to defect to the FRG altogether. An image of four KG men guarding the border crossing at the Brandenburg Gate on 14 August 1961, which had been taken to be used as propaganda, was quietly buried in the archives as all four of the young men on it had disappeared into West Germany.

Naturally, the boys and girls of the Free German Youth also had a role to play. The Secretariat of the Central Council of the FDJ immediately issued orders to its district representatives on 13 August 1961. Among others these included:

- *The youth of the working class and all other young people must show Comrade Walter Ulbricht, President of the State Council, their approval of the governments' measures.*
- *To help under the direction of the People's Police, especially in the cities, to ensure that agitators and idiots cannot do their devious work – not in cinemas, or restaurants or elsewhere.*
- *Every help that we can give to the units of the National People's Army and the other armed forces of our republic is to be made available by the members and leaders of the FDJ.*[6]

The deployment of the youth served two purposes. One was to impress on young people that the GDR needed to be defended as Walter Ulbricht had himself declared in 1960.[7] This was in itself an aspect of the regime's intention to hold the entire country in a state of combative readiness in case internal or external enemies threatened the republic. FDJ members visited NVA troops with whom they were supposed to spend time to increase voluntary recruitment. While plans to introduce conscription in line with the *Bundeswehr* in West Germany and the GDR's fellow Warsaw Treaty nations were under way and would be implemented in January 1962, this always sat somewhat uneasily with the regime – as evidenced by its acceptance of conscientious objection from 1964, the only Eastern Bloc country to do so.[8] It was deemed best to use opportunities of NVA deployment such as in August 1961 to involve the FDJ and give them an opportunity to bond with those already in the army.

The other purpose of FDJ deployment at the closed border was that their bright blue shirts all across East Berlin were highly visible and intended to reinforce the idea that the young generation supported the closing of the border. They would try to reassure alarmed Berliners as well as get into brawls with those opposing the wall, especially in West Berlin. They demonstrably sat in restaurants, cafés and other social spaces to act as additional security, as visible extensions of state power. It made many in the FDJ feel important, gave them a sense of power and, most importantly, a stake in the young republic which they had volunteered to protect.

On 16 August 1961, the mayor of West Berlin, Willy Brandt, spoke to 300,000 of his citizens in front of the City Hall in Schöneberg. His words were also broadcast on the American radio station RIAS, which, as he well knew, could be received in East Berlin too. In his fiery speech, he called the new border a *Schandmauer* (wall of shame), a term which would be used in official parlance in the West for nearly a decade until Brandt himself, then as Chancellor of West Germany, worked towards rapprochement between the two Germanies from 1969 onwards. In his role as mayor of West Berlin, he was angry. With real emotion, he urged Western politicians, including Konrad Adenauer and the new young US President, John F. Kennedy, to intervene. He pleaded with East German border forces to show humanity and refrain from shooting at those who wanted to cross. And he suggested that there would be support for his 'compatriots behind the barbed wire, behind the concrete bollards and behind the tanks; our compatriots in the Zone, who are watched today by troops of the Red Army so that they can't show what they want . . . We know that it is only the tanks that stop them from expressing their outrage.'[9]

But Brandt's was a lone voice crying in the wilderness. Adenauer and Kennedy both reacted sluggishly and with words rather than actions. The West German people showed concern but no powerful civil unrest emerged, while the East German population remained largely quiet in the weeks and months that followed. As cruel as it had seemed on a human level, from a political point of view, the Berlin Wall served to calm the situation in Berlin. Nobody said it but Adenauer, Ulbricht, Kennedy and Khrushchev all knew it. While the situation in the divided city remained tense, in the rest of East

Germany things settled down almost immediately. For all the aggravation and anger that the renewed acceleration of Ulbricht's 'building socialism' programme had caused, it had now simply become a fact of life. The Berlin Wall no longer allowed people to move to the West. This meant that the middle classes and skilled workers had to find a way to live with the situation while the rest of society stopped worrying about the lack of doctors, dentists, scientists and builders. There were notable exceptions, but on the whole it was as if the country shrugged its shoulders collectively and returned to work.

For those, however, who had loved ones in the West, and those who had begun to build a new life on the other side of the barrier but hesitated to leave until it was too late, the GDR became a prison with higher walls than the crude early structures in Berlin indicated. The authorities were keen to put an end to the brain drain to the West and they wanted to show that they meant business. The heightened tension among the political elite combined with the patchy nature of the first-generation Berlin Wall led to a deadly situation. East Germans minded to leave were to be deterred by border guards and their bullets. The next few years, before the divide in Berlin became a sophisticated and almost impregnable border, would be the bloodiest.

The Long Shadow of the Wall

East Berlin, 17 August 1962. The atmosphere in the city had been tense for months. Hardly a week had gone by without bloodshed along the Berlin Wall. In total, twenty-three people had lost their lives trying to cross over the inner-German border since it was closed a year earlier. The events that unfolded on this summer's day would shock the world and shape how the GDR would go down in history.

Just after 2 p.m., shots rang through the warm air of the Zimmerstraße, a long, built-up thoroughfare near Checkpoint Charlie, perhaps the best-known of the border crossing points in the city. A teenager lay bleeding on the ground at the foot of the Berlin Wall, screaming in pain and pleading for help.

The young man was Peter Fechter, an eighteen-year-old brick-layer from East Berlin. Frustrated with the East German regime's refusal to let him see his older sister in West Berlin, he spent his lunchtime breaks fantasizing with his colleague Helmut Kulbeik about escaping to the West. When, one day, the pair discovered a semi-ruined building by the Wall, the seeds of temptation were planted. Two days later they walked past the house again and decided to go inside. Although it turned out to be a working joinery, they managed to walk unnoticed into the back of the building. Fearing their footsteps would give them away, they took off their shoes and walked around in their socks. On the ground floor, they discovered a window facing the Wall that had yet to be boarded up.

In the year that had passed since the first border closures between East and West Berlin, the authorities had made systematic efforts to close gaps and eliminate weaknesses. Gone were the days of the Spanish riders supported by soldiers and volunteers; in came walled sections, barbed wire and armed guards. The building in which Helmut and Peter stood was supposed to form the easternmost part of the fortifications, but by sheer chance it still had an open window. The two men looked out and saw that they were low enough to jump down but also that, once on the ground, there was no cover. To get to West Berlin, they would then have to climb over the first fence, cross the 10-metre-wide 'death strip' and then traverse a 2-metre-high concrete wall topped with barbed wire. All in full view of one of the guard towers. It was a lethal obstacle course.

Suddenly, the men were disturbed by the sound of footsteps and voices. Panicking, they jumped out of the window. It was now or never. Still in their socks, they bolted the few metres to the first fence separating them from West Berlin and pulled themselves over it. The strip of land between them and the solid wall on the other side was only a few strides wide. Success was tantalizingly near. All of a sudden they were spotted by Guard Post 4, whose two officers opened fire immediately. Twenty-four bullets were aimed in their direction. Helmut would later describe how being shot at galvanized him to run as fast as he could. He reached the outer wall on the West Berlin side of the border, jumped and dragged himself over. The barbed wire cut into his foot, arms and chest, but the guards stopped shooting, knowing that to continue would send bullets whizzing into West Berlin.

In his torn clothes Helmut stood on top of the wall, turned around and shouted down to his friend, 'Quick! Quick! Come on!' But Peter was rooted to the spot, paralysed by fear. After a moment's hesitation, he snapped out of his trance and ran towards the outer wall. He reached it and jumped. But officers from Guard Post 3 had managed to move in closer and opened fire. The teenager was hit in the lower back while in mid-air, and fell back off the wall onto the East German side. Writhing in pain, he dragged himself behind a re-enforcement block by the wall for shelter, while the guards continued to shoot at him. Before long, he collapsed.

On the Western side, the sound of gunfire attracted a sizeable crowd. West Berlin police received their first call at 2.12 p.m. and immediately sent reinforcements to the area. The East German guards could hear the ambulance siren. Journalists also rushed to the scene, joining around 250 angry West Berliners. Furious shouts of 'Murderers! Murderers!' were aimed at the East German guards while West German police officers were urged to 'Shoot! Shoot!', which made it extremely difficult for them to simply stand by, as their orders required. They took their positions and pointed rifles at the East German border guards on the other side. The American units at Checkpoint Charlie were also subjected to a barrage of demands by the West Berliners to do something. But they too had strict orders to 'Stand fast. Do nothing.'

In the midst of this escalating chaos, Peter's desperate cries for help filled the air on both sides of the Berlin Wall. They started as loud shouts but were soon reduced to feeble whimpers. In the long minutes that followed, they faded altogether, as his life drained away. Nobody came.

While West German police officers on ladders threw bandages

and first aid material down to Peter, they dared not try to retrieve his body. To cross on to East German territory was a border breach that could end in bloodshed on an altogether different scale. American hands were tied too. Intervening to save Peter would have been tantamount to an invasion – at a time when Cold War tensions had never been greater. The East German border guards too would have taken their lives into their hands if they had tried to rescue the teenager. Only three days before, one of their own, Captain Rudi Arnstadt, had been shot by West German border guards in an incident at the Wall. The rifles now pointed at them from the West frightened the men, many of whom were themselves barely older than Peter.

And so hundreds watched for fifty desperate minutes while the wounded teenager cried and begged. When he eventually lay still, the East German guards set down a smoke screen for protection, ran out and recovered his body. No amount of propaganda or explanation by the regime could prevent the images of a slowly dying young man from going around the world, causing shock, anger and condemnation.

Conscious of the international and domestic tension created by a border still too insecure to deter those determined to leave yet guarded fiercely enough to cause frequent death and injury, the authorities were keen to develop the Wall into something more substantial. But in the early 1960s, the GDR still lacked the material to build housing on the scale required, let alone to fortify the 155-kilometre-long border around West Berlin. The earliest incarnations of the Berlin Wall were haphazard constructions made of whatever material was available. Where buildings such as blocks of flats marked the border, the inhabitants were simply evacuated and the windows and doors of the houses bricked up, so that the entire structure served as a segment of the Wall.

This happened along the Bernauer Straße in Berlin-Mitte. The north side of the street and the street itself belonged to the district of Wedding in the French sector while the houses on the south side belonged to the Soviet sector. This led to a bizarre situation whereby those who lived in the houses in the Soviet sector walked into West Berlin the moment they left their own front door. That was the case for fifty-eight-year-old widowed nurse Ida Siekmann who lived in Bernauer Straße 48 and regularly visited her sister Martha in her home in the Lortzingstraße in West Berlin, just a ten-minute walk away. When the border between East and West Berlin was closed overnight on 13 August 1961, Ida was initially still able to leave her house through the front door, immediately stepping on to a West Berlin pavement. But the authorities had put strict controls in place for all residents of the southern side of the Bernauer Straße while they began to brick up their doors and windows, creating new rear exits from 18 August. Three days later, on 21 August, it was the turn of Ida's house. With her entrance blocked, she was now cut off from her sister. Overnight, she worried that her window would be bricked up too and, seeing it as the only possible means to see her sister again, she made the fateful decision to take matters into her own hands.

On the morning of 22 August 1961, a day before her fifty-ninth birthday, she had made up her mind to get to West Berlin, no matter how. The window had still not been bricked up. Her flat was on the third floor. The fire brigade in West Berlin had begun to organize jumping sheets to help others in her situation, but how long would they take to come? In her panic, Ida decided she could not wait. She threw a few personal belongings out of the window, followed by her duvet and some blankets in the hope that they would cushion her fall onto the hard grey cobblestones, three storeys below. Then, she jumped. As her body crashed into the pavement, Ida was fatally wounded. She died on her way to the hospital.

Ida Siekmann's tragic death quickly became politicized on both sides of the Berlin Wall. In West Berlin, her funeral at the Seestraße cemetery was attended by a number of high-ranking politicians, including Mayor Willy Brandt. The urn was interred draped in the colours of the city. A memorial was also erected where she had died and it would be visited by politicians who were keen to have their photo taken with it to signal support for West Berlin. Among them were the West German Chancellor Konrad Adenauer and President Kennedy, neither of whom had done anything to help people like Ida Siekmann when they were cut off from friends and family in the West. In fact, Adenauer's first visit to the city coincided with the day that Ida died, nine days after the border had been closed.

The West German press sensationalized her death, labelling it as her 'deadly jump into freedom'. In reality, little is known about Ida's motives. As she was originally from Gorken, an area ceded to Poland after the Second World War, and lived on her own according to the records, it is not unlikely that her sister in West Berlin was her closest contact after she had found a new home in Berlin. She had lived in the Soviet sector for over fifteen years, happy to walk to her sister a few streets down. The fact that she did not move West then, as millions before her had done, would indicate that her motivations for the jump were far more likely to be of a private rather than political nature. As the doors were bricked up, panic broke out in the street as is well documented by other residents. The fifty-eight-year-old might have contemplated the prospect of spending her retirement alone in her bricked-up flat with no one to care for her as she got older. One can only speculate as to the true motives behind Ida's despair, but neither the press in the West nor the police in the East did her the courtesy. The East German police report flatly states: 'On 22.08.1961, around 6.50 a.m., Ida Siekmann, who lived alone . . . threw herself out of the window of her flat which was in the front part of the building, on the third floor . . . S. was removed by the Western fire brigade. The pool of blood was covered with sand.'[10] A martyr in the West, Ida was not to be remembered in the East at all. The only interest the GDR authorities had in her case was that it served to show how urgently the remaining gaps in the Berlin Wall had to be closed to avoid further bloodshed.

Two days after Ida Siekmann's death, twenty-four-year-old tailor Günter Litfin threw himself into the Humboldthafen bay in Berlin-Mitte to swim to West Berlin. A couple of days before the border was closed, he had furnished a flat in Charlottenburg where he planned to move in order to be able to continue to work there. He had completed his apprenticeship in this Western sector and since then commuted back and forth like nearly half a million Berliners. The events of 13 August had taken him by surprise and he began to investigate possibilities to move to West Berlin. On 24 August 1961, at 4 p.m., Günter climbed over the crude wall by the Humboldthafen, perhaps to cross over the bridge there. But guards spotted him. They were transport police officers who had been trained to regulate traffic rather than fire live ammunition at those trying to leave the GDR. They had strict orders to shoot but never received proper firearms training. The two policemen followed protocol, confronting Günter, ordering him to freeze. The young man panicked and ran. The guards fired warning shots. Günter knew this was his last chance to get back to his life in Charlottenburg. In a desperate effort to make it there, he jumped into the water, attempting to swim the 60 metres across. Now, the two policemen aimed directly at him and fired several shots, one of which hit Günter in the head and killed him.

Three hundred West Berliners watched the horrific scenes from the other side of the bay as the Eastern fire brigade was finally able to recover the body three hours later. This time, the GDR authorities could not remain silent as they had done with Ida Siekmann. In a cynical attempt to disgrace Günter, they launched a vicious media attack on him in *Neues Deutschland*, portraying him as a deviant criminal and playing to the mores of the time as they called him a 'homosexual who was well known in certain circles in West Berlin'. They even went as far as to claim that 'the Volkspolizei caught him red-handed in criminal activities not far from Friedrichstraße station. He avoided arrest by jumping into the Humboldthafen where he met his death.'[11] The same article also jeered that 'they will probably build "Puppe" ["Dolly"] a memorial in West Berlin'. Another person's death at the Berlin Wall was politicized, the individual behind the file callously discredited.

The GDR government was keen to limit further bloodshed in Berlin, especially in one of the 'hottest' periods of the Cold War, where such individual cases always had the potential to escalate into a calamitous conflict between the superpowers. It hastily fortified the Berlin Wall by any and all means.[12] John Bainbridge's report for the *New Yorker* of 27 October 1962 paints a vivid picture of the frantic efforts to close the border:

> At the base of the wall, there is usually a row of upright prefabricated concrete slabs about four and a half feet square and a foot thick. These were not set into excavated foundations but merely laid on the ground. As a result, when the ground heaved during last spring's thaws the wall fell down in a few places, and East German workers had to put it up again. On top of the slabs there may be a couple of rows of regulation-size concrete building blocks and, above them, a piece of smoothly finished concrete about thirty inches long and twelve inches square. All these blocks and slabs are held together with mortar that drips messily down the sides. Surmounting the structure at intervals of about three feet are Y-shaped pieces of metal, on which are strung strands of barbed wire that have become rusty. These are the usual components, but they are not always assembled in the same way. Sometimes, the master builders slapped a second piece of finished concrete on top of the first. Other times, they didn't. Occasionally, they put up a stretch using building blocks exclusively. Not surprisingly, the wall varies a good deal in height. As a rule, it is about ten feet high, but in some places it is twice that, and it may vary by a couple of feet as many as three or four times in the course of a city block. There is, however, one consistent thing about the wall, and that is shoddy workmanship. It looks, as a Berlin sculptor has remarked, as if it had been thrown together by a band of backward apprentice stonemasons when drunk.[13]

In the end, the GDR achieved what it wanted. The flow of skilled labour to West Germany was stopped. Between 1961 and 1989, 140 people would lose their lives in desperate attempts to cross the border. Eventually, the number of incidents at the Wall sank as it was secured more tightly. As watchtowers, anti-vehicle devices, searchlights and other additions fortified the Wall, it became increasingly unlikely that one could make it across to the other side successfully. This limited the number of people who tried to do so and thwarted many attempts before the would-be escapees entered the 'death strip'. While many more attempts were famously undertaken, some in hot-air balloons and through tunnels, the vast majority of those who contemplated moving West legally now simply resigned themselves to their fate. Meanwhile, most East Germans continued with their lives as they had done before 13 August 1961. They heard about the events in Berlin in the newspapers or on the radio, talked about it with friends and family, but were otherwise more concerned with housing, work and their private lives. If the GDR could develop reasonable living conditions in East Germany, most of its citizens could live with the Wall in Berlin.

Work Hard, Play Hard

Wismar, Mecklenburg, 1 May 1961. At four o'clock in the afternoon a beaming Jutta Mierse waved down at the crowds in the harbour from the deck of the GTMS *Fritz Heckert* as it left the Baltic port to go on its maiden voyage. The blonde stewardess would work at the dance hall and day café of the brand-new cruise ship for the next seven years. The young woman's nickname on board was 'Max', and she got on well with many of the other 180 crew members who sailed under Captain Willi Leidig. As they began to set up work routines together and practise rescue manoeuvres, they also found time to enjoy the eleven-day journey. They baulked at the price of goods in Helsinki shops. They marvelled at the treasures in the Winter Palace in Leningrad (now St Petersburg). They were touched by the enthusiastic welcome they received in Riga where thousands of people had flocked to the port to greet them. When they returned to Wismar on 12 May, Jutta was tired and worn out from her first voyage as 'the balance between work and rest had yet to be found', as she put it. She sought to find relaxation in the cinemas, clubs and restaurants of Wismar, while the *Fritz Heckert* was being prepared for its next journey. It was during this time that Jutta met a young plumber called Erich Kuhfeld who also worked on board the cruise ship. They got married and would sail on the *Fritz Heckert* together between 1961 and 1968.[14]

State-owned cruise ships like the *Fritz Heckert* were one way in which the GDR authorities attempted to offer their citizens a comparable standard of living to that achieved during the economic miracle years in the West or perhaps even trump it. But this was not without problems. Due to a permanent shortage of oil, the *Fritz Heckert*'s diesel engine was supported by a gas turbine – temperamental new technology that frequently failed and had to be repaired en route. Another issue with sea voyages quickly became obvious once the Berlin Wall had been built: taking people to non-socialist countries bore the risk of losing passengers in every port. When the *Fritz Heckert* set off from Rostock on 3 January 1962 to take its 400 guests down to the North African coast and through the Mediterranean, the Free German Trade Union Federation (FDGB), which organized these and other holidays, had tried to ensure that the backgrounds of those on board had been checked so that the voyage would remain free of the embarrassment of people leaving the GDR via its own 8,000-ton vessel. Sure that the passengers were aboard to amuse themselves in the cinema, dance halls, swimming pools and bars of the cruise ship, the tour went ahead as planned, including a trip to Casablanca where guests enjoyed the local nightlife. After a night in the Moroccan city, the crew noticed that twenty-four passengers were missing. They had arranged flights back to Europe via the West German consulate, a journey that received widespread coverage in the West German media. When another three guests went missing in Tunis, the captain received orders to return home immediately, even though a heavy storm had been brewing over the Mediterranean.

The leadership of the *Fritz Heckert* asked for permission to dock on the Portuguese coast to sit out the storm but were told to return at once to avoid further embarrassment if more passengers disappeared. On 21 January, as the ship made its way through the Bay of Biscay and up the French Atlantic coast, the terrible storm began. It was the worst Erich and Jutta Kuhfeld had ever experienced. As the guests lay on the floor in their cabins and feared for their lives, the cruise ship began to swing up and down on the waves with dangerous velocity. Cracks appeared around the windows, and the gas turbines caught fire, which was luckily anticipated by the crew who stood by with fire extinguishers. The *Fritz Heckert* was so susceptible to the currents that its course had to be corrected on various occasions, and just when it was on the home stretch, sailing through the Kattegat between Denmark and Sweden, the electrical system broke down temporarily.[15] When the shaken passengers left the ship after a journey that was memorable in all the wrong ways, the entire saga was kept under wraps. The authorities decided not to sail to capitalist countries any more and various technological improvements were undertaken on the ship. Eventually, it was decommissioned in 1972 and taken to the port of Wismar where it was used as a floating hotel for workers.

Other cruise ships such as the *Völkerfreundschaft* (Friendship of the Nations) continued their voyages well into the 1980s. It was only sold in 1985 after twenty-five years of active service for the GDR during which time it had sailed to 117 ports in twenty-five countries. Its most dramatic journey was a trip to the Cuban capital of Havana in October 1962 where it crossed the American line of blockade during the missile crisis with German and Czech holidaymakers on board. Accompanied by a US destroyer for three hours, the cruise liner continued its course to Havana and eventually docked there safely. Other incidents included a collision with a West German submarine chaser which attempted to help East Germans off the ship. Eventually, the oldest of the cruise ships (it had originally been launched by Sweden in 1948 before the GDR bought it) was in need of substantial rebuilding, too much for East Germany to undertake. The *Völkerfreundschaft* continued to be used as a cruise ship, most recently under the name MV *Astoria*. It was sold last in July 2021 to American tour operators who intended to use it in and around Portugal. At the time of writing, it was the oldest passenger liner still in use.

It has often been a point of criticism that the cruise liners were merely a propaganda project for the GDR – an expensive indulgence that was fraught in its technical execution and served only the lucky few who obtained a ticket. But the *Fritz Heckert* alone would allow 63,000 passengers an opportunity to go on a cruise between 1960 and 1972 – that's one in every 270 citizens. In those twelve years it sailed to fifty-nine ports in twenty-four countries, even if it was mainly in the Baltic Sea after its problem-laden journeys into the Mediterranean and the Atlantic.

The FDGB collated monies donated by citizens and state-owned companies (VEBs) to create many different kinds of subsidized holiday opportunities for the masses. The vast majority of GDR citizens went on holiday within the Eastern Bloc where the FDGB or the VEBs themselves offered places in their holiday homes. Many of these were in seaside destinations such as the popular island of Rügen, but there were also hotels, campsites and bungalows in mountain regions, forests or lakeside resorts. Margit Jatzlau, a technical drawer in a factory, remembered how popular holiday places were in her workplace. Almost everyone applied and managers had the difficult task to decide who would get to go each year. Paid holidays were enshrined in the constitution, so getting time off was not a problem, but the availability of affordable holiday accommodation still was. Some places were reserved for those who had achieved commendations at work, but the rest could be allocated to anyone.

While it is often claimed that the best places were only given to those who were eager to tow the party line, Margit remembered this as a fair process whereby 'everyone got to go every four to five years or so'.[16] Ultimately it depended on those who ran the VEBs and other workplaces how they allocated places for subsidized holidays, and recollections of how fair the process was vary accordingly from praise to scorn. There were also private opportunities to rent holiday homes which were advertised in newspapers and ranged from simple chalets to luxury accommodation with swimming pools and West German TV reception. Young people between sixteen and twenty-five could arrange holidays through an agency set up by the FDJ. Overall, holidays were a staple of family life in the GDR.

The vast majority of GDR citizens went on holiday within the GDR itself. For people like Margit, who grew up in a working class household, foreign holidays were financially out of reach even where they were legally possible. Later, when families wanted to go on holidays without arranging this privately or through their work-place, they could book it at the state-run travel agency, which had branches across the GDR. It dealt with everything from train tick-ets to visa applications, and holidaymakers could decide whether they wanted to travel individually and arrange their own holiday or in a group with a fixed programme and travel guide. Former GDR travel guide Rolf Beyer from Leipzig explained that the East Ger-man agency would be in contact with their counterparts in the other socialist countries to regulate the number of tourists they would allow in and out. He would direct tours to Poland, Hungary and even Cuba,[17] although the latter remained out of reach for most people who were not on a direct work or student exchange due to the expenses involved. The amount of money that could be exchanged proved to be another hurdle. Due to the huge economic imbalance between socialist countries, currency fluctuations caused by holidaymakers were feared and so only small amounts of East German marks could be exchanged in Eastern Bloc countries, not enough to pay for food and other expenses once there. The solution was that East Germans would fill up their Trabant cars (affection-ately known as 'Trabis') with tins and other groceries at home and take what they could on holiday with them, so that they still had enough of their allowed foreign currency left to buy souvenirs and foreign food such as the desired exotic fruits that were permanently out of stock at home.

Despite such teething problems, GDR holidays were popular and afforded East Germans an experience not entirely unlike that of their Western counterparts. Both countries enshrined eighteen days off work a year in law. In the West only a third of households trav-elled away from home at the beginning of the 1960s and even by 1968 the majority still stayed in the country rather than venture abroad.[18] With organized and heavily subsidized holidays, Ulbricht's regime had managed to create a remarkably successful system that allowed the masses to enjoy themselves in the 1960s. This helped calm the tensions caused by the Wall.

Holidays were one part of a wider programme that the GDR government wanted to pursue in the 1960s to build a settled and prosperous society. The frantic repression of the late 1950s began to make way for a readjustment of relations between the ruling SED party and its people. Between 1961 and 1965, nearly 16,000 prisoners were released who had been incarcerated for 'political crimes'[19] as the government was on a course of reconciliation. Ulbricht also realized that with the flow of people stopped both ways, he could no longer blame any expressions of discontent from the workers, such as strike action or demonstrations, on 'Western agitators'. Now that he held his people captive, he had to offer them a life that was worth living. This not only demanded higher living standards, but also the creation of a society where people felt they had a stake and gained satisfaction from the hard work expected of them. Ulbricht wanted to win the German competition not only on an economic level but also by creating the better society he had promised.

The New Economic System – Making Socialism Work

Sonneberg, Thuringia, 1964. The Head of Development at the Institute for Toys, Siegfried Umbreit, was delighted when he was offered a career opportunity in Berlin. He had steadily worked his way up from his humble origins as a builder to more and more sophisticated work with wood and metal before he got involved with the design of toys at the VEB in Sonneberg. There he worked under Professor Erwin Andrä, who shared his passion for design and functionality. It was he who recommended his Sonneberg colleague to lead a new department for toys at the Ministry for Light Industry in Berlin. Siegfried was thrilled. The professor's word was enough to get this huge career jump approved and the fifty-year-old suddenly earned 1,200 marks a month rather than the 700 he had received in Thuringia. It was worth moving to the capital and he even considered it worth leaving the church for. This was the only condition the authorities pinned on his new job. Siegfried reluctantly agreed – he had just inherited his parents' house and had to pay out his five siblings.[20]

The new Department for Toys which Siegfried Umbreit was building up involved several sub-sections such as 'Stuffed Toys and Dolls', which he took over himself, 'Wooden Toys' and 'Mechanical and Electromechanical Toys', each with its own specialized engineers. Their main task was to oversee the development of high-quality products and quality control. The vast majority of these toys were made for the export market, which was a lucrative source of revenue for the GDR economy.

Indeed, the GDR became a leading manufacturer of toys in Europe. A previous leader of the VEB Sonneberg, the GDR's largest producer, still maintains that 'Sonni', as it was affectionately called, 'produced the highest standards in Europe'.[21] Around 8,000 Sonnebergers were employed at the works, making toys which would be tested and approved by Siegfried Umbreit's department in Berlin. The output was then shipped to thirty-two different countries, including West Germany. There, new inventions like a doll which could be taken into the bath became immensely popular. As it turned out, children's tastes and desires transcended the ideological divides of the Cold War. In the Soviet Union too, East German dolls were a hit and ad-hoc orders of over 20,000 were sent frequently. As this proved such a fruitful source of revenue, the GDR scaled up production in the course of the 1960s and 1970s so that by the 1980s, 87 per cent of toys produced in the GDR were exported rather than sold internally.[22]

What seemed an astonishingly capitalist thing to do for a communist regime was part of a wider plan to make the GDR's isolated economy work. Walter Ulbricht was astute in his realization that 'We have little plaster, so we'll have to think faster'[23] – meaning we do not have much by way of natural resources so we will have to build up an economy based on sophisticated industry and skilled work such as new technology and desirable consumer items. He believed that the national economy would grow by 30 per cent through higher education, something that appealed to the new young elites, including people like Hans Modrow. The rising star of the SED was in his early thirties then. Ambitious and academically minded, he wanted to gain qualifications and experience in the real world rather than becoming a career politician. When Walter Ulbricht began to put an emphasis on specialized skills and asked his young cadres to set a good example for the rest of society, Modrow did not have to be asked twice: 'Finally! This met my own ambitions exactly.' He began a dissertation on the sociological development of leader personalities for the industrial sector.[24]

The wider policy to modernize, specialize and improve the GDR economy was laid out at the 6th Congress of the SED in 1963. Many of the delegates would later note that there was a real sense of optimism in the air when the discussion centred around 'building socialism' rather than communism. This suggested that Ulbricht was happy to put the brakes on the relentless pace of his economic reforms and reflect upon the mistakes made in the 1950s. By 1963, the GDR economy had reached a good platform from which to launch the modernization programme. The Soviet Union had begun to send food and supplies in the wake of the border closure in Berlin in a (mostly successful) attempt to calm the situation through material welfare. In view of what Ulbricht knew to be fickle Soviet support, the politburo had set up several commissions and working groups to come up with strategies to make the GDR economy viable without permanently depending on Moscow. Ulbricht accepted the conclusions these think-tanks presented him with. By the end of 1962, he admitted that the 'theory of the prevalence of politics over economics' must come to an end – 'economic tasks will have priority'.[25] At the Party Congress in 1963, a policy U-turn was announced in the shape of the 'New Economic System' (NES).

The NES was so radical in its move away from planning

principles that the West German newspaper *Süddeutsche Zeitung* even speculated that the GDR might be 'returning to a form of capitalism'.[26] More responsibility and freedom over development and production methods was handed back to the individual VEBs. Economic planning would take on the form of a wider framework with more room to manoeuvre. This was in the hope that highly specialized companies with long and proud traditions of research and development would get a free hand to do what they do best: develop world class technology to help the GDR's lucrative export industry. Carl Zeiss Jena, for example, a company that to this day creates world class lenses and other high-precision engineering in the field of optics, complained in January 1962 that the demands placed on it by the centralized economic planning were stopping it from 'concentrating on the development of the data processing technology needed for the completion of Zeiss' own measuring devices'.[27] For any central board to intervene in the planning and development of a high-tech company like Carl Zeiss was sheer madness and the frustration radiating back from the confident staff of such high-calibre enterprises was palpable. Ulbricht seems to have listened. For his NES, he enlisted people such as Erich Apel, one of the rocket engineers who had worked on Nazi military projects in Peenemünde during the Second World War. Apel was made president of the new economic planning commission and understood the needs and frustrations of his highly specialized colleagues across the country. Money was invested in technology that was groundbreaking and genuinely new, mainly in the field of electronics, manufacturing of specialist devices and space exploration.

The results of this economic reform were immediately visible. East Germany's GDP was higher in 1964 than it had been when the NES was introduced and this trend continued while the policy was active. Between 1961 and 1967, even the West German Cologne Centre of Historical Social Science reckoned that the GDR was beginning to catch up with the West, having advanced by around 5 per cent in this period.[28] While this may not seem rapid, given that the economic output was still only about half that of the FRG, there was a general sense that things were moving forward and the GDR was becoming a stable state with a viable economic system. This in turn raised both the possibility and the expectation that East Germany's society should be modernized in step with its economy.

Housing

Halle, Saxony-Anhalt, 15 July 1964, 2.30 p.m. Horst Sindermann, First Secretary of the SED district administration, was sweating in the summer heat as he laid the foundation stone for a new town, Halle-Neustadt. Jovially abbreviated to Ha-Neu (pronounced 'Hanoi') by East Germans, the utopian building project foresaw the design of an entirely new concept of how societies could live and work together. Sindermann had a broad smile on his face. A plastic helmet on his head, he shook hands with workers, leaving enough time for the photographer to immortalize this visible solidarity of the SED with its people – a fitting symbol of the new society the GDR was building with new towns like Halle-Neustadt.

The aim of the ambitious project was to provide 70,000 workers, mainly from the nearby chemical works in Schkopau and Leuna, with modern living. The run-down Old Town of Halle had been largely spared by the bombs and artillery fire of the Second World War but the economic problems of the post-war years had allowed for little investment, and housing standards became increasingly inadequate. The new estates could be built on the cheap thanks to the development of prefabricated concrete blocks, but they would provide warm, well-insulated, spacious housing with electricity and hot water. What to an outsider seemed like rows and rows of monotonous blocks became hugely desirable living spaces to GDR citizens. One of the architects of Ha-Neu, Peter Morgner, remembered: 'Yes, everybody wanted to move there. In this way, great diversity evolved. In Neustadt, the professors lived next door to the taxi driver. [Pause] Not any more.'[29] By the time that the Berlin Wall fell, over 90,000 people lived in Halle-Neustadt, using its infrastructure, childcare facilities, parks and communal spaces adorned by fountains, sculptures and wall art.

There were problems too. The GDR regime decided not to have street names in Ha-Neu and instead invented a complicated system of numbers for blocks, which was not only so confusing that the inhabitants had to come up with their own ways of remembering where they lived, but many also found it anonymous and claustrophobic. Architect Morgner himself bemoaned the monotonous design: 'If you live in a block with a digit or number, you begin to get the impression you don't live in a real city but on a chicken farm or a concentration camp.'[30] But people found ways around that. They celebrated birthdays in communal party rooms, hung up their washing together on the lines provided outside and had barbecues with their neighbours. For the first time a sense of normality and quality of life was beginning to emerge in the GDR.

Trabant

Fürstenwalde/Spree, Brandenburg, 1965. Inge Schmidt gasped as her husband turned up at their flat in a 'marvellously beautiful blue-grey Trabi'. Her unbridled joy at the sight of the car quickly gave way to concern as the thirty-seven-year-old bookkeeper ran the finances through her head. 'For God's sake, what if we can't afford the payments?' The young family had moved into a bigger and more modern flat which cost over 50 marks a month, nearly twice as much as the previous one. But she need not have worried. Waiting times for the GDR's new Trabants were so long, often running over ten years, that the little two-stroke cars retained their value extremely well. A used car would find a buyer close to the original price, sometimes even more. If the family ran into financial trouble, selling their new Trabi would not be a problem. Inge's husband was optimistic. Selling the car was the last thing on his mind. His parents-in-law had tragically died within days of each other a couple of years earlier, forcing Inge to sell their grocery store in Berlin which the family had run for generations. It had nearly broken her heart and the little Trabi was just the bit of luck the young family needed. 'We went everywhere in it, it was just beautiful,' Inge remembered. The family embarked on city trips to Prague, holidays by the sea near Rostock and to the scenic lake districts of Angermünde, closer to home. The next Trabi was immediately applied for in the full knowledge that selling their first one would easily help pay for it.[31]

The Trabant has now become an icon. Still beloved by many enthusiasts in eastern Germany to this day, in the West, the drab, outdated car symbolized the underachievements of the GDR as a whole. Its undersized engine produced only 23bhp even in later models, while the smell and sound of its output were distinctly reminiscent of decades gone by when models that were practically unchanged since 1963 rolled across the open inner-German border in 1989. But this is not how many East Germans see and recall it. Even if waiting times were long and frustrating, car ownership rose steadily. In 1965, Inge still belonged to a very lucky minority as only 8.2 per cent of all households owned a car, but this figure had more than doubled over the previous five years. By 1988, just over half of all East German households had a car,[32] which was only slightly behind West Germany and on a par with Britain.[33] This gave many people a sense of freedom, personal enjoyment and achievement. For working class families car ownership had previously seemed out of reach. The Weimar Republic had made no real headway into affordable, mass produced cars, and while Hitler had promised that he would, introducing the aptly named 'People's Car', the Volkswagen, he had dangled the prospect in front of workers and never fulfilled it as the war directed resources elsewhere. If the Trabi had to be applied for a few years in advance, this did not seem a big deal to most workers in the 1960s. One day, they would have their own car. And when they did, its air-cooled engine and simple mechanics made it durable and easy to fix.

A well-looked-after Trabi became the pride and joy of many East German families in the 1960s when it was still comparable to the small cars of the West such as the VW Beetle or the Mini. The trouble began when the government refused to work on technical innovation and only allowed incremental changes in engine size or interior design. By the 1980s, the Trabi had indeed become the dated and underpowered relic that the West so ridiculed.

In the early 1960s, however, the Trabi helped to support Ulbricht's New Economic System and get the public on board. A special new edition had been developed for the 6th Congress of the SED in 1963: the 'Sachsenring Trabant 601'. Built in Zwickau, Saxony, it bore resemblance to the British Triumph Herald, following the same design techniques, which were indeed modern and considered fashionable at the time. It had a little more legroom, a bigger boot and came in different editions once mass produced a year later. One could get an estate version, a DeLuxe edition with two-tone colouring or the *Sonderwunsch* (Special Edition) which came with optional fog lamps and other additions, embodying the spirit of progress Ulbricht's economic reforms were designed to evoke.

But the economic realities caught up with East German car manufacturing quickly. Some problems could be circumvented. The lack of aluminium and other metals, for example, was side-stepped by using a material known as Duroplast for the body. This was a mix of synthetic resin, cotton waste from the Soviet Union, paper and additional chemicals that were pressed into a durable material that proved to be astonishingly useful. It did not rust, was lightweight and when the government threw a few cars down a cliff to stress test them, they showed the same safety standards as comparable small cars at the time. But the process of making Duroplast proved to be arduous and time-consuming. The time the material took to harden when it was pressed was much longer than all the other steps in the production process, slowing everything down and reducing productivity and output. This was only one of the many headaches triggered by the ongoing crisis over raw materials. Only small incremental changes were introduced each time a new Trabant model came out, making it laughably outdated within a decade.

The name 'Trabant' itself dates back to the origins of the car in the 1950s. A word of Slavic roots, it meant 'companion' just like the Russian 'Sputnik'. As the latter was the name of the first ever artificial satellite shot into space in 1957, it was associated with technological development and the manic space craze of the time. The Trabi in the 1960s represented wider optimism about the future of the GDR and the possibility, not only of the country's economic survival, but of achievements its people could one day be proud of. This was particularly true of the car industry and its evocative role in the national German psyche. Unlike other socialist states such as Poland, the USSR or Yugoslavia, the GDR never really imported technology from Italy (as the others had done with Fiat) or elsewhere. Car technology was the way to the hearts and minds of East Germans.

Youth

Kino Babylon, East Berlin, 25 February 1966. *Alfons Zitterbacke* premiered at the iconic cinema in Berlin-Mitte. Over 2.5 million people would view this popular family movie in East German cinemas over the next twenty-three years. Key to its success was the eponymous protagonist, a cheeky ten-year-old boy. Affectionately nicknamed 'Alfi' by his mother, he struggles at school where he gets bullied for his last name, which translates as 'Wobble-Cheek'. He feels misunderstood by his teachers. Alfi's father has extremely high expectations of him and frequently criticizes him for his supposed physical shortcomings. In one scene, he squeezes Alfi's arm and tells him that there are no muscles there, 'nothing, no courage, no strength – try harder so that you will one day be a real Zitterbacke!' Only his friend Micki is always loyal to him even though she does not always understand Alfi's antics either. Annoyed and keen to prove himself, the boy decides to become a cosmonaut,[34] tackling a series of comical challenges he sets himself to train for space exploration. He begins by eating dozens of raw eggs to build up his muscles. Assuming that cosmonauts only eat food from tubes, he then embarks on a diet of toothpaste, mustard and anchovy paste before training for the weightlessness of space on a swing ride at the local funfair. All of this makes him violently sick. He also gets into trouble at school as he turns up with cotton wool in his ears in an attempt to get used to the near-total silence of space. Micki and Alfi eventually decide to hitchhike to Moscow so that they can attend the cosmonaut training centre there. But this plan fails as well, and the two friends have to come up with a new one.

The film was so popular because it captured the zeitgeist. Many children and teenagers were fascinated by the idea of space exploration. With Yuri Gagarin the Soviets had sent the first man into space in 1961, and in 1963 Valentina Tereshkova became the first woman, orbiting the earth forty-eight times in her three-day solo tour. When the pair visited the GDR in October 1963, they received a hero's welcome. Many people were genuinely excited to see the famous cosmonauts.[35] They were relatable. A steel and textile worker respectively, they seemed to prove that anyone can achieve their ambitions. Here were two young working class people, still in their twenties, who had become space explorers and internationally celebrated heroes. The idea enthused many boys and girls in the GDR who began to dream of becoming cosmonauts themselves one day. Alfons Zitterbacke, an ordinary boy with ordinary problems, gently and humorously represented their fantasies.

The GDR authorities were keen to channel this enthusiasm of the young. One means of doing so was the Free German Youth, the mass organization for young Germans aged between fourteen and twenty-five. The problem was that the initial enthusiasm for it had begun to wane. When young people such as Regina Faustmann had joined it in the late 1940s and early 1950s, they had usually done so because they wanted to help 'build the new young democracy we had been gifted'.[36] Over two thirds of the age group had flocked to the FDJ by 1952, but the widespread dissatisfaction in 1953 and the shockwaves of the popular uprising on 16 and 17 June in particular, had led to a mass exodus with numbers falling sharply to around 40 per cent of the cohort. While there was a mild recovery in the years that followed, numbers never returned to pre-1952 levels.[37] The FDJ retained its stuffy image as an organ of Ulbricht's government and was led by morally conservative, even prudish, individuals like Erich Honecker who was responsible for Youth Affairs within the Central Committee. He considered Western influences on youth culture 'decadent' and 'morally corrupt'. Modern dances such as the wildly popular Twist were particularly frowned upon. As a result, the FDJ had lost its touch and contained not even half of the fourteen- to twenty-five-year-olds in 1963. This was despite a giant budget of 100 million marks with which it ran its programmes such as holiday schemes and events.[38] Ulbricht was unhappy with this, but knew that he needed to go beyond Honecker to find answers and ideas for reform. He found his man in Kurt Turba.

Turba was the thirty-four-year-old editor-in-chief of the FDJ's student newspaper, *Forum*. It was meant to be a propaganda outlet for FDJ directives but became a relatively independent, modern and provocative paper under Turba, who ended up embroiled in permanent conflict with the FDJ leadership as a result. Ulbricht read the *Forum* often as he deemed it to be a good indicator of mood among young intellectuals beyond the slanted view he would receive from Honecker who was ever keen to promote his own career. In July 1963, when Honecker was away on holiday, Ulbricht summoned Kurt Turba and asked, 'You talk about problems in your paper, don't you want to tackle the problems in reality?'[39] Turba gave Ulbricht a number of reasons why he was not the man to do so, including the fact that he was not from a working class background (his father had worked in a bank) and that he was in charge of the rebellious newspaper *Forum*. Ulbricht merely laughed and asked sardonically, 'Why did you think I wanted you in the first place!?'[40] They sat down and Turba explained why and to what extent young intellectuals were fed up with the FDJ and more widely the situation in the GDR. They felt patronized and hemmed in by the stiffness and old-fashioned morality of the regime. Ulbricht was horrified. According to Turba, he ended the conversation by saying, 'Well, Comrade Turba, if only half of what you say is true, the situation is terrible!'[41] It was a done deal: the journalist would become the leader of the Youth Commission of the politburo and was immediately charged with the task of re-engaging young people.

Turba worked all summer to create a communiqué for the politburo that would convince young intellectuals that the SED genuinely wanted to be more inclusive towards young people. The result was published in the SED newspaper *Neues Deutschland* on 21 September 1963. Under the headline 'Trust and Responsibility to the Youth', the party explained that it wanted its intentions understood as 'encouragement to think independently, not as dogma'.[42] It went on to complain that 'too often our young people aren't trusted enough' and demanded that 'Once and for all, we need to put an end to a practice whereby teenagers are tempted into opposition through the bureaucratic behaviour of leaders and teachers, through nagging and stubbornness.'[43] Even the constant question regarding Western influences on youth culture was addressed with remarkable tolerance: 'We see dancing as a legitimate expression of happiness and joie de vivre. Some people seem to find it difficult to grasp the difference between a dancing event and a political gathering . . . Nobody is telling young people that they have to express their feelings exclusively in Waltz or Tango rhythms. Which music young people dance to is up to their taste, so long as they stay tasteful!'[44] And with this, the Twist was back on.

Keen to show that deeds would follow these words, some political leaders took to the dancefloor themselves. Horst Schumann, First Secretary of the Central Council of the FDJ, looked a little comical in his suit and with a receding hairline as he showed his best hip shake in front of the camera. But the message was loud and clear: if the youth wanted beats, Beatles and bass, they could have it. The only obligation was that the ever-present 40/60 ratio of foreign and East German music be maintained. GDR bands sprung up everywhere and imitated the American style they adored. Manfred Krug's 'Twist in der Nacht' (Twist in the Night), Susi Schuster's 'Jodel-Twist' and 'Oho, Susann' by Die Amigos were all 1963 hits that got the GDR's youth on their feet. With the beats, new youth cultures developed too. Mainly in the cities, boys grew their hair longer to look like their idols from Britain and the US; girls shortened their skirts. There was little that parents, teachers and FDJ leaders could do about it. The party had told them not to be dogmatic and to let it be.

When the youth met for their next Germany Convention in May 1964, half a million youngsters turned up, including 25,000 from West Germany. The programme and accompanying music was broadcast to the entire country via the Berliner Rundfunk radio station under the title *DT64* (short for the festival's name – Deutschlandtreffen 1964). They played an astonishing amount of beat music during the festival itself, even when compared to West German radio stations at the time.[45] After the festival was over, *DT64* became a regular programme that played fashionable pop music interspersed with casual chat every afternoon. This was so popular that the West German stations RIAS and SFB felt compelled to introduce similar programmes.[46]

The SED leadership was very satisfied with its efforts to win back the youth. In a self-congratulatory statement the politburo concluded that the Germany Convention clearly showed 'that the youth of the German Democratic Republic has a healthy relationship to its state . . . All speculation that the youth of the GDR was against the state and that the state was dogmatic has been disproved by the Germany Convention.'[47]

Women

Beiersdorf, Saxony, 1965. 'She should do what? Why?' Karin Tobianke's father stared into the face of his daughter's physics teacher in disbelief. The thirty-six-year-old had rushed into school after a hard day's work at the quarry and still had a million things to do on the little farm the family ran at home. But he had answered the invitation to see his oldest daughter's teacher, not really knowing what to expect. She had always done reasonably well at school. While never top of the class, her grades had been good on the whole and perfect in history, her favourite subject. Karin's teacher patiently explained again that she was a very capable girl and that he would like to put her forward for one of the coveted places at the extended secondary school (*Erweiterte Oberschule*; EOS) to gain qualifications for university entry.

This came as a complete shock to Karin too. Her mother was a poor teenager when she arrived in Germany in 1945 as a refugee and had to give up her training as a paediatric nurse in Breslau. She was a housewife and famer now, looking after the animals and crops while her husband, a trained carpenter, worked in the quarry by day and helped on the farm when he got home. No one in her family had ever progressed to a higher level of schooling, let alone to university, and her father was painfully conscious of this. He always attempted to speak a clear high German, rather than his native dialect, when in the presence of strangers to conceal his humble background. His biggest fear was that Karin might fail. The embarrassment! What would he tell his family and friends? But in the end, he gave in. Karin had long suspected that her father had been more ambitious than his situation would suggest and seeing his daughter thrive filled him with pride. 'Go on then, girl,' he said to her, 'but don't bring shame on us and fail!'

The words rang heavy in Karin's ears as she struggled through her first year at the EOS where she felt like a small fish in a very large pond. But she worked hard and by the second year she had proved that the trust her parents and teachers had put in her was well placed, mastering both the academic side of her curriculum as well as the obligatory vocational part. For the latter, Karin could choose between three pathways: an agricultural one in dairy production, an engineering one with train technology or a metalworker course at the local motorworks. She chose the latter and when she was finished, all pathways, vocational and academic, were open to the girl who grew up on a farm, expecting to be a sales assistant at a local shop. In the end, she decided to go on to further study in

Dresden to become a history and Russian teacher. She was paid study money: 80 marks at first, then over 100 marks due to her excellent results. Karin was even able to visit the university's partner institute in the Russian city of Smolensk in 1972, an experience which left a lifelong impression on her from the cultural experiences gathered at Orthodox church services and in people's homes, to a visit to Lenin's mausoleum in Moscow which filled the young woman with awe.

The trajectory of Karin's life from the mid-1960s was a direct result of deliberate state intervention. For both pragmatic and ideological reasons, the GDR was keen, right from the beginning, to create gender equality and encourage women to take part in society at all levels, on a par with men. While state-produced imagery and cultural output created an ideal of the working woman, reality initially lagged behind. Women in factories, laboratories and offices often appeared in newspaper articles and TV features, but by 1960 only a quarter of students at universities were female and the ratio at vocational schools was only marginally higher.[48] As historian Mary Fulbrook has rightly pointed out, the government underestimated that the obstacles to full gender equality at home and at work went beyond enshrining equal pay in law and creating opportunities for childcare; they included 'not only practical but also psychological barriers to equality of opportunity'.[49] Frustrated with this, the SED looked into the matter in 1961 and concluded that 'a completely unsatisfactory proportion of girls and women fill middle and upper leadership positions despite the fact that 68.4% of all women between 16 and 60 who can work do so'.[50]

With astonishing honesty, a party communiqué, published in *Neues Deutschland* in December 1961, laid bare the problems that women still encountered in the workplace and at home:

The Politburo of the Central Committee of the SED is of the opinion that the great skills and achievements of girls and women are not currently used enough to further their own development and wider societal progress. The main reason for this is that many – men in particular, including those in

> *leading positions in party, state, economy and trade unionism – still under-*
> *estimate the role of the woman in the socialist society . . .*
>
>   *Often women who are already in leading positions are burdened with*
> *an unmanageable workload without recognition of their duties as mothers*
> *and housewives. The demands made of them are often higher than of a*
> *man in the same position. Some leaders are, without saying so outright, of*
> *the opinion that women have to 'prove themselves' through special achieve-*
> *ments. Instead of helping women and girls to tackle the higher demands*
> *placed on them, they invent arguments that supposedly prove that the*
> *deployment of women in middle and senior leadership positions was*
> *impossible . . . There is even an 'argument' that claims women showed*
> *less understanding for technical, organizational and economical problems*
> *than men.*
>
>   *All of these incidents and similar ones go against the grain of our state.*
> *They hold back the development of the woman and with it of our entire*
> *society.*[51]

The SED urged schools, universities, employers, clubs, societies, in short 'the entire public', to address this problem as a matter of urgency. It asked organizations to discuss with women directly and 'frankly' what problems they had encountered, what obstacles might be in their way and seek solutions at all levels. In April 1962, a decision ratified by the Council of Ministers decreed tasks to help women and girls gain a better experience in their apprenticeship and work lives. It ordered 'state institutions supported by mass organizations to hold clarifying discussions regarding the outdated attitudes towards the role of women in society and work through them carefully'.[52] Karin's teacher too would have been encouraged to identify talented girls in his school who might be persuaded to embark on higher education or an apprenticeship for a skilled job. Her father's reluctance was typical for the time. Schools and work-places got increasingly better at persuading girls and their families to pursue higher careers than they would have chosen without intervention.

The East German historian Stefan Wolle points out that there were severe limitations to the success of this programme. Through-out the GDR's history women began to fill lower and middling leadership ranks but were very rarely found in elite positions of the state, party or economy. None of the universities and institutes of higher education reached a ratio of female lecturing staff much above 15 per cent and no woman was ever a full member of the pol-itburo of the Central Committee.[53] But is it realistic to expect this of any state in the 1960s? By 1981, 91 per cent of women were in employment, the highest rate in the world. By 1986, 50.3 per cent of university students were female. By and large women were finan-cially and otherwise independent of their husbands in a way that was unusual in many other societies, including West Germany. This is reflected in higher divorce rates, for example, and in the fact that more people cohabited rather than got married (which is also linked to religious reasons in an increasingly atheist society). On the whole East German women enjoyed greater professional and economic autonomy than their Western counterparts. Wolle was right to conclude that 'the state did everything it could to support women'.[54]

Tragedy and Progress

The building of the Berlin Wall in 1961 was undoubtedly a human tragedy that broke families apart, split a city in two and brought misery and even death to those wishing to cross it. Vocal protests in Berlin notwithstanding, there was surprisingly little pushback against the drastic measure within the GDR itself in the early 1960s. Many former East Germans remember this period as a time of stability.

This apparent paradox is easily reconciled by looking beyond the Wall at the wider context of both the Cold War and the situation within the GDR. Kennedy, Khrushchev, Adenauer and Ulbricht were all aligned in their relief that the dangerous waves of Cold War hostility had found a breakwater in Berlin. Similarly, the economic problems and paranoia caused by the open border had put the GDR authorities permanently on edge until it was closed.

With the ideological divide cemented, a period of calm set in. Repressive measures in East Germany were scaled back and the regime began to concentrate on creating a better economy and society. The most abiding memories many East Germans have of this time are shaped by the large-scale building projects, new professional opportunities especially for women, families obtaining their first cars, going on their first holidays and moving into their first modern flats.

None of this takes away from the national and personal cataclysm of division in Berlin and Germany, but it complicates the picture. The early 1960s were a time of both tragedy and progress as the GDR was always more than the Wall in its capital.

6.   The Other Germany (1965–1971)

Our workers' and peasants' state counts for something in the world after all.

1965 – Ending the Thaw

Döllnsee, Brandenburg, 7 October 1964. Leonid Brezhnev was bored and more than a little irritated. As the highest-ranking member of the Soviet delegation that had been sent to the GDR to celebrate its fifteenth anniversary, he felt Walter Ulbricht owed him more respect. The location he had been invited to was grand enough. Ulbricht's guest house at the shores of the Döllnsee, around an hour's drive north of Berlin, was beautiful. It had been built by Hermann Göring in 1934 as a hunting lodge and was surrounded by acres of forest. Brezhnev had not unreasonably expected to be taken hunting or perhaps at least on a relaxing walk by the lakeside. Instead, Ulbricht had incessantly lectured him from the moment he took his coat off.

The East German leader was concerned that the economic and cultural liberalization he had introduced might find a stern critic in Brezhnev, who was now the deputy leader of the Communist Party, the second most important man after Khrushchev. Ulbricht droned on and on over dinner about the advantages of the New Economic System and about how much progress his state had made socially. Eventually, his guest had enough. After dinner, he excused himself, claiming he was feeling a little unwell and had to lie down. Ulbricht was fuming. He suspected that Brezhnev was merely trying to avoid confrontation.[1]

As Brezhnev was a keen hunter and Ulbricht was not and did not want to embarrass himself, he sent his underling Erich Honecker to accompany the expedition into the surrounding forests. The two hunting partners got on like a house on fire and in the woods around the Döllnsee a friendship was born that would last the best part of two decades.

Honecker, nearly twenty years Ulbricht's junior and for a long time his most loyal supporter, had begun to distance himself from the First Secretary. He was unhappy when Ulbricht tasked Kurt Turba with the re-engagement of the GDR's youth behind his back, especially as he considered the FDJ his project and any criticism of it a direct attack on himself. But there was more to it than political guile. Both he and his wife Margot, who had become the Minister of National Education in 1963, were concerned that Ulbricht had let liberalization go too far. On one level the couple were driven by political concerns. Margot Honecker had annotated one of Kurt Turba's drafts for the 1963 SED communiqué allowing greater freedom for the youth to dance as it pleased with the comment, 'Should be stricter in its stance against the imitators of the so-called American way of life. This is not just about dancing alone . . . Add something about when dance stops being dance and begins to become politics.'[2] A group of like-minded conservative politicians began to gather around the emerging power couple to stop the invasion of consumerism and Western lifestyles through music. But there was also something prudish and old-fashioned about the moral objections they held against some strands of youth culture. Erich Honecker repeatedly called Western culture 'decadence of the worst sort' and even began to manipulate crime figures to exaggerate the degrading influence American and British pop music supposedly had on decent young East Germans.[3] That a man who drank West German DAB lager out of cans[4] and was well known to have had a wild streak in his youth – he 'loved girls and enjoyed the occasional drink' as Wolfgang Seifert, a former colleague, remembered – might not be in a position to lecture teenagers on the immorality of their hairstyles does not seem to have bothered Honecker.[5]

The party had also done its best to keep a tight lid on the origins of the Honeckers' marriage in order to preserve the facade of morality at the highest level. After the tragic death in 1947 of his first wife Charlotte, Erich Honecker married an FDJ leader called Edith Baumann in December 1949 and they had a daughter, Erika, in 1950. Just a few days after the wedding, he travelled to Moscow to attend Stalin's seventieth birthday celebrations. There, he began a passionate affair with Margot Feist, the youngest member of the People's Chamber who had been chosen to congratulate Wilhelm Pieck for his election to the office of President just a couple of months before. Margot was nearly twenty years younger than Honecker's wife and by all accounts an intelligent and charming young woman. When Edith found out about the affair, she tried to get Pieck and Ulbricht to intervene, but to no avail. Her husband continued his affair and two years later, on 1 December 1952, while the couple were still married, Margot gave birth to her lover's daughter, Sonja.

The politburo were not pleased. How could they tell the people to live 'clean' and 'decent' lives while their own rank and file were engaging in extramarital affairs? Walter Ulbricht's office intervened and sent Margot on a course in Moscow. The young mother was separated from her baby daughter and her lover, a decision that Honecker was still bitter about when he recounted the events in 1990: 'The intrigues that existed and which I could not prevent of course saw to it that just in the most beautiful time of togetherness, that is with a newborn baby, Margot was sent to the Youth Academy in Moscow by order of the Secretariat of the Central Committee.'[6] Honecker had to temporarily relocate his parents from the Saarland in West Germany to Berlin to look after his baby daughter while he continued to tend to his political career. In 1955, Edith finally agreed to a divorce and Erich was able to marry Margot.

Despite the fact that Honecker knew what it felt like to have his life dictated by politics and ultimately by the morality of others, he began to plot a crusade against what he saw as the moral decay of the GDR's youth in 1964. In the Soviet Union Nikita Khrushchev was voted out of office on 14 October of that year, less than a week after his successor Leonid Brezhnev had been enjoying himself at the Döllnsee, kindling his friendship with Erich Honecker. As the new Soviet leader immediately declared Khrushchev's de-Stalinization complete, his German hunting partner sensed it was time for a seachange in his country too. A series of brawls that took place at concerts and dance events in Leipzig in the early autumn of 1965 gave Honecker the impetus. Through the FDJ, he had adherents of youth subcultures condemned as 'indolent', 'long-haired' and 'scruffy'. He supported FDJ campaigns that encouraged students to forcefully cut the hair of their classmates if they deemed it too long and hailed the benefits of hard labour in order to help youngsters return to a more 'normal' lifestyle.[7] While Walter Ulbricht was on holiday, Honecker called an extraordinary meeting of the Secretariat of the Central Committee on 11 October 1965 which effectively reversed many of the freedoms the youth had been given two years earlier, even withdrawing licences to play certain types of music.[8]

This 'Beat Ban' meant that only five of the forty-nine bands who had been active in the Leipzig area were allowed to continue to play music. Angry with this, around 1,000 young people gathered on Wilhelm-Leuschner-Platz in the town centre on the night of 30–31 October 1965 to demonstrate against the restrictions. The writer Erich Loest, then thirty-nine years old, remembered what happened that night:

> There were no banners, no chants and no leaders; and the lads just hung around a little; and I am convinced that they would have quietly gone home after a while . . . One minute later a strange spectacle took place. State power rolled over the Leuschnerplatz: at the front, a jeep with police officers, behind it two lorries loaded with deployment police, in the middle the centrepiece – a vehicle, like an elephant, the driver's cabin equipped with little viewing slits, like a tank; on top a dome with a lowered pipe – a water cannon.[9]

The authorities' response was brutal. With bloodhounds, truncheons and said water cannons, they dispersed the crowd into

Leipzig's alleys, arresting 264 people in the process. Of those, 107 were convicted and sentenced to a 'several-week-long, supervised work detail as a necessary correction method' in the brown coal mines of Regis-Breitingen. This was less born out of fear as out of a desire to exaggerate the threat the beat bands had caused. The GDR authorities sent in FDJ youths and SED members to make the numbers of those who had assembled look bigger and more threatening. Some historians have estimated that only 500 of those in attendance were genuine protesters.[10]

But Honecker's scheme had the desired effect. Ulbricht was now isolated and under pressure to deal with the supposed evidence of moral decay that his liberalization methods had caused. Two days after the beat demonstration in Leipzig, he sent out a memorandum in which he claimed that 'it was a mistake that the Central Council of the FDJ organized Beat Band competitions and that it spread the idea that contrary to West German pop music and beat music this would have no damaging effect here'.[11] He even publicly denounced the Beatles shortly after in a speech: 'Is it really the case that we have to copy all the crap that comes from the West? I think, comrades, with the monotony of the "Yeah, Yeah, Yeah" and what not, yes, we should put an end to it.' Erich Honecker agreed. At the 11th Plenum of the Central Committee in December 1965, he proclaimed that 'our GDR is a clean state. In it there are immovable goal posts of ethics and morality, for decency and good manners.'[12] He went on to list specific radio programmes, such as the popular *DT64* as well as films like *Das Kaninchen bin ich* (*The Rabbit is Me*) which offended with its sexual and political themes. In this adaptation of a book by Manfred Bieler, produced by the state-owned DEFA, the protagonist, nineteen-year-old Maria Morzeck, is devastated when her brother Dieter is imprisoned for sedition against the state shortly after the Berlin Wall was built. In the process of trying to get him released Maria falls in love with Paul Deister, who is not only much older than her and married but also turns out to be the judge who convicted Dieter. Maria quickly works out that Paul gave her brother a harsh sentence to further his own career and distances herself from him. Despite this, when Dieter is finally released from prison and finds out about the affair, he beats up his sister. Maria realizes that she needs to take her fate into her own hands and successfully reapplies for a place at university which she had originally lost due to being deemed 'politically unreliable' as the sister of a criminal. Alongside many other cultural works, the film was banned for the entirety of the GDR's existence, which is why East Germans sometimes called banned movies 'rabbit films'.

The same plenum also undid many of the GDR's economic reforms in line with Brezhnev's more conservative policies in the Soviet Union. Moscow now demanded renewed subjugation of its brother states and their economies to Soviet needs. Private enterprise and the people's engagement in their respective economic systems were not part of the plan. The increase in deliveries of crude oil and steel that Ulbricht had petitioned Khrushchev for now fell on the deaf ears of Brezhnev. Erich Apel, the leading figure behind the GDR's New Economic System, was charged with the task of hammering out a new support plan with the Soviet Union from 1966 to 1970. On 3 December 1965, he was still opposed to a new scheme with Moscow, which he believed was wrong and harmful to the GDR's interests. But Moscow loyalists in Berlin, Ulbricht among them, overruled his judgement and ordered him to sign it. When Willi Stoph tried to call him at the ministry early in the morning, nobody picked up. A secretary opened the door to his office shortly before 10 a.m. and found the former rocket scientist slumped in his armchair. The cartridge of his service pistol lay by his feet. There was a lot of blood. Whether Apel had commited suicide or was murdered could never be fully established. The economic reformer was dead and was swiftly replaced by Günter Mittag, a strict supporter of the concept of the planned economy. He would direct East German economic policy right up to 1989.

Between 1965 and 1968, the GDR aborted many of its reforms and liberalization measures. While Ulbricht had certainly not initiated this process himself, he was all too happy to follow the tone set by Moscow and reinforced by the growing power circle around his former protégé Erich Honecker. While he had once been a steadfast ally to Ulbricht, even standing by him during the crisis year of 1953, Honecker was now beginning to build his own power base in firm alliance with his powerful friend at the Kremlin. By 1968, Ulbricht had bowed to pressure from Honecker's camp. The regime was so keen to tow the Soviet line that they eagerly supported Moscow's plans to suppress the Prague Spring,[13] a reform movement in Czechoslovakia under the leadership of the Slovak politician Alexander Dubček. When in the late hours of 20 August 1968 an invasion force of 500,000 Warsaw Pact troops threatened to crush any resistance in the Eastern European country, the GDR's NVA forces were among the support units. While not directly deployed in the front lines and never actually crossing over the border into Czechoslovakia, East German troops helped with the supply lines and were directly under Soviet command. It was a decision made in Moscow not to deploy NVA troops in open combat, not in Berlin.

Those in the GDR who had hoped the reforms of the early 1960s would last and be extended were now bitterly disappointed. The so-called Brezhnev Doctrine, which the Soviet leader reiterated in a speech in November 1968, made it clear that 'When forces that are hostile to socialism try to turn the development of some socialist country towards capitalism, it becomes not only a problem of the country concerned, but a common problem and concern of all socialist countries.' There would be no reform. Not in Eastern Europe, and not in the GDR.

Mielke's Stasi Empire

Berlin-Lichtenberg, 1962. Erich Mielke, Minister for State Security since 1957, moved into the purpose-built new headquarters of the Stasi at Ruschestraße. The seven-storey building, called Haus 1, was at the centre of an ever-expanding complex that would in the end span 2 square kilometres. Between the Ruschestraße in the west, the Gotlindestraße in the north, the Magdalenenstraße in the east and the busy thoroughfare of the Frankfurter Allee in the south, old buildings such as blocks of flats, a church and a police station were razed and a new layout established. The infamous Normannen-straße that is most often associated with the Stasi headquarters would cut straight through the middle of the grounds as they extended northwards and had to be closed for traffic from 1979 as the entire area was secured and guarded.

Mielke's offices were on the 'Minister Level' of Haus 1, on the first floor. They contained his own office, meeting rooms, an ante-chamber for his secretaries as well as private quarters complete with bathroom and kitchen. There was nothing grand about the place. Built in the same drab, grey, prefab concrete as many of the large-scale housing projects all over the GDR, the building was functional rather than impressive. Inside, wood-panelled walls, basic chairs and filing cabinets made it look like a regular office building. There were few personal touches and they mainly celebrated Mielke's hero Felix Dzerzhinsky, the Polish nobleman who had established the Cheka. Dzerzhinsky's statue stood in the entrance hall and his image adorned the hall on the first floor where Mielke's office was. The Stasi's Guards Regiment was named after him from 1967. Mielke admired the spirit in which he had set up the Soviet secret police force and quoted him often: 'The Chekist must have a cool head, a hot heart and clean hands.'

In 1962, Mielke moved the entire Stasi leadership into Haus 1. This included his own office staff, such as his closest colleague, Hans Carlsohn, who had worked with him since 1951 and would lead the Stasi secretariat from 1971. At thirty-two, Carlsohn was still rela-tively young when he followed his boss into the new offices in 1962 but he had already proved that he was up to solving 'the often diffi-cult tasks, which require a firm party conscience and a lot of energy . . . with circumspection and the necessary tact' as a report from 1959 attested.[14] He had joined the SED in 1946, when it was founded, and embarked on a career in the Barracked People's Police which quickly took a political turn as he worked in supervisory roles, installed by the party to control the police. In this capacity, he came to Mielke's attention, who immediately saw in the young man the steely ideological conviction that he sought to instil in all his staff. Carlsohn switched to the Ministry for State Security in 1951, at the age of twenty-three. He became a powerful figure as Mielke's right-hand man, controlling access to him, filtering documents and prioritizing tasks. The two men were also friendly in private as Carlsohn was a frequent visitor to Mielke's hunting residence in Wolletz, in the lake district of the Uckermark, north-east of Berlin. He would stay loyal to his boss right up to Mielke's death in 2000. Mielke also expected and received such loyalty from his personal secretary, Ursula Drasdo, and her husband Herbert who worked for him as a driver and bodyguard. There were four other secretaries who worked for his office in a shift system.

While the vast new premises in 1962 gave the impression of a burgeoning Stasi empire, the position of Mielke's ministry was perhaps at its weakest at this point. Construction had begun in 1960, before the border in Berlin had been shut. Then, the Stasi could justify the expansion of its premises, staff and remit with the argument that Berlin was an uncontrolled and uncontrollable haven for saboteurs, spies and foreign agents. The ability to cross state boundaries freely in Berlin while the rest of the inner-German border had been fortified for nearly a decade made politicians edgy. Mielke was able to use the ebb and flow of paranoia in the late 1950s, particularly after the Hungarian Uprising of 1956, to reinforce the image of the Stasi as the SED's 'Sword and Shield'. While the idea of a Ministry for State Security that had its eyes and ears everywhere to detect hostile activity was comforting to some in the politburo, it was frightening to others. Mielke had begun to tighten his grip on politicians too, not just the population.

When the SED leadership and their families moved into the secure Waldsiedlung at Wandlitz in 1960, the Mielkes were there too. They lived at number 14, a corner property at the north-western edge of the settlement, right next to Edith Baumann, non-voting candidate member of the politburo and Erich Honecker's ex-wife. There, Erich Mielke lived among the political elite with his wife

Gertrud, their twelve-year-old son Frank and their fourteen-year-old foster daughter Inge Haller whom they had taken into their care in 1955. Both of his children and their spouses would eventually work for his ministry as well. Mielke did not reside in the Waldsiedlung merely as a neighbour – he ran the place. All security was provided by the Stasi through bodyguards and men from the Felix Dzerzhinsky Regiment. Every single employee in the settlement, from butcher to hairdresser, was employed by the Ministry for State Security and vetted by them as to their backgrounds and ideological reliability. Any special requests that the residents might have also landed on the desks of Mielke's staff. This ranged from tailored suits for Erich Honecker to specialized hunting equipment and maternity wear. The Stasi boss had begun to control every aspect of the lives of the politburo members and candidate members who lived in Wandlitz. He knew everything about them, from their past marriages to their favourite exotic fruit.

The ministry had grown at a frightening rate since Mielke had taken over. In his first three years at the helm, it had expanded its staff by 3,521 employees, and by 1961 the total had reached nearly 20,000 even without the Guards Regiment, which weighed in with another 4,395 men.[15] To justify the expense, and because he genuinely believed in it, the Stasi boss invented a concept in 1957 which he called 'politico-ideological diversion' or PID: the idea that the enemy was no longer just trying to overthrow the GDR government through direct action such as terror attacks, incitement to unrest and spying, but also through the ideological erosion of the citizenry. Through Western music, dance, consumer items and politics, the population and even key politicians were softened up and made susceptible to corrosive ideas, which they would then use to undermine the society the GDR was trying to build and the socialist system overall.

PID was as vague as it was seductive. Anything and everything could be construed to be politically or ideologically corrosive – from Ulbricht's attempts to liberalize culture and entertainment in the GDR to suggestions of 'third way' economic reform. Mielke gave a name and a framework to the shapeless angst that had set in in the wake of the 1953 uprising, de-Stalinization, the Hungarian Uprising and the ongoing brain drain to the West. The politburo of the late 1950s was haunted by existential fear and Mielke presented himself as the crusader who would defend party and state. Because PID was a concept that did not need spies on park benches or saboteurs in factories, it gave Mielke the justification to look for subversion everywhere – in people's family connections to West Germany, in their tastes in music, in their views on any given issue, in their conversations and in their lifestyles. In other words, it allowed the Stasi to become the invasive superstructure that would make it infamous the world over.

To many in the upper echelons of the party, the building of the Berlin Wall brought an opportunity to curtail the powers of the Ministry for State Security that had begun to stretch its tentacles into every government department. Instead of taking a step back after 13 August 1961, as many had expected Mielke to do, given that the influx of foreigners was now physically blocked, the Stasi boss launched a wave of arrests. For the first three weeks alone after the border was blocked, 6,041 people appeared in *VoPo* and Stasi reports, half of whom were placed in protective custody. By the end of 1961, there would be 18,000 convictions for 'crimes against the state'.[16] Herein lay the problem. Had Mielke's vision for the Stasi been limited to a pure security organization, it would have been cut down at this point. He was told in December 1961 that his waves of arrests were unacceptable as they did not help build the 'socialist people's community' which Ulbricht wanted to foster at this point with his economic and social reforms. This happened in tandem with the 22nd Congress of the Communist Party of the Soviet Union a month earlier, which had also pushed for further reform, more adherence to the rule of law and a softening of the persecution of opposition forces. A year later, in December 1962, the Central Committee of the SED issued another paper in which it demanded of the Stasi that it cease its 'extraordinary' measures as they would not be necessary under the newly established conditions in the GDR. Ulbricht's trusted right-hand man Hermann Matern made it clear to Mielke that he was to stop monitoring vast swathes of the population as well as tampering with the affairs of other state departments. Attempting to shorten the leash of the Stasi man, he explained:

> *We have to change something in the way some comrades think, in their ideology. These comrades are of the opinion that the branches of the Stasi have a special position when compared to other branches of the state apparatus . . . This is wrong. The Stasi is a centrally led branch of the state, a part of the state apparatus which has received a very clear and limited set of tasks from the Party and the Government.*[17]

In other words, Mielke's department was nothing special and if he or some of his staff still laboured under that misapprehension, they needed to change their outlook.

On the surface, Mielke seemed to accept that he had a limited remit after the Berlin Wall had been erected. He told his regional staff that the Stasi had to slim down and make cuts because the 'Republic has stabilized' so they should each begin to 'rethink their structures and ways of working'.[18] He himself began to trim down management hierarchies, outsourced areas such as arson prevention to other state departments and lowered active surveillance down to specific companies and institutions rather than attempting to coordinate this at regional and district level. But in contrast to other departments that had to take severe cuts so that Ulbricht might be able to raise living standards to the desired levels, Mielke's Stasi stagnated, rather than shrunk. Between 1962 and 1964, the Ministry of the Interior, for example, lost a third of its budget. Meanwhile, the Ministry for State Security gained 0.7 per cent with which it was able to employ thirty-five additional staff. Compared to the mushrooming of his department in previous years Mielke took a hit, but he did not sit idly as he awaited the return of better financial times.

From 1962, the Stasi took over passport controls at all of the

GDR's borders: the inner-German one, the Berlin Wall and the eastern boundaries with Czechoslovakia and Poland. This seemingly small move meant that Mielke kept tabs on all traffic in and out of the country: emigration, immigration, tourism, exports, imports and family visits. He also gained control of a special unit within the People's Army, the so-called *Verwaltung 15*. Later called Working Group of the Minister Task Group 'S' (AGM/S), this elite special operations branch of the NVA was in effect a terror organization trained for deployment in West Germany. Alongside the armed Guards Regiment, this became one of Mielke's favourite projects. His son Frank and son-in-law Norbert Knappe would later serve in these organizations. The Guards Regiment also continued to provide the security for each and every state building, event and occasion, from preventing unrest in the night of 13 August 1961 to guarding bunkers, ministries and of course the Waldsiedlung where the politburo members and their families lived. As the GDR's state structures grew and expanded, so did the Stasi's armed divisions. The Felix Dzerzhinsky unit counted only 1,475 men in 1955; ten years later, its numbers had risen to 5,121 and by 1980 it was a division of 10,000 troops.

When, with the era of Brezhnev, an icy wind began to slow the thaw of relations between the East German government and its people, Mielke was in an excellent position to petition Ulbricht for more funding for his department. He had run a lean outfit at only 10 per cent of the overall budget for security in 1962. Yet, he had managed to keep the borders shut, secure public buildings and events, build up armed and secret deployment units and run an efficient and professional-looking outfit from the functional new headquarters in Berlin. The Honecker-led push against Western influences that were supposedly corrupting society seemed to confirm Mielke's PID concept. Everything now came together for the Stasi as it had patiently waited in the wings and consolidated its remit. Between 1960 and 1965, it had only grown by 6,000 members, from 23,000 to 29,000 (including the armed units). By 1970, it employed 43,000 staff. The budget it was allocated grew from 400 million marks in 1960 to only 500 million in 1965 due to the stagnation after the building of the Berlin Wall. But then it shot up to 1,300 million marks in 1970 – more than tripling its funds over the course of the decade.[19]

Despite this rapid expansion, Erich Mielke took care to keep all the power in his own hands. Everything was strictly handled on a need-to-know basis as he said in 1967: 'The MfS [Ministry for State Security] is a military-conspiratorial branch. Within it, it is impossible that everyone knows everything.'[20] This streak had already shown in the early days of the Stasi when Mielke took it upon himself to vet every single employee from the guards in front of his cells to the secretaries. He also still liked to intervene in questioning techniques and in the psychological methods with which prisoners were to be softened up and broken so that they might confess whatever it was that the Stasi wanted them to say. In this area, he never moved away from the sinister methods he had learned from his role model, the Cheka: sleep deprivation, solitary confinement and deception would all be used consistently throughout the history of the GDR.

Mielke even regulated the banalities of everyday office life. A set of notes found on record cards in one of his secretary's desks showed the extent of his neurotic need for order and cleanliness. They contained reminders to 'draw the curtains on the two windows at the front near the minister' but to leave 'the door to the cloakroom' open. One of the desks was supposed to have a 'fountain pen/filled up', '1 piece of paper for fountain pen' and '1 brown file'. They contained reminders to sharpen pencils, readjust the location of stationery and equipment on the desks, position the 'wastepaper basket in the corner between desk and telephone'.[21] Mielke specified exactly how he wanted his breakfast – 'two eggs, boiled for 4.5 minutes, pierced beforehand' – and his secretary kept a labelled drawing of where the individual breakfast items such as milk, salt, bread, knife, plate, white napkin and so on should be positioned.

Mielke was pedantic in every walk of life. His house was spotless, almost sterile. He saw to it that litter he spotted in the streets was cleaned up and public clocks had their time corrected. He hated it when people were late or not doing their jobs properly, which he checked by walking in on their work unannounced.

The increase in workload and constant desire to control everything took their toll on Erich Mielke. On 3 January 1968, shortly after he had celebrated his sixtieth birthday with many guests, he collapsed. He was taken to the state hospital on the Scharnhorststraße where staff diagnosed that he had suffered a stroke. He recovered in hospital for three weeks and then for another four at his hunting retreat at Wollnitz. His chief doctor, Helga Mucke-Wittbrodt, suggested that he might visit a health clinic in Moscow, following which he should take a step back and reduce his workload. She recommended more exercise, fresh air, sleep and general relaxation. Whether he stuck to this is not entirely clear. He seems to have reduced his alcohol consumption and quit smoking, but he could not change his restless urge to control and correct. Markus Wolf, the elusive 'faceless man' who directed foreign intelligence within the Stasi from 1952 to 1986, would later remember that 'it was indeed very difficult to pin down Erich Mielke for a few minutes in order to have a serious, calm conversation. Ten, fifteen minutes to talk to him? Impossible . . . With this hectic rush, with this loud nature, he distracted perfectly from the fact that he was overworked.'[22]

Mielke had his controlling position enshrined in the 'Statute of the Ministry for State Security of the German Democratic Republic' in 1969, with the principle of solitary leadership explicitly mentioned in section 8(1). That this was in stark contrast to the principle of collective leadership otherwise prescribed in socialist ideology does not seem to have bothered anybody, least of all Mielke himself. For the first time, so-called unofficial collaborators (IMs) are mentioned as well. They were defined as 'working people' and 'honest patriots' whose task it was to support the Stasi to 'maintain the security of state and society and to reduce and prevent as far as possible acts of sabotage or factors that hold back further development'. This statute stayed in place right up to 1989. Mielke had successfully used the 1960s to create a power base for himself with far-reaching responsibilities. Instead of being scaled down and made responsible to ministers who would give him 'clearly defined tasks' as Ulbricht and many in the politburo had demanded in the wake of the closing of the border in Berlin, Mielke had been allowed to build and extend his reach. By the end of the 1960s, he presided over a security empire which was allowed to deploy citizens to spy on citizens. He decided who and what entered and left the country. He guarded buildings, events and houses. He decided if ministers would have bananas in their fruit bowls at the Waldsiedlung. Mielke had made himself indispensable to the GDR's inner workings. His neurotic urge to control became the Stasi's.

Moving Forward

Alexanderplatz, East Berlin, October 1969. Erich Kuhfeld, then twenty-nine years old, stood on the large square in Berlin-Mitte with a Free German Youth delegation. Having worked on the *Fritz Heckert* cruise ship for seven years, he had left it in 1968 to take up the position of youth secretary for the shipping company in Rostock. In this role, he had been invited to the transformed Alexanderplatz. The square was enormous, an impression that was enhanced by the fact that it had been pedestrianized – no cars or buses blocked the view. At 80,000 square metres, it was four times as large as the original space before the Second World War. As it had been badly damaged in the conflict, it offered a unique opportunity for socialist city planning to be put into practice, a *tabula rasa* to create a beating heart for the new capital.

Where there had been a bustling black market in 1945 between the rubble of the Protestant Georgenkirche and the ruined Teachers' Union building, Ulbricht envisioned a socialist square that could be used for rallies, events and general enjoyment. With ruthless efficiency, the government had not only had the rubble cleared, but also the remaining thirty-four houses torn down. It relocated over 500 households and diverted the traffic of the 3,600 cars, 136 trams and 60 buses that had crossed the square every hour according to a survey undertaken in 1966. What was left was a rectangular concrete square with endless possibilities. In the same way that the inspiration for the wide thoroughfare of the Karl-Marx-Allee had been taken from Moscow's wide, open roads, Alexanderplatz was to become a space similar in style and function to Red Square in the Soviet capital. In 1964, a competition was held for ideas for the 'Redesign of the Alexanderplatz' and the winning entry put in practice from March 1966. In 1969, the Centrum Warehouse was added at the north-western end (now Galeria Kaufhof), next to the 120-metre-high Interhotel Stadt Berlin, the second-highest building in Berlin then as now. At the north end, the Haus des Berliner Verlages, the Haus der Elektroindustrie and the Haus der Statistik formed a tall row of blocks that oozed modernity as well as bland functionality. To give the square a pleasant, more pedestrian atmosphere, artists were also invited to add decorative elements. Ulbricht's favourite, Walter Womacka, created the large *Brunnen der Völkerfreundschaft* (Fountain of International Friendship). Inaugurated at the twenty-first anniversary of the GDR in October 1970, its 6-metre-tall fountain pumps the water up before it trickles down the copper, glass and ceramic structure. Womacka also designed a giant mosaic, made of 800,000 stones, which runs like a wide belt around the outside of the then newly erected House of the Teacher. Titled *Unser Leben* (Our Life), it features idealized depictions of GDR society. Perhaps one of the most popular features is the World Clock, a turret showing the time in 148 cities around the world.

Erich Kuhfeld's FDJ delegation had come to Berlin to see Alexanderplatz's neighbour and East Berlin's most spectacular newcomer: the Fernsehturm, Berlin Television Tower. At a height of 365 metres, it was designed as a breathtaking monument to modern technology. Still Germany's tallest building today, it was hailed as a 'masterpiece of socialist architecture'. It embodied the spirit of progress that Ulbricht was keen to evoke. It was functional, acting as an effective means of broadcasting TV and radio signals and also stylish and luxurious with its viewing platform and revolving restaurant. Sitting in the Telecafé, 207 metres above ground, a visitor could enjoy a drink while slowly being shown the entire 360-degree panorama of Berlin as the platform took an hour for one full rotation. On a clear day, visibility can reach 42 kilometres. Erich marvelled as he stepped into the elevator and was 'shot up in the air' within forty seconds before being released into the sphere of the tower. 'That was quite something and impressed on us how far we had come technologically,' he remembered.[23]

The Fernsehturm had only been opened on 3 October 1969, 4 days before the twentieth anniversary of the GDR. A high-ranking delegation that included Ulbricht and his wife Lotte, Honecker, Mielke and other members of the politburo had visited the viewing platform and symbolically switched on the transmission for DFF 2 – the second channel of GDR TV and the first to be broadcast in colour.

By 1958, 300,000 televisions were registered within the GDR. Viewers could then see a morning programme (initially just a repeat of the evening programme intended for those who worked late shifts) and programmes such as the popular children's bedtime show *Abendgruß*, which included *Unser Sandmann* (Our Sandman). It became a feature in almost every child's life as the little bearded man with his triangular hat took his audience on his adventures before he ended the show with a goodnight song, marking bedtime for millions of East German children. While West Germany had its own Sandman, the GDR's ultimately proved more enduring. It is still broadcast today. Apart from being a comforting childhood feature, the Sandman also embodied the technological progress of the age as he travelled into space as a cosmonaut or drove around in futuristic cars. The show also featured a popular cast of animal characters such as Frau Elster (Mrs Magpie) and Herr Fuchs (Mr Fox).

Technological advances were to be accompanied by social progress. In 1965, the government introduced a range of educational reforms that were to ensure that a classless society would be established. Enough highly qualified personnel needed to be available in the future to continue the pace of progress, which in turn was the only way to eventually overcome the perpetual economic drawbacks that the GDR's lack of natural resources caused. To this end, all children attended comprehensive schools called polytechnic secondary schools (POS) for the first ten years of their education. These would provide general schooling as well as a range of practical skills that would prepare the majority of children for their future jobs in agriculture and industry. In contrast to the three-tier system in West Germany which streamed children according to ability from a young age, this was supposed to ensure that disadvantages in the cultural environment at home had time to be levelled out through education, so that a more meritocratic system would be established. In the 1950s and early 1960s, around one in five students would then be recommended to continue their studies towards qualifications for university entry in consultation between teachers, parents and the child – a much higher proportion than in the West, although this would change in the course of the 1960s and 1970s when the FRG caught up.[24]

Those on track to go on to university were still obliged to complete vocational training at the same time, usually with a choice of agriculture or industry, so that they left with both academic and vocational qualifications. This fulfilled the dual purpose of giving them a backup option if the teacher's judgement had been wrong and the high academic standards of the extended secondary school (EOS) proved too much, while also keeping intellectuals, academics and other professionals culturally linked to the working classes. Those who entered university and white collar professions had an understanding of what life as a machine worker or dairy farmer entailed. All children were acquainted with manual labour from a young age. At primary level, they learned to use tools, how electrical circuits worked and fundamental agricultural principles in school gardens. This was followed by more advanced skills such as technical drawing, socialist economics and stints in factories or harvest support at secondary school. Altogether work skills accounted for 10.6 per cent of the curriculum.[25]

This system was the practical implementation of the GDR's emblem: where the USSR had only workers and peasants represented on its flag with a hammer and sickle, the GDR added a compass to its hammer and ring of rye. It was a mission statement: maintain an intellectual elite but integrate it with the workers and peasants. Ulbricht believed that technology and progress were the GDR's only chance to survive economically. He could not afford to alienate the middle classes culturally now that he had locked them into his state.

In addition to the EOS route, higher-skilled professions could also be learned at technical colleges as well as through adult education centres and polytechnic universities. The goal was to provide high-quality education for anyone who had the skills and the ambition to access it. The state also tried to ensure that those options remained open to everyone throughout their lives to further the education of ambitious individuals at any stage. While this led to unprecedented upwards social mobility for those from humble backgrounds, the proportion of those in leadership positions who came from genuine working class backgrounds was as low as one in five. The GDR's own figures estimate only around 50 per cent.[26] Nonetheless, access to university for working class students was not only made possible through financial and structural support but also encouraged. This was so effective that by 1967 around a third of university students in the GDR came from working class backgrounds[27] while it was only 3 per cent in West Germany (and would never rise above 5 per cent until reunification).[28]

While this indicated an astonishingly rapid pace of social progress, politically the GDR was beginning to regress. In 1968, a new constitution replaced the 1949 version, which had been designed to be compatible with West Germany's. The new incarnation accepted the political realities of the situation and made no qualms about the political differences between East and West. It explicitly referred to the GDR as a 'socialist state' and indeed mentioned the word 'socialism' 145 times within its 108 articles. Article 1 also enshrined the SED's unrivalled leadership over the state into its foundation document. While it maintained the right of association, meaning the ability to form or join clubs and political parties, it was only 'under the leadership of the proletariat and its Marxist-Leninist Party' that socialism would be realized. All associations that ran contrary to this idea would not be protected. The SED granted itself the role of arbiter of who and what would be tolerated.

At the same time, Ulbricht made good on his promise to deliver better living standards and this is what many East Germans remember most vividly in their recollections of the 1960s. Household products and consumer items in particular became more readily available as the economy was refocused on this sector. While in 1960 only 6 per cent of households had a washing machine, by 1970 just over half no longer had to do their laundry by hand, making life significantly easier for women who were now often working full time as well as looking after domestic chores. While the rise in scooters and mopeds in the GDR is often attributed to the sluggish rollout of cars, this is only a partial explanation why one in five GDR citizens owned one by 1970. They were rapidly gaining the same cult status as they did in the West, complete with leather jackets and individualized helmets.

The GDR consumer industry's crowning glory was its progress in supplying fridges. In 1960, only 6 per cent of households had one and people had to cool perishables in 'ice cupboards' – larders cooled with ice blocks that were provided by mobile horse-drawn ice suppliers or local ice producers who sold blocks of frozen water for 50 pfennigs. By 1970, however, 56.4 per cent of households had a fridge, which trumped West Germany's 28 per cent by quite some margin. Access to telephones, on the other hand, lagged behind significantly. By 1970, half of all West German households had a telephone at home, while in the GDR it was only 6 per cent. Distribution was slow and often on a case-by-case basis.

On the whole, East Germans' lives improved enormously during this decade. Saturday work was abolished in 1967 and weekly working hours were reduced to 43.75 for the same pay. The monthly minimum wage rose from 220 to 300 marks with an instruction to raise anyone's wages gradually if they were still below 400 marks. Child support rose from 40 to 60 marks for the first child and from 45 to 70 marks for additional children. Subsidies for rent, food, cultural activities and public transport made them affordable. It only cost 50 pfennigs to go to the cinema, for example.[29]

As people now had more time and money, a lively leisure culture emerged. East Germans wanted to enjoy themselves and gastronomy became a particular area of expansion. 'Deluxe' chicken shops sprung up everywhere selling 'Goldbroiler' while the Gastmahl des Meeres chain sold seafood, fish and battered 'Rostocker Fischsticks'. By 1968, almost every household had a radio and three quarters had a TV. By the end of the next decade, nearly every household had both. In 1969, both East and West Germany introduced colour TV, and new stereo systems also gave those who could afford it cutting edge technology in their living rooms. In 1968, the GDR even produced a portable, battery-powered stereo device called 'Bändi' but this was difficult to acquire as the Versandhaus Leipzig, a mail order service, had secured rights to sell it exclusively and found it difficult to satisfy the demand.[30] Nonetheless, the inexorable move towards modern living was visible everywhere, even down to the slow demise of the corner shop, which mirrored the same trend in the West. By 1970, over 70 per cent of goods were sold in supermarkets. Even West German observers reported in newspapers in the FRG that the GDR seemed to have 'settled', its people had 'gotten used to the situation' and there was a degree 'of pride that their own individual achievements and the achievements of their society will have to be recognized outside of the GDR'.[31]

The relative prosperity and real optimism of the 1960s helped the GDR regime consolidate its power. The changes in the new constitution went almost unnoticed by the population in the face of the overwhelming feeling that things were finally getting better after the difficult post-war years and the GDR's shaky beginnings. The 1960s also saw the first GDR-born and -educated generation grow up – young men and women who grew into a distinctly East German identity without the ideological baggage of their parents and grandparents. They were fully-fledged citizens of the German Democratic Republic. The GDR was here to stay, and so were its citizens whether they wanted to or not.

Recognition

Valley of the Kings, Luxor, Egypt, 26 February 1965. Walter and Lotte Ulbricht stood in the dry air of the famous archaeological site on the west bank of the Nile and marvelled at the ancient monuments around them. Dressed in a full suit, complete with tie, the seventy-one-year-old First Secretary's only nod to the location was a white panama hat. His wife would later write a gushing travelogue for the women's magazine *Für Dich* which was turned into a book entitled *Eine unvergeßliche Reise* (An Unforgettable Journey). She described how 'happy and excited' she was: 'For the first time we went to a country which was not part of the Warsaw Pact and it was Egypt, which we have known from school age for its ancient cultural treasures and which we had always taken for a dream location, out of reach. Now I will see the pyramids and temples.'[32] She felt the need to point out that such impressive monuments could only have been achieved through exploitation – 'The [pharaohs] did not care how many people were kept from doing useful work and paid with their property or even with their lives.'[33] Still, the couple were hugely impressed by everything they saw and experienced – from the long journey on the cruise ship *Völkerfreundschaft*, which Lotte Ulbricht admitted had been a 'secret wish' of hers, to the 'beautiful and intelligent face' of President Nasser who welcomed them with great fanfare as *Neues Deutschland* reported: 'Triumphal drive to the Koubbeh Palace. Thousands of people cheering: Welcome. The flags of both countries in the streets. 21 shots from the cannons in Cairo and Alexandria. Welcome ships are out at sea. State banquet in honour of the guests from the GDR.'[34]

It was a huge diplomatic triumph for the GDR. Since West Germany's Hallstein Doctrine of 1955 proclaimed Bonn's expectation to be recognized as representing all Germans, East and West, the GDR had been diplomatically and economically isolated. The political weight of the bigger and more prosperous FRG was enough to coerce the rest of the world not to recognize East Germany as a state nor trade with it or invite its political representatives on state visits. Doing so would have drawn the ire of a mighty West German export economy. But Ulbricht was able to exploit the foreign political tensions that ensued when Bonn agreed to grant Israel a $60 million credit for arms purchases. For the first time relations between the FRG and the Arab nations of the Middle East were seriously compromised. It was in this context that Walter Ulbricht wrote a warm letter to Egypt's President Gamal Abdel Nasser. The letter did not ask for a state visit. It claimed that Ulbricht was ill and that his doctors had recommended he spend some time in warmer climates. He asked for Nasser's permission to have a few days' holiday in the Egyptian sun. Keen to spite Chancellor Ludwig Erhard's government in Bonn for their support of Israel, Nasser consented. Bonn's clumsy response was to publicly accuse Nasser of political games and dangle the threats of the Hallstein Doctrine. But instead of being cowed by the prospect of a damaged relationship with Bonn, Egypt's ire further increased. The country upgraded Ulbricht's holiday to a full state visit. On 31 January 1965, the West German ambassador was told that Nasser was considering recognizing the GDR as a sovereign state, thereby blowing a hole into the wall of the Hallstein Doctrine. The years of diplomatic humiliation seemed to come to an end.[35]

Lotte Ulbricht's words reflect just how deeply this affected the East German government: 'I was filled by a deep sense of gratification. The government in Bonn had tried everything to prevent our visit . . . but the times in which the German imperialists could force their will on to other peoples with impunity are over . . . Our workers' and peasants' state counts for something in the world after all.'[36] The response from Bonn was as harsh as threatened – all economic

The Other Germany (1965–1971)

aid to Egypt was cut and Israel recognized as a state. In turn, Egypt and many of the other Arab nations cut their diplomatic ties with Bonn.

Over the course of the late 1960s, as relations between Bonn and the Middle Eastern nations deteriorated further (particularly in the context of the Six-Day War in June 1967), the GDR declared its support for them. Compounded by pressure from the USSR, this became a springboard for East German interests in other developing countries, which meant it provided loans to spread its economic and political influence. On 30 April 1969, Iraq was the first non-communist state to recognize the GDR diplomatically. Then followed Cambodia, Sudan, Syria, South Yemen, Egypt and Algeria. It had taken the GDR two decades to break its diplomatic isolation and to be recognized by the world as a sovereign state.

While the GDR was keen to become an independent player on the world stage, at home it was still considering how a reunification of Germany might be achieved in its own way. Walter Ulbricht had naively assumed that the Social Democratic Party in West Germany might be amenable to working towards a common socialist framework, either directly or through a confederation. He had put out feelers throughout the 1960s, suggesting meetings and closer collaboration between his SED and the SPD. In 1968, when West Germany was run by a 'Grand Coalition' of the SPD and the CDU/CSU alliance – the first post-war government to include the Social Democrats – Ulbricht made several suggestions. These included that all European nations be allowed to have normal relations with each other, that the UN (to which neither German state had yet been admitted) should accept both Germanies as members and that violent force would not be used to resolve conflict between the two German states. While this initially came to nothing due to the Prague Spring, Ulbricht tried again a couple of years later, in 1970. This time he was talking to the first West German Chancellor from the SPD, Willy Brandt.

The former mayor of West Berlin had become a more pragmatic and astute politician since the tense years that followed the building of the Berlin Wall. When the SPD man took office in the autumn of 1969, he immediately pledged that he would establish better relations with the GDR and the Eastern Bloc as a whole. He spoke openly about 'two states of two nations in Germany', acknowledging the GDR as a separate entity. This marked the beginning of Brandt's new *Ostpolitik* with which he aimed to establish more normal relations between East Berlin and Bonn. Things were not only looking up for East Germany's diplomatic future with West Germany but also for its relations with the rest of the world. If it was no longer blocked by the FRG, the GDR could begin to import and export freely. It had become a nation in its own right, acknowledged and respected by the world. But while this would be economically powerful, it was hardly the stuff that inspired the kind of national pride that would get the GDR through a crisis or over periods of insufficient supplies. A more emotive and psychologically powerful vehicle for nationalism had to be found.

State-Sponsored Sport

State Council Building, East Berlin, 8 November 1968. Walter Ulbricht and Erich Honecker cut strikingly comical figures as their sober, dark suits were complemented by giant sombreros on their heads, complete with drawstrings and tassels. The high-ceilinged banquet hall with its large glass windows looked festive, its long tables laden with food and drink and decorated with fresh flowers and folded napkins. Only the best would do for the distinguished guests the head of state had invited into his offices. The building itself must have had an effect on the young group of men and women about to be honoured there.

It had only been opened four years earlier and struck a peculiar balance between the GDR's desire to project modernity and its need for history and political heritage. The asymmetrical front is typical of the functional objectivity (*Funktionale Sachlichkeit*) style of other new buildings in East Berlin but the facade was clad in red rhyolite, a volcanic stone sourced from Saxony-Anhalt, which contrasts sharply with the grey elements that run horizontally at the top, middle and bottom of the building. Its most interesting feature is the Portal IV, rescued from Berlin Palace before the latter was demolished in 1950. The SED leadership had been reminded by the Marx-Engels-Lenin Institute that it was from this portal that Karl Liebknecht, the founding father of the KPD, had declared Germany a 'socialist republic' on 9 November 1918, the day Wilhelm II abdicated. The Kaiser himself had also chosen the same spot to inform his citizens that they were at war on 1 August 1914 and urge them to unite behind him, a call that Karl Liebknecht, initially alone among the parliamentary deputies, had refused. This historical piece was deemed worthy of preservation and strikingly integrated into the modernist facade.

It was through this portal that Ulbricht's young guests would enter, walk past the huge stained-glass windows in the corridors with their idealized scenes of working class life and into the festive hall with its 1 million-piece mosaic depicting the state emblem of the GDR. At the post-speech reception, the sombreros and general joviality clashed with the socialist modernist surroundings as much as it did with the grand Prussian entrance.

The sombreros on Ulbricht's and Honecker's heads were a nod to the fact that their distinguished guests had returned from a journey to Mexico where they had represented their country. The 1968 Olympic Games in Mexico City held enormous importance for East Germany. For the first time, the GDR was admitted with its own national team whereas it had previously been part of an all-German squad fielded in the Games of 1956, 1960 and 1964 (itself a remarkable diplomatic feat given the necessary collaboration as East and West German athletes competed for places in the qualifying stages). With its own team, the GDR could now celebrate its athletes as national heroes. Honecker would later write about the sporting stars of the GDR that they were 'role models whom others will strive to follow. New generations will be won over to the field of sports. Together, competitive sport, mass sport and systematic physical education at school have contributed to the prestige of our socialist state and gained us more than a little recognition in other countries.'[37] The national insecurity that had haunted the GDR since its foundation still ran deep, and sport seemed a powerful way out of it.

A desperate hunt for talent had begun in the 1950s with children as young as three or four identified as potential future elite athletes. Systematic measuring and testing in kindergartens would identify those with ideal physical proportions and natural talent for specific sports. Referrals to training programmes and, from 1952, specialized Sport Schools for Children and Young People would follow. An example of the success of this broad and ruthlessly efficient programme was Ingrid Krämer. Born in 1943 in Dresden, her talent was recognized early, and she began to train for the Olympic discipline of diving at the local Sportclub Einheit, founded in 1954. At the tender age of fifteen, she became GDR champion from the 3-metre springboard and two years later, in 1960, she was sent to the Olympic Games in Rome to compete for the all-German team. Her spectacular victory there, at the age of seventeen, ended the longstanding and unbroken series of US triumphs – American women had won gold in diving since 1924 – and set a record that would not be broken for three decades. She became the only person ever to be named sports personality of the year by both East and West Germany and was chosen to carry the flag for the all-German team (a tricolour with Olympic rings) at the next Games in Tokyo in 1964 where she won more gold medals. With her pixie face and bright blonde hair, she became a global icon. Her lifestyle fitted the zeitgeist of the early 1960s when many young people longed to break the conservative shackles of their parents' generation.

At each of the Olympic Games of 1960, 1964 and 1968, she competed under a different surname as she had married twice in that timeframe. She raised even more eyebrows by inviting her friend and competitor, the American diver Paula Jean Myers, to be her bridesmaid. There is a bronze statue of Ingrid on the roof of the largest public swimming pool in Dresden, built in 1964 and still in use today. In 1975, she was inducted into the International Swimming Hall of Fame in Fort Lauderdale, Florida, and in 2011 into Germany's Sports Hall of Fame. Her disarming charm combined with her astonishing sporting success to make Ingrid Krämer-Gulbin, as she is now known, an enduring international icon and one of the first GDR sporting heroes. Young stars like her gave the GDR a sense of self-worth and national pride domestically as well as recognition and praise internationally.

At Ulbricht's Mexican party in the State Council Building in November 1968, a new sporting star was rising, one that exemplified both the success and the challenges of elite sport in the GDR. Margitta Gummel, a twenty-seven-year-old from Magdeburg, had won gold in the shot put event, setting a new world record and becoming the first woman to break the 19-metre barrier. On 8 November 1968, she beamed at the specially decorated cake the SED had ordered to celebrate this remarkable achievement. Ulbricht pointed at the elaborate arrangement of sugar and marzipan which formed a miniature shot put range and joked, 'Your 19.61m are measured here exactly but the confectioner has left some space for the next world record.'[38] It was Margitta who ceremoniously bestowed Ulbricht and Honecker with their 'real' Mexican sombreros brought back from the Olympic Games as a souvenir. She in turn was awarded the Patriotic Order of Merit (Silver) for her 'outstanding contribution to the state and society in the field of sport'. The GDR came fifth in the medal ranking that year, beating West Germany by three positions. The athletes who had helped to achieve this astonishing result were treated like victorious soldiers.

However, Margitta Gummel's success story also shows the dark side of the GDR elite's addiction to sporting success. Under Manfred Ewald, a complex character with a murky past during the Nazi years, sporting victories became an obsession for the SED. In various roles, which included a place in the Central Committee of the party from 1963 and the presidency of the GDR's Olympic Committee from 1973, Ewald shaped and built the GDR's 'sporting miracle'. He saw sport as a means of winning the class struggle which legitimized the relentless pursuit of perfection. This meant tough training regimes that compromised young people's education and family life (young Ingrid Krämer, for example, needed one-to-one tuition to complete her EOS course). Ewald did not shy away from the more sinister manipulation of sporting outcomes through doping. Margitta Gummel was one of his first guinea pigs. Research later revealed that she was given her first dose of the steroid Turinabol on 28 July 1968, three months before her record-breaking success in Mexico, which marked an improvement of nearly 2 metres from her previous training results. The GDR's own research records show how her results increased steadily as the dose of Turinabol was increased from 10mg daily until she managed shot put results of well over 20 metres. The research team concluded that steroids were particularly effective in female athletes and permanently changed their physique, so that even when doping was paused, they still achieved much better results than they would have done through training alone.

As a result, the GDR began to administer steroids to teenage girls. Manfred Ewald was convicted for this in 2000 when a German court concluded that he had 'aided the physical harm of twenty female elite athletes who were given harmful steroids without their knowledge which caused damage and danger to their health'. Ewald himself defended his actions in his 1994 autobiography *I Was Sport: Truths and Legends from the Wonderland of Victors* in which he claimed that sport had done more good than evil for East Germany and that doping had been more widespread than his leadership at the top had been aware of. Margitta herself, who appears in the doping records as number 1/86, continued on a steep trajectory on the back of her victories. She retired from her Olympic career in 1972, had a family and completed a doctorate in 1977. Even after the fall of the Berlin Wall, she continued to sit on the reunified National Olympics Committee until the documents were leaked that showed her doping records. Those who were given steroids at a younger age and sometimes without their knowledge had to live with the physical side-effects for the rest of their lives. When administered to teenage girls, Turinabol and similar substances cause irreversible changes such as a deeper voice, hair growth, suppressed development of breasts and other ways of making the body more masculine.

The story of GDR sport has two sides. It is too easy to brush off the immense success of the small state as entirely related to the widespread doping schemes. Margitta Gummel, for instance, had become an immensely strong athlete before she received her first doses of steroids, and the 20-metre mark was later reached by other female athletes too, including three from West Germany. While it is unlikely that the GDR would have been as miraculously successful as it was without doping, its achievements cannot be explained with this alone. The little state dominated the sporting scene for decades, winning 755 Olympic medals in total of which 203 were gold. From the Winter Games of 1972 until the end of its existence, the GDR came either first or second at every single one of the Olympic Games – summer and winter – beating the giants of the USSR and the USA alongside its main rival West Germany. Of course, systematic doping enhanced athletic performance but this would have been ineffective without a wide base of athletes to select from.

Sport became an integral part of growing up in the GDR. Young children did physically demanding exercise at kindergarten level. Those showing talent and considered suitable were selected for elite programmes, but everyone else continued to be physically active at school too. Even at university, students had to complete a certain number of sporting hours each term to pass their academic qualification. Many older East Germans remember with a mixture of nostalgia and discomfort how they began a day of lectures with a shivering hour in a draughty swimming pool at 7 a.m. Team games like football remained social activities for many GDR citizens well into their adult years where they stayed in sports clubs which doubled up as communities and friendship groups.

Sport brought immense national pride to a state that had been browbeaten over its economic struggles in the 1950s and 1960s, and the international successes of the 1960s coincided with the diplomatic, political and economic stabilization of the GDR. It helped

East Germany gain an international profile and develop a sense of nationhood.

By the end of the decade, Walter Ulbricht could say with some justification that he had made East Germany work for many of its citizens. The regime still cracked down hard on those who opposed it. Those who attempted to leave the country were still regarded as 'fugitives' and imprisoned, bullied and, in the most horrific cases, shot outright at the Berlin Wall. At the same time, for the majority of East Germans life in the GDR had become acceptable. Many working class Germans would go further as they appreciated the educational and professional opportunities the system had afforded them. Ingrid Krämer, for example, had been a shy, podgy, slightly awkward girl whose father, a metalworker, had no intention of sending her to ballet school as she had pleaded with him to do. But Eveline Sibinski, a twenty-year-old assistant coach at the diving centre in Dresden, saw something in her and took her under her wing. The immense funding pumped into the sector by the GDR authorities and the support for the ambitions of individual athletes and trainers created a climate where hidden talents like those of little Ingrid Krämer's could be discovered.

Similarly, talented students and workers were encouraged and financially supported to continue to train, learn and study in the field that matched their talents. It has been pointed out that this came at a loss for the middle and upper classes who often found it harder to gain entry to academic pathways or to have their achievements recognized by the politicized structures within the education system, but it is worth remembering that the reunited Germany has perpetuated the social rigidity of West Germany. A 2018 UNICEF study ranked Germany in the bottom third for equality of chances of primary school children from different social backgrounds.[39] While this does not justify disadvantaging a particular social group so that another may thrive, it explains why many working class Germans began to accept the GDR as a system that worked better for them than previous German states had done.

Ulbricht's Fall

A hospital in Moscow, 28 July 1970. Leonid Brezhnev to Erich
Honecker:

> *Believe me, Erich, the situation as it developed at your end so unexpectedly
> is troubling me deeply. The GDR is for us, for the socialist brother states, an
> important outpost. It is the result of the Second World War, of our achieve-
> ments, paid for by the blood of the Soviet people. Until recently, the GDR
> was something to us that could not be shaken. But now, a danger lurks . . .*
>
> *We still have troops in your country, Erich, never forget that . . . Without
> us, there is no GDR.*
>
> *Let us talk frankly as fellow communists. Walter has his strengths . . .
> but he is old . . . In two to three years he won't be able to lead the Party
> anyway.*
>
> *Yes, and another thing: I will tell you honestly from one communist to
> another that there is a certain arrogance in your country towards the other
> socialist countries, their experiences, methods of leadership, etc. Even
> towards us . . . The GDR developed or is developing the best model of
> socialism. Everything is done better in the GDR, everyone must learn from
> the GDR, GDR socialism must be a beacon to other countries – the GDR
> gets everything right.*
>
> *I know from my own experience how Walter treats these questions. I
> mean his behaviour in his dacha. He puts all my delegation members in a
> corner while he works on me in a hot room – I sweat – he doesn't relent –
> this may not be the most pressing issue but you cannot and must not treat
> anyone like this.*[40]

As this conversation testifies, Walter Ulbricht was seriously beginning to fall out of favour in both Berlin and Moscow. Erich Honecker,
once Ulbricht's disciple and only loyal supporter during times of
crisis, had long been presenting himself as his successor – a plan
supported by Brezhnev. While age is often quoted as the main
reason for Ulbricht's inability to continue to run the party and

government, his stubbornness and failure to read a room were bigger problems. Ulbricht became evermore pleased with himself and his country the older he got, and he remained tone-deaf to how this was perceived at home and abroad. At the end of the decade he had a habit of comparing himself with Lenin, Stalin and even Marx – an act akin to blasphemy to many of his comrades.

While still somewhat in awe of Soviet Russia, Ulbricht became more and more dismissive of the Eastern European states. In 1968, for example, he told a group of Czech reformers that the GDR had moved beyond the social upheaval they were experiencing in their country during the Prague Spring. He arrogantly proclaimed that East Germany 'was moving on a much higher stage of development than is the case in Czechoslovakia'.[41] When he welcomed a Polish delegation in Berlin the following year, he opened proceedings with the words, 'Even if you try very hard, you will only get where we already are in ten years.'[42]

The economic and social advances made by the GDR in the 1960s had gone straight to Ulbricht's head. He had never possessed an instinct for the effect his words and actions had on others, had always been wooden and sometimes embarrassingly off-key with his remarks. The comparatively high living standards of the GDR and relative political stability had only confirmed his inherent arrogance. One by one, his comrades in Berlin and elsewhere turned against him. The USSR's defence minister Marshal Grechko was so annoyed after another one of Ulbricht's clumsy missteps that he exclaimed, 'The old man is useless now!'[43]

Apart from Ulbricht's personality, many of his policies were also beginning to worry Moscow. His pride in the achievements of the GDR had led him to believe that it required more independence from Moscow and a bespoke system that befitted its unique virtues as a 'socialist German nation state' as he called it publicly at an international conference in January 1970. The German-American historian Dietrich Orlow has convincingly argued that 'Ulbricht, the quintessential Moscow man, began to resent the heavy-handed tutelage of his Kremlin mentors.'[44] This was especially true when it came to inner-German policy. As we saw, when Willy Brandt became Chancellor, Ulbricht sensed a chance to further socialism on both sides of the Wall. The ageing First Secretary had sub-scribed to the 'magnet' theory ever since Germany was formally divided in 1949. According to this doctrine, the German nation will always be drawn together, seeking unification. A divided Germany was akin to placing two magnets on a map – the attraction between them is tangible and will eventually bring them back together. The big question was if the capitalist or the socialist magnet had more pulling power. If Ulbricht could establish good relations with Brandt – a known left-winger even within his centre-left party – then perhaps socialism could be made attractive enough to West Germans to increase the weight of the East German magnet.

Without Moscow's consent, Ulbricht embarked on a course of *Westpolitik* which was mirrored in Bonn by Willy Brandt's more famous *Ostpolitik*. The FRG's Chancellor met Willi Stoph, the GDR's new Chairman of the Council of Ministers, twice in 1970 – first in Erfurt (East) and then in Kassel (West). While nothing much came of the meetings of the two Willies, these efforts had not been approved by Moscow nor indeed the Central Committee in Berlin. Orlow points out that this was neither Brezhnev's course nor that of the central committee of the SED, but Ulbricht's own plan which he pursued for reasons 'both personal and patriotic'.[45]

Closer inner-German cooperation would also have helped fur-ther the GDR's economic ambitions. Being able to import energy resources such as coal from West Germany (perhaps in exchange for valuable uranium) would have reduced economic and political dependency on the USSR, which had so often proved fickle in times of need. Ulbricht could not help but instinctively believe that his countrymen on the other side of the border would prove a more natural partner. West Germany would also be a large and prosper-ous export market for the specialized manufacturing industry of the GDR. To this end, Ulbricht had happily proclaimed that social-ism was not a mere transitionary period on the way to communism but could work in its own right. This went directly against Soviet doctrine and marked a clear ideological diversion from Moscow's path. It also indicated that he was willing to compromise the economic system if this led to more productivity and compatibility with trading partners.

Brezhnev had seen enough. According to the GDR's main Russian translator, Werner Eberlein, who sat in on most important state occasions that required his services, Honecker's meeting with the Soviet leader on 28 July 1970 became particularly agitated when the conversation shifted to the relationship between the SED and the SPD. Brezhnev bluntly told his interlocutor that 'the Communist Party of the Soviet Union is against a normalization of relations with the FRG. The meetings between Brandt and Stoph in Erfurt and Kassel were unwelcome. Why is Walter working towards closer cooperation with Brandt's SPD? He cannot make political decisions without us.'[46] Eberlein remembered that he had never heard Brezhnev speak so directly before.[47] The General Secretary of the Communist Party of Soviet Union was indignant about the way that Ulbricht treated him like an equal. Gone was the subservient man who had prostrated himself in front of his idol Stalin. The relative success of the GDR had bolstered Ulbricht's confidence to the brink of arrogance. He even demanded that the USSR's own building of relations with West Germany should be tied to the demand that Bonn must fully and officially recognize the GDR's status as a nation state. Enough was enough for Brezhnev. Ulbricht's days were numbered.

As the Ulbricht era came to an end, the GDR looked back on a tumultuous couple of decades. They had been marked by some of its most excessive injustices. The regime had virtually sealed its decision to imprison East Germans behind a wall. It had authorized the shooting of those who dared cross it. And it had built an extensive security apparatus that ranked among the most complex and ruthless in world history.

Many ordinary East Germans, however, remember the 1960s as a decade of modernity and blindingly quick progress. Its partner, the Soviet Union, showed it could compete with the US in the space race which led to a space craze in East Germany, especially among the younger generations. The economic and political situation stabilized as the brain drain to the West stopped because of the Wall. Housing programmes provided more and more affordable homes while the opportunities for the working classes to learn, study, work and better their standing in society had never been greater. Sporting and diplomatic successes gave the GDR a national identity and sense of patriotism and self-worth.

East German society accordingly began to split into two groups. The smaller one was deeply unhappy and felt oppressed, exploited and suffocated by the politicization of many aspects of life. But the vast majority of people had come to terms with living in the GDR. Large-scale demonstrations, strikes and unrest as observed in other parts of the Eastern Bloc, such as the Prague Spring of 1968, remained largely absent from the GDR's factories and streets. Ulbricht handed a comparatively steady East Germany to its new leader Erich Honecker.

7. Planned Miracles (1971–1975)

We were in the middle of the Cold War, neither side worked with silk gloves.

Honecker Strikes

Marx-Engels-Platz, East Berlin, late April 1971. It was around 1 p.m. when Yuri Bassistov, a senior member of the Group of Soviet Forces in Germany (GSFG), pulled up in front of the headquarters of the Central Committee of the SED. An imposing square of stone and concrete, it was built by the Nazis to house the Reichsbank. One of the few purpose-built office blocks in Berlin to survive the Second World War, it has been in use ever since it was finished in 1938. Bassistov had not come to admire the bombastic architecture. He was on a top-secret mission. In the morning, he had received his briefing from his immediate superior Leonid Maltsev, a Belarusian officer freshly graduated from Kyiv Higher Military Command School who would later serve as Minister of Defence of Belarus from 2001 to 2009.

Bassistov was to pick up the Central Committee member Werner Lamberz from Marx-Engels-Platz pretending that the politician was meant to give a talk in front of Soviet officers. Only Bassistov, Maltsev and the Soviet ambassador Pyotr Abrassimov were in the know. In the presence of Lamberz's colleagues, Bassistov chatted with well-feigned interest about the supposed talk and he continued to uphold the charade in the car where a Stasi officer accompanied the Central Committee member as usual. Bassistov knew the security man would be difficult to shake off. But the Soviets had come up with a cunning plan. When they arrived at the GSFG headquarters in Zossen-Wünsdorf after a 50-kilometre drive south, Maltsev had coffee ready for everyone. Conversation remained on the 'talk' and the logistics of it. Maltsev informed the other three men that he wanted to host it at a military base near Magdeburg. He told the Stasi man that he would not have to travel the two to three hour journey with his charge. They would use a military vehicle and Soviet security personnel. The politician would be delivered back to the office the next day, courtesy of the Red Army. Satisfied that Lamberz was in safe hands, Mielke's man went back home to Berlin. Bassistov remembered how, a few minutes later, the luxurious GAZ-13 Chaika they had come in 'passed through controls as reported by checkpoint Zossen and we had the green light to begin with "the talk". We rushed to the military airport of Sperenberg, just a few kilometres away. A twin turbo-prop AN-24 plane stood on the runway, ready for take-off. It is worth pointing out that even the crew had no idea who their only passenger was. The next day, the plane returned from Moscow as expected. Lamberz was in a good mood and briefly reported that everything had gone well and the decision had been made.'[1]

A few days later, on 2 May 1971, Walter Ulbricht asked to resign from his office as First Secretary of the Secretariat of the SED. Lamberz had been sent to Moscow to confirm that it was indeed the will of Leonid Brezhnev to replace the ageing Ulbricht with his understudy Erich Honecker.

Presenting it to the politburo as 'an act of kindness', as Hans Modrow, then Secretary for Agitation and Propaganda, would later remember, Honecker graciously accepted his former mentor's resignation.[2] Yet, he had himself helped push Ulbricht from the throne. Sensing that the build-up of a power base in Berlin was going well and that Brezhnev might be susceptible to a leadership change in the GDR, he drafted a letter to Moscow. Dated 21 January 1971, it contained a litany of complaints about Ulbricht and asked Brezhnev to remove him:

Comrade Walter Ulbricht won't stick to resolutions and agreements . . . Not just domestically, but also in our policy towards West Germany, Comrade Walter Ulbricht follows a personal line which he insists on stubbornly.

> *We think this is connected to his advanced age. This is probably a human, a biological problem. We understand – and everyone in the Party will understand – that, at the age of seventy-eight, it is extremely compli-cated to process the great volume of work and duties . . .*
>
> *This is why it would be so important to us and an immeasurable help if Comrade Leonid Ilyich Brezhnev had a conversation with Comrade Walter Ulbricht in the next few days, with the result that Comrade Walter Ulbricht himself asks the Central Committee of the SED to be released from his pos-ition as First Secretary of the Central Committee and the SED on grounds of ill health.*[3]

The letter had not just come from Honecker alone but was signed by thirteen of the twenty-one members of the politburo. This was a clever move by Honecker who had long been seen as the 'Crown Prince'. Instead of appearing divisive and ambitious, he played into the communist cult of the 'collective' by presenting the decision to oust Ulbricht as one the Central Committee had reached together. They had convinced themselves that forcing the stubborn leader to retire as he clearly could not fulfil his duties any more was the kind thing to do. Egon Krenz, at the time Secretary of the Central Coun-cil of the FDJ, remembered that, on balance, he agreed with the decision:

> *Walter Ulbricht was, for me too, a great man and a great strategic thinker. He was also, even if some dispute this today, a great friend of the Soviet Union. But of course he had grown old, and older people have a tendency (not always but sometimes) to think they know better about everything. He viewed some things only from his own perspective and this of course was fraught with the danger of creating division within the party. And a div-ided party is never great, not even today. Ulbricht had brilliant achievements and ways of thinking, but he wasn't receptive any more, unable to under-stand the new times . . . Erich Honecker was much more flexible at that time. He was younger, not yet sixty, and he had the trust of the Soviet leadership . . . In the end, the solution was reasonable and pragmatic, at least when viewed from the outside.*[4]

On 3 May 1971, the day had come. Walter Ulbricht officially resigned and suggested Erich Honecker as his successor. In the afternoon, TV and radio presenters read a brief communiqué to inform the public that Ulbricht had 'out of health reasons, asked the Central Committee to release him from the position of First Secretary of the Central Committee of the SED so that the position might be passed into younger hands . . . The Central Committee reassured Comrade Ulbricht that under the leadership of its First Secretary, the Comrade Erich Honecker, in line with the ideas of Marxism-Leninism, it will continue the great task of building the socialist society in firm lockstep with the Communist Party of the Soviet Union and the entire international communist movement, and it will do so united, as one and with success.'[5]

Hans Modrow remembered how 'what looked like an obvious, harmoniously agreed process had roots that were anything but democratic, obvious and harmonious'.[6] Ulbricht had been well and truly overthrown by his former disciple and, as if that was not enough, Honecker would spend the next two years ensuring that the former First Secretary of the SED would be politically silenced. While Ulbricht technically remained in office as Chairman of the State Council, a position that ostensibly gave him a role as elder statesman, he was sidelined by Honecker with systematic ruthlessness. Ulbricht was monitored by the Stasi at Honecker's behest. Even Lotte Ulbricht felt the cold grip of the new regime keenly. Cast in the role of an East German Lady Macbeth, she became a 'persona non grata', as she put it,[7] and was alleged to have steered her husband towards the supposedly treacherous decisions he made. In her 1996 memoirs, she complained bitterly about the way she had been gradually isolated since the late 1960s at the behest of the SED leadership.[8] She was barred from all public appearances as early as autumn 1970 and even twenty-six years later remembered 'how painful this was for a communist woman who had fought for the communist cause since she was sixteen'.[9]

Walter Ulbricht himself took it very badly, both mentally and physically. He found it difficult to comprehend what was happening

to him and complained to his wife that almost the entire politburo
had turned against him. Lotte told him gently, 'Well, then you must
have done something wrong, if everyone is against you.'[10] In mid-
March 1971, Ulbricht's personal physician Arno Linke had still noted
that his patient's 'clinical parameters were even better than expected
at his age'.[11] A few months later, following his forced abdication, the
seventy-eight-year-old was gravely ill with arteriosclerosis. Stubborn as ever, Ulbricht remained determined to cling on to power for
as long as he could, at least until Honecker's official election would
put an end to his long reign. 'I have to hold out until the end of June,
then you can do with me what you please, doctor,' Ulbricht told
Linke each time the physician warned the old man about the stress
he continued to subject himself to.

The very fragile Ulbricht could not help himself and had to be
fully involved in the 8th Congress of the SED, which took place
from 15 to 19 June 1971 and would officially appoint Erich Honecker
as the new leader. Brezhnev arrived in person on the eve of the
event and Honecker had planned to greet him with the customary
'brother's kiss' at Berlin-Schönefeld Airport in front of the TV cam-
eras. Before Ulbricht could spoil the moment for him, Honecker
roughly shoved his former mentor out of the way and barged past
him to greet the Soviet leader first.

Later that day, around 10.30 p.m., Arno Linke's telephone rang
and the doctor was urgently called to the Wandlitz settlement.
Ulbricht had collapsed. Linke remembered that when he arrived,

> Ulbricht lay on his bed, slightly raised through the support of a pillow.
> Dark rings had formed around his eyes. He looked at me anxiously through
> dilated pupils . . . Deep wrinkles lay around his mouth. On his pale face
> was a sheen of cold sweat. His breathing was laboured and shallow, and I
> was shocked when I took his pulse. Three hours ago, it had been relatively
> strong, now his pulse was weak, fast, irregular and barely detectable.[12]

Ulbricht was in no position to attend the conference as planned.
Unable to read his leaving speech on which he had worked for so

long, he lay in his bed alone as colleague after colleague denounced him. Honecker spoke of 'some comrades, who have forgotten the value of criticism and self-criticism . . . they think they are infallible and untouchable', while others chipped away at Ulbricht's economic policy and rapprochement with West Germany. Lotte Ulbricht caused a scandal when she expressed her contempt by refusing to clap after Brezhnev's speech on the second day.

As his political work and personality were under attack, Ulbricht's physical condition continued to deteriorate further. A makeshift intensive care unit was installed at Wandlitz and the former leader was only allowed to leave his bed to go to the toilet and to wash himself. He was given oxygen three times a day and monitored constantly. On 18 June, he collapsed again with extremely painful angina attacks. 'Doctor, my heart,' he breathed at Linke, 'I have taken more oxygen but it doesn't help.'[13] Still, he would not cancel a visit from Brezhnev himself the next afternoon. The Soviet leader stayed for a long time, talking in calm and reassuring tones to the man he had ousted from power. Ulbricht could not bring himself to let go of the political life he had led since his teenage years. Watching Honecker take over, he prophesied that the younger man's rule would be one of 'soulless, administrative activity, which has nothing to do with Leninism'.[14]

Even when he suffered a heart attack on 14 July 1971 that hospitalized him and left him partially paralysed on the left side due to temporary lack of oxygen to his brain, he suspected that the medical advice to fully retire was a plot to push him out of politics for good. He railed against the doctors and politicians who had supposedly colluded to keep him isolated. Hospital staff dutifully reported his every word back to Honecker, who responded by further sidelining and humiliating Ulbricht. When Ulbricht celebrated his seventy-eighth birthday on 30 June 1971, Honecker visited the visibly ill man in his home. This was no private courtesy call. Bringing a camera team and photographer, Honecker showed the public a frail old man in a dressing gown, unable to get out of his armchair. As a sprightly Honecker leaned down to him, squeezing his hand with both of his with apparent warmth, the rest of the politburo stood by with concerned and benevolent expressions on their faces. The message was clear: Ulbricht was not even fit to fulfil the role of elder statesman. It would fall to Honecker – and Honecker alone – to move the country into the next decade.

Dawn of the Honecker Era

Vilm, Baltic Sea, July 1971. Lothar Herzog tried hard to please Erich and Margot Honecker. His superiors had told the twenty-eight-year-old waiter that his career would be finished if the First Secretary came back from his summer holiday reporting that he did not get on with him. Like all employees in the sealed-off community of the Waldsiedlung, where Lothar had worked since 1962, he was a member of the Stasi. Erich Mielke ran a well-oiled machine at Wandlitz. Lothar would have to leave this position if Honecker didn't want him around any more – there was no room to avoid one another and Mielke was keen to keep life at the Waldsiedlung as harmonious as possible.

So Lothar followed the instructions he had been given to a tee. The most difficult part was to do his job without being seen. Vilm is a beautiful tiny island, covering less than 1 square kilometre. It lies in the Baltic Sea just off the coast of the much better-known and larger island of Rügen. Vilm had been left relatively untouched and declared a conservation area since the early 1930s. The SED elite decided to use it exclusively for the members of the Council of Ministers and their families as a private holiday island. Eleven guest houses were erected in the style of a finishing village, complete with a communal clubhouse where everyone would eat lunch together. In such intimate surroundings, Lothar found it hard to remain invisible to his charges whom he served all day, every day. When the weather permitted it, the Honeckers liked to enjoy their afternoon coffee at the beach for which tents had to be erected complete with camping furniture. To avoid disturbing them, coffee and cake were delivered by a silent electric vehicle. Erich Honecker was also fond of swimming naked. But unlike the vast majority of East Germans, who frolicked happily in public on one of the many nudist beaches along the Baltic coast, the First Secretary seems to have been a little shy. Lothar had to wait until everyone was back at the clubhouse for dinner before he could venture out to the beach to clear the coffee table. The four-week holiday went smoothly and he remained Honecker's waiter and bodyguard until 1984.[15]

To Honecker, those four weeks of splendid isolation were the proverbial calm before the storm. Before he left for Vilm, he had announced big plans for the GDR at the 8th Congress of the SED. With old Ulbricht out of the way, Honecker wanted to be the breath of fresh air that the country needed. While not particularly distinctive in looks, charisma or oratory, Honecker had one thing going for him: relative obscurity. Even though it had long been obvious to the political elite that he was a strong contender to succeed Ulbricht – some had even taken to calling him the 'Crown Prince' – to the public, he was a relatively blank slate. At 1.68 metres tall and with his slight build and receding hairline, he came across as a bit boring, even shy. He was awkward around other politicians, particularly in meetings with foreign leaders. Even in the famous colour photograph that hung in every official building in the land, Honecker looks bland in his mustard-coloured suit and thick, horn-rimmed glasses. His voice, while not quite as grating and reedy as Ulbricht's, was by no means confident and neither was his register or tone. His clumsy sentence structures, limited vocabulary and nervousness quickly became trademarks of his public persona.

But Honecker did not want or need to rely on charisma to win over East Germans. He was determined to do things better and wanted to take the people with him. Under the somewhat mundane-sounding motto of 'Unity of Economic and Social Policy', the new First Secretary's five-year plan promised something quite revolutionary: the value produced by the workers would be reinvested immediately to their benefit. The harder they worked, the better the country would become. But this needed to be tangible and immediate if the image of the dawn of a new era was to be made credible. The time for 'unplanned miracles', as Honecker put it in a clumsy attack on Ulbricht's economic liberalization, was over. Planned miracles would be the order of the day instead. Johannes Kuppe, then a thirty-five-year-old academic working on a 'GDR Handbook', later remembered that the public saw the transition of power to Honecker as a 'sign – "Something is happening!" The forced separation of 1961 would be easier to bear if all the drudgery in an economy that never produced enough might be reduced a little and properly rewarded.'[16]

Back from his beach holiday, Honecker set to work to turn his promises into reality. The first step was to take economic power firmly back into state hands and centralize methodology and processes. Ulbricht had tolerated the entrepreneurial remnants that still lingered in parts of the economy – in 1971, there were still over 11,000 independent businesses, self-employed people and semi-private enterprises which accounted for nearly 40 per cent of the production of consumer goods in the GDR.[17] To Honecker this not only smacked of capitalism but had also evidently not produced the living standards he dreamt of for his people. By the spring of 1972, practically all of those vestiges of private business had been nationalized into VEBs. Those responsible for economic planning across the various government departments breathed a sigh of relief. The unpredictability of economic forces did not mix well with the constant political pressure to achieve results in the planned economy. Better to have direct control over production and be responsible for one's own decision-making than for the whims of the market. As the economic historian Jörg Roesler put it, 'The stress caused by the constant pressure to reform and experiment with new managerial methods was over. One simply did not speak about economic reform any more'.[18]

Similarly, the ambition to compare the GDR's economy to that of West Germany went out of the window. As Honecker had promised the Soviets to place East Germany firmly back within the Soviet Bloc, the inner-German comparison simply lost its special place, at least for a while. Honecker even had the phrase 'German nation' removed from the constitution in 1974 in order to emphasize that the GDR had become an independent state that was here to stay. Many things were renamed to prove that Honecker was no longer looking West for the goals and ambitions of his country. The Deutschlandsender (German Channel) radio station, for example, became Stimme der DDR (The Voice of the GDR) in November 1971. The dawn of the Honecker era would not be measured by East Germany's relative success but rather, in the First Secretary's own words, by 'the continuous improvement of the material and cultural quality of life of the population'. From housing to consumer products – Honecker promised to do it better.

Blue Jeans

Olbersdorf, Saxony, May 1978. Andrea Rudat looked at herself in the mirror and liked what she saw. A slender fourteen-year-old girl with wavy brown hair, she had recently joined the FDJ and wore her neatly ironed blue shirt with pride. It looked good on her and even better tucked into the gorgeous Levi's denim skirt she had just received from her uncle, Dieter. He lived in Hildesheim, in Lower Saxony, West Germany, and regularly sent over second-hand clothes which his friends and relatives had discarded. He knew how much joy the sought-after brands brought to his family in the East. The light-blue denim skirt with its distinctive red label was no exception. Andrea was delighted when it appeared in one of his 'West Parcels', surrounded by the usual gifts of coffee, chocolate and brandy. It even had braided belt loops! She wanted to show her friends, especially Nora who was widely regarded as the coolest girl in her year. Her peers were suitably impressed, even a little envious.

Fräulein Neumann, however, was not amused. She was the strictest teacher in the school and it was she of all people who called Andrea into her office at breaktime. 'Fräulein Rudat,' she began. Andrea flinched, expecting a tirade. 'I am very disappointed. You are the best pupil in your class – a student representative, a member of the Council of Friendship even! How could you?' Andrea's heart sank. She hadn't meant to be provocative. All she had wanted to do was to show her friends her new skirt. 'I really wouldn't have expected this from you,' Fräulein Neumann continued in a disconcertingly quiet tone that hit Andrea more than a dressing down could have done. 'You of all people. What were you thinking?'

What was she thinking? What would her parents say? They were humble factory workers who took immense pride in their bright daughter's academic achievements. They argued each time over who would go to her parents' evening appointments to receive glowing praise. On the whole, jeans from the West were perfectly acceptable by then. They were even sold in the GDR whenever the state could get hold of some. But of course, it suddenly registered with Andrea, wearing a Levi's denim skirt with her FDJ-shirt tucked into it was a different matter. She had inadvertently turned herself into a walking display of the class struggle. Luckily, Fräulein Neumann had a soft spot for Andrea. She did not flag up the incident, nor did she tell her parents about it. Instead, she continued to support the promising young student and fought tooth and nail for her to be allowed to go on to the extended secondary school in nearby Zittau where she would be able to gain entrance to higher study and university – against the express wishes of her parents who were fiercely class conscious and wanted her to learn a 'proper trade'. Fräulein Neumann knew that there was nothing depraved about wearing 'Blue Jeans', as the desirable American clothing was called in the GDR. Everyone did it, even Andrea.[19]

Erich Honecker understood this too. As the founder of the Free German Youth, he had not completely lost touch with the wishes and desires of the young. He sensed that he would lose the next generation of East Germans if he continued in the stuffy vein of his predecessor. He wanted to pay heed to their needs, and the never-ending allure of the American 'Blue Jeans' was high on the list. The sought-after jeans were extremely hard to come by in the GDR and those who had them usually relied, like Andrea, on Western relatives to procure them. But in November 1971, the *JuMo* (short for

Jugendmode, 'Young Fashion') departments of the GDR's shopping centre chain Centrum suddenly had original Levi's in stock. East German youngsters were ecstatic. They flocked to the stores in their droves. Werner Jarowinsky, the member of the politburo responsible for trade and supplies, reported back to Honecker, 'Given the large amounts of stock selling so quickly and the great interest of the young people, temporary mass appearances of shoppers are unavoidable. It has been decided that the shops will have to deploy more retail assistants – even draw staff from administrative roles – and make more changing rooms available.'[20] In four days in late November 1971, the GDR's shops sold nearly 150,000 pairs of jeans.

But branded American jeans were expensive – even in West Germany they were out of reach for many. In the GDR they were offered at affordable prices, heavily subsidized by the government in the hope that they were a passing fancy. But their popularity just would not wane. On the contrary, throughout the early 1970s jeans suddenly appeared everywhere – in schools, in discos, even on FDJ leaders.

The GDR film industry too made use of the popularity of 'Blue Jeans', be that in the many cowboy films produced by the state-owned production company DEFA or in the cult classic *Die Legende von Paul und Paula* (*The Legend of Paul and Paula*) from 1973, which Erich Honecker himself cleared from potential censorship. The former icon of rebellion was suddenly an acceptable feature in popular culture and everyday life.

This meant that the demand for the fabled clothing could not permanently be supplied with expensive imported stock from the West. There was another problem too: the original American brands were so popular that chaos broke out every time they were on offer as people stormed the *JuMo* departments and overwhelmed both staff and security. When the Ministry of Light Industry ordered an astonishing 1 million pairs of Levi's directly from the US in 1978, they had learned their lesson from previous incidents and wanted to be more cautious – not least in an attempt to distribute the wares fairly and avoid stockpiling. The solution was to sell the trousers through universities, workplaces and other organizations (even the Stasi got its fair share of American jeans). Employees and students couldn't believe it when they received the message: 'Special sale of jeans, original American Strauss-Levis. Work/Student ID required.'[21] The batch of 1 million jeans sold out in no time and yet the population of only 16.7 million could not get enough of them. The situation was unsustainable.

The Honecker regime tried to deal with the high demand for jeans by launching its own lines of production. From the mid-1970s, brands with evocative names like Wisent (European bison), Boxer and Shanty tried to imitate the Western flair of the original, but as ever, the GDR had a resource problem. It did import some cotton from the US, particularly for the Boxer brand, the most popular and comfortable of the domestic offering. But it was also the most expensive as a result. Much of the cheaper stock was made with lesser materials. The main source of cotton was the USSR and the raw material sourced from the brother state had short fibres, unsuitable for jeans production. It had to be mixed with synthetic fibres, leaving the trousers stiff, uncomfortable and difficult to wash. They did not have the desired washed-out effect and often the cut was a little off. To get the tight-fitting look of the original, some East German youths resorted to putting their jeans on in a bathtub full of water – this would soften the fibres and stretch them. When they dried again, they sat on the proud wearer as if spray-painted. But to many, the GDR jeans were better than no jeans at all and the East German 'Nietenhosen' (rivet trousers), as they were still called by many, sold en masse. Wisent jeans, for example, were produced in the VEB Clothes Factory of Templin, about an hour's drive north of Berlin. Templin exclusively made jeans. The factory's 400 female workers worked in three shifts to produce up to 6,000 pairs a day. Initially, these were exported into West Germany as well, which worried the Levi Strauss company in America so much that it intervened, arguing the GDR was plagiarizing its designs and methods (particularly the stitch design on the back pockets). The legal solution was that Honecker was allowed to continue to produce jeans for the domestic market only but not for export.

But the experience of wearing a pair of Wisent jeans did not come close to the Western original – materially or psychologically. No matter how hard Honecker tried (and by the end of the 1980s, every East German teenager owned two pairs of jeans on average), the allure of the forbidden West remained high for GDR youths for whom an imported pair of Levi's or Wrangler's was often a satisfying outlet of political or personal rebellion. The young Angela Merkel – then Angela Kasner – took pride in wearing Western jeans and parkas sent by her relatives in Hamburg (despite the fact that GDR jeans were produced in her home town of Templin): 'The jeans which my aunt sent or brought over with her were our hope. I almost never wore a piece of clothing from the GDR.'[22]

The immense effort Honecker put into procuring jeans for the population and in particular for the young showed how far he was willing to go to make life in the GDR not just bearable but enjoyable. When he took over from Ulbricht in 1971, he was not seen as the stubborn old apparatchik many would remember him as later on. Well into the middle of the 1970s, Honecker and his five-year plan worked for many East Germans, even the young. Long-haired youths who wore jeans and parkas while listening to the Rolling Stones or Pink Floyd had more to fear from their parents and teachers than from the First Secretary.

Red Woodstock 1973

East Berlin, 28 July 1973. It was a glorious summer day when thirteen-year-old Uwe Schmieder from the sleepy little town of Zeitz in Saxony-Anhalt proudly beat his marching drum in the heart of the capital city. Surrounded by his older friends from the local secondary school, he soaked up the atmosphere of the 10th World Festival of Youth and Students as if in a trance. Not old enough to join the Free German Youth yet, he had nonetheless been allowed to don its bright blue shirt as his local group were desperate for another drummer. Uwe found the atmosphere 'intoxicating; the peace, friendship and the chants. We had never practised those, we just joined in . . . I felt very close to the country at that moment.'[23]

Nearby, West German journalist Manfred Rexin shared the feeling of unfettered joy and openness. Sent 'over' from West Berlin to report on the mass event on the other side of the Wall, he was taken aback by the 'impression of a GDR that wasn't as stuffy as we had experienced it in the 1950s, and even worse after the building of the Wall. But it was – it seemed – a GDR in transition and this raised hope.'[24]

Gregor Gysi, then a twenty-five-year-old lawyer, also found it impossible to resist the lure of the excitement in East Berlin. 'I constantly went to Alexanderplatz and the other venues. I experienced how young people from West Germany debated with teenagers from the GDR. It was exciting, it was rewarding – the arguments were very different. There was such freedom. Music was played everywhere.'[25]

For nine hot days in the summer of 1973 East Berlin was transformed into a bustling, multicultural festival ground. The World Youth Festival is an international event that has been hosted by different cities since 1947. It provides a platform for a wide-ranging programme of music, debate and art by left-leaning youth organizations and clubs from all over the world. When it was time for the GDR's capital to host the festival, the FDJ went into overdrive. Organized by 1.7 million of its members, the 10th World Festival of Youth became a mass event on an unprecedented scale. It was visited by 8 million people from 140 countries. This included many West Germans, 800 of whom directly took part with floats, displays, lectures, music performances and other activities. Many – especially West Berlin teenagers – had turned up out of sheer curiosity. Gregor Gysi remembered with astonishment that 'even the Young Union, the youth organization of the CDU [Christian Democratic Union], came over from West Germany'.[26] Among the many Western visitors were sympathetic, high-profile American guests too. Angela

Davis led the US delegation. A prominent far-left activist and academic, she had spent some time in prison in the US while an incident was being investigated in which a weapon belonging to her was used in the storming of a courtroom in California during which five people died. Extensive campaigns in support of Davis were mounted in the GDR under the slogan 'Freedom for Angela'. When she was released, she immediately went on a tour of Eastern Europe including East Germany where she was received by tens of thousands of people in September 1972. Honecker appreciated the charisma the young black woman radiated and attempted to make use of it. Davis was given an honorary degree from the University of Leipzig and an invitation to lead the US delegation to the 1973 festival. She duly appeared for the opening ceremony as a guest of honour and held a speech to rousing applause.

With such international flair, the festival was exhilarating for young East Germans. From the spontaneous jam sessions to the heated political debates – the sense of openness, spontaneity and pride to be host to such a huge and popular event mingled with curiosity about the international crowds. Ina Merkel, then a sixteen-year-old schoolgirl, remembered that the many visitors from developing countries held a particular fascination for GDR citizens: 'They still evoked revolutionary zeal, rebelliousness, resistance. And this was attractive to GDR citizens as the GDR didn't have that any more. The GDR had become a little bit boring.'[27] The spirit that had gripped the first FDJ generation in the late 1940s and early 1950s had indeed evaporated. Gone were the days when youngsters felt they were rolling up their sleeves to build a better Germany in the face of a world of enemies. The GDR had come of age. At the end of the festival summer, on 18 September 1973, it would be admitted into the United Nations alongside West Germany. The Basic Treaty of 1972 had seen both Germanies accept each other as sovereign states, which meant East Germany was free to establish diplomatic relations with the rest of the world. By 1980, there were East German embassies and missions in nearly 200 countries. Ina was right, the GDR had become 'a little bit boring' – it seemed to be a state like any other now and life had become comparatively comfortable.

As if another sign was needed to show that the shaky foundation period of the GDR was over and a new era had begun, Walter Ulbricht died in the midst of these nine days of free music, love, debate and drinking. In the course of the previous two years, Erich Honecker had completely silenced his erstwhile ally and mentor. In a move not dissimilar to de-Stalinization in the USSR nearly two decades earlier, Honecker's 'new course' had promised that the winds of change were blowing. While nominally remaining Chairman of the State Council until his death, Ulbricht's work was erased from the canon of state ideology and was rarely mentioned in public any more. Indeed, the stadium where the Youth Festival had held its opening event had still been called Walter-Ulbricht-Stadion up until a few days before the festival when it was renamed Stadion der Weltjugend (World Youth Stadium). On occasion, the fragile old man had been rolled out again, always ostensibly to contrast him with the sprightly Honecker. The popular East German singer Frank Schöbel remembered an incident where he was asked to perform at an event at the State Council Building in 1972 with Ulbricht in attendance. The latter 'sat for the whole time, visibly frail, possibly only kept upright by his medication. Erich Honecker was standing next to him . . . I sang the chorus relatively quietly because I thought every loud noise might be too much for the old man. At the end he came up to us to say thank you with his typical reedy, high voice. I had the feeling he hardly recognized anyone any more, a mere shadow of himself.'[28]

By the high summer of 1973, Walter Ulbricht's name had slipped out of view along with the man himself. The founding father of the GDR quietly passed away on 1 August 1973 at 12.55 p.m. at the age of eighty. He died in the guest house of the SED, on the fringes of Berlin, the fringes of the festival and the fringes of public life. The official TV and radio channels interrupted their regular programmes and broadcasts of the festival to announce the death of Walter Ulbricht and then continued with what they deemed suitably dignified classical music. The SED newspaper *Neues Deutschland* dedicated its front page to the passing of the country's former leader. But the festival itself was not interrupted. Frank Schöbel played his two-hour concert at the base of the TV tower as planned and signed the silk scarves of his fans. The carefree atmosphere of the summer of 1973 would not be marred by the death of the man who had built and dominated the GDR for over two decades. The GDR had moved on.

On 7 August 1973, two days after the end of the Youth Festival, Walter Ulbricht received a full state funeral. Flags were lowered to half mast, the newspapers were full of condolences from all over the world and delegations from fellow Warsaw Pact states were invited to the State Council Building for the official ceremony. Soviet leader Leonid Brezhnev himself appeared at the East German embassy in Moscow to pay his respects. If Honecker thought Ulbricht had been forgotten by ordinary people, he was mistaken. From early in the morning, long queues had begun to form on Marx-Engels-Platz in front of the State Council Building as people wanted to say goodbye to the man who had built their state. 'He has achieved more than a little,' said one of the men in the queue.[29] Ulbricht's body lay in state for much longer than planned that day as the authorities had not anticipated such long queues. After the ceremony, which included the renditions of the national anthem, Beethoven (performed by Dresden's philharmonic orchestra) and the Internationale, Ulbricht's oak coffin – draped in the GDR flag – was driven to the crematorium through the streets of East Berlin on an open military vehicle. People lined the streets to pay their last respects. On 17 September Ulbricht's ashes were interred at the Memorial to the Socialists in Friedrichsfelde where many other communists such as Karl Liebknecht, Rosa Luxemburg and Wilhelm Pieck are buried.

Ulbricht's last journey was dignified and emotional. But his death did not have the deep psychological impact of Stalin's sudden demise twenty years earlier. Most people remember the summer of 1973 not for some profound sense of loss or shock but for the Youth Festival, the hot weather and a vague sense that things had settled in the GDR. East Germany's quiet farewell to its founding father stood testimony to the confidence and stability the country had gained since he had helped create it.

Ostrock

Rauchfangswerder, East Berlin, spring 1974. It was a Friday when the reporters of the *Freie Welt* (Free World) magazine turned up at Dean Reed's house – a 'black Friday' as his wife Wiebke informed them when she opened the door. Their old house on the tranquil shores of the Zeuthen Lake just south-east of Berlin was still in dire need of restoration and Reed had attempted to do some of the work himself that morning when he cut his wrist with the blade of an axe, causing a deep flesh wound that had needed stitches. A gleaming smile flashed over the American's handsome face as he shrugged off the whole episode and decided to go water-skiing regardless. That suited the magazine reporters just fine. They had come for pictures that underlined the image of the freedom-loving cowboy. Wiebke sighed, 'Dean will risk life and limb.' Her husband kissed her and retorted, 'My wild years are over.'[30]

But Dean Reed's wild years were not over yet. Born in Denver, Colorado, in 1938, he had spent the early days of his career attempting to build an image as a charismatic singer and actor with Capitol Records. He became a huge sensation in South America when he toured Chile, Brazil, Peru and Argentina in the early 1960s but the experience politicized him deeply – something he would later explain was caused by the social inequalities he witnessed. In March 1966, he invited Che Guevara to his house in Buenos Aires and the two men talked all night, which left a profound impact on the American and contributed to his expulsion from Argentina for 'communist activities'. When his contract with Capitol ran out in the autumn of 1966, he decided he would try his luck in the Soviet Union where he gave thirty-nine concerts in eight cities for the state-run events agency. Dubbed 'Red Elvis', Reed's hip shake,

charisma and rock'n' roll sound made him a superstar behind the
Iron Curtain. He sold millions of records and got many acting roles
in the bloc and in Italy. Without a trace of irony, he saw the commercial success he gained with his American image and his pop,
rock and country tunes as a means of funding his political campaigning against capitalism.

Reed became a prominent anti-Vietnam protester and politically
supported Salvador Allende in Chile. In one of his most dramatic
stunts, he washed an American flag in a bucket of water outside the
United States embassy in Santiago declaring, 'This North American
flag is dirty with the blood and tears of the millions of people of the
majority of the countries of South America, Africa, and Asia who are
forced to live in misery and injustice because the U.S. government
supports the dictatorships which keep these people in bondage.'[31] The
flag still hung proudly from a pole behind his house in East Germany
when the reporters of *Freie Welt* came to visit in 1974.

When he met Wiebke, an East German teacher, at an event in
Leipzig in November 1971, the two instantly fell for each other. Years
later, Wiebke still remembered every detail of their first meeting: 'It
just happened, I don't know what possessed me. When I stood in
front of him, I went weak at the knees and breathed in the little bit
of English I had, "You are the best looking man of the world."'[32]
Reed moved to East Germany in 1972 and the couple married in
June 1973.

Erich Honecker instantly recognized that he had struck pop-
culture gold. In the midst of the frenzy for all things American from
jeans to rock'n' roll, the GDR had acquired its very own communist
cowboy. Dean Reed incorporated the perfect combination of popularity and politics – and would not even need much convincing to
act the part. As Stefan Ernsting put it in his biography of Reed, 'He
wanted to be a hero and believed in heroism as firmly as only an
American can.'[33] Throughout the 1970s, he tirelessly gave interviews
and concerts (among many other events, he also played at the Youth
Festival in 1973), always staying on message. He had, as he told the
Volksstimme newspaper, 'the feeling that I have changed my life at

the decisive moment; I realized that Marxism-Leninism is the only humane philosophy'.[34] Throughout the 1970s, he continued to fill concert halls and act in many films which financed his political campaigns around the world.

Reed's star had long since waned when in 1986, after a series of deep personal crises and a fair degree of disillusionment with the GDR (but not with socialism itself), he was found floating in the lake behind his house. He had cut his wrists and overdosed on sleeping pills. His fifteen-page suicide note, addressed to Eberhard Fensch, an SED functionary responsible for TV and radio, was only released by the authorities after 1990 and blamed his last wife, Renate Blume, for his unhappiness. It is more likely, however, that the cowboy felt restless in the GDR, to the point of deep depression. For one thing, he was desperately homesick. Despite his fervent belief in socialism, Reed had never really been able to give up his American identity. He listened to American military radio stations while in the GDR and returned to his home country several times. There, he became more frustrated and disillusioned with each visit as his ideology was rejected by US audiences. It was his peculiar mix of unadulterated American flair and political activism that made him such a huge success in the GDR. This tension became too much for him to bear.

13 June 1974, Frankfurt am Main, West Germany. Frank Schöbel and his background dancers had been crouching in a huge colourful ball in the middle of the Waldstadion for what seemed an eternity. Not only was it incredibly cold and wet for the time of year, but he was worried about how the crowds might react. As they waited in the small, damp space for their turn to perform, the tension became almost unbearable. There were 62,000 people in the stadium. They had come to watch the opening of the FIFA World Cup, the first ever to be hosted by Germany. Each participating nation had been invited to introduce itself in a five-minute show segment. The GDR had chosen thirty-one-year-old Fränki, as his friends called him. This was a huge opportunity for the young pop star from Leipzig.

During Ulbricht's brief phase of cultural liberalization, he had had successful hits with American-inspired songs such as 'Looky, Looky' and 'Party Twist' in 1964. He was even allowed to star in the 1966 state-produced DEFA musical film *Reise ins Ehebett*, wearing a pair of jeans which were then still considered risqué. But his career had suffered when Ulbricht began to tighten the cultural reins again, forcing Schöbel to conform. His earlier hits were mothballed for a few years and he was ordered to appear in uniform to improve the image of the National People's Army.

When Honecker took over in 1971, he saw Schöbel as a good way to impress the young. The singer was even allowed to perform his 1971 hit 'Wie ein Stern' (Like a Star) on West German television in 1972, the first East German singer to be afforded this privilege by the GDR authorities. Honecker saw huge potential in the handsome young pop idol who was often described as an East German Dean Martin or Cliff Richard. 'Wie ein Stern' was released as a single in East and West Germany. It was popular all over the Eastern Bloc as well as in Austria and Switzerland.

Schöbel had become a star. And yet, the singer remembered being very nervous in the Waldstadion in 1974 when the huge ball he was crouched in unfolded around him, forming a flower pattern on the stadium floor and 62,000 pairs of eyes in the audience were revealed, all gazing expectantly at the famous East German. 'Would they boo when the GDR was announced?' he wondered. They did not. He played his song 'Freunde gibt es überall' (There are Friends Everywhere) without hiccups – although he would rather have played a football song he had composed specifically for the occasion: 'Der Fußball ist rund wie die Welt' (The Football is as Round as the World). Nonetheless, Schöbel was pleased. He was later told that 600 million viewers watched his performance worldwide.[35]

Many other East Germans have very fond memories of the 1974 World Cup. The little GDR won its group even though it included the West German hosts who had by then built a fearsome reputation as a football team. The only ever football match between GDR and FRG took place in the group stages. Remarkably, the East won

1–0 with a beautiful goal scored by Jürgen Sparwasser. Even though West Germany eventually won the tournament and became world champions for the second time, that too had many East German households cheering. Gerd Müller, Franz Beckenbauer, Sepp Maier, Paul Breitner and many other West German star players were seen as all-German heroes. Schöbel had provided the soundtrack to a fondly remembered summer of football.

Given the scale of global public attention, Honecker was keen to ensure Schöbel and his band would not step out of line. Someone from the Culture Ministry was sent with the men to remind them that they must not wear jeans or anything else considered too outrageous. 'We have a political mission,' the man from the ministry reminded the band. So Schöbel and the others hatched a plan. To begin with, they would wear the formal suits they had worn at their confirmation ceremonies – hideously outdated outfits that consisted of white nylon shirts, thin ties, tight trousers and pointy shoes. As they walked past some West Berliners at the border checkpoint, they were laughed at, 'Look! Easterners!' But their chaperone loved it, 'Just what I had in mind!' Once on the train, they quickly got changed – not quite into jeans but at least into flared trousers that were popular at the time. In doing so, they struck a compromise that exemplifies countless others. East Germans were finding ways to live with a regime that permanently oscillated between the need for popularity and the need to control.

Many musicians managed to carve out enough artistic freedom for themselves in the GDR. The rock band City, formed in East Berlin in 1972, had a huge hit with their 1977 song 'Am Fenster' (By the Window) which was also released in West Germany a year later and sold over 10 million copies in total. They were one of the few bands to be allowed to sing in the West and even made an English-language LP called *Dreamer* in 1980 with the American producer Jack Rieley who had previously facilitated the Beach Boys' comeback in the early 1970s.

Karat were another rock band formed in East Berlin. From 1975 they produced music that was both popular and approved by the state. The band received the Art Prize from the Culture Ministry in October 1977 and was produced by the state-owned label Amiga from 1978. A year later, they had their first commercial appearance in West Berlin where their biggest hit 'Über sieben Brücken mußt Du geh'n' (You Must Cross Seven Bridges) also became popular. It was covered in 1980 by West Germany's most successful singer Peter Maffay, who had a huge hit with it himself. Karat continue to be commercially successful to this day.

Female singers too became an intrinsic part of East German rock and pop music. Ute Freudenberg had been discovered in 1971 at the age of fifteen, and went on to receive formal musical education at the University of Music Franz Liszt in her home town of Weimar in Thuringia. Her 1978 hit 'Jugendliebe' (Young Love) is widely regarded as a classic of the GDR. So is Nina Hagen's 'Du hast den Farbfilm vergessen' (You Forgot the Colour Film), produced by Amiga in 1974. In it, Hagen chides her boyfriend Michael for only taking a black-and-white camera film on their holiday to the Baltic Sea rather than a colour one:

> So angry my bare foot is stomping in the sand
> and from my shoulder I flick off your hand
> Micha, my Micha, and it all hurts so
> do that again, Micha, and I'll go
>
> You forgot the colour film, my Michael
> Now nobody will believe how beautiful it was
> You forgot the colour film, oh my soul!
> All the blues and whites and greens later were no more!

The nineteen-year-old Nina Hagen – not quite yet the punk icon she was to become – sang with an endearing, almost child-like petulance which was in turn set off by the cheerful, catchy music. It was an experience almost every East German could empathize with. Colour films were not easily available and the vast majority of private GDR photographs were taken in black-and-white. The song became

so iconic that Angela Merkel chose it for her official retirement ceremony in 2021.

In contrast to other popular artists, Nina Hagen could not find a
cultural and intellectual niche for herself in the GDR. Her mother
Eva-Maria Hagen had been in a relationship with the singer and dis-
sident Wolf Biermann, which had political consequences that stifled
her creative life. The authorities regarded her as a political liability
and kept a tight lid on how and where she was able to perform. She
gained a few roles in DEFA films in the mid-1970s but then decided
to leave the GDR at the end of 1976, which she was allowed to do
due to her association with Wolf Biermann who had just been
stripped of his citizenship and expatriated. A successful career as a
punk artist in the US, Britain and West Germany followed.

What Nina Hagen would not or could not do – adapt her style
and output to the regime's needs – others found acceptable. The
most popular and most successful East German rock band is also
the one that knew best how to navigate the narrow path between
regime and people: the Puhdys. The band had existed in various
configurations since the late 1960s but in 1970 they were banned
from performing in the GDR's most populous district of Karl-
Marx-Stadt (now Chemnitz), Saxony. The head of the council's
culture department had personally inspected one of their concerts
in the little Saxon village of Clausnitz. He was not impressed with
what he saw and heard over the course of the three-hour performance. 'The titles played by the ensemble were exclusively sung in
"English,"' the official complained. 'Normally, well-equipped
ensembles own sound systems with an output of 70 or 80 watts.
This ensemble, however, carries a 200-watt sound system.' The biggest problem was the effect this noisy group had on its impressionable
listeners: 'Some of the "songs" on offer were served up with screams
and inarticulate noises to an audience consisting mostly of teenagers who, whipped up by the music, carried out degenerate motions.
The ensemble was unable to manage the sequence of titles in such
a manner that any kind of chaos among the teenage dancers might
have been avoided.'[36] The inspectors lost no time in banning the

Puhdys from performing in their entire district, 'due to repeated grievous violations of the principles of our socialist cultural policy'.

In the face of such strong official objection during the repressive atmosphere of Ulbricht's last years, the Puhdys understood that their options were limited. If they wanted to be successful in the GDR, they would have to adapt. They held talks with local government officials to ask what they would need to do and promised to change the concept of their band accordingly. On 23 October 1970, two months after they had been banned, the Puhdys received a letter from the authorities: 'Your understanding and your promise to keep working on your programme and to reduce English-language singing contributed decisively to our decision [to lift the performance ban]. We wish you all the best for your continued work in the culture-political field.'[37]

And the Puhdys stuck to their promise. Gone were the days where they played covers of British and American hits in village halls and pubs. As they began to write their own material in German, their venues became bigger and eventually their freedoms greater. Stylistically, their role models remained Western rock bands like Uriah Heep and Deep Purple, but they wrote German songs and became extremely successful creating music for GDR films and staging big concerts such as at the 1973 Youth Festival in East Berlin. They also performed in the Eastern Bloc and West Germany, selling over 400,000 copies of their albums by 1977. Having regained the trust of the authorities and in the somewhat more open cultural atmosphere of the 1970s, the Puhdys were eventually able to return to the language of their Anglo-American musical heroes. In 1977, they produced the album *Rock'n' Roll Music*, their first English compilation, which exclusively consisted of cover songs. They were allowed to continue producing more English-language music and even toured the US in 1981. A year later, they were awarded the National Prize of the GDR for artistic achievements and by 1989 they had sold 20 million albums, more than any other East German rock band.

The Puhdys' initial adaptation to the requirements of the regime was not a mere act of submission as many of the more critical intellectuals and artists in the GDR would often charge them with. Their willingness to sing in German was crucial to their elevation as a band that shaped rock music in the GDR. In a strange way, the pressure from petty-minded authorities forced them to become more creative, to find their own voice. The same is true for many other musicians in this period. Collectively, the sound of 'Ostrock' that emerged from the GDR in the 1970s was inspired by the West but made distinct by the experiences and conditions of the world the musicians lived in. Their popularity beyond the state's borders stands testimony to the quality of output. Ostrock may have been influenced by political pressures but it was not made by them.

Westpolitik

Bonn, West Germany, 24 April 1974. It was 6.30 a.m. when the forty-seven-year-old Günter Guillaume opened the door of his flat in Ubierstraße 107 in the Bad Godesberg district of West Germany's capital city. 'Yes?' he asked the uniformed men from the Federal Criminal Police Office who had knocked on his door. They explained that they would need to arrest him and his wife Christel as well as his mother-in-law Erna Boom. Still in his pyjamas and now gripped by panic, Guillaume blurted, 'I am an officer of the National People's Army of the GDR and I work for the Ministry for State Security. Please respect my honour as an officer.'[38]

There it was: proof that one of West German Chancellor Willy Brandt's closest aides was in fact an East German spy. Guillaume and his wife had received special training for this purpose – they appear under the code names Hansen and Heinze in the Stasi files from the 1950s. Their task was to move into West Germany, infiltrate the system and move up the ranks as far as they could. At first, their cover story seemed watertight. Christel's mother Erna Boom lived in Frankfurt am Main and so her daughter and son-in-law 'fled' the GDR in 1956, ostensibly to be with her. Using the start-up capital of DM10,000 which they had received from the Stasi, they set up a coffee and tobacco shop called Boom am Dom after Christel's maiden name and its location near the cathedral (*Dom* in German). They waited a year before they joined the local branch of the Social Democratic Party.

Nobody suspected anything as Günter Guillaume's quiet efficiency and impeccable work ethic saw him steadily climb the political ladder. By 1972, he had reached the top. As Willy Brandt's personal aide, he attended top-level meetings, had access to classified documents and gained insights into the Chancellor's private life. The two men developed a close personal relationship as Guillaume accompanied Brandt on business trips and supported him on the campaign trail. He was even invited to join the Chancellor's family at their private home, attended garden parties and went on Sunday walks with them. Brandt first found out about the double identity of his confidant when he returned from a trip to Cairo and Algiers. As his plane landed and he walked down the gangway, he was informed that Guillaume had been arrested that very morning. A mere twelve days later, Brandt handed in his resignation as West German Chancellor. The Guillaumes spent years in prison before they were released back into the GDR in 1981 as part of a spy swap between the two Germanies. Back home, the couple were celebrated as heroes. Both received the Order of Karl Marx (the GDR's highest honour with a prize of 20,000 marks) and high officer ranks within the Stasi. They held almost star-like status and were invited as VIPs to events and dinners.

While new research, such as Eckard Michels's biography of Guillaume, has shown that he was by no means the master spy he was hailed as in the GDR, this high-profile episode nonetheless reveals a lot about inner-German relations in the 1970s. Bonn and Berlin may have been centrepieces in the much larger puzzle of Cold War relations, but they were far more obsessed with one another at this point than they were with their superpower allies and enemies. Willy Brandt's Chief of Staff, Horst Ehmke, had aptly summarized the top three priorities of the West German Federal Intelligence Service as 'GDR, GDR, GDR'.[39] This was reciprocated in the East as Erich Mielke saw espionage of and by West Germany as the main concern at all levels of his organization. As the Stasi invested considerable resources in the FRG as its main target, it was able to build a sizeable network of spies in the political and administrative structures of the other Germany. Stasi expert Jens Gieseke counted 170 strategically placed sources of which five had been successfully planted in areas of the Chancellery, the office of the President, the press office and the security group of the Federal Criminal Police Office. This included a secretary in the Chancellery, a journalist, and a member of staff in one of the sub-committees of the Chancellery. Similar numbers applied to all other core government departments, including the Foreign Office, and all of the major political parties.[40]

Paradoxically, this obsession with each other also found its expression in closer German-German ties despite the fact that when Honecker replaced Ulbricht, he was initially keen to prove to Moscow that he was going to turn his back on such fraternization with the class enemy. Many of those who had been sceptical of Ulbricht's previous flirtations with the Western Social Democrats were relieved, such as East German Foreign Minister Otto Winzer, who had called West German rapprochement under Willy Brandt's *Ostpolitik* an act of 'aggression in felt slippers'. Honecker himself also still told troops during an inspection on the island of Rügen in 1972 that 'our Republic and the FRG have the same relationship with one another as each does to a third state. The FRG therefore is a foreign country and more to the point: it is an imperialist foreign country.'[41]

However, the Saarlander could not quite let go of his intrinsic ties to the West despite being convinced that the brutally enforced separation of East and West Germans was a necessity that helped preserve the peace in Europe. In 1974, he pointed out that the rules of engagement for border forces had not changed. If someone attempted to break through the fortifications of the inner-German border, the guards were to call, then fire a warning shot, and, if there was no possibility to apprehend the target, 'firearms are to be used without reservation and comrades who have used their fire-arms successfully are to be praised'.[42] Keen to prove that he too could live with such restrictions, Honecker chose not to attend his mother's and father's funerals in the Saarland when they died in 1963 and 1969, respectively. But like many other East Germans, he could not quite shake off historic sentiments of German nation-hood after only two decades or so of separation. The lure of his countrymen on the other side of the Iron Curtain remained great, and while the Social Democrats were in power in the FRG, there was political will there to normalize German-German relations.

Brandt and Honecker began the process of inner-German rap-prochement with the Transit Agreement, signed on 17 December 1971, which allowed better access from West Germany to West Berlin and at least thirty days of travel a year for West Berliners into East Germany (which could be extended on a case-by-case basis). The transit of people and goods was to be as 'simple, fast and cheap' as possible, which meant, for example, that the searching of car boots and people who were just passing through GDR territory was to stop. A further traffic treaty was signed on 26 May 1972 which made it possible for East Germans to visit relatives in the West for 'urgent family affairs' – something that had previously been extremely difficult if one was not a pensioner, for whom exceptions were made as they were not deemed economic assets any more.

The biggest breakthrough came with the Basic Treaty signed on 21 December 1972. Its Article 1 agreed on 'the development of good neighbourly relations on the basis of equal rights'. The dry formal tone of these words belies their significance. For years, West Germany's Hallstein Doctrine had meant that the GDR was to be shunned by the Western world, not recognized as a sovereign state, while Bonn claimed to speak for all Germans. The Basic Treaty marked a seachange with its 'neighbourly' rhetoric and 'respect for the independence and sovereignty of the two states'. This shift allowed the FRG to normalize its relations with East Germany and it afforded other states the opportunity to do so too. The pinnacle of this inner-German thaw was the establishment of 'Permanent

Missions' in Bonn and East Berlin. While the GDR proudly called its emissary an 'ambassador', the FRG could not do so as it still had the demand for reunification written into its constitution and recognized all Germans as its citizens (by contrast, the GDR had introduced its own citizenship in 1967). Bonn therefore deliberately avoided the word 'embassy', and called its man in East Germany its 'Permanent Representative *by* the GDR', not *'in* the GDR'. East Berlin was considered not to be part of East Germany, just the same as West Berlin was not governed by West Germany under the Four Power Agreement of 1972, which had confirmed the responsibilities of the occupying powers for the city.

For the GDR the 'German Question' was more or less resolved from 1974. The two states existed as separate, sovereign entities with separate capital cities, citizenship and governance. It considered the FRG a foreign country but one that could be negotiated with. Bonn meanwhile retained reunification as a constitutional aim until 1990 and only partially accepted the idea of East German citizenship. Importantly, however, it accepted the GDR's sovereignty. The Permanent Missions and the new foundations laid for bilateral relations allowed the two Germanies to build closer political and economic ties during the 1970s. Honecker had successfully walked the tightrope of convincing Moscow of his unquestionable loyalty to the Soviet course while simultaneously establishing unprecedented links to the other Germany.

Doing Business with the West

Leipzig, Saxony, spring 1974. Alexander Schalck-Golodkowski was busy. The forty-one-year-old Deputy Minister for External Trade was in his element amid the hustle and bustle of the Leipzig Trade Fair – a proud tradition in the Saxon city since 1165, when the first fair was recorded. Not even socialism could break with such a longstanding tradition of commercial zeal. The GDR had celebrated the 800-year anniversary of the Leipzig fair in 1965 and given it its own mascot: a pipe-smoking tradesman with an orange globe for a head and a briefcase in his hand inscribed with the destination 'Leipzig Trade Fair'. The Trade Fair Man was so popular that over 400,000 copies were made in various sizes and he made regular appearances in *Unser Sandmann*, the children's TV programme. People associated him with the excitement and internationalism of the fair itself at which Western delegations, companies and journalists were present every spring and autumn. It fell to men like Schalck to make these commercial encounters with the capitalist world as fruitful as possible.

The Leipzig Trade Fair was more than just a marketplace for new products. It was a networking event for one of the GDR's most important financial props: trade with the West. Schalck had the skills, creativity and temperament for the task even before he had completed his degree. In 1956, when he was only twenty-four, he was already appointed as a head of department within the GDR's Ministry of Foreign Trade, and in 1966, he helped initiate and build the *Kommerzielle Koordinierung* (Commercial Coordination) enterprise, known as *KoKo*, which tried to acquire foreign currency for the GDR. The Leipzig Trade Fair had become an indispensable event in Schalck's calendar and he was all the more surprised when he was called to Berlin in the middle of the 1974 spring fair. 'I was told to appear in front of the General Secretary immediately,' he would later recall. 'This invitation would become my first personal encounter with Erich Honecker.'[43]

When he arrived in Berlin, Schalck was summoned into Honecker's bright office where he found himself face to face with the man himself. Stasi boss Erich Mielke and the Secretary for the Economy of the Central Committee Günter Mittag were also present. The men gazed quizzically into Schalck's round face. They were looking at a natural salesman with a head for factual detail and a calm manner that made him seem trustworthy to the political class of the GDR as well as his Western trading partners. What the powerful trio really needed to know and the reason they had seen fit to pull their most important money maker away from the fair was:

how much profit had been made by selling prisoners to West Germany?

Honecker elaborated: 'Comrade Mielke explained to me that all such income is processed through the department you control. Is this true?'[44] It was. Since 1962, the GDR had begun to make financial deals with the West German government, charities, lawyers and individual families for the release of its political prisoners and others who wanted to leave East Germany. The first 'sale' happened in December 1962 when twenty adult prisoners and twenty children whose parents had already emigrated were sent to the West in exchange for three wagon loads of fertilizer. What started as an unofficial ad-hoc transaction of willing human cargo against much-needed materials and goods quickly proved so lucrative that the operations were scaled up. By 1989, the GDR would 'sell' 33,755 people to the West and the average 'price' per person more than doubled from DM40,000 to DM95,847, although the 'value' of prisoners varied significantly depending on how much they were deemed to be worth to those who wanted to free them on the other side of the Berlin Wall. By the time Honecker asked Schalck for an itemized account in the spring of 1974, he had made nearly half a billion West German marks in goods and cash.[45]

The selling of humans from one half of a divided state to the other was an act of economic desperation. It should be noted, however, that the term many West German observers used for these transactions – *Menschenhandel* (human trafficking) – doesn't reflect the fact that the prisoners themselves were often actively involved. Both the Protestant and Catholic churches, for example, used their inter-German networks to draw up lists of East German members of their communities who wanted to leave the GDR and then organized for them to do so via this system. Government agents, both East and West, were assigned to the tasks to negotiate prices for individuals or groups, often keeping fairly close and amicable 'business' ties with one another for years. Both East Berlin and Bonn tried to keep a lid on this dubious practice in order to avoid public scandal. The operation reached a peak in 1977/78 where 12 per cent of all those who left the GDR legally did so by being 'bailed out' with Western money.

Once Honecker had spoken to Schalck, the infamous *Honecker-konto* (Honecker Account) was set up for the funds from these transactions. Account No. 0628 was established with the Deutsche Handelsbank in East Berlin on 29 March 1974 and its trustee was none other than Schalck himself. The name 'Honecker Account' is therefore somewhat of a misnomer – the First Secretary never had any direct access to it but ordered the funds to be used via the *KoKo*. The intended purpose of the money acquired through the sale of people (nearly DM3.5 billion in total) was not to fund the privileges of the GDR elite, as has often been claimed, but to ensure there was enough security for Western creditors to keep lending the GDR money and to fund imports of consumer goods such as shoes, exotic fruits (including the famously elusive bananas) and textiles such as the much-desired original American 'Blue Jeans'.[46] On 7 August 1980, DM32 million was listed for 'bicycle tyres, biscuits, chocolate, wine, socks for men, underwear for adults, terry towels, outdoor shoes, cleaning cloths, tea towels'.[47] Other imports for sectors such as health and sport were also funded through the *Honecker-konto*, as well as millions of marks spent in foreign aid for Poland and Nicaragua. The account also doubled up as a rainy-day fund for the permanently cash-strapped GDR. Some of the money was carefully invested in Vienna, Copenhagen and Lugano; some of it was used to buy gold reserves. In December 1989, there were still DM2.2 billion credited on the account with around DM100 million available in cash and the rest invested in foreign banks so it could serve as loan securities for creditors.

Due to its small size, lack of industrial capacity and ongoing problems with energy procurement, East Germany was reliant on foreign trade and imports even for such essential things as gas, oil and machinery. There was not a single year between 1969 and 1980 where the GDR's exports to capitalist countries exceeded its imports from them. Nonetheless, the system worked remarkably well in the early 1970s. Between 1969 and 1973, productivity rose by 23 per cent (a trend that continued, if not quite as fast, throughout the decade) and by 1975 real wages had increased by 30 per cent.[48] Despite the fact that some caution is required when dealing with economic data produced by the GDR, most historians now agree that the economy increased steadily in the first half of the 1970s, including a stable growth of GDP. At the same time, Honecker was keen to make good on his 1971 promise to 'increase the material and cultural living standards of the population'. Life was to move on from the make-do endurance spirit of the Ulbricht decades towards the 'arrival' of the GDR at a sustainable normality.

As a result the state invested enormous sums into housing, welfare and entertainment. By 1975, building activity had reached a level of 128.5 per cent compared to 1970, which improved accommodation and workplaces by modernizing and extending them. Rents were so heavily subsidized that GDR citizens did not have to worry about affordability once they had found a suitable flat. From 1971, the rates paid were means-tested, allowing working class families with children privileged access. A four-person household in West Germany spent around 21 per cent of their net income on rental costs while a similar household in the East only needed 4.4 per cent. While this focus on newly built housing meant that older buildings were left to decay in town centres up and down the country, which made for very unsightly impressions on foreign observers, the prefab blocks came with central heating, insulation, bathrooms and plenty of space. Honecker was also able to oversee rapid progress in supplying the population with consumer goods. By 1975, more than a quarter of households had a car, compared to only 15 per cent in 1970, and the figure would rise to 38 per cent by the end of the decade. By 1980, almost every household had a fridge, a TV and a washing machine.

But all of this had to be funded somehow. Western countries borrowed billions from their banks and other domestic and foreign financial institutions to fund their own welfare states – by 1980 West Germany had accrued a national debt equivalent to €239 billion. This was more difficult for the GDR which operated in an

economic system dominated by the Soviet Union and was dependent on Moscow's needs. Borrowing money from West Germany
therefore became a lucrative option. Backed through the funds
from the Honecker Account, the GDR found it increasingly easy
to win Western creditors. By 1980, these creditors had lent their
socialist neighbour DM25.3 billion already and the interest was eating heavily into any economic progress made. The GDR made up
for some of this by selling refined oil back to the West. Finished in
1964, the oil pipeline Druzhba (Russian for 'friendship') delivered
oil from Russia to Eastern Europe, including East Germany, which
the latter then refined in its own sophisticated installations and sold
to Western Europe – a lucrative business, especially since the oil
crisis of 1973 had hit the world hard. Prices and demand had shot
up while import costs from the USSR had been fixed in a five-year
plan. Indeed, business was so good, the pipeline reached full capacity in the early 1970s and a second pipeline, Druzhba 2, was laid
parallel to the first in 1974. However, on 18 June 1975, the Soviet
Ministry for External Trade sent a formal note to its opposite number in East Berlin stating that oil prices must unfortunately be
adjusted in light of recent economic developments. The price of a
tonne of crude oil more than doubled from 14 to 35 rubles. Werner
Jarowinsky, politburo member with responsibility for trade and
supplies, wrote to Honecker, 'This would mean further costs for
1976 of an additional 725 million marks.'[49]

Honecker's steady economic progress was killed by this decision
in Moscow. So creating an illusion of progress became state policy.
Where previously genuinely improved products were imported or
produced, the GDR now began to package old goods into new
boxes and increased their prices while the cheaper products just
vanished from the market. The incremental and artificial 'improvements' of the Trabant are a striking example – there was no real
progress in terms of the outdated, two-stroke engine, or the size
and comfort of the car. The inability to import cotton from the
Soviet Union meant that huge amounts of textiles had to be bought
expensively from West Germany. Modern new factories which

now ran efficiently on oil and gas from Russia had to be recon-verted to run on domestic brown coal supplies, making them inefficient and dirty again while reducing output and increasing prices by default. This archaic technology had a devastating impact on the environment and workers who had to put up with the heavy fumes and continued to labour in the coal mines. In this context, Schalck's work in creating economic ties to the West became indis-pensable. Accordingly, his methods of revenue creation became increasingly creative. Apart from its prisoners, the GDR sold con-fiscated paraphernalia from the Nazi era, art and artefacts it had 'nationalized' during the early post-war years and anything else that could be turned into cash. By 1989, the *KoKo* had made DM50 billion according to Schalck – around half of that flowed immedi-ately into the coffers of the state while half remained with the *KoKo* for reinvestment.

No wonder Honecker mused in 1990, 'I would like to say that Schalck, in my view, did valuable work for the development of the GDR's external trade with the Western world . . . Unfortunately, the GDR had few businessmen like him.'[50] The businessman in question had no sleepless nights after the fall of the Berlin Wall. He would later remember, 'I was a convinced citizen of the GDR, and I have always acted in the interest of my state. That this was not always done in the manner of honourable Hanseatic tradesmen was due to the situation of the divided Germany. We were in the middle of the Cold War, neither side worked with silk gloves.'[51]

8. *Friends and Enemies (1976–1981)*

All the coffee is gone!

The Churches and Other Enemies of the State

Zeitz, Saxony-Anhalt, 18 August 1976. At 10.20 a.m., a light-grey Wartburg 311 came to a halt on a junction on the Braustraße in front of the entrance to St Michael's Church. Zeitz was an industrial hub of around 45,000 inhabitants. Once the area around the church had been characterized by mediaeval timber-framed houses and cobbled streets, but seven Anglo-American air raids during the Second World War had dropped over 3,200 tonnes of bombs on the town. Much of it was in severe need of repair or rebuilding. But as Zeitz was taking in large numbers of German refugees from Eastern Europe, housing space took priority over the restoration of the historic town centre. As elsewhere, modern, large-scale prefab housing blocks were built on the outskirts while the centre was left to decay. By 1976, the streets around St Michael's looked more than a little tired with the bright facade of the mediaeval church forlorn in a square surrounded by shops.

Nobody was paying much attention when the Lutheran pastor Oskar Brüsewitz parked his Wartburg in front of the church entrance and got out wearing the black gown of his office. No one was surprised when he put a hand-painted sign on the roof of his car which read: 'A message to everyone ... A message to everyone ... We indict communism for: the oppression of the churches in schools of children and teenagers! [*sic*]' Forty-six-year-old Brüsewitz was well known in the community for his vocal opposition to the GDR authorities and his unusual means of expressing it. One Christmas, he had installed a huge illuminated cross on top of his church. The locals reported that he rang the church bells at night, let sheep and pigeons roam the church during services and drove across a field in a Trabant with a plough attached. While these claims are to be taken with a pinch of salt as they were later used by the Stasi to assert that Brüsewitz was insane, the pastor was well known to be somewhat eccentric in the way he expressed his opposition to the GDR. He had previously used posters and placards to spread his messages and became increasingly frustrated that his flock did not seem to care. The Deputy Bishop of Magdeburg Friedrich-Wilhelm Bäumer claimed that he had become unapproachable and 'entangled himself in a dark web, in his own lonely thought processes'.[1]

When Brüsewitz started installing yet more political messages on his Wartburg that morning, it seemed to be just another one of his antics. But then he opened his boot, took out a 20-litre milk can and poured its contents all over himself until his black gown was completely drenched. He took out a match. Before any of the bystanders knew what was happening, a ball of flames erupted around the pastor, engulfing him, the back of his car and the road surface. Brüsewitz ran 20 metres from his car on to the church square where an NVA man happened to be standing near a telephone booth. The startled soldier tackled the burning pastor to the ground. Just as Brüsewitz hit the pavement, the church bells of St Michael's began to ring out.

Brüsewitz's suffering was brought to an end when another driver got out of his car and came running with a heavy woollen blanket which was quickly wrapped around him to stifle the flames. The whole tragic spectacle was over in three minutes. Some 150 onlookers had now gathered around the square. Brüsewitz was immediately transferred to the local hospital where he received emergency treatment, but he had suffered second degree burns on around 80 per cent of his body, including his head, and died four days later.

It is clear from the Stasi's detailed files on the case that the authorities were immediately concerned about the effect of Brüsewitz's self-sacrifice on the public mood in the country and abroad. They

A Welder at Rostock Shipyard.

At VEB Schwermaschinenbau Karl Liebknecht, Magdeburg.

Break time at the VEB Elektrokohlefactory, East Berlin.

Free German Youth, 1973.

X World Festival of Youth and Students, 1973, East Berlin.

Beginning of the summer holidays, Berlin, 1972.

Toys, 1982.

Palace of the Republic, 1976.

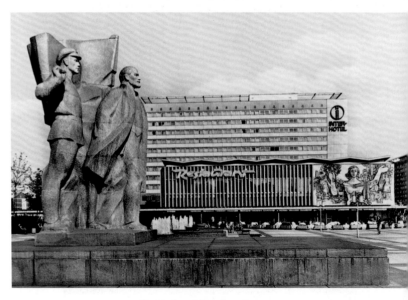

Dresden's socialist reinvention, 1979.

Border Guard, 1980s.

Kiosk, East Berlin, 1971.

A man shovels coal from the street to his basement in Halle, February 1990.

Pioneers celebrating 25 years of the Berlin Wall.

Boy washing car, 1975.

Contract Worker from Mozambique, 1984.

Couple in the Oderbruch region.

questioned witnesses at the scene and asked them if they could remember the messages on the pastor's billboard which had been hastily removed by the police. Much to the Stasi's relief the 'overwhelming majority' could 'only remember fragments of the slogans' and 'took a negative view of the deed and distanced themselves from it'.[2] There were several indicators that this was not just wishful thinking on behalf of the Stasi. Brüsewitz had struggled to fit in with the community for a long time both personally and professionally. The son of farmers was drafted into the *Wehrmacht* in the last phase of the war, at the age of fifteen, before he was captured by the Red Army. When he was released, he moved to West Germany, became a cobbler, got married and had a daughter. But this life fell apart with his marriage and he moved to the GDR for a fresh start in 1954. There, he lived with a Christian family, found his faith and began to pursue training as a priest. This was initially aborted when he struggled with psychosomatic problems. He improved, returned to the cobbling business, married again and had two daughters and a son. But health problems continued to plague him and, tragically, his son died of illness in 1969.

Brüsewitz sought refuge from his problems by throwing himself wholeheartedly into his religious work. He was ordained as a pastor in 1970 and in this time he became increasingly erratic and political. This did not always earn him the admiration of his flock and fellow church leaders. The conflict came to a head when the community suggested in 1976 that he seek transferral to a different parish, ideally in West Germany. It was in this context that Brüsewitz's tragic end needs to be seen. His wife and daughters confirmed that he had been deeply troubled for some time. He had even dug his own grave before his suicide and wrote a letter in which he spoke of a 'war raging between light and darkness. Truth and lies are standing side by side.'[3]

Brüsewitz was a broken man who had suffered too many tragedies to integrate into communities in East and West Germany that largely just wanted to get on with their lives regardless of the politics of the Cold War raging around them. Brüsewitz could not live like that. He was restless and wanted to fight the injustices of the world, while his own mind and health repeatedly dealt him blows and setbacks. As a result, his death was not that of a martyr, angrily avenged by a wave of church resistance. The sad truth is that people had never understood him and the churches had largely found a way to go on within a hostile system. To them, Brüsewitz was a troublemaker. Shortly before his death, the leadership of the Lutheran church in Saxony issued a statement to the parish in which it condemned the actions of the pastor: 'We know that Brother Brüsewitz saw his service as bearing witness to God, even if he sometimes pursued this with unusual means. But we cannot condone the deed of our brother . . . We are of the opinion that it is our duty to work within society . . . We reject any attempt to use what happened in Zeitz as propaganda against the German Democratic Republic.'[4]

The problems that were to spring from Brüsewitz's suicide for the GDR authorities were not so much caused by a backlash from church communities or wider society, but by their own aggressive response. They had not been able to shake off the permanent, pathological paranoia of their early years. The system was still run by people like Honecker and Mielke who had gone through a formative phase of political persecution and responded to the resulting sense of threat with methods learned from Joseph Stalin. If the quiet and distanced reaction from Brüsewitz's family and the parish could have convinced the apparatchiks that there was not going to be any trouble, the media attendance at the funeral shattered their fragile confidence. No fewer than nine major West German media outlets had come to make political capital out of the pastor's tragic death. In turn, the Stasi deployed an army of its own security personnel and informants who spied on religious leaders as well as preventing political messages and wreaths to be laid by the grave outside the official funeral service. The Stasi report on the funeral notes with palpable relief, 'Around 2.50 p.m., the funeral concluded without any disturbances.'[5]

But Mielke's men also noted that some church leaders and one of Brüsewitz's daughters had given interviews. A camera team from the West German public broadcaster ZDF had also filmed in Zeitz. Knowing that the majority of East Germans had access to West German TV and would be able to watch the interviews and reports, the SED decided that defamation was the best strategy. Before the funeral an article in the party newspaper *Neues Deutschland* had already called the pastor 'an abnormal person who had pathological tendencies and suffered from paranoia', in an attempt to reinforce the idea that his suicide had personal reasons.[6] The political reporting in the West triggered the familiar defensive reflex in the GDR authorities. The result was a clumsily worded and inflammatory article on 29 August 1976, when most East Germans were already beginning to forget about the incident.

In this much longer piece, the paper released a complete history of Brüsewitz's alleged antics which the Stasi had gathered from people in Zeitz. Without fact-checking the gossip the Stasi had received, *Neues Deutschland* retold stories of alleged madness such as when the pastor is supposed to have climbed onto a tractor during heavy rain, declaring that God would now send the deluge to drown the infidels. The paper then proceeded to declare that the idea that the churches were persecuted in the GDR, as the West German media claimed, was nonsensical as the state allowed 'everyone to pursue happiness as they see fit'. For proof, the newspaper listed that 'the Lutheran church has 4,000 pastors, the Catholics 1,300. At six universities there are departments of theology. Lutheran charities run 52 hospitals with 7,000 beds, 87 homes for people with disabilities, 280 old people's and care homes with 11 places as well as 112 recuperation centres, 23 orphanages, 326 nurseries with 17,000 spaces and other such institutions. Not to mention that all children in our society enjoy the benefits of higher-level education. In the Federal Republic this is only available for the children of the wealthy.'[7] While the majority in both church communities had indeed come to terms with the way things were in the GDR, this bragging about religious freedom and equality on the back of a public suicide by a Lutheran pastor was too much for many.

An eight-page Stasi report details how the *Neues Deutschland* article caused the leaders of the Lutheran church in Saxony to write a collective response, which was to be read out in churches and sent to the West German press. A committee was formed which investigated the Brüsewitz case in detail and then sent the findings to all church leaders and the State Secretary for Church Questions. The Stasi report noted that 'it is probable that this will contain negative comments about the state . . . and express the "hardships of Christians in the GDR".'[8] The East German leaders also invited West German colleagues to a meeting in East Berlin where they discussed how action might best be coordinated. In their formal declaration, which was sent to *Neues Deutschland* but not published, the church leaders explained that they felt it was necessary to speak out because they believed the pastor was done an injustice by both the West's 'attempt to make a political martyr out of Brüsewitz' as well as the East's 'portrayal of him as an insane person'. This was followed by a detailed correction of Brüsewitz's biography and the demand that the letter be published in full as 'we find it shameful that the dignity of a human being and his reputation in death have been harmed. Such practices destroy all efforts to establish trust between Church and state.'[9]

It is true that trust had been strained before 1976 through the GDR's constant erosion of church practices, for example by replacing the coming of age ceremony of confirmation with a secular equivalent called *Jugendweihe* (youth consecration) or the demolition of sixty church buildings, not all of which were war-damaged. It is also true that the majority of Christians had found a way to live with the system and the system with them. Angela Merkel, for example, grew up in Templin, around 80 kilometres north of Berlin, as the daughter of a Lutheran pastor. The family retained its Christian identity, yet Merkel was able to adapt to life in the GDR too. She later volunteered for an active FDJ role in 'Agitation and Propaganda' – a position that allowed her to take part in and organize cultural events and activities. She would later say this was '70% opportunism',[10] but in contrast to the Nazi regime, with which the GDR is still often compared, there was room for private withdrawal. In a rare comment on her East German life, Merkel would later say, 'I always had my retreat. There were no shadows over my childhood.'[11] For the majority of Protestants and Catholics, this remained the attitude after Brüsewitz, but the regime's excessive response to the case became a watershed moment for opposition circles in the GDR. Through the *Neues Deutschland* articles and other distasteful defamation of the dead man's character and state of mind, the authorities had lost moral standing and made it very easy for those who wanted to attack it. The incident highlighted a vindictive strain in the collective psyche of the political leadership.

St Nicholas Church, Prenzlau, Brandenburg, 11 September 1976. On the same day that the church committee finalized its letter about Brüsewitz, a related event was carefully watched by the Stasi: a religious evening with songs, book sales, food and lectures. Somehow the thirty-nine-year-old singer and political activist Wolf Biermann had managed to secure a slot on the programme despite having been banned from performing in the GDR for nine years. While he did not know it yet, this would be his last concert in East Germany before 1989. Amid the heightened tensions between state and churches, Erich Mielke naturally had his eyes and ears on the concert. The fact that 300 people watched Biermann play did not overly worry the Stasi. Its report somewhat gleefully noted that, 'While his first performance, the "Che-Guevara Song", received attention and applause, the rest of his programme resulted in more and more of his audience turning to the other attractions such as the book sale etc.; some even left the church.'[12] Biermann's own recollections, which he shared in the West German magazine *Der Spiegel*, differed vastly as he described roaring applause and much bigger audience figures. The Stasi meanwhile did not seem too concerned about his reception at this point. What was concerning it was that Biermann openly addressed the highly sensitive matter of the pastor's suicide in Zeitz and politicized it in the same manner that the West German media had done, claiming Brüsewitz had 'fled the republic into death'.[13]

The Stasi had long perceived Biermann as a political threat. The son of a Jewish communist, who had been active in the resistance against the Nazis and was murdered in Auschwitz, Biermann grew up in Hamburg with strong political convictions. Like his father, he was a communist from a very young age and wanted to continue the political struggle. So he moved to the GDR in 1953, only sixteen years old, while his mother stayed in Hamburg. In East Germany, he became involved with an artistic community from around 1961, which led him to try his hand at stage directing and songwriting. Both activities immediately drew the ire of the state due to his heavy criticism of the Berlin Wall. His theatre was closed in 1963, a temporary performance ban issued and his application for SED party membership denied. When Biermann then proceeded to perform political work in West Germany, a permanent performance ban was issued by the Central Committee in December 1965. But when he continued to record music illegally in his flat in East Germany, as well as officially in West Germany, the Stasi began to develop a systematic plan for his *Zersetzung* (decomposition). *Zersetzung* was still a relatively new concept at this point. It was officially introduced in Directive No. 1/76 on the Development and Revision of Operational Procedures in January 1976 and encompassed 'silent' (i.e. psychological) methods of undermining and attacking individuals in the hope that they would give up the perceived activism or opposition. According to Biermann, the Hamburg branch of the KPD, the German Communist Party, colluded with the Stasi and encouraged his mother to distance herself from her son.

The concert at St Nicholas Church hit the GDR authorities at a point where the tensions and fear over the Brüsewitz case had reached its pinnacle. The timing of the event and his explicit politicization of the pastor's death were enough to seal Biermann's fate. When he applied to be allowed to go on a concert tour in West Germany, which he had been invited to by the trade union organization IG Metall, Honecker is said to have intervened to allow him to leave. During the tour, he repeatedly criticized the GDR, which was then used by the state to rid itself of a vocal critic forever. On 16

November 1976, the politburo tabled a motion for the 'Expatriation of Wolf Biermann' and announced this decision in the afternoon.

As had been the case with its response to Brüsewitz, the regime's overreaction to Biermann also backfired. When they heard of their colleague's expatriation, an influential group of writers, musicians and other artists met on the same day in Berlin to draft and sign a resolution that urged the government to 'think again'. When *Neues Deutschland* refused to publish the resolution, the artists gave it to Western media agencies such as Reuters who ensured it was widely publicized. West German public broadcaster WDR showed a recorded Biermann concert in solidarity on the same day. When a couple of days later, the FRG's biggest public broadcaster ARD showed the concert in full, many East Germans were exposed to Biermann's music for the first time. Many of the GDR's artists, actors and musicians who had previously decided to live and work within a regime they may not have loved but found tolerable now became openly resentful. The GDR lost one of its most popular actors, Manfred Krug, who had his application to emigrate granted and left the country in 1977. It drove out Biermann's ex-girlfriend the actor Eva-Maria Hagen and her daughter Nina Hagen too. Other signatories who did not leave were now targeted with *Zersetzung* techniques, imprisonment and performance bans. In one of its most self-destructive moves, the GDR had alienated some of its most creative artists in one fell swoop.

The year 1976 could and should have been a continuation of the cultural opening initiated by Honecker in the first half of the decade. True, Honecker made it clear that he was also looking backwards when he reverted his title back to General Secretary and also assumed the role of the Chairman of the State Council in October. This effectively restored his leadership to the status Ulbricht's had had before his powers had been curtailed. Yet, there were encouraging signs of reform too. When East Germany became one of the signatories of the Helsinki Accords on 1 August 1975, it agreed to uphold basic human rights just as the other European and North American signatories had. It gave East German artists, church leaders and opposition leaders hope that the GDR was evolving, modernizing. Christa Wolf, for example, had been successful in the GDR with her political fiction. Her 1963 novel *Der geteilte Himmel* (*Divided Heaven*) was a hugely popular critique of politics and society in the GDR. The book describes a young couple struggling to come to terms with the moral and economic realities of the GDR. Manfred, the male protagonist, flees to West Berlin just before the Wall is built while Rita, unhappy but also disillusioned with the materialistic West, tries unsuccessfully to convince him to return. Rita attempts suicide and the story is told from her perspective as she wakes up in hospital. Wolf was very open about the fact that the book was semi-autobiographical. Despite the overt and desperate criticism of the GDR and Germany's division, it was a bestseller in the East. It was also widely read in West Germany and translated into many foreign languages. Yet, when Biermann was expelled in 1976, Wolf was one of the first signatories of the resolution to revoke the decision. Talented creative minds like hers were stifled by a regime too blinkered by its own paranoia to trust the people who had chosen to live and work within its rules.

The churches too were no mortal enemy to the GDR. Manfred Stolpe, Head of the Secretariat of the Federation of Evangelical Churches, said in 1976 that all that the churches wanted was 'neither to be a transmission vehicle for the Party nor a trojan horse for the counter revolution'. Indeed, even the possibility of a 'red' socialist church was attractive to many religious leaders, including Angela Merkel's father Pastor Horst Kasner. But the crass defamatory remarks about 'Brother Brüsewitz' turned many moderates into vocal critics.

The great irony of 1976 was that neither Brüsewitz nor Biermann themselves triggered the opposition movements they eventually inspired. Neither of the two men had a particularly high profile on their own. Both had voluntarily moved to the GDR from West Germany. Both were somewhat lost souls with difficult pasts who, perhaps somewhat naively, believed that their messages would make the country a better place. Neither had found much of an audience, let alone triggered organized resistance from high-profile individuals and groups. Instead it was the ever-present, systemic fear that the survivors of Nazism and Stalinism, who had built socialism in the GDR, had baked into its very foundation. The terror of subversion, itself a product of police states that had gone before, sat so deep within the very heart of East Berlin that neither Ulbricht nor Honecker ever really found the courage to face and overcome it. Like a child who never grew out of the night-time terrors of infancy, the GDR never stopped looking for monsters under its bed.

Coffee Crisis

Potsdam, Brandenburg, summer 1977. 'All the coffee is gone! They have no more coffee!' Axel Wladimiroff's mother told her twenty-three-year-old son in genuine despair. She had gone out in the morning together with Axel's grandmother to try to procure a pound of roast beans but to no avail. There was none. Axel still remembered years later how difficult it was to tell her, 'Mutti, I can't get you any coffee either, they just haven't got any.' Coffee was more than just an optional lifestyle accessory to his mother and grandmother. Having endured the war, displacement and the tough economic situation of the 1950s, to them coffee meant stability and material comfort, something that both women were experiencing for the first time in their tumultuous lives. Afternoon coffee had become a daily ritual, not just comforting but essential as a psychological crutch. When relatives from the West sent parcels, they usually included coffee. Millions of East Germans remember to this day what it was like to open a 'Westpaket' and inhale the wonderful smell of roasted beans it exuded. The idea that good-quality coffee was not an everyday commodity that could be obtained in any quantity and at any time had long contributed to the mystique of the drink and its attendant rituals.[14]

Up until 1977, there had been coffee in the GDR. The government had made sure of it even when the Soviet Union stopped its exports of the precious beans to the GDR in 1954. Ulbricht's men were instructed to find enough hard currency to buy coffee on the world market – to the tune of around DM150 million a year. From the imported beans, around 50,000 tonnes of coffee were produced by seven different plants across the country with brands such as Rondo, Mona and Kosta offering different types and qualities. While the end product was not exactly cheap (collectively, East Germans spent 3.3 billion marks annually on coffee, which was nearly the same as for furniture and twice as much as what they spent on shoes), demand was always higher than supply. The government knew full well that millions of their citizens awaited parcels from West German friends and relatives with an aching longing which was in no small part due to the expected coffee supplies. But rather than resent this fact, it became part of their economic calculation. Around one fifth of East Germany's coffee demand was supplied through Western gifts – one fifth that did not have to be bought on the world market. The only trouble was that the classic 'counter gift' that East Germans sent back to the West was *Dresdner Stollen*, a traditional fruit bread eaten during the Christmas period. This in turn contained many ingredients that had to be imported such as candied orange peel, raisins, almonds and a variety of spices. So the ongoing coffee shortage sometimes inadvertently caused a shortage of *Stollen* at the other end.

But 1977 was different. This was not a temporary issue or just a question of checking a number of shops before finding one that stocked coffee. This was a crisis. Honecker had been warned that this might happen at the end of 1976, when bad harvests in Brazil combined with the existing economic troubles caused by the oil crisis to create a perfect storm of global coffee shortages. Suddenly the GDR's import costs had more than quadrupled to an eye-watering DM667.2 million in 1977. Honecker's fixer Schalck-Golodkowski coldly suggested the only plan that seemed economically feasible without taking the beloved product off the shelves completely: 'Not all of the types of roast coffee produced and offered in the GDR will be produced any more after 01/07/1977.'[15] There should only be one type of brew and it would consist of only 50 per cent coffee, the other half to be made up from substitutes. Other economic advisors added that they recommended banning the sale of coffee in restaurants completely and reducing the overall available amount by 80 per cent, leaving the population with only a tiny bit of coffee mix. The politburo member Albert Norden was so alarmed by these suggestions that he wrote to Honecker saying, 'I just find this unbelievable . . . these measures will not be met with understanding but cause great dissatisfaction.'[16]

With Honecker on his customary summer holiday at this point, it was left to his men and women in Berlin to come up with a final plan. On 26 July, the politburo passed the 'Decree for the Supply of Coffee'. From 1 August 1977, all institutions, the army, workplaces and most restaurants were only allowed to serve the new coffee mix. This was to consist of 51 per cent coffee, 34 per cent rye-barley mix, 5 per cent chicory, 5 per cent sugar beet fibre and 5 per cent ground spelt. Only the more expensive brands of Mona, Ronda and Mokka-Fix Gold were to stay on the market in the hope that the increase in cost would drive demand down.

Unsurprisingly, the population hated 'Erichs Krönung' (Erich's brew), as people began to call the awful coffee mix. They grumbled loudly and openly about its horrendous taste and the regime's inability to procure proper supplies. The late 1970s were supposed to be a time of progress and stability. East Germans refused to just make do. Or at the very least they would grumble rather than take the hit quietly. Still, Axel Wladimiroff remembered how his mother just could not let go of her beloved afternoon ritual despite the terrible taste of 'Muckefuck', as it became referred to by East Germans: 'She shook in revulsion at every sip of it, every sip. But she forced the stuff down nonetheless. Because it was still coffee to her.'[17]

A year later, the situation had eased a little. World prices for coffee began to normalize and in the GDR too availability and pricing improved somewhat. Nonetheless, the coffee crisis of 1977 had not only shown the authorities how precarious their reliance on coffee imports from the non-socialist world was, but also how expensive it could suddenly become if the market fluctuated. The open grumbling of an otherwise relatively contented East German public also troubled them. A permanent solution to stabilize coffee supplies had to be found. While the plants would never grow in the GDR, perhaps a socialist partner state could be found to trade goods with, so that foreign currency would not be needed.

Since the end of the Vietnam War in 1975, the tropical state in South-East Asia had been struggling economically. Vietnam had been exploited for its resources for decades under French colonial rule before it came under brutal Japanese occupation during the Second World War. After 1945, the French returned and began a desperate struggle to hold on to their colonies in Indochina, culminating in the bloody battle of Dien Bien Phu in 1954, the upshot of which was that they left their colonies but Vietnam was split in two. Fearing that the leader of the north, Ho Chi Minh, would unite the country under one communist regime, the Americans took over the baton to control the region. Throwing the might of Western military force at the tiny state for the best part of two decades, the conflict bled the country dry – materially, psychologically and literally – with an estimated overall death toll of around a million Vietnamese people. The problems did not end in 1975 either. Over 40,000 civilians have fallen victim to landmines since then. Nearly one fifth of the forested areas of Vietnam had been sprayed with the toxic chemical Agent Orange which would contaminate the soil and groundwater for years to come. The harsh requisitioning of food and resources by the communist militia groups during the war itself had led to widespread starvation and outbreaks of disease. With the war over, the salvation they had promised the civilians if they just held on and continued the struggle did not set in. The country was in desperate need of economic recovery.

The GDR saw a golden opportunity. East Germany could help the brother state rebuild itself while solving its own coffee problem at the same time. In December 1977, Erich Honecker visited Hanoi and Ho Chi Minh City himself and brought with him Günter Mittag, the politburo member responsible for the economy, and Margarete Müller, candidate member of the politburo and an expert in agrarian production and plant cultivation. In order to impress on the Vietnamese brethren how much there was to gain from economic cooperation with the GDR, Honecker had brought a feast. A special plane carried the best of East German cuisine, complete with a team of chefs to serve it up. Lothar Herzog, Honecker's bodyguard, remembered a banquet that included 'Radeberger beer, Rotkäppchen sparkling wine, wine from Meißen, Thuringian sausages, pork knuckles and of course the obligatory Kassler [gammon]'.[18] The German opulence seemed out of place to Lothar in 'Vietnam, which lay broken, starving and exhausted, two years after the decades-long war'. It seemed Hanoi struggled to put up the East German delegation somewhere suitable and organize enough food and drink for the guests. 'But the visit in Vietnam was an important political gesture, which was meant to show that the solidarity will go on.'[19] The SED elite came away convinced that economic cooperation would help both countries and steps were taken when they arrived back home.

Siegfried Kaulfuß, the forty-nine-year-old deputy director of the state-run business group for groceries and coffee, was charged with the task to build up coffee production in Vietnam. 'I didn't know what I was getting into,' he would later remember, 'but looking back I am grateful for this mammoth task.'[20] He travelled to Vietnam over fifty times, planting and cultivating the 6,000 coffee trees that would form the nucleus of a future-proof industry. He was taken aback by both the extreme poverty and the can-do attitude of his Vietnamese business partners. 'The people there had nothing. Nothing to wear, nothing to eat. But they were very friendly and helped us. To this day I feel a deep connection to Vietnam.'[21] Following a 1980 development treaty between the GDR and Vietnam a massive undertaking began. In Dak Lak province, 600 metres above sea level, an area of 10,000 hectares was cleared for the coffee plants. Machinery was delivered and roads, settlements and schools were built for the 10,000 people who migrated from the coast to the mountain areas to work on the plantations. The workers were trained there and in the GDR. East Germany sent lorries, farm machinery and equipment for the installation of complex irrigation systems. In Dray H'Linh, a hydropower plant was built, costing the equivalent of $20 million. In exchange for this enormous aid package, the GDR was to receive half of Vietnam's coffee production for a duration of twenty years.

This project was hugely successful, perhaps one of the most effective aid projects ever conducted. Vietnam is now the world's second largest producer of coffee, producing around 30 million 60-kilogram bags every year, and its industry employs 2.6 million people. Its Robusta beans have a high caffeine content and are ideal for granular and instant coffee, which is drunk in large quantities around the world. Only 6 per cent of the produce is used internally, while the rest is exported at an estimated annual worth of $3 billion.

East Germany stood to gain half of this yield – more than enough to supply its own demand and create additional revenue through exports – but coffee plants take years to mature and produce their beans. The first harvest of the East German coffee project in Vietnam only came in 1990 – too late for the GDR, which ceased to exist in the same year. As Vietnamese coffee production grew by 20–30 per cent each year in the 1990s, and the South-East Asian country established itself as a major force on the worldwide coffee market, East Germans too consumed the produce they had once helped to sow. But they did so as capitalist consumers, not socialist brothers and sisters.

For a short time in 1977, another, more disturbing path to coffee procurement was also trialled. Werner Lamberz, a competent and well-liked politburo member, had risen through the political ranks far more swiftly than most of his colleagues and Honecker trusted him to explore possible trade deals with African countries, despite the fact that he was neither responsible for foreign policy nor the economy. Lamberz was indeed very successful on this mission. In 1977, as many African countries were in the process of shaking off their imperial ties, he visited coffee-producing nations such as

Angola, Zambia and Ethiopia to offer their emerging socialist movements ideological and economic support.

Ethiopia was Lamberz's main target. In February of that year,
Mengistu Haile Mariam, a socialist army officer, had become the
new head of state in a bloody coup. Indeed, there were rumours
that it was he who had killed Emperor Haile Selassie in 1975 by
smothering the ageing leader with a pillowcase. Lamberz met the
revolutionary, and offered him a range of GDR products such as
lorries, machinery and farm equipment in exchange for coffee.
Mengistu, however, was more concerned with squashing resistance and 'counter-revolutionary' movements in his country as
well as preparing for war with neighbouring Somalia. He needed
either weapons, or hard cash to buy weapons. Due to the worldwide coffee shortage, he could easily exchange his country's
precious produce for the latter, which put Lamberz on the back
foot. The only thing the GDR had that Mengistu wanted was military support. So the two men hammered out a 'coffee agreement':
'blue beans against brown beans'. Lamberz offered firearms worth
53 million marks in exchange for 5,000 tonnes of coffee. Pleased
with the arrangement, Mengistu visited East Germany in October
1977 and told Honecker and Lamberz that, 'thanks to the GDR's
aid, it was possible to equip and feed 100,000 men of the people's
militia. In this way, the GDR played a significant role in the revolutionary development of Ethiopia.'[22] What the chairman of the
military junta Derg did not spell out is that the weapons were used
in the so-called Qey Shibir, the Red Terror that accompanied
his revolution during which tens of thousands of people were
killed.

This arrangement did not last very long. When Lamberz flew
back to Ethiopia in December 1977, he was already struggling to
convince Mengistu to commit to more coffee deliveries. The
ongoing shortages on the world market meant that the price for
the 'black gold' had risen further and its value was now higher than
the weapon deliveries from the GDR. Lamberz offered more aid,
lorries, infrastructure projects and machinery for agriculture which

he argued would help stabilize the country better than violence but Mengistu was not interested. In 1978, he terminated the agreement altogether and told the GDR that he would only accept hard cash, something it did not have in the quantities required. The relationship began to crumble less than two years after it had begun. Lamberz himself came to an unfortunate end under mysterious circumstances in a helicopter crash in the middle of the Libyan desert where he had just negotiated a financial deal with Libyan leader Muammar Gaddafi.

From 1977 onwards coffee supply remained a huge and costly issue. East Germans consumed pure coffee when the world market allowed the government to buy and import some or when their Western friends and relatives sent it. Many grudgingly began to get used to the idea of drinking the unappealing ersatz coffee. Indeed, many of those who were teenagers in the later 1970s or in the 1980s associated the taste of coffee with the GDR's coffee mix as that was often all there was.

Guest Workers

Eberswalde, Brandenburg, 17 October 1979. Jorge Noguera was tired and cold. The day before, he had been a world away. Thousands of kilometres now separated the young man from his home and he was beginning to feel it. He had said goodbye to his friends and family, boarded a plane and touched down at Berlin-Schönefeld Airport twelve hours later. He was bundled on to a bus together with his forty-nine fellow travellers and gazed out of the misty windows at the strange, grey landscape. The one-hour journey to Eberswalde, around 50 kilometres north-east of Berlin, took them past houses, factories and fields. Everything looked so modern and different, so unlike Cuba.

Jorge's journey from Cuba to East Germany had begun when he opened his local newspaper in San Luis, Santiago de Cuba, one day to find an ad by Cuba Técnica, the umbrella organization for the technological sector of the planned economy. They were looking for people who wanted to spend some time in the GDR to learn a technical skill so that they could return and contribute to the advancement of the local workforce. Jorge was intrigued. He filled in a registration form at the job centre in Santiago.

A couple of months later, a representative of Cuba Técnica turned up in San Luis and explained to those who had signed up what they would be expected to do in East Germany. Qualifications were not required. They would live and work in the GDR for the duration of a fixed-term contract. Accommodation was provided, but the 900-mark salary would be split between the workers, who received 40 per cent, and the Cuban state, which received 60 per cent. Extra provisions consisted of an opportunity to fly back home for forty-five days every two years as well as holidays and day trips in Germany subsidized by the company they would work for. Jorge and dozens of other men and women from the local area signed their contracts. None of them spoke any German or had any idea what to expect.

In Eberswalde, Jorge was employed by VEB Kranbau, a manufacturer of high-quality slewing cranes used to lift cargo in ports. Engineering, development and construction were all done in-house by the company's 3,000 employees and Eberswalde cranes enjoyed an excellent reputation for quality and workmanship worldwide. They can still be found in many ports today. While most of the company's output went to the Soviet Union, it also sold a lot of equipment to countries in South America, Africa and Europe, creating lucrative cashflow for the GDR. Jorge and his group joined the 450 trainees at VEB Kranbau to learn as much as they could before taking their skill and knowledge back to Cuba.

Jorge's first task was to adapt to life in his host country. He had arrived just on the cusp of winter after having lived a life in the tropical humidity of Cuba. He gratefully accepted the set of winter clothing provided by the company as a starter kit. But neither the boots nor the warm coat could prepare him for the sight of snow. 'I was shocked at first,' he remembered years later, 'what is this snow?

It was the first time I had seen any. But then we went outside with lots of other people and had a snowball fight.'[23] Work life, on the other hand, was strictly regulated. Jorge's group was split into different specialisms: steel workers, technicians, welders and so on. Jorge himself had been chosen for depot and logistics work where he learned how to operate cranes and forklifts. He also had to learn German, which he found extremely hard. Having worked from Monday to Friday in a shift system, he spent four hours each Saturday and Sunday learning German so that he could make himself understood to his co-workers after only a few months. Each Monday, the Cubans received language and vocational training, which they were then to apply throughout the week. The company also organized trips to Berlin and to museums and out into the countryside. In their spare time, the Cubans loved to gather to play their national sport: baseball. Jorge regularly travelled to Halle, Nordhausen or Fürstenwalde to meet up with his friends to play this most un-German of ball games.

While Jorge made many German friends too, there was also friction at times. One incident in particular went so far that the local authorities nearly dissolved the Cuban enclave in Eberswalde. A misunderstanding at a fairground, where much beer had been consumed by the locals and the Cuban workers alike, led to a mass brawl between them. The authorities initially planned to distribute the workers out to new places and Jorge was designated for a place in Eisenhüttenstadt. But in the end things calmed down and everyone was allowed to stay. In a country as ethnically homogeneous as the GDR, Jorge was always conscious that he looked and sounded different. 'I am obviously a foreigner. You can see it from a distance. I'm not white. I'm not blond. And everyone knows I'm a foreigner.'[24] But he adapted to life and work in Eberswalde where he got married and wanted to stay even when his four-year contract had come to an end. Jorge was chosen for a programme of further qualifications alongside eight Cuban colleagues – 'only the best, with the best discipline,' as he proudly recalled. He was allowed a forty-five-day break to visit family in Cuba before he began another two-year course in Eberswalde. In 1985, his son was born and the small family wanted to settle permanently.

Jorge was one of a rising number of foreign contract workers in the GDR. The programme had begun in 1965 and 1967 when agreements were made with the Polish and Hungarian governments, respectively. Further agreements were signed with Algeria (1974), Cuba (1975), Mozambique (1979), Vietnam (1980) and Angola (1984), followed by smaller projects with Mongolia (1982), China (1986) and North Korea (1986). Most of the workers were under thirty-five and returned to their home countries after their contracts expired. The idea was not for them to integrate and stay in the GDR but to learn a skill and return to their home countries. They were housed in accommodation near their workplace rather than left to find their own place to stay. As the second most developed economy in the socialist world and with a long track record of German engineering, the GDR was well placed to help its brother states, who also gratefully accepted the extra flow of money that reached them through the salary schemes. The GDR's economy had a chronic shortage of labour and the temporary contractors helped plug the holes in the market to some extent. While this aspect has been the focus of discussions concerning foreign labour in the GDR, the numbers alone indicate that labour shortage was at best a secondary concern. When Jorge arrived in 1979, he was one of only 21,000 foreign workers in the GDR. While this number accelerated through the 1980s, even the highest figures never exceeded 94,000. In a workforce of 8.55 million, they made up around 1 per cent. By comparison, West Germany had contracted 14 million foreign workers between 1955 and 1973. In the last year of that process, they made up nearly 10 per cent of the workforce.

The GDR's guest workers were not recruited out of sheer economic necessity, nor were they segregated from the German population out of cynical or even xenophobic reasons as some have suggested. Such reflections are born out of modern sensibilities and take little account of the economic and ideological context in which the GDR operated. In the bipolar world of the Cold War, where the socialist side had a lot of economic catching up to do, it was seen as paramount that a state with the level of education and comparatively high state of development like the GDR should help developing countries strengthen their economies. East Germany's relationship with Cuba is a prime example. The number of Cuban guest workers was well below 10,000 in any given year. Of course they provided their labour for the GDR economy, but at 900 marks a month, Jorge cost the state the same in 1979 as the average salary of German workers and he needed training, education, language tuition, travel costs, clothing and a place to live. Meanwhile, the GDR invested large amounts of economic aid into Cuba. It bought sugar and citrus fruit for above-market rates, built schools and hospitals on the island, donated machinery and agricultural equipment and constructed entire refineries for sugar, rum and other products. The VEB Zementanlagenbau in Dessau built a giant cement plant in Nuevitas, Cuba – still Latin America's largest today. The GDR invested far more into the development of other socialist nations than it ever received in terms of the paid labour provided by the workers.

This is not to play down the human tragedy that ensued when workers did not want to return to their countries of origin. This is particularly true for the 15,000 guest workers who had come from Mozambique. In contrast to Cuba, Poland or Hungary, their country was torn apart by civil war. Stable work was difficult to come by, and where it could be secured, pay was nowhere near the levels they had received in East Germany. There was also military conscription, which added another layer of danger. When the Berlin Wall fell and the concerns of the young Mozambicans slid down the order of priorities during the reunification process, a decision was made to deport them back to their home country without financial or other support put in place. Instead of receiving well-paid jobs as specialist workers, as they had been promised by their government, they faced unemployment and poverty. They felt let down, both by their own country, where they are called 'Madgermanes' (those made in Germany), and which had offered them to the GDR as part of a programme to pay off debt, and by a reunified Germany which sent them back without a second thought.[25]

By far the biggest group of foreign workers, numbering around 60,000, came from Vietnam. They made up around two thirds of all contractual workers and contributed to over 700 companies in the GDR. The promising start of the coffee programme was followed by a wider economic agreement struck in 1980. In contrast to the other countries, Vietnam sent many women. Not only had the country lost many men during the Vietnam War, but it had also become more used to the idea of female labour and wider participation of women in society, outside the home, than other affiliated nations. Anecdotal evidence suggests that Germans found it very easy to work with Vietnamese colleagues and vice versa as there were fewer cultural differences. Vietnamese women with enviable sewing skills filled an important niche and were much appreciated for it. As with the workers from Mozambique, many Vietnamese labourers also found it hard to return to a country that was scarred by prolonged conflict and civil war. Those who were mid-contract in 1989 and had banked on the money they were to receive for the whole duration of their contracted time struggled particularly when they were simply sent back. In total only around 5,000 Vietnamese people stayed after reunification.

Despite the difficulties faced by those contractual workers who found conditions in the GDR preferable to those back home and wanted to stay, the programme as a whole does not deserve the intense and one-sided criticism it has received from Western historians. The GDR ran its foreign labour programme as an exchange programme born out of ideological concerns rather than immediate economic benefit to the GDR. The comparison to the post-colonial situation in Western nations is misguided, even absurd, given that East German propaganda had fiercely attacked the entire principle of what it called 'imperialism'. When countries in Africa, Asia and South America managed to gain independence, the GDR sought to support the socialist movements that often sprang from this. This was, of course, not done purely for humanitarian reasons but also because it helped steer such countries away from the capitalist orbit and aided economic recovery within the socialist one, opening up desperately needed markets and resources for international trade. The GDR was always looking for ways to obtain raw materials – a nightmare that never ceased to haunt its economy.

Reliance on Soviet Russia was proving increasingly damaging, particularly in the 1970s when the oil crises had seen it withdraw support from its socialist brother states. Autarky, or economic self-sufficiency, was not an option for the tiny GDR. The idea was to strengthen the socialist world overall, economically in individual countries and politically via a strong diplomatic network and inter-dependencies. Rightly or wrongly, the plan was never to transition the GDR to an immigration society, akin to those the Western nations were becoming. To project ideals of ethnic and cultural diversity, arising from mass immigration to capitalist nations, on to the GDR would be anachronistic and misleading. The internation-alist ideology of socialism combined with the economic challenges of the GDR and led to a desire to build a global market of like-minded countries. The concept of 'peoples' friendship' was more than a platitude.

A Military Society

Berlin Wall, January 1981. Andreas Weihe's night shift seemed endless. The nineteen-year-old border guard sat in his concrete watchtower and shivered as subzero winds whipped across the wide no-man's land that surrounded West Berlin. It wasn't the first time that the heating had broken down. But Andreas and his col-leagues had learned to make do with a rudimentary 'stove' fabricated from heating elements out of hot plates which warmed up concrete slabs carefully arranged around them. These home-made solutions were so common that many of the watchtowers emitted the red glow of heating spirals at night, and they sucked so much electricity out of the system that the guards had to manipulate the central switchboard as there was a serious risk that the main spotlights of the border system would blow. As Andreas later remarked, 'The border was never as sophisticated as many think.'[26] While the Berlin Wall reached its most complex state in 1980, this 'fourth-generation' still relied on human observation to stop East Germans from crossing into the West. Young men like Andreas sat in the towers staring into the sanded area known as the 'death strip'. The mood in the draughty guard towers above it oscillated between intense stress and equally intense boredom.

Every man was alone with his thoughts. Personnel rotation and unpredictable shifts made it difficult to form friendships or build real camaraderie – a deliberate system designed to prevent collusion on escape plans or schemes to help others across the nearly unbreachable border. It also bred suspicion and mistrust. The men knew that border guards had been killed by their own colleagues who had tried to flee across the border. One incident happened only a few months previously, in November 1980 when Andreas had just joined the border company. The thirty-four-year-old Ulrich Steinhauer was shot five times by his nineteen-year-old colleague Egon Bunge. One of the shots from the latter's service pistol hit Ulrich in the back and went straight through his heart. Egon ran across the border into West Berlin as his colleague bled out on the ground. Like so many of his fellow border guards Ulrich had not even wanted to be there. He had been a carpenter in his home town of Ribnitz-Damgarten by the sandy beaches of the Baltic Sea and travelled the length and breadth of the GDR every summer from his savings. But in November 1979, he was drafted into Border Training Regiment 40 in Oranienburg, north-west of Berlin. Neither of his parents were party members, and Ulrich was not particularly political either. When he began to be deployed at Berlin's borders in the spring of 1980, he told his commanding officer that he would only be willing to shoot 'in an extreme emergency' and his Stasi file complained that he would only go as far 'as he himself deemed right'.[27] Ulrich hoped sincerely that he would get through his eighteen months' service without ever being put in a position where he would need to use his weapon in earnest, as he told his younger sister Ilona. 'The time in the army can't be over fast enough,' he wrote to his parents in April 1980. 'This time next year, things will look much brighter.'[28] Even his last letter, written two days before he was killed, was signed off: '172 days to go.'[29] By the time it reached his family, Ulrich had already been dead for three days.

Three months after Ulrich Steinhauer's death, Andreas Weihe was guarding the same stretch of the border with West Berlin. The young recruits had been shown the exact spot where Ulrich had bled to death and told to be vigilant at all times. Trust no one. They were reminded again and again that even those who were on guard with them had to be carefully watched. Shortly after, their entire border company was named 'Ulrich Steinhauer', making it impossible for the men who served in it to forget what happened to one of their own who, like many of them, did his job reluctantly and under immense psychological pressure.

Like Ulrich, Andreas sought solace in writing letters to his parents when he could. Often half a year would pass before the guards were allowed to visit friends and family at home, and some found it difficult to cope with the pressure and isolation. Andreas remembered how the limp body of a fellow officer was carried past him on a stretcher one day. The man had taken his own life with his service pistol. The nights in particular were long and lonely – all the time in the world to contemplate the situation one found oneself in. The minutes crawled by as Andreas stared intently into the brightly lit quiet of the night. He was tired and aching from sitting still in an awkward pose that avoided touching the dangerous heatsource he and the others had built. He was also rigid with anticipation. He had seen colleagues struggling to uncurl a trigger finger held in the same cramped position throughout a tense long shift. Agonizing thought circles swirled through his mind. What if someone ran across the illuminated area in front of him right now? Would he have it in him to shoot? 'The spotlights began to dance in front of my eyes, and I began to see things that weren't there,' Andreas recalled. 'I was always hugely relieved when my replacement appeared.'[30]

Like many of the young men who sat in the Berlin Wall's watchtowers, Andreas had ended up there as a result of 'coercive volition', as he put it. Born in September 1961, a few weeks after construction of the Wall began, he grew up 250 kilometres east of it in Abbenrode, a small border community in the Harz mountain range. His family had roots there that stretched all the way into the nineteenth century, which meant that even the immediate proximity of the West never held any serious allure for him. But living so close to the inner-German border still shaped every aspect of his life. Residents of this 'restricted zone' had to carry their papers with a special stamp identifying them as legitimate residents wherever they went. A football pitch and a public swimming pool ended up within 500 metres of the border, rendering them unusable to the residents, much to the dismay of the local children. The pitch was simply moved when a new fencing system was built diagonally across the old one, but the swimming pool fell out of use altogether.

In the 1970s, the 'green' border between East and West Germany had been ruthlessly extended and fortified irrespective of local infrastructure or sensibilities. The process included not just NVA border personnel but also civilians such as Manfred Rudat, then in his early thirties. 'Manni' had initially served part of his compulsory military service at the border between Thuringia and Lower Saxony, at Klettenberg barracks. Like Andreas, he 'prayed every day that nobody wanted to make an escape attempt during my shift. We had all been ordered to shoot in the legs. If you didn't do it, you would be in trouble.'[31] During that time, Manni fell in love with Ingrid, a local girl. He was devastated to learn that he would not be allowed to enter freely the 'restricted zone' she lived in following his military service. So he decided to marry Ingrid in 1967 and move to her area permanently. Needing a job, he began to work at the Klettenberg barracks again, but this time in a civilian role.

When the government decided to beef up systems all along the rural border, it fell to people like him to help bulldoze the old border and install the next generation of concrete reinforcements, barbed wire and 3-metre-high fencing. This would be lined by a mined area right by the fence. It was Manni's job to deliver the materials to the border in a lorry. He had also been trained to drive and repair industrial and agricultural vehicles before he was drafted for military service. So one of his tasks consisted of laying a met-alled path parallel to the mined fence for motorized patrols. He then drove up and down the road he had built delivering goods and materials where they were needed. One of the strangest things he had been tasked with was feeding the German shepherd dogs that roamed the border on their long leads, trained to take down those who tried to flee across more inaccessible wooded areas. He remem-bered that the dogs looked ferocious and powerful and wondered if it was the excellent veterinary care they received or the hearty diet of beef and soup that he brought them. As all his jobs required entering the highly sensitive area immediately by the border, Man-ni's behaviour and private life was carefully monitored by the Stasi and its helpers. Did he watch West German television? Why was he so reluctant to join the party? Would he be tempted to join his rela-tives in West Germany? 'You never knew who spied on you and I hope I will never know. What if it was your friend, your neighbour or your colleague?'[32]

Sixty kilometres to the north, in Abbenrode, the increasingly heavily fortified border also meant that those who guarded it were stationed locally. A 100-man company was permanently located in the area. The majority of the men came and went with their period of service but some married into the community as Manni had done. Abbenrode children like Andreas Weihe came to know the guards. They visited them regularly for special occasions, some-times even at Christmas, and met them around town.

While living in the border zone also had its perks, such as a 70-mark 'zone bonus' for each family member, it also brought many inconveniences. When relatives came to visit, they had to apply at least six weeks in advance as well as register their arrival and depart-ure with the local People's Police officer. When Andreas married in 1985, it was no use that he was a local man with three years' military service, including a stint at the Berlin Wall, on his record. The rules applied to him too. His wedding guests had to arrive and leave together in one bus so that it would be easier to account for anyone who might have used the chance to slip over the 'green' border unnoticed while the festivities went on. Much to Andreas's dismay, one of his guests was indeed missing when the bus was due to leave again the morning after his wedding. As it turned out, however, the young man in question had not attempted a daring dash across the border. He was found shortly after in a nearby field where he had retreated with a local girl.

While a real escape attempt could have had serious consequences for everyone associated with it, the incident was largely laughed off by the Abbenroders. To them, the nearby border had been a fact of life from birth. Even those who had not served directly as guards like Andreas had often been involved in the complex processes of deterrence and monitoring. Andreas's father, for instance, had served as a civilian auxiliary to 'border protection' forces. This involved patrolling the village to check that all the locals had chained up their ladders so that they could not be stolen and used to climb over border fencing, as well as keeping an eye out for anything suspicious and reporting it.

By 1980, when Andreas was asked to join the SED and serve at least three years in the NVA in exchange for a place at university, the border held no terror at all for him. He had grown up with it and imagined that if he volunteered to serve as a guard, he might be able to spend the three long years in his home region just like the border guards he had seen come and go since childhood. When he was sent to the Berlin Wall instead, it came as a shock, but Andreas had learned to accept that life in the GDR didn't always afford free choice. 'I was part of a generation that was raised in socialism, through and through. I was definitely a little bit proud of our country,'[33] Andreas remembered later. What was three years' service doing something he had seen others do since childhood? In exchange he would gain education and work opportunities that, as the son of working class parents, he thought of as a privilege to be earned, not an inherent right. Through a mixture of education, incentives, pressure and immersion, military service became a part of life for an entire generation of East Germans.

Philippsthal, Thuringia, July 1981. Thoralf Johansson was not enjoying himself. The sixteen-year-old and his classmates had been sent on a twelve-day 'Defence Education Camp', a new initiative for his year group which the authorities had introduced only in May. Guided by young NVA officer recruits, who in turn were supposed to hone their leadership skills, the boys went through an eight-hour programme of drills and team-building activities every day. Girls were taking a course on 'civil defence' of equivalent length. Thoralf was very ill at ease. A clever boy, interested in science and technology, he found the physical activities he was being asked to undertake awkward and uncomfortable. 'We did target practice with small-bore rifles, not proper weapons, just small-bore rifles. I really never hit the target and got into a spot of trouble over it,'[34] he recalled. There was no respite. When they were not at the shooting range, the boys ran around the camp with compasses, trying to complete missions in teams. At night, they slept in army-issue tents. By day, they practised marching, standing to attention and were reminded that the enemy lay just a few metres away, behind the inner-German border that ran right through Philippsthal. 'The West wants to attack us,' Thoralf and his friends were told again and again, 'we have to defend ourselves.'

Thoralf had little choice but to attend. He wanted to go to university, so not only was military education obligatory for him as it was for everyone else in that position, but he also had to sign up for an extended period of military service. Apprentices too had to undergo training. The way the state saw it, extended military service was fair recompense for extended education. At school, Thoralf could have refused to attend the camp by talking to the headmaster, but the alternative would have been to join the girls in their twelve-day 'civil defence' course, which did not really make a difference beyond the fact that it was not held in a camp but as a day course and lasted only six hours a day as opposed to eight. So most teenage boys did not bother switching from one to the other and risk humiliation on top of military training. The camps were organized by the *Gesellschaft für Sport und Technik* (GST), Sport and Technology Association, a mass organization founded in 1952 with the aim to prepare and recruit young people for military service.

The tense geopolitical atmosphere of the period and the fact that the GDR was on the front line of the Cold War led to an increasing conviction among East German officials that citizens should be in a state of constant readiness. Society would need to be militarized to a point where it had both the skills and the mindset to defend itself and the communist bloc from the expected Western invasion. By the end of its first year, the GST already had half a million members. The enormous public funding the organization enjoyed made membership attractive. Apart from military recruitment, it fulfilled many other functions. Members could take driving lessons and acquire licences for cars, motorbikes and lorries. It offered exciting and otherwise inaccessible activities such as flying gliders and planes, diving and shooting. There were ranks, rewards and easier routes into certain professions. Despite several mass walkouts (for example, in protest at the crushing of the Hungarian Uprising in 1956), membership rose steadily, reaching nearly 650,000 in its last year of 1989. Even those who were not members regularly came into contact with the GST through its pre-military training programmes in schools and other organizations, such as the camp Thoralf attended.

While paramilitary organizations and the NVA itself had been part of the GDR's DNA almost from the beginning, the late 1970s and early 1980s still marked a sharp increase in the government's efforts to militarize society as a whole. Many school subjects such as history and physical education had long had an element of pre-military content to them. Active recruitment for the NVA, the Stasi's Guard Regiment and other paramilitary organizations had also been intense in schools and within youth organizations. But it was paradoxically during a Cold War thaw that the politburo came to the conclusion that it needed to 'help young people orient themselves within the complex situation of international class war, possess a clear idea of who the enemy is and be ready at all times to act for socialism and defend it', as Erich Honecker put it.[35] On 1 September 1978, 'Defence Education' became a compulsory subject in its own right at polytechnic secondary schools, the comprehensive schools all children attended. All boys and girls aged between fourteen and sixteen had to take it and attend the four double lessons together, only splitting when the boys attended their camp at the end of the school year. The educational mission of the programme was to 'familiarize girls and boys with selected basic skills of national defence and further their preparedness'.[36]

Military education was extended even to the earliest stages of education. The centralized curriculum for four- to five-year-olds stipulated that the 'relationship of the children to the armed forces be strengthened. They should collect images and talk about them with the teachers; establish friendly relations to a member of the armed organizations if possible'.[37] Students aged six to seven were meant to build on this:

> the children's knowledge of the soldiers of our National People's Army is extended. The existing relationships to such people are fostered. Through these tight relationships with individual members of the armed organizations, their love and affection for them will be developed further. They know that our soldiers are also workers. They protect the people and their labour and watch over their ability to play happily.[38]

This was combined with a comprehensive programme developed through the other subjects. Even music and art were often directed towards military subject matters. Children learned how to play military marches or were asked to draw tanks and battle scenes. Surveys in the GDR showed that this was met with mixed success. Just under half of fourteen- to sixteen-year-old students said they enjoyed 'Defence Education' while 43 per cent said they did not and 8 per cent admitted that they did not enjoy it 'at all'.

Those who wanted access to higher education often had to make the difficult decision whether they could accept that the price for this was extended military service. Conscription for men had been introduced in 1962, the year after the Berlin Wall had been built and six years after West Germany had done the same. Compulsory service normally lasted eighteen months and the only option to object was to cite religious reasons, in which case the time still had to be served but in a non-combat role as a so-called *Bausoldat* (construction soldier). But men who wanted to study at university had to prove their worth to the state as the government openly argued from 1970 onwards. Not only could they not opt out, but they had to sign up to a three-year temporary commission as officers. Even the brightest and most promising would-be academics, scholars and scientists were forced to undergo a lengthy spell of military training before they were allowed to study at university. Some, like Thoralf, were brave enough to cheat the system: sign up to the 'Voluntary Extension' of their conscription duties to gain a place at the extended secondary school and then brazenly tell the authorities that they had changed their minds. In this way, Thoralf served only eighteen months rather than the full three years he had originally signed up for.

More often than not, male university students paid the price for their education in three years of military service. Many marriages between East German graduates tended to have a three-year age gap between husband and wife. Graduates who got to know one another as students of the same cohort did so with the female partner having been allowed to join three years earlier than the male, straight from school. Couples who had known one another before military service tended to break off their relationship while the boyfriend was away almost constantly for three years. The NVA wanted the young men to itself to fully instil the military ethos in them. So it often based its recruits as far away from home as possible and then gave very little leave where the men could have returned home to visit family, friends and girlfriends. This isolated them deliberately in an effort to bind them psychologically to one another and the state.

There were obvious drawbacks to this strategy for the regime. It forced many bookish, less active and outright hostile individuals to complete military service for which they were ill-suited. This meant it often increased or even created opposition to the authorities in individuals who might have otherwise accepted the conditions in the GDR. On the flipside, it also allowed opportunists access to the coveted higher education pathways even if they were not academically suited to them. Schools and teachers were supposed to recommend the best and brightest for the few available places, but had been under pressure since the early 1970s to fulfil recruitment quotas for the NVA. There were regular inspections and checks of teachers, schools and districts to see if they had persuaded enough boys to sign up. The result was a mix of coercion and promise. Margot Honecker, Minister of National Education and wife of Erich Honecker, even complained about this in a report to the Central Committee of the SED. She was worried that 'the measures put pressure on headteachers and teachers to produce results, which has the effect that recruited students aren't always suited to fulfil the demands of the military vocation, politically, academically, character-wise and physically, which also shows in the fact that . . . in individual cases careerists were furthered, who used the opportunity to get access to the EOS [extended secondary school]'.[39] Despite such clear warnings from within, officer recruitment targets for schools were not retracted, nor even reduced, while fulfilment of them continued to rise and eventually even exceeded the targets throughout the 1980s.

However, the militarization of society also had positive effects. Both East and West Germany tried to break up the social exclusivity of the officer ranks which were formerly dominated by the aristocracy. The FRG managed a remarkable feat in pushing the landed gentry out of it, but it was mostly the educated middle classes that benefited from this. In West Germany, it was still extraordinarily difficult in the 1970s to be admitted into officer ranks without *Abitur*, an academic qualification that grants access to university after twelve or thirteen years of schooling. Yet the streamed school system still made it difficult for poorer children to access higher education. As a result, only 15 per cent of officer recruits came from working class households.[40] On the other side of the Wall, the systematic and all-encompassing militarization of society in East Germany had many drawbacks, but it also opened up the military to all social classes. For the first time in German history, officer ranks were filled en masse with young men from working class backgrounds who found rewarding roles for themselves within the NVA. The single largest social group that officers were drawn from was a working class background right from the beginning. In 1956, nearly three quarters of officers had working class parents and this figure remained high despite the wider social reconstruction of the GDR. In 1989, working class recruits still filled 60 per cent of officer ranks in the NVA[41] – this figure naturally reduced over time as the children of parents who originally came from humble backgrounds but had entered traditional middle class professions were no longer classed as workers.

The common argument that officer recruits were universally blackmailed into accepting temporary commissions in exchange for university places is simplistic. The prestige that came with rank and degree would have been out of reach for the vast majority of them without the social engineering the GDR engaged in and many working class boys saw it as an opportunity rather than a chore. Eckehardt Neudecker, for example, joined the NVA in 1962, not for political reasons or because he was forced to but because he craved the stability and structure it offered. The eighteen-year-old had grown up in the tumultuous period of the post-war years. His mother had died when he was just a child and his father was very old and had come back from the war changed and unable to give his son the care and attention he craved. The army provided young Eckehardt with the structured and safe environment he had never known at home. They gave him a bed, a stable income, camaraderie, rules and a home. In addition, the NVA did not cap his ambition and career to ordinary infantry roles but encouraged him to become an officer with all the education, training and social prestige that came with that role.

However, the net of militarization was cast so wide that it affected virtually everyone whether they wanted to or not. Those at the top continuously feared a Western invasion and sought to imprint this tension onto the entire East German society. Their ideological convictions held that capitalism is inherently expansive. In its search for new markets it would destroy socialism. This idea was particularly powerful in the GDR with its precarious position on the fault lines of the Cold War divide. The result was the impression that the country was permanently under siege. This trickled down into society and eventually permeated all stages of state education. Female undergraduates were made to run drill missions in NBC suits, protective clothing that seals off the wearer completely against nuclear, biological and chemical attacks and was particularly unpleasant to practise in during the sweltering summer heat. The young girls and boys of the Ernst Thälmann Pioneer Organization had a collective ritual where their slogan, 'For peace and socialism be ready – always ready', was turned into a salute-like gesture. The teacher or leader would call 'Be ready' and the group of pioneers (six to fourteen years old) would answer together 'Always ready' while raising a stiffened hand above their forehead, thumb down and little finger up. Standing still, walking neatly in groups and saluting teachers and leaders were all regular parts of cultivating a collective spirit of combat-readiness which allowed nobody to opt out.

To further uphold and intensify alertness, there was a dense network of sirens set up across the republic – in schools, factories and public buildings. While West Germany had this too, there the sirens were only tested twice a year, once in March and once in September. On the other side of the German border, they were tested every Wednesday at 1 p.m. – a regular reminder that the threat was constant even if the country seemed to be at peace. National defence was a matter for all citizens, not just border guards and soldiers, as far as the government was concerned. It followed that this required not just a degree of training for virtually everyone at some point in their education, but also a constant level of tension. Under Honecker,

the militarization of society had reached new heights. It had become
a systemic feature of the GDR.

A Golden Age?

Anklam, Mecklenburg, late June 1982. Erika Krüger returned from
the Workers' Festival of the GDR in Neubrandenburg brimming
with excitement. The twenty-nine-year-old mother was a proud
member of the 'brigades' that produced shelving systems at the
works in her home town of Anklam, a settlement of 20,000 that had
been hastily rebuilt after having had the rare misfortune of having
been shelled by American, Soviet and German attacks during the
Second World War. Anklam had risen from the ruins, complete
with a new town hall, theatre, airport and the GDR's very first 'People's Swimming Pool' in 1968. It was also home to several large
state-owned companies such as a cement works as well as the VEB
furniture maker 'Wilhelm Pieck' where Erika began to work in production as a fifteen-year-old in 1968. As she was the daughter of a
blacksmith and a tailor, who had three other children to feed, an
apprenticeship or even university were out of the question. She
needed to be financially independent as soon as possible. She had
proved a capable and enthusiastic worker making the iconic,
Bauhaus-inspired shelving systems that featured so prominently in
many East German households.

The quality of these GDR-made products was so good that over
90 per cent of them went into export, mostly to the Soviet Union
but many also to West Germany where large mail order companies
distributed them to their consumers. 'The Russians loved polished
tropical wood. To the NSW [non-socialist economic sphere] we
usually sent local woods such as pine, beech and oak,' Erika remembered. Some of it came all the way from Cuba in an effort to help
the socialist island which was struggling under the American trade
embargo. Erika and her colleagues produced over seventy shelving
units a week but many East Germans had to save for years to afford

the 6,000-mark pieces. Over the years, the young woman took great pride in 'working with my hands – anything but rotting at a desk!' She found the rewards for hard work and innovation satisfying and received financial bonuses for them as well as medals and certificates. She greatly enjoyed the social aspects of work, too, founding a crocheting and knitting circle. She and fellow enthusiasts met every other week after work for needlework and company. Erika's drive and enthusiasm were recognized and she was chosen for an evening course in woodworking techniques in 1977, which she completed and in turn received a better salary. But a degree still seemed completely out of reach.

That changed at the Workers' Festival of the GDR in 1982 where a delegate from the local department of culture asked to speak to her: 'Your socialist engagement honours you, Frau Krüger. Why don't you start studying for a degree in textile design? You could do this while continuing to work at the company.' Erika couldn't wait to tell her husband Gerhard. He had been a constant companion and pillar of strength to her since the two had met years earlier at the furniture factory where he polished the shiny front surfaces of the cupboards. 'Do it, Erika!' Gerhard said and meant it, whole-heartedly supporting his wife by looking after their two young sons while she went to evening lectures and weekend seminars. 'And why not?' both thought. They might have been from humble backgrounds, but Honecker's reforms in the 1970s had allowed Erika the luxury of further education. Working hours had been reduced to forty a week. Erika earned 870 marks a month plus 260 marks extra for the high quality of her output. The government's building programme had produced 1,091 new flats in Anklam and the couple secured a four-bedroom one with a balcony for themselves and their boys. Life had become rather comfortable and there was room for ambition.

In their spare time too, the Krügers reflected the relative material comfort that the 1970s had brought. Like many families, they obsessed over their little garden, spending time there after work and at the weekends. Germany has a long history of allotment gardening which is intrinsically connected to its industrial heritage. Workers living in cramped urban environments with little outside space, which they had done since the nineteenth century, often treasured a small plot of land to cultivate. The GDR's allotment gardens are sometimes dismissed as bourgeois due to the often comically specific rules about how they are to be used and managed. But their origins reach back to workers' movements. An allocated plot of land was seen as a means to solve supply problems in many European countries. They provided a sense of community among those belonging to the organizations that managed the gardens as well as a sense of individuality thanks to the privacy of an enclosed plot of land. Erich Honecker understood that and supported the system to counterbalance the building of flats rather than houses. The GDR had 650,000 allotment gardens, giving access to a piece of land to 1.5 million citizens or every eighth family. Nearly two thirds of them belonged to workers like the Krügers who kept rabbits there, planted flowers and grew fruit and vegetables. The produce could be sold on to shops which in turn sold them to consumers for subsidized prices. While this may have led to bizarre situations whereby gardeners bought their own produce back from the supermarket shelves rather than consuming it directly, it solved some of the supply problems and ensured better availability of seasonal produce as well as providing families with extra income.

Erika would later remember that they were quite happy with life as it was in the 1970s and early 1980s. 'In the holidays we would travel to FDGB resorts in Oberhof, the Harz mountains or Zittau . . . We only paid 190 marks for fourteen days, full board.' Life may not have been luxurious but to Erika and her family it seemed safe and full of little rewards. 'We worked, received our regular wages as well as extra bonuses for hard work. We got by and had nothing to worry about . . . It was only when I visited my sister-in-law for her sixtieth birthday in West Germany in 1987 that I understood what having too much looked like. Behind Oldenburg's supermarkets were bins from which groceries were overflowing. Furniture parts that were outdated just went straight from the stores into giant containers. What was missing in the East was thrown away there.'[42]

Not everyone was happy to get by on Eastern produce alone. By the end of the 1970s, there were nearly 500 'Intershops' in the GDR. They sold Western products for West German currency. Initially, the first such outlets were opened in the 1950s in the port cities of Rostock and Wismar as well as in Leipzig where international travellers flocked to the trade fairs. Then further shops were opened at airports, upmarket hotels for foreign visitors and along the transit railways – all intended to serve well-heeled capitalist visitors while in the GDR and out of view for East Germans themselves who were not legally allowed to possess West German currency in any case. However, as tensions between the two Germanies eased in the 1970s, the authorities became more relaxed about the Intershops and eventually relented by legalizing the possession of foreign currencies from 1 February 1974. Many other factors played a role too. If East Germans bought products, particularly imported ones like coffee, with their own Western money, then the state killed two birds with one stone. It became less of a concern to obtain those products for the population as they supplied themselves while also putting foreign currency into the coffers of the state with which other things might be purchased on the world market. Forum Handelsgesellschaft, the company which ran the Intershops, more than tripled its income of West German marks between 1974 (DM286 million) and 1984 (DM955 million).[43] This even allowed it to pay Intershop staff a bonus of DM30 a month. Adding to the allure of the Intershop with all its foreign wares was the fact that its goods did not come cheap. Cassettes for tape recorders came in at 5 marks, Matchbox cars were 2.50 marks and an original pair of Wrangler jeans 50 marks.

The eye-watering prices for Western goods only heightened their appeal. Intershops were quasi-magical places that featured large in the collective culture of East Germans. The closely guarded shelves held the stuff of dreams. The moment you entered, you were hit by garish colours and shiny plastic wrappers that looked alien in a socialist world of muted colours that did not rely on advertising or appealing product design. Going to the Intershop became a family outing for many as children might be allowed to pick a Western toy as a treat once enough Western currency had been saved up. Many a proud child would show off their stuffed Monchhichi toy monkey from Japan to their friends. Husbands bought expensive Western make-up or perfume as a special gift for their wives. Young parents secured a tin of the coveted Penaten baby cream for their newborns. Teenage girls would spend years' worth of savings on a fashionable skirt or a jacket. But the thing that East Germans remember most is the scent of the Intershop: an evocative mixture of intensely perfumed washing powders and soaps combined with the comforting aroma of roast coffee and the oddly exciting smell of new plastic products. 'It just smelled of the West,' many East Germans still reminisce. Many took this smell home and savoured it. Lux soap bars were placed in between clothes or towels in the cupboard while they gave off their scent and were only used for their intended purpose long after it had faded. Renate Demuth refilled empty Rémy Martin cognac bottles with the cheap East German equivalent Goldbrand – her party guests never noticed the difference and would rhapsodize about the exquisite taste of the supposedly Western tipple.

Such was the magic of the Intershop that anything that was hard or impossible to get in the GDR seemed to be available there – so long as one had ready access to Western currency. Forum Handelsgesellschaft, the company that ran them, became a byword for making things possible with West German marks. The phrase 'Forum geht's' captured this idea: a pun on the question 'Worum geht's?', meaning 'What's happening?', which was turned into 'Forum geht's' – 'Forum makes it happen'. If you wanted your Trabant fixed but the spare part you needed was not available, a bit of foreign cash could work wonders – *Forum geht's!* Need your shelving system quicker? *Forum geht's!* The most extreme form of this was exemplified in a GDR-owned company called Genex. This was a mail order catalogue from which West Germans could order presents for their East German friends and relatives. The product range was vast and consisted of things that were difficult or impossible to get in the GDR. Western benefactors could buy anything from televisions and dining tables to motorbikes, cars and even houses for their Eastern beneficiaries. Due to the awkward political situation between the two Germanies, the complicated financial proceedings behind Genex involved partner companies in Switzerland and Denmark. West Germans chose a product from the catalogue, paid for it into a West German bank account and named an address in East Germany to which they wanted the gift delivered. While the GDR had tried to set up a domestic mail order service in the 1960s, it quickly realized that it just could not guarantee the required stability of supply. More and more orders remained unfulfilled and the formulaic excuses consumers received after weeks of waiting only led to more disappointment. In 1976, the authorities decided that this did not work. They closed their own mail order down and relied solely on Genex to cover people's consumerist desires.

The authorities tolerated the phenomenon of a two-currency system even as many of its own staff became consumers of Western goods. While uniformed men and women were told not to enter Intershops in their official garb, a policeman remembered that he often had to remind party members to at least cover their SED badge before they entered. This tolerance meant that the government explicitly acknowledged that there were two kinds of shops in which you paid with two kinds of money, which meant two types of people shopped in them. Those with generous Western relatives and those without.

Despite the many remaining problems, the 1970s were a high point in East German living standards and many people experienced the decade as a time of relative material comfort and stability. GDR citizens had the highest living standards in the communist world and did not need to worry about getting by on a daily basis. Subsidized rents, even in the brand-new centrally heated flats with toilets and kitchens, only cost them a fraction of their salaries. Fridges,

TVs and washing machines had become everyday items. At the same time, average monthly income steadily rose from 755 marks in 1970 to 1,021 marks in 1980. While Trabant cars are often ridiculed and historians tend to stress how long it could take to obtain one, by 1980 nearly 40 per cent of households had one. Honecker's desire to put his subjects' needs and wishes front and centre had paid off.

In addition, the state opened many avenues for lifelong learning and opportunities for social advancement in all walks of life, not just within the military. People from disadvantaged backgrounds began to fill leadership positions as they went to university, embarked on apprenticeships and were advised on how to further their career while on the job. In factories, where targets were not always perceived as a means of oppression but led to a genuine sense of achievement, collective spirit became a source of identity and belonging to many.

Still, the proximity to the West and the little pockets of consumerism Honecker opened up in his desperate struggle to compete also created windows through which the alluring scent of capitalism wafted into a GDR that had begun to appear a little stuffy. The revolutionary zeal and can-do enthusiasm of the early years had waned and young people, who had neither experienced the fascist enemy they were supposed to fight nor were brought up in the rough street battles of the Weimar Republic, were comfortable and a little listless.

This was acutely felt by the Stasi whose leader Erich Mielke began to see the ghosts of the counter-revolution everywhere. Deeply suspicious of Honecker's opening up of the GDR to aspects of Western consumerism, the Stasi boss saw a potential beginning of the end of the entire state. In 1992, two years after reunification, he still mused that 'The opening to the West which Honecker supported brought problems. It was obvious to me that the constant increase in visitors from the FRG – of politicians as well as private citizens – must have a destructive effect.'[44] This worried him so much that he even mistrusted the General Secretary himself. Mielke began to collate damning documents about his boss in a red leather briefcase which he kept locked away in his offices until they were discovered in December 1989. They contained files about Honecker's trial for high treason in 1937, during which he had made confessions that implicated fellow members of the communist resistance. There were also letters that his father Wilhelm had written to the Nazis to try to save his son's life. They professed a change of heart in his son who he claimed had denounced communism and 'now saw that his youthful ideals are realized within this state'. In addition there were letters from Honecker's second wife Edith Baumann and from his third wife Margot Feist, who had both written to Walter Ulbricht to plead for his support while defaming each other. Perhaps the most unsavoury item was a document that showed how the state had financed building works on a holiday home that belonged to Honecker's secret lover.

The fact that Erich Mielke was collating damaging evidence against the leader of the GDR is a clear sign that the Stasi and its leadership had begun to look inward for enemies too, not just among the wider population. Mielke saw potential enemies everywhere. Accordingly he changed the ethos of his spy organization to one that not only sought to detect current enemies of the state but also attempted to predict future changes in the mindset of individuals. Even if one was a loyal, hardworking citizen of the GDR, this could change at any moment, and the sooner the Stasi detected the seeds of discontent in an individual, the better. On 3 April 1981, Mielke gave a talk that he wanted to reach all levels of his organization. The key question was 'Who is who?' Who was reliable and who was not? How could the Stasi best work this out? Mielke broke the question down further: 'who is the enemy, who has a hostile-negative attitude, who might become an enemy due to the effects of hostile-negative and other influences, who might be vulnerable to the influence of the enemy and who might be abused by the enemy, who takes a wavering position and on whom can party and state depend at all times and lean on reliably'.[45] The fact that Mielke's listing of types of citizens contained five enemy types and only one type of trustworthy subject speaks volumes about the heights of paranoia he and his organization had reached. The rest of the politburo were watched too and often controlled by the Stasi. Mielke's grip became tighter each time Honecker took another step towards liberalization and Westernization.

There is something intrinsically insecure about a leadership which constantly looks abroad for comparison and then hastily inwards to see if anyone else is looking too. In its pursuit of material comforts and pockets of consumerism the government hoped that this might satisfy the population in the short term. But in the process, Honecker's GDR overstretched itself economically and ideologically. The transformation of society under Ulbricht, including unprecedented social mobility, was part of a long-term vision of a classless society where people would voluntarily forgo the luxuries at the top end of the economic spectrum in order to avoid the deep poverty at the other. Realistic or not, Ulbricht believed in a more modest society in which the collective stood higher than the individual. Free education and healthcare, subsidized housing and food for all came at the costs of waiting for a car or a television set. Honecker, however, identified material desires as a core element of dissent and worked hard to satisfy them in the form of fragments of Westernization. Buying truckloads of American jeans or allowing people to obtain Western washing powder in Intershops merely increased the desire for more and sharpened the perception that the GDR was at best a half-hearted imitation of the West, at worst a jealous onlooker. The material comfort Honecker imported for East Germans may have temporarily increased happiness and life satisfaction but it also sowed the seeds of doubt in people's minds and left the GDR wandering through its third decade without a clear sense of direction.

9. *Existential Carefreeness (1981–1986)*

To be or not to be, that was the question.

Quarrel among Brothers

Crimean Peninsula, 3 August 1981. Erich Honecker had always enjoyed visiting Leonid Brezhnev at his summer residence. It was a world away from the austere atmosphere in East Berlin or the bombastic receptions in Moscow. In Crimea, visitors were greeted by palm trees swaying gently in a warm summer breeze filled with the sounds and smells of the sea. Drinks flowed freely. These meetings had become a familiar ritual. Every year, the Soviet leader would retreat to the village of Oreanda at the southern tip of the peninsula. His villa at the shores of the Black Sea was surrounded by extensive grounds and featured a pool – the perfect place to impress foreign visitors and put them at ease. In 1971, Brezhnev had gone swimming there with the West German Chancellor Willy Brandt, who was not too shy to borrow a pair of swimming trunks from the Soviet leader according to the latter's personal photographer Vladimir Musaelyan. In 1974, Brezhnev hosted lavish dinner parties there for US President Richard Nixon. Oreanda was both a pleasant place and historically evocative, close to the Livadia Palace, the elegant residence of the Romanovs where the Yalta Conference had been held in 1945. Crimea projected a picture of the Soviet Union as a world player entirely at ease.

While Western politicians were only occasionally treated to Brezhnev's hospitality, he invited the leaders of the socialist brother states to Crimea every year from 1971. Honecker saw these 'meetings in a friendly, open and constructive atmosphere' as 'excellent opportunities to exchange opinions and experiences in a detailed and unconventional manner so that plans for the future could be coordinated'.[1]

This eleventh meeting between the two men in August 1981 was different. Brezhnev, now seventy-four years old, was no longer able to play the congenial host. The troublesome 1970s had broken him both mentally and physically. His acrimonious home life had become so toxic that he considered divorcing his wife and disowning his children. Drowning his sorrows in alcohol only worsened his depression. Plagued by crippling insomnia and unable to find any respite from his troubles, he became dependent on tranquillizers. The Soviet leader had long been overweight and smoked heavily for years. During the 1970s the relentless economic crises of the Soviet Union piled insurmountable political problems on top of his private ones. Unable to withdraw into his home life for respite, Brezhnev eventually buckled under the pressure. He suffered a series of minor strokes, followed by a heart attack in 1975 and another, more severe, stroke in the same year. Despite his failing health, there was no rest for the ailing leader. Fearing the political turmoil that would come with a power struggle, the Soviet elites decided to keep the frail old man in place. Political initiatives were prepared behind the scenes and a ghost-like Brezhnev was literally wheeled out on state occasions to announce them. In public, the old man appeared lifeless and apathetic. East German translator and politician Werner Eberlein, who saw him in February 1981, remembered how shocked he was to find 'a senile geriatric who had been more or less propped up by his doctors especially for this party congress. In his conversations with Honecker, he read every word from a piece of paper.'[2]

When Honecker met him six months later in Crimea, the Soviet leader was a mere shell of the man who had once been his friend and ally. Honecker found Brezhnev's inability to engage with his concerns extremely frustrating. Brezhnev mechanically recited his brief: the Soviet Union needed to look after its own economic affairs for the foreseeable future and the GDR would no longer be able to rely on Soviet credit. Worse still, he could not guarantee that the supply of oil would remain stable. This was a huge blow to Honecker. His country had banked on the annual delivery of 19 million tonnes of oil contractually agreed with the Soviet Union.

As we have seen, East Germany's only viable domestic source of energy was brown coal which was environmentally disastrous, technologically backward and economically inefficient. The USSR's vast oil reserves in the Ural region, Siberia, Kazakhstan and Turkmenistan had seemed the ideal solution to solve the entire Soviet Bloc's energy needs in the long term. The Druzhba pipeline, which had been completed in 1964, was extended in the 1970s to connect Western Siberian oil fields directly with Eastern European refineries. A network totalling more than 5,000 kilometres of pipes, it was a gigantic industrial effort that suggested longevity. So the GDR had adapted its own economy accordingly. A giant refinery had been built in Schwedt by the Polish border and begun operation in 1964. Its 30,000 workers produced nearly 400 different products with the oil it received. Alongside petrol, diesel and heating oil, this included tar and lubricants. Entire branches of the GDR's economy depended on its output. The complex chemical products it made were needed in the textile industry, the agrarian sector, washing powder production and furniture factories to name but a few.

Energy consumption in the GDR had also begun to lean on imports from Soviet Russia. In 1960, coal still accounted for 97 per cent of domestic energy use; by 1980, oil had taken over 17.3 per cent and gas 9.1 per cent.[3] As oil is five times as effective as brown coal in terms of energy production, the economy was shifting towards the deliveries from the Soviet Union while investment in domestic brown coal had begun to slump. The oil crises of the 1970s had made this an increasingly expensive undertaking – by 1980, the GDR was paying the equivalent of $15 a barrel of crude oil compared to $2–$3 in 1972[4] – and as a result local brown coal once again had to be sourced in higher quantities. Nonetheless, crude oil from the Soviet Union could still be turned into hard cash in the GDR's refineries. Their oil-based products were sold to many non-socialist countries on the world market, including West

Germany. So successful was this that, among the non-producing nations, East Germany had become one of the biggest exporters of fossil fuels. By the time Honecker received the worrying news from Brezhnev under the palm trees of Crimea, oil-based products accounted for 28 per cent of its exports to non-socialist states.[5]

Honecker's desperate pleas fell on deaf ears. Brezhnev retorted that 'the recipients of the deliveries of Soviet oil and oil-based products sold those on to capitalists', making enormous profits in the process. He argued that this was not only an unfair economic advantage but closer financial ties to the West, particularly to West Germany, handed 'leverage of various kinds of pressure' to the class enemy which could have 'grave consequences' as the current crisis in Poland showed 'in a dramatic manner'.[6]

This kind of rhetoric added insult to injury as far as Honecker was concerned. The leader of the GDR had sought closer relations with West Germany not only for financial reasons but also because both Bonn and East Berlin feared the possibility of Cold War tensions spilling over into nuclear war on German soil. The Social Democratic Chancellor of West Germany Helmut Schmidt had signalled that he was open to a German-German summit and Honecker was keen to arrange one. But Brezhnev intervened, explicitly forbidding such a meeting and meddling directly in the domestic affairs of the GDR. Ostensibly, this was because Bonn was not to be rewarded for its support for NATO's Double-Track Decision in 1979, which deployed more US medium-range nuclear missiles in Europe while demanding bilateral negotiations for arms control with the Soviet Union. In reality Moscow was increasingly concerned about inner-German collusion. It is telling that Brezhnev had himself kept cordial relations with Schmidt and received him with full diplomatic honours in Moscow in July 1980. But he was concerned that the GDR would rise to the role of intermediary between the two, a position that would have gained it substantial political capital.

Honecker was bitterly disappointed by the lack of trust his erstwhile ally showed him. According to Egon Winkelmann, East

Germany's ambassador to the Soviet Union from 1981 to 1987, Honecker talked himself into an angry rant when he briefed him about his role in Moscow. 'They threatened me not to meet Schmidt. What nonsense!' he fumed.[7] While a devoted socialist, loyal to the ideological legacy of Soviet communism, Honecker was also a patriot who resented the idea that his country was used as a pawn in a dangerous war game played by others. He did not know how many nuclear-armed SS-20 'Saber' missiles had been stationed on his soil nor indeed where they were. On a day-to-day basis, the GDR's government was not even told the number of Soviet troops stationed on its territory (still around 350,000 in the 1980s). For an estimation Honecker relied on guesswork based on water use in Soviet military installations.

The summer meeting in Crimea did absolutely nothing to restore the broken trust between the former hunting mates who used to be politically aligned. Mentally and physically unable to respond to Honecker's arguments, Brezhnev's hollow repetition of the lines that had been impressed on him by those pulling his strings confirmed the GDR's worst nightmare: it would have to fend for itself among the economic giants that surrounded it.

Indeed, not long after Honecker's return to Berlin he received formal notice of Moscow's change of policy. Breaking prior arrangements, the Soviet Union reduced its oil exports to the GDR by over 10 per cent, from 19 to 17 million tonnes, so that it could offer more on the open market and reduce some of its own economic problems. Moscow's costly invasion of Afghanistan, which had dragged since December 1979, the spiralling costs dictated by the renewed arms race with the West and a series of bad harvests had plunged the Soviet Union into a deep economic crisis with supply problems so severe that they threatened to cause social upheaval of the type witnessed in the Solidarność (Solidarity) trade union movement in Poland. The Soviet Union was withdrawing into itself, making the 'Friendship' pipeline on which Honecker had pinned his hopes for East German prosperity look like a cynical joke.

The German leader was unable to hide his despair. In two pleading letters to Moscow, Honecker asked Brezhnev to think again. But to no avail. All his former friend could do was send the Secretary of the Central Committee of the Communist Party of the Soviet Union, Konstantin Rusakov, over to East Berlin on 21 October 1981, where he was to impress on Honecker that the Soviet leader's hands were tied. Rusakov assured Honecker:

> *We know what great difficulties we cause you with this. But please believe us, we have taken the hardest measures in our own country. In the course of the existence of the socialist community of states, we have helped you so often in so many difficult situations. Now we are asking for your help. We can see no other way. Comrade Brezhnev told me, 'When you speak with Comrade Honecker, please tell him that I cried when I signed this off.'*[8]

Brezhnev's tears in Moscow stirred no one in Berlin. Coldly, Honecker retorted, 'Please ask Comrade Leonid Ilyich Brezhnev openly whether two million tonnes of oil are worth the destabilization of the GDR.'[9]

Honecker's despair was understandable. Whatever the reasons, the Soviet Union had left the GDR in an impossible situation. Abandoned by its benefactor in the East and forbidden from engaging with potential markets in the West, the small East German state stood isolated. It lacked the natural resources to run an autarkic economy and, following Moscow's decision in 1981, it lacked the means to acquire what it needed from elsewhere. Total economic collapse loomed as politicians were anxiously observing the political turmoil across the border in Poland. The GDR's Eastern neighbour was about to declare martial law in response to the social unrest that a deep economic crisis had triggered there. While still shielded from the crises that were unravelling rapidly behind the scenes, East Germans clearly sensed that something was afoot. A common joke at the time asked why other socialist states were called 'brothers' rather than 'friends'. The answer was all too fitting: you can choose your friends but not your brothers.

Economic Crisis

Dresden, Saxony, autumn 1981. Klaus Deubel shook his head in disbelief at the circle he was supposed to square.[10] And not for the first time. The thirty-nine-year-old researcher at the Institute for Rationalization in Dresden had been given the unenviable task of increasing efficiency in the local area. His hands were tied. He just had to try, however acrimonious it would be. The order came right from the top, from the Ministry for Electrical Engineering and Electronics, and cascaded down to each state-run business. Klaus's impossible task included finding ways to cut down on the resources spent on management and administration, which had amounted to 20 per cent of expenditure and was to be halved. Klaus found this especially difficult as he was friendly with his colleagues and reluctant to suggest changes to their detriment. He worked hard to create a bundle of measures that included sensible suggestions to increase productivity with limited impact on his colleagues' established roles. One such idea was that individual organizations would once more be allowed to concentrate on their core business rather than producing consumer goods outside of their natural expertise to help Honecker with his initiative to keep the population happy. LEW Hennigsdorf in Brandenburg, for example, had been making locomotives since 1913 but had recently been forced to produce radios, garden furniture and sauna heating systems to supply East Germans with the types of things their Western relatives owned. In view of the mounting economic crisis, Klaus sensibly suggested concentrating on the original specialisms of each branch of industry. In a fifteen-minute meeting at managerial level, his carefully designed solutions were dismissed out of hand and a blanket reduction of management and administration to 10 per cent of expenditure was decided instead.

Direct state interference in the day-to-day running of highly specialized industries was nothing new. The planned economy, by definition, worked over long periods of time and in broad brush-strokes. But in the second half of 1981, centralized, ill-considered measures were cranked up rapidly because of the impending economic crisis, which led to absurd developments. Having cut the management level in businesses down to its bare bones, the planned economy became chaotic and ineffective. Measures decided at ministerial level could no longer be delegated down efficiently. Klaus remembered how the State Secretary of the Ministry for Electrical Engineering and Electronics, who was reporting directly to the minister, personally rushed around factories distributing component parts. Individual companies had also been given a rigid formula to cut down on work times. In the case of the Centre for Research and Engineering of Microelectronics in Dresden, Klaus remembered, the formula came out with a result that legally obliged the institution to save more working hours than it had actually been allocated for its current projects.

Nonsensical and haphazard efficiency measures intensified in 1981. This was in part due to the fact that the SED Party Congress of April 1981 introduced a new five-year plan. The 'main task' remained as before to make the GDR's economy viable. This meant increased productivity, rationalization and improvement of quality. Günter Mittag, Secretary for the Economy of the Central Committee, pointed out that there were severe problems on the world market which affected production in the GDR: 'this is particularly the case in price developments in energy sources, raw materials and in the increased spending on the development of a basis of domestic resources'.[11] Mittag was convinced that the answer could only be to introduce a degree of economic self-interest at every level of the economic chain. He had supported Walter Ulbricht's New Economic System from 1963, which had advocated replacing the five-year plans with a more dynamic model. But political resistance at the time made it difficult for this vision to be fully implemented. Mittag's other firm economic conviction was that 'a national economy can only survive internationally if it works at the highest technical standard'.[12] Ulbricht had wholeheartedly agreed and wanted to invest large sums in computer technology as well as other seemingly futuristic projects for the 1971–1975 plan. But with his health in decline and his days numbered, he had been ridiculed for such views by many party colleagues and his ideas were brushed off as the fantasies of an old man in search of a legacy to build.

Ten years later, much had changed. Ulbricht was dead and the Soviet Union was about to abandon the GDR economically. Much later Mittag bitterly commented that when it came to a possible push in technological development, 'we still laboured under the illusion that it was possible for the GDR to do this in close coopera- tion with the Soviet Union'.[13] In 1981, it became clear that Brezhnev was increasingly reluctant to even deliver raw materials as planned, never mind develop new technologies like microelectronics with the GDR. For Mittag the solution was obvious: the future lay in high tech, and if Moscow could not or would not open its eyes to that, then East Germany must begin to look for other partners, if need be outside the socialist sphere.

As the GDR looked for a model whose efficiency and technology might be emulated, one country stood out as a natural candidate: Japan. Throughout the 1970s, the two countries had already begun to collaborate and trade chemicals, metals and electrical engineer- ing. The latter had been of particular interest given that the GDR needed radios, TVs and stereos to compete with Western consumer culture. Erich Honecker travelled to Japan himself in May 1981 on a full state visit where the two countries concluded trade deals total- ling $440 million. Japan would deliver a car clutch plant as well as an iron foundry to East Germany. The GDR would in return send machinery to Japan. Honecker was also deeply impressed by Japa- nese work culture which valued discipline and efficiency while retaining a sense of collective effort over individual careerism. He marvelled at the automation processes which used robots to make high-end products. When he returned from his visit, he began to push for industrial modernization.

Political pressure to achieve tangible economic progress was immense. The more the GDR managed to fulfil the desires of the population, the more it demanded. By 1980, there were 105 television sets per 100 households, but this also meant that more and more people were exposed to Western culture, including advertising. According to the GDR's own statistics, more than 70 per cent of the population watched West German programmes where they saw appealing new consumer products advertised such as cassette players and recorders. Karl Nendel, State Secretary of the Ministry for Electrical Engineering and Electronics, was tasked with finding a solution to mass produce the desired devices quickly. He charged the VEB Electronic Components in the city of Gera with production of an affordable cassette recorder but the company found this difficult as it simply had neither the know-how nor the staff to comply. Nendel, frustrated with the lack of results, summoned the director of the VEB and demanded answers. When he was told again that the company simply had neither the staff for the task nor adequate equipment for it, Nendel snapped. 'You must understand,' he screamed in the director's face, 'that it is politically necessary to finally have our own recorders!' It was too much for the director. He clutched his chest and Nendel ran out to alert the secretary to call a doctor. The director had suffered a heart attack. 'Today, I think that I went too far in cases like this,'[14] Nendel remembered later in his memoirs, but not without repeating the same mantra that had given the director a heart attack: 'It was ideologically essential to supply the population with modern consumer goods.'[15]

In the end, the decision was made to import the entire production line and a deal was struck with Toshiba. The Japanese industrial giant already had a footing in the GDR where it was helping to establish factories for the production of colour TV sets in Berlin and Ilmenau with imports to the tune of DM850 million. On 13 May 1982 it added a factory for audiotechnology with the capacity to produce 750,000 cassette recorders and 30,000 hi-fi cassette decks. The chosen location was Berlin-Marzahn where the largest of Honecker's house building projects had already produced the lionshare of the country's over a million new flats (it would be nearly 2 million by the end of the decade) – new jobs in the area were highly welcome. A brand-new production hall was added to the existing VEB Stern-Radio Berlin, the state-owned radio production company, and filled with Japanese systems and other parts imported from the US. Herbert Roloff, General Director of International Trade for the Import of Industrial Technology from 1980 and responsible for overseeing the process, remembered that the success of this huge undertaking was limited: 'Yes, we managed to put new types of entertainment electronics and household appliances on the market. Instead of one model, there were two or three. But on the shelves in the West – and that includes our Intershops – there were twenty models.'[16]

Focusing on microelectronics and rationalization wasn't enough to heal the GDR's festering economic wounds. Many Western countries responded to the severe problems caused by the oil crises of the 1970s by introducing cuts to their welfare systems in the 1980s – from Helmut Kohl in West Germany to Margaret Thatcher in the UK and Ronald Reagan in the US. Honecker had no such option. The GDR's subsidies to essentials such as rent, food and childcare had become a fact of life. When prices for textiles rose briefly in 1977, it had immediately led to stockpiling by disconcerted citizens while rationing of everyday luxuries such as coffee and chocolate also caused consternation. Honecker was trapped between the spiralling costs of socialism and the inability to meet them with increased income from the oil trade since Brezhnev had cut him short.

Borrowing was not a solution either. The Soviet Union had made it clear that it could no longer afford to grant the GDR the credits it relied on, so the only option was to turn West. However, the West lost trust in markets behind the Iron Curtain because both Poland and Romania ran into deep financial problems in 1981. (Poland went bankrupt and martial law was declared in December 1981.) This had direct consequences for the GDR when, in the first half of 1982 alone, 40 per cent of Western investments were pulled out of the small country with no options left to replace them.[17]

The situation was made worse by the fact that the looming economic disaster was papered over by the government while people could see the evidence day in and day out in their own lives. As wages and prices were artificially kept stable, such figures do not reveal the true picture. Werner Krolikowski, member of the Central Committee of the SED and of the Economics Commission, noted in a report in March 1983 that 'purchasing power is developing disproportionately in relation to goods on offer'.[18] In other words, while workers retained their wages as before and had enough money left in their pockets after paying for the subsidized essentials such as rent and food, there was less and less on the shelves for them to buy. Krolikowski went on to report that 'The population voices much criticism about shortcomings in the supply situation, which can be described as a permanent state of affairs.' For Krolikowski what was worse than the economic situation was that the government lied about it to its people. He listed an increase in industrial production for the beginning of 1983 as 2.6 per cent 'while, in public, EH [Erich Honecker] speaks of an increase of industrial goods production of 4.3% ... i.e. the embellishment of the situation through lies and deception continues, directly ordered by EH and GM [Günter Mittag]'.[19]

As Krolikowski indicated at the time, East Germans could not be fooled forever. The discrepancy between politicians' words and their everyday experiences was too great. Wolfgang Dietrich, a thirty-seven-year-old mechanic who opened his own garage when economic reforms in the 1970s made this possible, really felt the squeeze on his business in 1981.[20] He had struggled from the outset when he opened in 1977. Car parts were always scarce and had to be ordered a year in advance from Leipzig. Loans were not available and he had to fund all business expenses out of his own pocket. He scraped together enough money to buy one ramp only and as he was initially not allowed to employ others, the service he could offer was tied to his own work time. When he was eventually allowed to employ another mechanic, the wages for him were tightly controlled and kept unattractively low. Even a bunch of flowers, which he had bought his employee for his birthday, was rigorously struck off the expenses list Wolfgang handed in annually for his tax review.

In the 1980s, the situation became increasingly difficult. His garage was only allowed to order three replacement engines a year as all machinery and industrial output, in general, became increasingly scarce. But Wolfgang was creative and branched out his business in other directions. He built his own tow truck and offered breakdown cover in the local area. This service was incredibly popular as Wolfgang could repair almost anything on wheels – from cars to tractors. He had learned (and learned to love) to maintain farm machinery in his apprenticeship as a fifteen-year-old boy in 1959 in the village of Trebus in rural Brandenburg. It was a challenging task, made especially difficult by the fact that he did not have his own telephone in the garage. This meant that anyone who broke down or needed help on a farm had to find a public payphone or ask the police to call Wolfgang's home number where his wife would pick up the phone a few kilometres away from the garage. Then she had to come out to let him know the details before Wolfgang could drive his tow truck out to assist. This convoluted system only changed when a government vehicle broke down near Storkow with the Deputy Minister for Postal and Telecommunications in it. Wolfgang came to the rescue and offered the VIP and his party his sofa while the car was being repaired as there was always a shortage of hotels and guest houses in the GDR. Sure enough, shortly after the incident, a telephone line was laid to the workshop.

Incidents like this not only revealed the dire situation of the economic infrastructure of the GDR but also how highly attuned East Germans were to it. In the long run, this was unsustainable and the politburo was well aware of it. Outside help was desperately needed, and if the Soviet Union would not provide it, the GDR had only one way out. Whether Brezhnev approved or not, help would have to come from West Germany.

Strange Bedfellows

Schleiz, Thuringia, German-German border, 5 May 1983. It was a beautiful spring day when Alexander Schalck-Golodkowski, the

GDR's main fundraiser, made his way through the Thuringian mountains in a spacious government Citroën. Outside, the seemingly endless dark green sea of pine trees rose and fell with the landscape. But Schalck wasn't there to admire the view. He was being chauffeured to the Bavarian border and it was paramount that he got there safely and on time. For that reason alone, Stasi boss Erich Mielke, responsible for logistics and security, would rather not have chosen the Citroën for such an important journey. They were difficult to make bullet proof and prone to breaking down. But his boss Erich Honecker had loved his 'Zitrone' ever since the French had given him a CX Prestige model to try. He had never looked back – the soft seats and smooth suspension had clinched the deal, according to bodyguard Bernd Brückner.[21] So thirty-five cars were ordered and now everyone had to live with them and their attendant impracticalities. But Mielke couldn't help himself. He always had Schalck's journeys backed up by a second vehicle.

Once the Citroën had reached the car park at the border with Bavaria, Schalck was no longer Mielke's responsibility. He was on his own and that was no bad thing as far as he was concerned. An armoured dark blue BMW 750 was already waiting and Schalck slipped into the back. As the driver passed from Thuringia into Bavaria, neither East nor West German border guards wanted to see any papers. Everything had been arranged to perfection. After a few hours' drive south, the limousine turned off the main road and on to a long, unpaved drive. A picture-perfect country house appeared in the distance, framed by lush green meadows and the clear blue sky. Schalck gazed at the Bavarian scene and wondered, 'Could the solution to the GDR's financial problems be found here of all places?'[22]

Schalck was sceptical. He was about to meet Bavarian Minister President Franz Josef Strauß, 'the ultimate Cold Warrior, the personification of Western imperialism', as he put it.[23] And he had come to ask him to save GDR socialism from financial collapse. At face value, the situation was absurd. Strauß had been a vocal opponent of West German financial aid for its socialist neighbour – 'Not a pfennig for the GDR,' he had reputedly insisted when he was Finance Minister of the 'Grand Coalition' in the late 1960s. But Schalck figured it was worth a try. By 1982, the GDR's economy was on the ropes and with it the state's very existence. The country had already geared its economy towards maximizing exports, making record profits of 5–6 million marks a year, but it needed almost all of that to pay the interest on existing debt. Investment was needed everywhere as technology and production methods were falling further behind Western standards. It stood to reason that if money could be borrowed from somewhere, even from the class enemy across the border, it could be used to rebuild and modernize the GDR, resetting the economy as a whole. The investment would eventually pay off.

It would take millions to bring the GDR's economy up to speed – sums that the Soviet Union could not afford and the West would not give. A sense of impending doom began to grip the GDR's economic fixers – 'to be or not to be, that was the question', Schalck mused.[24] Then Josef März, a close political ally and personal friend of Strauß, had approached Schalck at the Leipzig Trade Fair. The Minister President of Bavaria would like to meet him at März's guest house, Gut Spöck, in Upper Bavaria.

Schalck stepped out of the BMW into the warm Bavarian sun and took in the beautiful Alpine scenery. He was tense. 'How would communist-hating Strauß approach a representative of the "SED regime"?' he wondered.[25] The last diplomatic crisis had been all too recent. A month earlier, a West German man, who had travelled through the GDR, had died of a heart attack when questioned by border guards in a barrack in Drewitz, Saxony-Anhalt. As such, this was nothing out of the ordinary. The psychological pressure that East German border guards deliberately built up during questioning proved too much for an estimated 350 people in total who died of heart failure at inner-German checkpoints. But given the heated tensions of the early 1980s, when both superpowers continued their manic arms race in Europe as well as competing for influence in the Global South, this latest case sent the conservative end of the West

German press into a frenzy. Claims that the dead man had 'practically been beaten to death' circulated freely.²⁶ Chancellor Helmut Kohl cancelled a planned meeting with Erich Honecker. Weighing heavy on Schalck's mind was the fact that Strauß had been one of the most vocal critics, openly suggesting that the man's death had amounted to political 'murder'. So Schalck had no idea what would await him when the door to Gut Spöck opened and he was greeted by the hosts, März and his wife. From their generous living room he could see the surrounding mountains nestling round a beautifully still lake. Then suddenly the idyllic silence was shattered by the wings of an approaching helicopter which landed noisily right in front of the house. From it Strauß emerged – waving and with a wide smile on his face.

Despite all their political differences, the Bavarian and the SED man hit it off immediately. Over pork knuckles and potato salad, Schalck warmed to his congenial host. He found it hard to get a word in edgeways as Strauß waxed lyrical about his political battles as defence minister under Konrad Adenauer, West Germany's first Chancellor; about having chided an army general for buying cheap, subsidized toys for his children in the GDR ('wasn't he ashamed to buy products that East Germans needed urgently?'²⁷); about his political travels around the world, from Romania to Angola. Schalck, now sunk into a comfortable armchair, listened politely. There followed a lecture on just how much influence Strauß still wielded in the federal government ('Nobody gets past me in Bonn!'²⁸) and a treatise on the difficulties inherent in the social market economy. It was late when he finally addressed the reason he had invited his guest: 'Herr Schalck, now that I have got to know you personally and gained the impression that you can be trusted . . .'²⁹ a credit of DM1 billion could be made available to the GDR through West German banks.

Strauß knew better than to tie this offer to fixed terms and conditions. Should this financial arrangement come to pass, the FRG could not be seen to compromise on human rights standards in the GDR while the GDR could not lose face by allowing the FRG to buy domestic political reform from it. Strauß cautiously suggested that the General Secretary might want to think about easing restrictions for West German visitors in East Germany 'at a point in time that Honecker deems convenient'. It was then that Schalck knew a solution could be found. Strauß not only understood the delicate political situation in the GDR but he respected it. Schalck was delighted that 'a new "channel" had been opened, more exciting, more important than any that came before'.³⁰ He immediately got back into the BMW and rushed to Berlin. He arrived there at 4 a.m. and went straight to the office where he dictated the outcome of the conversation to his secretary who had stayed up to await his return. Then Schalck called his wife to let her know he would not be home anytime soon and waited for the arrival of Mittag and Honecker. Both men were excited to hear the good news and wanted to do everything in their power to proceed with the credit. Relieved that he had averted the financial collapse of the GDR, for now, Schalck sunk into an office armchair and fell asleep.

In the spur of the moment and desperate for the cash injection, Honecker promised a range of measures, so long as they remained secret and out of the eye of the West German press: border controls would become less aggressive; children up to fourteen years no longer needed to exchange a minimum amount of West German marks into East German marks on visits; and he even considered dismantling the 71,000 deadly automatic firing devices that covered nearly 450 kilometres of the inner-German border. Despite several diplomatic setbacks that ensured Schalck more sleepless nights away from home, the deal eventually came together. A credit agreement was signed between the two German states on 1 July 1983. On the same day the National Defence Council of East Germany decided to develop border security measures without automated systems and mines. In 1984, there was another DM1 billion credit while Schalck's *KoKo* enterprise also provided record sums of around DM3 billion a year. The GDR's immediate financial collapse was averted.

The financial ties between the two Germanies also had a thawing effect on their political relationship. Former Chancellor Helmut

Schmidt had made a start by visiting the GDR in December 1981 but relations remained fraught given the tension created by the nuclear arsenal stationed in both Germanies. The personal ties that began to develop between the politicians as a result of the Schalck–Strauß 'channel' made all the difference. Strauß, his wife Marianne and his son Max visited the GDR only weeks after the deal had been finalized. Schalck greeted the family at the border and escorted them to Haus Hubertusstock, the hunting residence of Erich Honecker by the beautiful Lake Werbellin, north-east of Berlin. When conversation over lunch remained somewhat stiff and formal, Marianne Strauß broke the ice. She sat opposite Honecker and told him openly how much she admired East Germany's extensive childcare system and the financial help for young couples as well as the support women received during and after pregnancy in the workplace. She regretted that the lack of such a support mechanism had led to a shrinking population in West Germany. Honecker, genuinely touched by this, immediately warmed to the Bavarian family – their connection outlasted the meeting and bridged political differences.

Bavaria and the GDR began to forge an unlikely cultural and economic connection out of the financial agreements struck in 1983/84. Cities and towns were twinned, research projects arranged and cultural exchanges became more frequent. The Bavarian National Museum held an exhibition in Dresden, for example, while Dresden's art collection was on display in Munich. A lot of trade began to flow back and forth as both Schalck and Strauß had intended. In the second half of the 1980s, trade with the Soviet Bloc still accounted for half of the GDR's exports and imports. Meanwhile, the trade volume between the two Germanies grew from DM10.9 billion in 1980 to DM14 billion in 1988.[31] Over 1,000 cooperative projects existed between East and West by 1988. Some of the Western products that GDR citizens craved, like Nivea skin cream, were produced in East Germany by West German companies. When West German companies were asked why they traded with the GDR rather than its cheaper brother states further to the East, they pointed to the highly qualified staff, German as a common working language and reliability. At the same time, the eased situation at the inner-German border and somewhat loosened travel restrictions led to more interactions between East and West Germans from all walks of life. The fear of 'the other' was beginning to dissipate. In the autumn of 1987, Honecker travelled to Bonn himself, following an invitation from Kohl. He was received with full state honours. It looked as if the two Germanies had found a way to coexist.

Martin Luther was East German

Wartburg Castle, Eisenach, Thuringia, 4 May 1983. It was an unseasonably cool day. Thick, grey clouds hung broodingly above the fortress, occasionally releasing spatters of rain. A biting wind whipped through the narrow passages between mediaeval walls. Surrounded by iron-grey skies, the Wartburg looked spectacular. Sitting on top of a 410-metre-high precipice in the Thuringian Forest it overlooks the picturesque market town of Eisenach. Its elevated position makes it an imposing landmark and also exposes it to the elements. Yet the weather did not dampen the mood of the 3,000 visitors to the castle who had flocked up the winding mountain road during the afternoon. As evening fell, they gathered in the inner courtyard of the Wartburg, huddled together and wrapped in heavy raincoats. None of them wanted to miss the historic occasion. Some people craned their necks to see the assembled VIPs.

West Berlin's mayor (soon to be West Germany's President) Richard von Weizsäcker was there. Born into an aristocratic family, a devout Christian and a member of the conservative Christian Democratic Union since 1954, he seemed to embody the opposite of everything the GDR stood for. Yet, he sat mere centimetres away from SED politician Horst Sindermann, who had come up with the term 'Anti-Fascist Protection Rampart' that was officially used to refer to the Berlin Wall. Such East–West harmony was a sight to behold for those present at the castle, and for those watching the proceedings at home. The event was transmitted live from Wartburg Castle to East and West Germany, as well as Austria and Switzerland. After all, the man they had all come to celebrate was not just an east German, he was integral to the history of all German speakers: Martin Luther.

Martin Luther had been born 500 years earlier, in Eisleben – officially called Lutherstadt Eisleben since 1946. His crucial role in the Reformation alone had made him a central figure in a majority-Protestant country. He is also a national figure. It was at Wartburg Castle that he translated the New Testament into a form of German that was accessible to ordinary people across regions with vastly differing dialects. In contrast to pre-existing translations, Luther deliberately used simple and emotive language, 'removing impediments and difficulties so that other people may read it without hindrance', as he put it. It worked. Luther's way with words and his ingenious use of the printing press meant that his translation was widely read. As people began to weave Lutheran expressions and morality into their local dialects and culture, the patchwork of German-speaking principalities became a somewhat more coherent cloth, an important step towards the very concept of German nationhood.

Luther has always been a problematic figure, however. His virulent antisemitism could not be brushed aside; his contribution to the split of Christianity is not a cause for celebration as far as German Catholics are concerned; and the centrality of his legacy to German Protestantism and his support of the bloody suppression of the, in his words, 'Murderous, Thieving Hordes of Peasants' in their revolt of 1524–25 made him a very tricky figure for the GDR, which wanted an atheistic society and viewed itself as the resolution to the long struggle of the oppressed. And yet the unifying aspect of Luther's work trumped all such concerns on both sides of the Wall. It has never stopped resonating among a people who saw division as an eternal curse on their nationhood. When the 'Luther Year' of 1983 approached, it was too good an opportunity to miss for the GDR. It desperately needed historical roots that reached deeper than the mud and blood of the Second World War. And Martin Luther was East German, after all.

Previously lambasted as the 'servant of dukes' and 'butcher of peasants', Martin Luther's metamorphosis into a progressive East German figure of world renown was well under way by 4 May 1983, the anniversary of Luther's arrival at the Wartburg where he undertook his translation of the Bible. Despite the sparse availability of building materials, the authorities had begun in the late 1970s to restore the town centres and historical buildings touched by Luther's life and work. This included his home town Eisleben; Wittenberg, where Luther is said to have nailed his famous ninety-five theses to the door of All Saints' Church; and of course the Wartburg and nearby Eisenach which was expected to be host to many international guests during the festivities in 1983. Honecker, an atheist originating from the Catholic Saarland in West Germany, now personally headed the Luther Committee and believed the money and resources flowing into the grand-scale renovation projects were well invested. Opening the newly restored Wartburg on 21 April 1983, after five years of renovation work to bring to the fore the castle's mediaeval character, he declared, 'To many citizens of the German Democratic Republic a visit to the Wartburg will mean a strengthening of their feeling for their nation and for their homeland.'[32]

Apart from bringing a sense of historical longevity to the young nation, the restoration projects were also designed to further the prestige of the GDR and give its citizens the feeling of being taken seriously by the international community. The authorities openly courted Western tourism as a part of the Luther Year of 1983 and expected visitors from West Germany as well as from other Western nations, primarily the USA. The state-run travel agency advertised Luther tours which included visits to 'authentic local restaurants' and the promise of 'Luther souvenirs'. While Western media remarked critically that the GDR hailed Luther's legacy in the same year it celebrated the centenary of Karl Marx's death, it also saw this careful extension of ideological comfort zones as a positive sign. The *New York Times* ran a front-page report on 8 May 1983, titled 'East Germany Finally Embraces Luther', which noted that Honecker's government had 'a growing self-confidence' and 'state restrictions on church activity, notably the construction of new churches, have been eased'.[33] American churchmen and women embarked on pilgrimages to Lutheran sites in East Germany, restoring a sense of local pride in communities whose heritage had at best been neglected and at worst actively eroded since 1945. The meeting of GDR citizens with church leaders and dignitaries from East and West Germany for a televised service at the Wartburg on 'Luther Day' in 1983 was more than a symbolic gesture. There followed commemorative stamps, a film series about Martin Luther, a 'Songs of the Reformation' LP as well as dozens of local events across East Germany.

The rediscovery of Martin Luther was only one part of a broader effort to give the GDR historical roots. Another supposedly East German legacy that lent itself to reinterpretation was that of the Kingdom of Prussia whose core lands had spanned the territory now occupied by the GDR. Initially, GDR historiography foregrounded the militarism and rigid class structures of Prussia. When the quadriga, the chariot drawn by four horses, on top of the iconic Brandenburg Gate was restored in the 1950s, in a rare early example of East-West cooperation, the East Berlin authorities removed what they deemed 'emblems of Prussian-German militarism' from the ensemble. On the night of 2 August 1958, they secretly took the quadriga into the Neuer Marstall building in Berlin-Mitte and removed its eagle and Iron Cross without which it stood on top of the Brandenburg Gate, high above the Berlin Wall, until it was fully restored in the 1990s (including the Prussian insignia).

A more nuanced image of Prussia as a country that also stood for liberalism and progress was already beginning to develop from the late 1950s onwards. Historians such as Ingrid Mittenzwei, Professor at the Central Institute for History at the Academy of Sciences of the GDR, contributed to this transformation as her influential biography of Frederick the Great asserted that 'Prussia is part of our history.' Ideological language and politicized narrative history were toned down so much in the 1980s that many works by East German historians were also commercially successful in West Germany – particularly the ever-popular genre of historical biographies. The publisher Edition Leipzig, which concentrated largely on exports, openly asked its authors to avoid 'export-reducing phrases'.[34] East German books such as *Battles of World History* were popular in the West despite attempts of the publishers there to block GDR rivals from the market.

The rethinking of German history continued to accelerate in the 1980s with the rediscovery of Prussia at its core. It helped that this had long been established in the military. In 1962, the NVA reintroduced the *Großer Zapfenstreich* (Grand Tattoo), a Prussian military tradition that originated in the nineteenth century and persists in the German army to this day. The ceremony was more regularly performed by the GDR's forces between 1981 and 1989 as part of a general renewal of traditions. Spectators flocked to see the *Zapfenstreich* in front of the Neue Wache (New Guard), the former guardhouse for the Royal Palace and a memorial to the Prussian-led Liberation Wars against Napoleon in 1813. The Neue Wache was itself an example of the blend of histories in the GDR. While the outside was restored in the 1950s, the inside was converted into a 'Memorial to the Victims of Fascism and Militarism'. The same principle was applied to the traditional 'Grand Guard Mounting' ceremony that had happened there, with interruptions, since 1818. Instead of Imperial Prussian guards, there were now soldiers of the Friedrich Engels Guard Regiment performing the ceremony every Wednesday – a major spectacle and popular tourist attraction in East Berlin.

Prussia was also evoked in the civilian sphere. The 1980 film 'Clausewitz – Life of a Prussian General' was broadcast on prime-time TV and showed Carl von Clausewitz as a reformer and Prussia as a progressive historical force. In the same year, an equestrian statue of Frederick the Great was restored to its central place on Unter den Linden after it had been moved to Potsdam in 1950. The

Marxist historian Ernst Engelberg even began to reinterpret Otto von Bismarck, Germany's first Chancellor, previously viewed as a reactionary Prussian Junker and enemy of socialism. In his 1985 two-volume biography of the Iron Chancellor, which appeared in East and West Germany simultaneously, he called Bismarck 'clever, human and empathetic'.[35]

In 1987, Honecker's efforts to fully restore East Germany's Prussian legacy took on astonishing proportions when he sent his media expert and former Culture Minister Hans Bentzien to Louis Ferdinand, Prince of Prussia, head of the now defunct Hohenzollern dynasty and the grandson of Kaiser Wilhelm II. His mission was to lobby the Prince – whom he was to deferentially address as 'Your Imperial Highness' – for a return of the remains of Frederick the Great and those of his father Frederick William I to Sanssouci Park in Potsdam as the former had wished for in his will. Louis Ferdinand was even offered the restoration of residential rights to Cecilienhof, the mock-Tudor palace that had been built during the First World War and hosted the Potsdam Conference after the Second World War. While not entirely averse to the idea, the Prince was somewhat reluctant to restore his ancestors' remains to a country that had nationalized much of his estate after the war and had previously declared the legacy of his family to be one of militarism and fascism. The remains of the famous Prussian kings eventually returned to Potsdam but not until 1991. Nevertheless, this episode shows just how much the GDR was beginning to embrace historical ties beyond its own short political existence. It began to understand that a nation can't grow without roots.

German Partnership or Socialist Brotherhood

Moscow, Soviet Union, 13 March 1985. The international delegation stood huddled together in front of Lenin's Mausoleum on Red Square. Some wore Russian-style fur caps against the cold. All did their best to look solemn and mournful as their thick, dark overcoats provided limited relief from the Russian winter. The gathering was a sight to behold: British Prime Minister Margaret Thatcher, Palestinian leader Yasser Arafat, French President François Mitterrand, West German Chancellor Helmut Kohl, Romanian President Nicolae Ceaușescu and the East German leader Erich Honecker were among the dozens of foreign dignitaries gathered in the heart of what US President Ronald Reagan had dubbed the 'Evil Empire' almost exactly two years earlier. Notably, the latter was absent, having 'an awful lot on my plate right now that would have to be set aside'.[36] But with the exception of the US, most of the leaders of major capitalist and communist countries had come to Moscow to bury Konstantin Chernenko, seventh General Secretary of the Communist Party of the Soviet Union. His short-lived reign had followed that of Yuri Andropov, who had himself only ruled for fifteen months after the death of Leonid Brezhnev in November 1982. The world leaders looked sombre enough when Chernenko's open coffin was carried past them, but they were unified in the hope that the era of interim leaders in the Soviet Union would come to an end. Chernenko's successor Mikhail Gorbachev had just turned fifty-four and seemed practically youthful compared to the frail Soviet leaders the world had become accustomed to in the decade or so since Brezhnev's health began to fail in the early 1970s. There was hope for reform, modernization and political stability in the Soviet Union on both sides of the Iron Curtain.

For the two German leaders, Helmut Kohl and Erich Honecker, Chernenko's funeral was particularly symbolic. Along with the man himself, they hoped to bury Soviet objection to inter-German dialogue. Indeed, it was on that cold evening in March 1985 in Moscow that the two men met in person for their first formal meeting. In the two-and-a-half-hour conversation they held there, Kohl reiterated his previous invitation to Honecker for an official visit to Bonn. A joint statement proclaimed that both sides would undertake all conceivable efforts to establish 'normal and neighbourly relations between the German Democratic Republic and the Federal Republic of Germany in the interests of peace and stability in

Europe'.[37] Honecker had previously tried to drive such a course
against the express wishes of the Soviet leaders. If Brezhnev had
been wary of German collusion, Chernenko had gone even further.
He had openly attacked inner-German reconciliation in a piece entitled 'On the Wrong Track' published on 2 August 1984 in *Pravda*, the
newspaper of the Soviet Communist Party: 'None of it is geared
towards the development of humanitarian aims, as West Germany
likes to claim, but towards the attempt to gain new channels of
political-ideological influence.'

Honecker tried his best to remain defiant, telling Philipp Jen-
ninger, the President of the West German parliament, that 'the
GDR's foreign policy is made in Berlin, not Moscow'. But Cherne-
ko's thinly veiled and very public criticism of Honecker was
politically dangerous for the General Secretary. After all, he had
himself used his predecessor Walter Ulbricht's rift with Brezhnev to
topple him. Honecker was keenly aware that his every move was
watched by Moscow, not only through KGB agents but also through
political enemies within his own ranks. There were members of the
Central Committee who regarded the closer political and economic
ties to the West with suspicion.

In addition, Honecker was beginning to develop a strangely personal relationship with Helmut Kohl via phone conversations in
which the two men openly discussed details of a meeting, irrespective of the deafening 'Nyet' from Moscow. The personal tone in calls
such as this one from December 1983 aroused suspicion within elements of the politburo:

> *Honecker: Yes, Hello?*
> *Kohl: Yes, this is Kohl, good day.*
> *Honecker: Good day, Chancellor, this is Honecker.*
> *Kohl: Yes, good day, General Secretary. How are you?*
> *Honecker: Excellent, I would like to say, if only the weather was a little*
>   *better.*
> *Kohl: How is the weather over there?*
> *Honecker: Misty, fog.*

> Kohl: *Yes, it's completely cloudy here, previously it was cold; now we have*
> *spring weather.*
> Honecker: *Yes, I know what you mean.*
> Kohl: *Much too warm. General Secretary, I just wanted to call you at the*
> *end of the year to exchange a few thoughts. The first thing I wanted to*
> *mention is that I see with great satisfaction that we managed this year,*
> *irrespective of the global political situation, to accomplish a number of,*
> *in my view, really sensible things . . .*
>
> *We, the Federal Government, want to do everything we can to*
> *secure what we have achieved and if possible to extend what political*
> *jargon calls 'the strands of our relationship', or as I would put it a*
> *little more simply, 'our sensible relationship' . . .*
>
> *My invitation to you stands of course. Just let me know when you*
> *take it up.*[38]

When Honecker proceeded to challenge Kohl on the stationing of
American intermediate-range ballistic missiles in West Germany,
Kohl did not respond in kind to what he knew were 'completely different standpoints'.[39] Instead, he reassured Honecker that he could
guarantee 'with absolute certainty that there will not be a war of
aggression from the Federal Republic or from NATO'.[40] He proceeded to remind Honecker that they were both Germans with a
historical responsibility to prevent war in Europe. He may have
been eighteen years younger than the General Secretary but,

> Kohl: *I too have experienced the war as a child, fully conscious of what*
> *was happening.*
> Honecker: *In the last moments, yes?*
> Kohl: *Yes. And at the end even as Flakhelfer ['air force assistant', i.e. child*
> *soldier]. I experienced air raids in my home town of Ludwigshafen. My*
> *brother fell in the war. My brother-in-law was incarcerated by the*
> *Nazis. I experienced everything that was typical of the fate of German*
> *families at that time . . .*

Sensing the lingering distrust in his interlocutor, the Chancellor added,

> Kohl: You are talking to a man who will do nothing to harm your
>   position.

The reminders of a shared German past alongside the indirect promise not to whip up opposition in the GDR softened the stance of Honecker who concluded the conversation in cautious agreement with his Western counterpart.

> Honecker: It is of course important, resulting from our responsibility
>   alone, that we preserve peace, i.e. avert a new war. I accept your
>   reassurances gladly. I nearly said, 'so God wills it', everything may
>   come to pass as you have expressed it . . .
> Kohl: Yes. Well, I wish you a happy start to the New Year.
> Honecker: Yes, you too have a happy start to the New Year. I heard you're
>   in the Ludwigshafen area. It's a beautiful part of the world.
> Kohl: I have to travel so much, I'm glad to be at home for once.
> Honecker: That's nice. Well, thank you very much. Enjoy New Year's Eve.
>   Goodbye.
> Kohl: Goodbye.[41]

This extraordinary conversation shows that while Honecker and Kohl were firmly committed to their respective blocs and had to take into account what Washington and Moscow made of their desire to forge closer bonds with one another, they were also acutely aware of a shared German fate. They felt they had a unique historical responsibility to maintain peace in Germany and Europe.

This burgeoning German consciousness that seemed to go hand in hand with the GDR's efforts to see itself beyond the ties it shared with the USSR strained the relationship between the brother states immensely. In an attempt to clear the air between them, Chernenko and Honecker met in Moscow in August 1984 to 'clarify a number of important questions in our relationship' as the official transcript of the meeting put it.[42] The General Secretary of the SED spoke for well over an hour to justify the need for closer German-German relations. When he was finished, an unimpressed Chernenko retorted that ultimately West Germany's role was that of the 'military, economic and ideological . . . executor of Reagan's policy on our continent. The forked tongue and the militaristic tendencies of politics in the FRG exceed everything done in Bonn under Adenauer. Bonn and Washington act in complete unison.'[43] He proceeded to disabuse Honecker of his notion that East German foreign policy was made in Berlin. 'How relations between the GDR and the FRG develop is a question for our common big policy. This question touches the Soviet Union directly.'[44] As if that was not explicit enough as an instruction to Honecker to give up his independent relationship with Kohl, the Soviet Defence Minister Dmitry Ustinov, who was also present in the meeting, made it abundantly clear that this was not a matter for discussion. Couldn't Honecker see that any and all reassurances he might have received from Kohl were mere 'pretence, just ideological deception'?[45] Ustinov went further. The more East and West Germans interacted with one another on any given issue, the more likely it was that security was compromised. 'We also ask, if one opens the gates even wider, will this not affect the soldiers?'[46]

This questioning of the loyalty of the GDR's armed forces to the socialist cause was too much for Honecker, who retorted angrily that he had no choice but to seek some sort of accommodation with West Germany since 'There are few citizens of the GDR who do not have relatives in the FRG.' By the end of the meeting 'it was suggested to Honecker that his very position would come under discussion if he did not abandon his plans to travel to Bonn,' as the GDR's main man for Western relations, Herbert Häber, later remembered.[47]

Häber, one of the principle Eastern architects of the idea of a 'Coalition of Reason' between Bonn and East Berlin, would himself fall victim to the increasing concerns in the politburo regarding the clashes with Moscow. Keen to maintain his position of power in Berlin and in Moscow, Honecker joined the ugly campaign that was mounting against Häber the following year. Eventually buckling under the pressure, Häber suffered a nervous breakdown on 18 August 1985 and was hospitalized for several months during which Honecker pushed him to resign from the politburo 'for health reasons'. Regardless of the close relationship the two men may once have had, the General Secretary needed a scapegoat to parade in Berlin and Moscow to prove that his conversations with Kohl and the vast Strauß loans did not amount to an ideological opening to the enemy in the West.

Just how fractious Honecker's relationship with the Soviets had become was evident in the fact that both Chernenko and Ustinov were openly discussing alternative candidates for the leadership of the GDR well before the clash at the meeting in Moscow. Egon Krenz, then the youngest member of the politburo, remembered how the Defence Minister of the Soviet Union had invited him for a private discussion in June 1984. 'Ustinov studied me and took a sip from his tea glass. Then he asked: "Don't you think your General Secretary's time is up? Don't you want to discuss this with your politburo?" I was surprised by this directness . . . Suspicions that Honecker might walk his own way with Bonn behind Moscow's back were great.'[48]

By the time Honecker and Kohl finally met in March 1985, Chernenko and Ustinov were both dead and a very different, much younger man had taken their place. Mikhail Gorbachev seemed to understand that the permanent course of confrontation between East and West was unsustainable in the long run. A year earlier, in February 1984, he had still been deemed too inexperienced to take the political rudder of the Soviet Union and Chernenko had been chosen to follow Yuri Andropov's short reign. Gorbachev had used the extra year this gave him wisely. He often stepped in for the gravely ill Chernenko, proving a steady pair of hands despite his relative youth. Many members of the politburo were impressed with Gorbachev's style as he chaired more and more of their meetings, and by the time of Chernenko's death, he seemed his natural successor. He had also held the role of chair of the Foreign Affairs Committee of the Soviet legislature, which, while technically more of a nominal position than one of political influence, had provided him with the opportunity to travel widely.

On his travels, he found that his desire to make contact with the West was reciprocated. The British Prime Minister Margaret Thatcher, for example, had written to several key figures in Moscow to invite them for a meeting. It was Gorbachev who took her up on the offer. Thatcher's recollections of their first meeting in December 1984 show how much more open than his predecessors Gorbachev was towards Western leaders:

> *Over drinks in the Great Hall Mr Gorbachev told me how interested he had been to see the farmland on the way to Chequers and we compared notes about our countries' different agricultural systems . . . It was not long before the conversation turned from trivialities – for which neither Mr Gorbachev nor I had any taste – to a vigorous two-way debate. In a sense, the argument has continued ever since and is taken up whenever we meet; and as it goes to the heart of what politics is really about, I never tire of it.*[49]

Gorbachev's openness to the West raised hopes in Honecker that he too might be allowed to travel to Bonn. But as quickly became apparent, Honecker, nineteen years Gorbachev's senior, had very different ideas about what openness to the West looked like. To Gorbachev, it meant a reduction of the expensive arms race that was destroying his country economically. And it was to entail a liberalization package under the twin slogans of glasnost (openness) and perestroika (restructuring). Honecker meanwhile kept a tight lid on reform movements in his country. To him, openness to the West meant that both sides accepted the status quo and began trading with each other without attempting to change the other's system of governance.

This clash of visions came to a head when Gorbachev visited the GDR in April 1986 to attend the SED Congress. Challenged again by Honecker about allowing a meeting with Kohl, the Soviet leader repeated his predecessor's counter-arguments. While he would himself receive West German President Richard von Weizsäcker with full state honours in Moscow just over a year later, Gorbachev remonstrated with Honecker about his plans to meet the Chancellor in Bonn: 'What can I tell my people, Erich, if you visit the Federal Republic in such a situation?' Honecker asked in turn, 'And what do we tell our people, who have the gravest concerns about peace and would therefore like me to undertake this journey?'[50]

Honecker was deeply hurt by the mistrust Moscow seemed to continue to harbour against him. Turning to an old friend, the Soviet ambassador to East Germany Vyacheslav Kochemasov, he complained, 'How should this be interpreted? As suspicion towards me or as a refusal to recognize that this trip is in our common interest? As it turns out, others are allowed to go but I'm not. And this at a moment when I am, for the first time, invited for a state visit and a possibility has opened up to establish bilateral relations with the FRG on equal terms.'[51] Honecker wanted to be recognized as a state leader in his own right and for the GDR to be a sovereign country rather than a vassal of the Soviet Union. His relationship to Moscow was beginning to break.

While Gorbachev later cautiously signalled to Honecker that he was willing to begin thinking about allowing a German-German meeting in the future, East and West German politicians had long continued establishing their own channels of communication, independent of Moscow. When it looked like Helmut Kohl's Christian Democrats might go into the 1987 elections politically damaged, the SED renewed its contacts with the Social Democrats in the West to whom they promised support in the election campaign in exchange for a pledge that the SPD would recognize East German citizenship fully should they win. When Kohl won the election, Honecker decided to continue to work with him despite ongoing political differences. The two men had already established a solid rapport, and Kohl's government decided in August 1987 not to modernize its Pershing 1a missiles. Combined with the 1986 agreement between the USSR and the US to reduce arms in Europe, the stage was set for the two Germanies to find a way to coexist peacefully.

On 7 September 1987, Kohl received Honecker with full honours in Bonn – despite the fact this was officially billed as a 'work visit' rather than a 'state visit'. President Weizsäcker too treated Honecker like a state guest and called him a 'German among Germans'. Over 2,000 journalists covered the event worldwide, granting the GDR the place among the nation states it so desired. As Honecker and Kohl discussed details such as ease of travel restrictions, common research and cultural projects as well as closer economic ties, both sides signalled their regret for the ongoing hostilities between their states. Kohl spoke in his dinner speech of a 'consciousness for the union of the nation' as represented in 'a common language, a common cultural heritage, in a long and ongoing common history'.

Honecker, visibly touched by a private visit to his younger sister Gertrud Hoppstädter, who still lived in the Saarland by the French border, admitted that 'borders are not how they should be'. He hoped that the day would come 'when the border will no longer divide us but unite us, just as the border between the GDR and the People's Republic of Poland unites us'.[52] While their visions for the future differed profoundly, both Chancellor and General Secretary shared the view that they were of one nation, but one nation that would have to continue to live in two different states.

Malaise

Berlin-Schönefeld Airport, spring 1986. Ulrich Struwe stood among a group of a dozen or so strangers and wondered whether he was doing the right thing. The thirty-four-year-old was married with two children. He had a job, a flat, an allotment garden – life was good. Why had he chosen to leave it all behind for two long years? He looked at the faces of the other men and remembered why. They all shared the same peculiar expression: a mixture of uncertainty and excitement.

'Ulli', as his friends called him, had hit a bit of a dead end. Born in Oelsnitz in the Vogtland region of Saxony, he had trained as a factory mechanic at the age of seventeen. Following his military service, he retrained as a welder in a tyre factory in 1976, where he had managed energy distribution ever since. But soon the monotony of the job started to grind. 'It was the same old drudge, day in and day out,' Ulli remembered later.[53] 'I was thoroughly fed up with everything in the factory. I had reached rock bottom. Was this really all there was to life?' By the beginning of 1986, he couldn't bear it any longer. But what to do? He had two girls at home, aged seven and nine, so giving up work altogether was not an option. Then it hit him – there was a way to earn significantly more money than he currently did and have the adventure of his life. During basic training in the army, the FDJ had shown up repeatedly, always looking for people who might be willing to go to the Soviet Union for a couple of years to work on the Druzhba gas pipeline. Unlike the more famous oil pipeline with the same name, which was completed in 1981, its sister network for gas was still being extended on a huge scale. All the brother states were required to help in exchange for energy from Soviet Russia. The GDR had been allocated three new construction sites for the period from 1982 to 1993. The work was to be organized by the FDJ as their *Zentrales Jugendobjekt* or Central Youth Project, and it worked together with employers to delegate a specialized workforce for two or three years. This was done entirely on a voluntary basis.

The men would be stationed in the Soviet Union for the entire time they signed up, with two holidays a year when they were allowed to visit friends and family at home. Apart from a higher base salary, the job came with multiple benefits. The nature of the working day meant that more money was accrued through extra hours. In addition, workers received 25 marks extra a day just for working on the pipeline. Up to half of the salary could be paid into a Genex account from which products could be bought that were otherwise difficult to obtain in the GDR, such as high-quality toys, household appliances or furniture. If the standard contract of two years was extended to three, pipeline workers received a special certificate which allowed them to procure a car of their choice. Trabants or Wartburgs were usually available immediately. The waiting time for a Lada was an extra six months. Given the usual waiting times for new cars of over ten years, this benefit alone was worth it to many.

To Ulli, the material perks were great arguments to convince his wife and children that what he was about to do was worth it. He himself mostly needed a break, something exciting. His life in the GDR was safe and fairly comfortable but it was also mind-numbingly monotonous. He needed to get out. A spell in the untamed Eurasian steppes seemed irresistible. Looking around at his fellow passengers at Schönefeld, he saw that the other men felt it too. None of them had known each other before they had signed up to work on the Druzhba network. Like Ulli, they had individually contacted their local FDJ offices one day or were contacted by them, and found out that workers with relevant skills were always desperately needed.

Once signed up, they embarked on a three-day crash course to prepare for the journey ahead. This included a lecture on behaviour. Under no circumstances were the workers to leave the site unattended. While they would largely work separately from the Russian workers, they would also collaborate with them. So they were told about cultural differences such as the importance of Victory Day on 9 May, when Russia commemorates the victory over Nazi Germany, which the East German workers were to respect. They were warned that they were subject to Soviet policing which included punishment for anything from actual crimes to political or work-related misdemeanours. They were to be aware that the safety and quality standards of the Soviet workforce may differ from their own (a substantial understatement as it turned out). For example, they might see local workers standing on the running board of fast-moving work vehicles. This was normal and not to be commented upon. Lastly, the group were asked to put a tie and suit jacket on for their passport photograph. Two months later, it was time to go. Ulli said goodbye to his wife and daughters and boarded a plane to Moscow.

'Then the madness began,' recalled Ulli. From Moscow, a train took them to the city of Perm in the Ural region, nearly 1,500 kilometres to the east. The twenty-seven-hour journey revealed little but barren land, broken occasionally by settlements and cities. They crossed over the famous Volga River, swollen with water from the melting ice. The weather was terrible. There was mud everywhere. Disheartened, Ulli stared at the unforgiving landscape that would be his home for the next two years. From Perm, the group was taken to the construction site of the gas pipeline, at Gremyachinsk, 170 kilometres north-east of the city. The irony that this was an area where many German prisoners of war had once been held as enslaved labourers sourcing timber, coal and stone under horrendous conditions did not escape some of his colleagues. Nearby, the infamous former gulag Perm-36 still operated as a prison for 'especially dangerous state criminals', which included many political opponents.

The camp attached to the Gremyachinsk construction site was not a bad place to be for Ulli and his German colleagues. They were allocated housing and work groups in the vast area according to their skill type. Carpenters, builders, cement specialists and electricians all had different roles to play. As a welder, Ulli was part of a work gang that set up giant turbines. While he was technically working under Soviet lead engineers, the living arrangements were kept well apart as German workers were fed, housed and looked after to a much better standard than their Russian colleagues. They lived in their own area of the camp, cut off from the Russians in container-style bungalows. There were usually five rooms in a house with two to three beds in each room and a shared toilet. Ulli remembers the place to be quite homely with carpets, armchairs and wardrobes. Efficient coal briquettes for heating were specially delivered from the GDR as was the food – including the popular Radeberger beer brewed near Dresden. 'I have to say we were very well fed throughout, but the highlight was the "Day of the Pipeline Builder" – a special occasion to honour our work out there. On that day, we were presented with a banquet that would put those you get on modern cruise ships to shame.'

The authorities were well aware of potential issues with morale given that the men were cut off from their homes, families and friends for so long. As a result, they kept a careful eye out for cynicism or troublemakers. Those deemed socially disruptive or harmful to the morale on the site were sent back to the GDR immediately. Those who stayed were entertained by a programme of cultural activities, for which they were taken to Perm and to discos, which the men dubbed 'Getting Drunk to Music'. There were fashion shows, cinema and theatre trips. What stuck with the workers the most was that all the stars of the GDR's music scene came out to play for them. Ulli saw bands like the Puhdys and the popular rock violinist Hans die Geige.

Entertainment and good food were necessary morale boosters given the heavy workload. Shifts lasted twelve hours each day and ran either from 6 a.m. to 6 p.m. or vice versa. Only on Saturdays did the men have some time off during which they could relax or enjoy the entertainment on offer. While housework such as cleaning and laundry was all done for them, the work on the pipeline could be backbreaking and was done under extremely difficult conditions. 'In the summer, the sun never really fully set and it was hot all the time. In the winter the reverse was true. It's disorienting. You lose all sense of time,' Ulli recalled. In addition, unlike their Russian colleagues, the Germans were not properly equipped for the job at hand. Their regular diesel went 'thick as custard' in the icy winter air before the men realized they had to use winter diesel. At $-44\,^{\circ}$C Ulli's extension leads froze solid and would have snapped had he tried to roll them back up outside. Instead, he took the frozen cable into a heated container before rolling it back up once it had defrosted. The synthetic headgear the welders were issued also became brittle in the cold outside while being prone to catching fire in the flying sparks produced by the welding. Ulli was kindly warned one time that his 'head was on fire' by one of his colleagues before it was too late.

The Russians were always happy to trade their own warm fur caps for the high-quality chocolates or liqueurs that the Germans had access to. The snow could also be useful. Ulli remembered that in the winter, when their huts were completely snowed under, he would store vodka bottles by opening his window and stuffing them in the snow outside. Yet the conditions were not always the stuff of fond memories. Workers could get frostbite very easily or even freeze to death without noticing it. Ulli and his colleagues never worked alone and always made sure that they would not walk between huts by themselves at night, especially when drunk. It did not take much to lose fingers, toes or even one's life in the harsh winter frost of the Urals.

Despite everything, Ulli loved his Russian adventure. He extended his two-year contract and stayed the full three years before returning home in 1989 and buying a beige Wartburg. Some men even stayed for ten years or more, enjoying the carefree existence that was spiked with adventure and a sense of achievement. Like Ulli, many men proudly brought cheap gold or jewellery back from Russia. They ordered toys for their children from the Genex catalogues. They marvelled at the tough Russian women who 'worked just like their menfolk' on the site. They gathered stories of near-misses in a strange land to tell their friends and family. To many, working on the pipelines seemed the perfect escape from the safe drudgery back home.

One man's drudgery was another man's stability. With some justification, Erich Honecker looked with pride at the changes in living standards that had been achieved under his leadership. Despite continuous problems with supplies and being behind technological standards in the West, the GDR felt like a stable country with comparatively high living standards. By design, there was full employment and the subsidized rents, food, cultural offerings and childcare meant that there were few existential concerns. At a time when West Germany was grappling with around 8 per cent unemployment and job security was a worry to many of those who did have work, East German families never really had to fear a sudden loss of income or not being able to pay the rent. By 1987, over half of all households had a car and all had at least one washing machine, fridge and TV.[54]

Products that were difficult to get hold of through regular routes were often obtained with the help of Western relatives who ordered them directly through Genex catalogues or provided the currency for a trip to the Intershop. Friends and family in the right places could also help. All in all, the economic shortcomings of the GDR in the mid-1980s, while reaching crisis level behind the scenes, appeared to many East Germans as nuisances rather than existential threats to their way of life.

This lack of existential concerns coupled with a solid life–work balance meant that East Germans had a fair amount of money and time on their hands without having to worry too much about having to make the most of it. As a result, they spent a lot more time socializing and enjoying leisure pursuits. Clubhouses, allotment gardens, restaurants, communal barbecue pits and party rooms in apartment blocks were popular retreats where friends, colleagues and neighbours would meet to relax. Accordingly, alcohol consumption in the GDR skyrocketed. By 1988, the average East German drank 142 litres of beer a year and 16.1 litres of hard liquor, twice as much as their West German neighbours and enough to make VEB Nordbrand the largest Schnapps producer in Europe.[55] The American academic Thomas Kochan has argued that this is not due to a need to escape the dreary realities of the GDR, as has often been claimed, but rather to the 'existential carefreeness' experienced by 'a low-competition collective society'.[56] Most East Germans drank not to forget their worries but rather because they had too little to worry about.

This state of relative comfort also led to a certain complacency in political terms. The contrast to the social unrest seen in Poland throughout the 1980s, which was in part triggered by rationing and spikes in food prices, could not be starker. Of course, the GDR also had opposition movements that were met with tight oppression by the state. But it didn't see mass dissatisfaction spill on to the streets in the way its neighbours did until the demonstrations in the autumn of 1989. In fact, the SED reached a record membership of 2.3 million people in 1986 as people began to get used to the idea that party membership was a lever to career advancement.

Nonetheless, Ulli was by no means alone in his feeling that life in the GDR seemed to stagnate. When Angela Merkel defended her dissertation on quantum chemistry in January 1986, she was thirty-one years old and had taken a leisurely seven years to complete the project. She had been comparatively well off and aimless at the same time. She held a permanent position at the Academy of Sciences in Berlin-Adlershof with an income of around 1,000 marks a month, which was higher than normal for white collar professions. There was no haste, no pressure. Higher positions were difficult to obtain without party membership, and Merkel had already let the Stasi know she would not spy on her colleagues for them either, making rapid career advancement unlikely.

Merkel was comfortable enough in 1980s East Berlin, not least because she took many opportunities to escape it. Fascinated with the political unrest in Poland, she travelled there three times in 1980 and 1981, twice officially through the FDJ's travel agency Jugendtourist (Youth Tourist), once privately together with colleagues from the academy. The latter trip was a particularly daring venture as private journeys required a letter of invitation. Merkel's colleague Hans-Jörg Osten, who spoke Polish, fabricated one so that the group of friends could travel.[57] The many conversations with young Poles captivated the twenty-six-year-old student as they openly talked of change and reform. She also used the opportunity to visit her mother's birthplace of Danzig (now Gdańsk) by the Baltic Sea. Upon return, GDR border guards searched her bag and found photos, a Polish newspaper and a badge of the independent trade union Solidarność which had been founded at the Lenin Shipyard in Gdańsk in 1980 and had been at the heart of the push for change in Poland. Merkel simply pretended she did not know what these things meant as she spoke no Polish and got away with it.[58]

In the summer of 1983, she embarked on an even bigger adventure: a three-week journey through the Soviet republics of Armenia, Azerbaijan and Georgia, some of the few areas of the bloc she had not already visited. This was also her riskiest trip. While study stints in Moscow, Leningrad and Prague were officially sanctioned and organized, Merkel wanted to tour the southern tip of the Soviet Union independently, which was difficult to do as freedom of movement in the USSR on official visas was extremely limited. Tours had to be officially organized and planned in advance, backed up by official invitations. It was an open secret among East German backpackers that if people claimed they wanted to travel to Bulgaria over land and sea, transiting through Poland and Ukraine, they would be issued with a three-day transit visa for the USSR, which could be used to get in. Once in, people just stayed and travelled, worrying about the return journey later. That's exactly what Merkel and her colleagues did.

Once in Kyiv, they did not board a train to Odessa to take a ship from there to Bulgaria as their visa stated. Instead they took the train to Georgia and then vanished into its mountains. 'No hotel, no official camping sites, no stations – they would have checked our papers everywhere,' Merkel remembered later.[59] Instead she and her two colleagues hitchhiked, pitched their tents where they could and asked the locals for help when they needed it. On the way to the ancient city of Gori, Stalin's birthplace in eastern Georgia, they hitched a ride only to notice in shock that the man behind the wheel was a policeman in uniform. The friends were initially lucky as the man was himself keen to stay under the radar. He had a dead deer strapped to his bonnet which he had illegally brought over from Azerbaijan. However, soon the car was stopped by traffic police for speeding. The officials were happy enough to let their colleague go but took the tourists and their dubious paperwork into the police station of the mediaeval town of Mtskheta.

Merkel once again proved apt at talking herself out of trouble. Georgia was simply too beautiful to leave after their visa had expired, she explained. How could they have travelled straight on to Bulgaria? The policemen took kindly to this charm offensive and let the three friends go, even advising that they must visit the capital Tbilisi before they left. They did and ended up sleeping in a homeless shelter at the station. As there were no direct flights home from Georgia, Merkel and her companions travelled to Sochi, a Russian city by the Black Sea. They knew punishment for their lack of visas would be light as they wanted to travel back to the GDR in any case – a temporary travel ban and a small fine would be the worst case scenario. As it turned out, the trio simply had to write a punishment essay entitled 'Why did I transgress the laws despite having studied and known them?'[60]

While her travels kept Merkel intellectually and physically engaged for a time, the aimlessness of her life in Berlin quickly caught up with her again. She kept herself busy organizing cultural events in the FDJ group of her institute. She remembered later that this entailed 'getting theatre tickets, organizing book readings and talks. We were also interested in everything that was critical of the GDR between the lines.'[61] Membership in the youth organization normally ended with the completion of an apprenticeship or vocational training, but for academics, whose education by definition took longer, it was often extended to the age of thirty. When Merkel reached this age on 17 July 1984, her father, a strict theologian, came to visit her for her birthday. In light of the incomplete doctoral work and his daughter's life as a long-term student, he chided, 'You haven't got very far.'[62] The young scientist knew he was right. Looking back on this period of her life later, she reflected on her difficulties to stay motivated: 'In the period when the Wall fell, I was glad I had not let myself down.'[63]

While Ulli Struwe and Angela Merkel found outlets for their restlessness within the confines of GDR life, others did not. The number of applications from citizens to leave the country legally and permanently rose yearly. Between 1973 and 1983, an annual average of 9,000 East Germans left the country this way (while between 20,000 and 30,000 applied). From 1983, when an official process for 'permanent leave' existed, 41,000 people filled in the form in the first year alone. Between 1984 and 1988, 113,000 applications for permanent leave were granted by the authorities.[64] Putting an application in was not risk free. The wheels of bureaucracy turned deliberately slowly as the Stasi searched for ways to criminalize the behaviour of those making the applications. On 15 October 1983, Margot Honecker, Minister of National Education, passed a directive in her department to declare that 'Educators who attempt to achieve their resettlement into non-socialist states or West Berlin are to be removed immediately from their direct teaching and educational work with children and young people with reference to their unsuitability to pedagogical work . . . The reason given for . . . the termination of their work contract must not include any reference to the attempt to reach resettlement.'[65] In other fields of work, those handing in applications to leave the country risked their jobs or the educational and professional prospects of close relatives, including children. But more and more people attempted to leave as groups and made the efforts of the regime to stop them public through demonstrations and campaigns. It became increasingly difficult for the authorities to keep a lid on such activities. As a result, more applications were granted and it became somewhat easier to travel West to visit relatives or for work and study.

Many Stasi files from this period paint a similar picture. A quiet dissatisfaction with the status quo was beginning to spread among some parts of the population and people found different ways of dealing with it. Wolfgang Mulinski, an electro-technician, married with two children, had once been described as a model citizen in an entry in his Stasi file from 1977:

> M. enjoys crafts in his spare time, which could be called a hobby of his. In terms of his character, nothing is said about M. in his local neighbourhood. He leads a perfect lifestyle, does not drink too much alcohol and is only rarely seen in bars. In the community, M. is committed to improving the appearance of the local area. He has taken part in two block assemblies to discuss pressing questions. On national holidays, he decorates the outside of his flat and donates money.[66]

However, by the 1980s, Wolfgang was beginning to feel a sense of dissatisfaction with the rigidity of life in the GDR. He found an outlet in politics and joined the Liberal Democratic Party to push for reform and political change. Accordingly, his Stasi files became more critical. The once-reliable Wolfgang was now 'together with his colleague and best friend [name blacked out] to be counted among those persons who show questionable application in their attitude to work'. The unofficial collaborator (IM) tasked with watching Wolfgang was told to 'ensure constant control and analysis of the activities of M.' and move on to 'investigate the spare time activities of M.'. Like many GDR citizens, Wolfgang knew he was being watched by the Stasi although he never found out the identity of the specific IM who reported on him. Yet, like most of his fellow East Germans, he never considered leaving his home and his country. He had become used to the conditions as they were and looked for ways to improve them from within.

Overall, most East Germans had come to terms with the system they lived in. It wasn't always easy. After all, the GDR was a rather small country which was difficult to leave even temporarily. To many, it was a little stuffy, even provincial. But for those who wanted to live a quiet life with the small comforts of home, it was a stable place with few concerns or worries. Increasingly, the state under Honecker had begun to forgive minor transgressions even while their monitoring was ramped up. The Stasi was reaching record levels of observation, but more often than not, it did little with the information it had gathered. Those who were willing to ignore the prying into their private lives largely did so. The GDR had mostly lost the freneticism of the first three decades and with it the firm grip over its citizens. By abandoning both the manic drive towards equality and progress of the early post-war years as well as ambitions driven by career advancement and consumerism, the GDR had left many of its people comfortable but aimless.

10. Everything Takes Its Socialist Course (1987–1990)

Forwards ever, backwards never.

Socialism in the Colours of the GDR

East Berlin, summer 1987. When Peter Claussen arrived in the East German capital to take up his post as Deputy Public Affairs Officer at the US embassy, he was not entirely sure what to expect. The American was ideally suited for the job as his north German family background meant his command of the language was excellent with only the slightest trace of an accent. This was deemed to make his task easier as he would need to win the trust of those segments of the East German population who might be interested in forging and maintaining connections to the West in the medium and long term. In short, Peter's mission was to find 'cracks in the façade'.[1] It was a task as intriguing as it was daunting. He had been briefed on the history of the GDR and warned about the inescapability of Stasi surveillance – both at work and in the flat he and his family would be allocated. 'We assumed that the surveillance was omnipresent. We were advised to look over our shoulders,' Peter later remembered.[2] Colleagues who had previously worked in East Germany told stories of the regime's attempts to intimidate them. One American diplomat returned to their flat after a short absence and the toilet had obviously been used but not flushed. Another came back from holiday to find the favourite toy of their five-year-old broken. In an effort to prepare for the complete lack of privacy that awaited them, the Claussens bought a 'magic' toy slate, so that they could write messages to each other in their flat and erase them immediately. 'In the end we never used it,' Peter recalled, 'you get used to anything. You get used to being spied upon, being bugged. And it didn't really do anything. It didn't destroy your life.'[3]

When Peter and his family reached Berlin in the summer of 1987, they found things had changed a fair bit from the unpleasant atmosphere that his predecessors had been exposed to. President Ronald Reagan had delivered a speech in West Berlin in front of the Brandenburg Gate on 12 June 1987, in which he demanded, 'Mr Gorbachev, tear down this wall!' But nobody could have foreseen that the fall of the Berlin Wall was just two years into the future. Reagan's speech was initially just a publicity stunt. The event that did make a difference to the way Peter and his American colleagues were treated in East Germany was Honecker's visit to Bonn in September. Keen to be seen as the leader of a nation worthy of respect, he worked to ease tension with Western nations which changed life within the GDR tangibly.

The American embassy was allowed to set up new cultural exchange programmes such as a Fulbright Scholarship scheme whereby nine PhD students and lecturers were sent to the US and the same number invited to the GDR for research and teaching. There was a free library in the embassy as well as a stand at the Leipzig book fair – in both cases conversations were started with those who showed interest in the books and their contacts maintained for later communication via letters and meetings. The embassy also knew how to play into the desires and obsessions of the East German public. Having learned how much love there still was for classic Western themes like 'cowboys and Indians' among all Germans, including in the East, the embassy invited the Assistant Secretary of the Interior for Indian Affairs to the GDR. The idea that a real-life Cherokee, indeed the former Principal Chief of the Cherokee Nation, would visit the provincial GDR caused a great deal of excitement. Ross Swimmer and his wife had a packed programme touring the country. Among many other stops, the couple visited the Karl May museum in Radebeul, near Dresden. The nineteenth-century novels of the German writer and his heroes

Winnetou and Old Shatterhand were still very popular. Yet the locals who came to meet this real-life 'Indian' in such hallowed grounds could not help but be a little disappointed. As Peter Claussen recalled, Swimmer did not exactly meet the expectations held by those who grew up with GDR-made Westerns on their TV screens: 'He looked like a banker. He didn't have long hair, no feather on his head. He just wore a blue suit and a red tie. He looked like a Republican. A perfectly normal politician.'[4] That was exactly what Peter's work entailed, dispelling myths about the West.

Some measures taken on the way to closer relations with the West went much further, particularly when it came to West Germany. On the morning of 28 August 1987 the party newspaper *Neues Deutschland* sold out in many places across the country. Normally full of political communiqués and dry reportage of events, it didn't have a reputation for exhilarating content. But on that late summer morning, the newspaper contained a piece that felt like history in the making: a joint paper published by the West German Social Democratic Party (SPD) and the East German Socialist Unity Party (SED). Titled 'The Competition of Ideologies and Common Security', it was the result of regular talks that had begun in 1984 and would continue until 1989. The committees met in alternating sessions in East and West Germany and over the years the delegates became friendly, even having a bowling night at Müggelsee where bawdy jokes were exchanged alongside political ideas.[5]

Neither of the two party leaders Willy Brandt and Erich Honecker took issue with the idea that their thinkers exchanged ideas and discussed the future of left-wing politics on both sides of the inner-German divide. A day before the written publication of the results of these discussions, representatives of both parties presented the paper together in both Germanies. The result was explosive. The parties had jointly called for 'a common policy of securing the peace, a policy of dialogue and of disarmament, of compromise, of a balancing of interests and of cooperation'.[6] No longer was there a demand for reunification of Germany under the banner of one ideology. Instead, the SPD and the SED argued that 'the peaceful competition . . . of both systems would make the biggest contribution to the solution of the big questions humanity faces'.[7] Consequently, 'both sides will have to accept that there will be a long time period during which they will have to coexist and deal with one another. No side should negate the right of the other to exist' nor 'meddle in the practical policy of other states'.[8]

Claiming to speak not just for themselves but for 'Western democracy' per se, the SPD delegates had practically called for the end of the Cold War. They had ambitiously declared that they aimed for a world order in which socialism and communism could exist alongside capitalism – in other words, the Cold War need not be won or lost by either side any time soon. The people themselves would decide which system worked best for them. Honecker was delighted. Having spent a lifetime fearing both real and imaginary threats to his ideology, he could now see a pathway to a secure future for the GDR. That the paper also contained demands for 'a culture of political discussion' and 'an unhemmed pluralism in culture, science, art and political opinion making' seemed acceptable in exchange for security.

The SED's main author of the paper, Otto Reinhold, sent a copy to his General Secretary for approval. When it eventually reached the politburo, Honecker had scribbled on it, 'This is a historical document.' Egon Krenz, who chaired the session, remembered that there were some objections against the document, for example from Alfred Neumann, a long-standing opponent of Honecker. But overall the mood was positive and the document was approved for release.[9] East and West, it caused controversy and debate across the political spectrum and opposition groups. On 1 September, it was discussed in a live show on GDR television and the Stasi too noted that the 'document was received with great interest particularly by members and functionaries of the SED and other progressive forces in all parts of the population of the republic and it triggered a large number of discussions'.[10] Regardless of the differences in attention and approach between the SED and the SPD, a good deal of their original aim had been achieved. A culture of debate was being modelled on a small scale as big ideas for the future of the two Germanies were discussed in party circles as well as in bars and on the street.

Krenz had good reason to believe that Gorbachev would be impressed with this development too as he had called on the GDR to consider the same reforms that he had planned for his own country. Krenz met with none other than Alexander Yakovlev, the member of the politburo of the Communist Party of the Soviet Union who had been the intellectual architect of the concepts of glasnost and perestroika. Krenz was convinced that what the SPD-SED paper suggested was the embodiment of glasnost – openness. But according to Krenz, Yakovlev was not impressed. He had read the document during his summer holiday in the GDR and found that it implicitly 'criticized Soviet power while the American strategy of confrontation and rearmament against the socialist states was not mentioned'. When Krenz, a leadership hopeful and Soviet loyalist, let on that he was taken aback by this reading of the paper, Yakovlev told him he expected the SED to interact with the SPD on a foundation of 'Marxism' not 'popular Marxism'. He ended his rebuke by telling 'Comrade Krenz' that he should try to 'rectify this failure. Else the document won't be worth the paper it is written on.'[11]

This unexpected private rebuttal was followed by an official one in November when the Soviet ambassador in East Berlin, Vyacheslav Kochemasov, passed on a message from his politburo which had studied the paper intensely. It had come to the conclusion that 'the SED had allowed the blurring of fundamental differences between communists and social democrats. The paper suggests that coexistence between socialist and capitalist ideology is possible.'[12] Kochemasov handed over the two-page document from his government which itemized the mistakes of Honecker's party, 'failings which, in our view, could have been avoided'.[13]

Many in the SED politburo were fuming. Left-leaning politicians in the West hailed the SPD-SED paper as a result of Gorbachev's openness while Moscow was trying to rein in the fallout from a document that in their view 'could be used to penetrate the GDR ideologically'[14] by the Social Democrats. This conflict further inflamed the existing anti-Gorbachev sentiments in East Berlin. Kurt Hager, chief ideologist of the SED, had long viewed attempts to reform the GDR with suspicion and rejected Soviet pressure to do so. In April 1987, in an interview for the West German magazine *Stern*, he was asked: ' "Perestroika" – does that mean restructuring the GDR too?' Hager replied that while 'We German communists have always felt great respect and admiration toward the land of Lenin . . . this does not mean – nor did it mean in the past – that we copied everything that happened in the Soviet Union.' When the interviewer pressed him, Hager, now clearly annoyed, responded with an analogy that would provoke fierce opposition in the GDR itself, where *Neues Deutschland* ran a full transcript of the interview the next day: 'Would you, by the way, feel obligated to paper the walls in your apartment just because your neighbour papered his?'[15] Hager rejected both the Soviet and inner-German concepts of reform. Following the release of the SPD-SED paper, he announced in a speech in October 1987 that 'We will not stop fighting the aggressive forces of imperialism as foes, as enemies of the peaceful life of humanity.'[16] Now under pressure from his own chief ideologist and from the Soviets, one of the architects of the paper, Otto Reinhold, was forced to publicly agree with Hager two weeks later.

Honecker's relationship with Gorbachev had hit a new low. Unwilling to carry out the same reforms as Moscow while still held back by it from pursuing closer relations with the West, Honecker became increasingly frustrated. His ambition to negotiate disarmament in Germany, eye to eye with Bonn, was also beginning to slip away as Gorbachev undertook his own efforts to reduce the crippling costs of the arms race with Washington. While the seventy-five-year-old General Secretary continued to travel a lot – after Bonn, he visited Belgium and Paris – he seemed increasingly out of touch with his younger colleagues in other countries. All eyes were on Gorbachev whose affable and intelligent manner stood in stark contrast to the wooden and increasingly frail East German.

Honecker reacted with a policy of active detachment from the Soviet Union. From October 1987, the politburo decided to censor speeches held in the country they had once so greatly admired. A year later, the German edition of the popular Soviet magazine *Sputnik* was taken out of circulation, which was practically akin to a ban. SED offices, the FDJ, the headquarters of the GDR's news outlets and several other institutions were swamped with letters and complaints demanding explanations and that the magazine be brought back. Opposition circles began to study the Russian language with renewed enthusiasm, so that original material might be obtained and read without interference from the East German authorities. Many young people found great delight in wearing T-shirts or stickers displaying Gorbachev's face or the slogans 'glasnost' and 'perestroika' – after all, teachers and university staff could hardly reprimand them for such zeal in supporting the 'brother' in the East.

Honecker meanwhile had no intention of giving up on his ambition to make the GDR a more independent player in the community of states, one that would be respected in its own right. He meant it when he told Gorbachev in April 1986, 'Good luck, dear comrades, with your perestroika, but we will walk our own path.'[17] Two years later, the General Secretary proudly proclaimed his country would find its own system. There would be 'Socialism in the Colours of the GDR'. In many ways, this was the GDR's de facto break with Moscow. For better or worse it was now on its own.

No End in Sight

Calgary, Canada, 27 February 1988, 8 p.m. A nervous twenty-two-year-old athlete looked up into bright spotlights and at the 17,000 expectant faces in the audience. It was now or never. She wanted to be the best. She wanted to be the only woman to win back-to-back Olympic gold in figure skating. Was her make-up right? Again and again Katarina Witt went back to the bathroom to check, reapplying the glossy red lipstick and bold eyeshadow that set off her figure-hugging dress. 'Kati' Witt knew that it would pay off to take '30 long seconds to flirt with the 9 judges and not just the 7 gentlemen', as she put it.[18] At the peak of her popularity, *Time* magazine had called her 'the most beautiful face of socialism' and her dramatic flamenco-inspired dress, with its transparent inlay that created a neckline down to her waist, reinforced her image as a boldly attractive young sportswoman. Witt remembered finding out in the autumn of 1987 that her chief rival, Debi Thomas of the United States, would also perform at the Olympics as Carmen to music from Bizet's opera. The media all over the world – East and West – lapped it up. The 'Battle of the Carmens' was almost too good to be true. In the USA, the event was watched by a third of the TV audience. In the GDR, the figure was closer to two thirds. Erich Honecker himself got out of bed in the middle of the night – it was 4 a.m. in East Berlin – when his star athlete began Carmen's dramatic last dance.

Witt herself remembered later how much the tension got to her: 'I felt weak and tired and almost wanted to stop.'[19] She instinctively knew that right then she didn't have the required chutzpah for the difficult triple loop jump that was part of her performance and went for a perfectly executed double instead. The remaining minutes went exactly as planned and an exhausted but immensely relieved Kati Witt collapsed dramatically onto the ice into Carmen's death pose. There was a tense wait while Debi Thomas got ready for her turn. Witt noticed that her rival had tried to high-five her coach but had missed his hand. She took that as a good omen, and she was right: Thomas was slightly off form, making enough mistakes to cost her the gold medal. Katarina Witt won and returned home to a hero's welcome. Perks like a Soviet-built Lada car and dinner with the SED elite awaited her.

The year 1988 is often seen as the beginning of the end of the GDR. But while economic, political and social difficulties were undoubtedly mounting in the background, most ordinary East Germans did not feel as if they were about to reach the end of an era.

Many aspects of East German life and society continued to evolve. Elite sports is one such example. For a small country of only 16.5 million inhabitants, it achieved extraordinary things in this field. In all Olympic Games in the 1980s – summer and winter – the GDR came second in terms of medals won, apart from the Winter Games of 1984 in Sarajevo, where it came first – ahead of both the Soviet Union and the USA. Of course there was also a darker side to this success, as widespread and systematic doping blurred the lines between sporting achievement and corruption. But elite sports remained a focal point for people's hopes and aspirations. It gave many confidence and pride in their small country – in defiance of the criticism from the West and pressure to conform from the East.

For women in particular, taking part in competitive sports from a very young age helped carve out a more confident role. Kati Witt has often been criticized for the way she allowed the authorities to exploit her sporting successes politically while she enjoyed privileges such as travel to Western countries and expensive gifts at home. But she was a confident young woman who knew exactly what she wanted and demanded privileges from the state in exchange for her achievements.

In other fields too, female ambition had become the norm. By the time Kati Witt won the battle of the Carmens, over 90 per cent of East German women fought their own battles in the workplace. The GDR had reached the highest rate of female employment in the world as women entered every last bastion of previously exclusively male domains. It was also during 1988 that the first female graduates left their four-year NVA officer training in Zittau. When they found out that they were not to be given the traditional 'honour daggers' that male graduates received, they complained to their superiors. Heinz Kessler, the Minister of National Defence, made a decision just two days before the graduation ceremony that women too were to receive the coveted symbol of their status as officers. There was a rush to get hold of the daggers directly from the traditional knife smith in Mühlhausen where they were produced. When the box with the daggers arrived just in the nick of time, the women officers' uniforms still had to be adapted so they could carry the dagger on the jacket as their male colleagues did. By the time the first female officers of the air force graduated in Kamenz the same year, things began to run a little more smoothly as the NVA began to adapt better to the specific requirements of its new female officers.

While women in officer roles were still a tiny minority – by 1989 only 190 were trained – the overall number of female recruits across the branches of the NVA rose to around 2,000 in the course of the 1980s. A military career was still seen as an unusual choice for a young woman but those who signed up for it often saw it as a means to do something new and different. Kerstin Haack, a nineteen-year-old typist from Stollberg in Saxony, had become rather bored after two years in her office job. 'I needed a bit of adventure,' she would later remember, 'I thought this can't be all there is to life.'[20] In 1984, she reported to the *Wehrkreiskommando* (regional commando office) and 'just said yes' to a new life in the military. A few months later, Kerstin was no longer typing documents in the office but throwing grenades, crawling through mud and shooting at targets. The fact that she was mostly among men during her basic training at the military-technical college of the air force of the GDR didn't bother her. 'Sure, you'd get the odd silly comment here or there,' she laughed years later, 'but overall the whole experience was hugely rewarding. I became fast friends with some of the men and we worked well together.'[21] The work was engaging too as Kerstin learned how to guide planes to and from the airfield using Russian commands. Once a freshly minted *Unteroffizier*, Kerstin was relocated to Jänschwalde-Ost and then to Marxwalde, both in the far east of the country, by the Polish border. Initially, she was a little disappointed about these placements. At basic training, she had befriended another female recruit who was now stationed elsewhere and they were separated. She was also the only woman in her company, which could sometimes make things a little awkward. While the men lived on site, Kerstin was billeted slightly further away and had to cycle to work every day no matter the weather.

The bitterly cold winter of 1986 was particularly memorable as she would regularly arrive at the airfield with her eyelashes and hair frozen stiff. There was no separate toilet or changing rooms for her. A superior officer would 'stand guard' in front of the communal facilities when she used them. But her work as a flight dispatcher was intense and rewarding, and Kerstin enjoyed the genuine camaraderie with the men in the company.

At the same time as women like Kerstin were carving out a role for female recruits in the armed forces of the GDR, West German women were still constitutionally banned from combat roles altogether. As a result, every single one of the 2,000 women who served in the NVA in 1990 lost her job, role and status after reunification. Only very few of them would later rejoin the *Bundeswehr*, often in civilian roles. While women in uniform were by no means universally accepted in East Germany – in the forces themselves or in wider society – the opportunity itself was a remarkable step towards equality. Even on the eve of its disappearance, the GDR was still shifting and changing.

As willing as the government was to drive a reform agenda from above, it was equally reluctant to engage with changes driven from below. While the majority of East Germans in 1988 neither wanted the state abolished nor dreamt of imminent reunification with the West, there was a discernible expectation that the GDR needed to modernize its politics. The inflexible structures of government and the lack of public discourse, transparency and accountability that came with them had long been at odds with the dizzying speed of social reform. The GDR was a highly literate, highly skilled and highly politicized society, confident and proud in its achievements and keen to move forward. It was fertile ground for the seeds of reform and democratization. Gorbachev's ideas for change in the Soviet Union and the increasing opening of the GDR to cultural influences from the West met keen minds that were ready for intellectual discourse beyond the narrow lines still prescribed by censorship and the stranglehold of the Stasi. With the hardships of the post-war years long in the past and Western countries increasingly willing to acknowledge the GDR's right to exist and engage with it, there seemed to be no reason to hold on to a permanent state of defensiveness. Attempts to open up the GDR were by no means attempts to destroy it – on the contrary, many young intellectuals and workers, saw it as a means to strengthen the state and socialism.

Increasingly it was obvious to many that Honecker was not the man to carry such change. His break with Gorbachev had made that abundantly clear by 1988. Walter Friedrich, leader of the Central Institute for Youth Studies in Leipzig, whose job it was to inform the government on moods, interests and developments among the country's youth, became increasingly worried by what he saw in the late 1980s. Knowing his warnings would fall on deaf ears if he approached Honecker, he instead turned to Egon Krenz, who was fifty-one years old at the time and regarded as the 'Crown Prince' to the position of General Secretary. The strictly classified analysis Friedrich sent him in November 1988 did not hold back: the 'shortcomings and weaknesses in our country (e.g. supply and replacement problems, information policy, window-dressing, real democratic participation etc.) are increasingly clearly perceived and increasingly criticized. The superiority of socialism is increasingly questioned. The non-opening in the direction of the perestroika strategy is making it worse.'[22]

Friedrich added a stark warning, which in hindsight reads like a prophecy:

> *The population's identification with our aims and values, with the policy of our party, can only be increased if we can find meaningful new ways to interact with the people (e.g. information, transparency, democratic participation). Or else the people will become detached from us within the next 1–3 years, to a threatening degree.*[23]

This was criticism from those who tried to strengthen the government through reform and Friedrich was by no means alone. The argument raged even in the politburo itself where Gerhard Schürer, a candidate member and chair of the State Planning Commission, demanded a new economic course as he saw inevitable bankruptcy looming under current conditions. Stubborn as ever, Honecker dismissed the warning and denounced Schürer as a 'saboteur' – a grave accusation in communist jargon. It was only a year later, in the autumn of 1989 and under Egon Krenz as General Secretary, that he was commissioned to pen an 'Analysis of the economic situation of the GDR with conclusions' – too late to make a difference. Even the powerful figure of Günter Mittag, who had been instrumental in defending the command economy against liberalization, seemed dejected. His ailing health may have contributed to this. In 1984, he had to have one of his legs amputated due to his diabetes and the other was soon to follow in 1989. Frail and confronted with mounting political and economic pressures, Mittag admitted to the politburo in September 1988 that 'We have reached a point where things could tip.'[24]

Wind of Change

While few expected an immediate end of the GDR or reunification with West Germany, change was in the air from early 1989. With no real way to affect politics at the top through active participation or elections, many critics of the regime had begun to organize themselves into groups outside of the political structures of the state. Many of these were pacifist and environmentalist organizations, not dissimilar in aims and structures to those that existed in West Germany. Fears over the stationing of nuclear missiles on German soil were further heightened by the Chernobyl nuclear disaster in April 1986 which sent radioactive clouds over parts of East and West Germany, exposing how little both governments were prepared for such catastrophes. This fuelled existing opposition to nuclear technology – civilian and military – on both sides of the Wall.

From the mid-1970s, some of those who had applied for permanent emigration, aiming to leave the GDR legally and settle in West

Germany, began to form networks to make their demands heard. As applicants were usually exposed to discrimination and intimidation that could even lead to losing their jobs, they wanted to go public with their plight rather than suffer individually. A very effective way to do this in a state that had a firm grip on the media was to look for support in the West German newspapers which were always keen to run stories about opposition in the GDR.

Powerful examples had been set by people such as the forty-six-year-old physician Karl-Heinz Nitschke who lived in Riesa, Saxony. He had long tried to leave the GDR in increasingly desperate ways. Shortly after the Berlin Wall had been built in 1961, Karl-Heinz planned and practised for his family to escape through the Baltic Sea on a rubber dinghy. This was of course extremely dangerous. Over 5,600 people tried to swim, float, surf or propel themselves to West Germany via 'State Border North', as the official jargon called the boundary in the Baltic Sea. Only 913 were successful. The rest were either arrested by the 6th Border Brigade Coast, had to abort their attempt or drowned. In order to give himself and his young family the best chance, Karl-Heinz asked his nephew in Düsseldorf, in West Germany, to smuggle a suitable boat engine into the GDR. The two exchanged the dangerous cargo on a motorway as the repercussions of being found out could be severe. The Nitschkes practised on a lake in Brandenburg while driving up to the coast from time to time to scout out a suitable spot. Eventually, they decided to cross from Born on the Darß peninsula in the direction of Denmark until a Western ship would pick them up. But a friend betrayed the young family before they could even attempt their risky escape. Karl-Heinz was arrested by the Stasi on 22 September 1964, a few days before he intended to leave. He received a two-year prison sentence.

When a further escape attempt in 1975 through Romania and Yugoslavia also failed, Karl-Heinz decided to try a different way. Perhaps he could beat the authorities at their own game. He filed thirteen applications to be released from East German citizenship. All were denied without giving a reason. As a highly specialized doctor, he was deemed indispensable by the authorities irrespective of his views. From 1974 to 1976 alone, the GDR had lost 404 members of the medical profession to West Germany and three times as many had applied to leave. So Karl-Heinz knew he would never be allowed to go legally if he continued to fight alone. He needed to go public. The GDR had just signed the Helsinki Accords, which included a pledge that all signatories would respect 'human rights and fundamental freedoms'. Accordingly, Karl-Heinz argued in his 1976 'Riesa Petition for the Full Accomplishment of Human Rights' that GDR authorities were compelled to allow their citizens free choice of their place of residence. There were only seventy-nine signatories, most of them from Riesa and Karl-Marx-Stadt (Chemnitz), which lies 75 kilometres south. As Karl-Heinz had neither much geographical nor popular reach, he sent his document to various human rights organizations in West Germany. Reports ran in many major newspapers such as *Berliner Morgenpost* and *Frankfurter Allgemeine Zeitung* and from there made their way back into the GDR where the matter was widely discussed among other opposition groups.

As the Stasi file about the incident points out, Karl-Heinz believed that 'One cannot achieve anything with individual applications and only through collective action can applications gain force.'[25] Apart from publicizing the petition, he also sent a copy of each of his applications to his sister who lived in West Germany and tried to help by contacting politicians, TV stations and newspapers. Initially Karl-Heinz's protest seemed unsuccessful. The Stasi used its terrifying arsenal of psychological warfare methods (*Zersetzung*) on him and many of the other petitioners. His every step was being watched to find further incriminating evidence until he was arrested by three Stasi officers in his flat on 31 August 1976. Many of the other petitioners withdrew their support under psychological pressure and the Stasi seemed satisfied with its efforts when it noted that 'The negative persons have been further isolated and are not given any more opportunities to concentrate or cultivate further hostile-negative activities.'[26] Many of those who did not bow to such pressure were arrested. At least nine of the original signatories were 'bought out' of prison by the West German government through the Schalck-Golodkowski scheme. In the end, the pressure Karl-Heinz had built via the Western media came to fruition. The Stasi had a show trial planned that was supposed to lead to a nine-year prison sentence. Instead, Karl-Heinz was deported to West Germany after twelve months in protective custody.

The idea of collective action was powerful as the Karl-Heinz Nitschke case demonstrates. Across the GDR other groups became more and more prolific throughout the 1980s. One particularly visible example was the so-called white circles. Beginning in 1982 in Jena, Thuringia, a group organized peaceful protests against denied applications for permanent leave by wearing white clothing in public squares or streets. The authorities couldn't do anything about it as the protesters didn't say a word. To all intents and purposes they were ordinary people who had chosen to be in a public place at the same time.

Other powerful groups such as the peace movement Swords to Ploughshares targeted the militarization of society and the arms race which had led to stationing nuclear weapons in East Germany. As the name with its biblical reference suggests, the movement was closely connected to the Protestant churches which helped it organize demonstrations and other activism effectively, including with their counterparts in West Germany. In the early 1980s, the GDR moved to have the group's distinctive emblem – a heroic male figure striking a sword with a hammer to bend it into a ploughshare – banned from schools, universities and public places, penalizing the young wearers who often jeopardized their educational opportunities and career prospects. The group struck back in a peaceful way. Instead of their symbol, they sewed round white patches onto their clothing, which could hardly be taken as a crime. Church days, discussion forums and Swords to Ploughshares services often attracted thousands of participants throughout the 1980s.

Environmental groups too grew in size and confidence. Buoyed by the support they received from the Green Party in West

Germany, whose members and politicians frequently travelled to the GDR to take part in peace marches, church meetings and discussion forums, the independent movement of East German activists grew steadily. In 1986, they founded an 'Environment Library' in the Zionskirche in Berlin. This church had been in the parish of Dietrich Bonhoeffer who had bravely organized powerful resistance against the Nazis and was executed at Flossenbürg concentration camp in 1945. This provided a powerfully emotive backdrop to the activists who now erected homemade shelves in its basement, where banned books and magazines were stored. It was also a meeting place for opposition groups who could organize protest action and print leaflets such as *Umweltblätter*, which began with a print run of 150 in 1986 and swelled to over 1,000 a year later. This worried the Stasi so much that it conducted a night-time raid on the library on 25 November 1987. Codenamed 'Trap', this operation involved an astonishing twenty agents who stormed into the basement shouting 'Hands up, machines out'[27] as they caught young activists such as twenty-two-year-old Uta Ihlow and seventeen-year-old Till Böttcher in the process of printing the new issue of *Umweltblätter*. They also dragged the fifty-two-year-old pastor Hans Simon out of bed and presented him with a list of items they had confiscated, such as the printers, before the activists were arrested.

This act of Stasi repression backfired immediately. The next day, 200 people gathered at Zionskirche for a vigil. When they were dispersed, yet more people turned up holding candles. The authorities responded by closing off the church and its square to the public, but by that stage Western media had been alerted to the situation and reported widely on it. The authorities relented after three days and released the group members from custody. They showed that peaceful opposition could be powerful, and coverage of Operation Trap gave it publicity on a scale they could never have achieved themselves with the leaflets alone. The Environment Library gained more and more visitors and began to link up with other groups such as the leave applicants and peace movements. Once again, the GDR's inherent paranoia proved to be self-destructive.

Inspired by the publicity and success of the Environment Library, other groups gathered for demonstrations, church services and disruptive action in larger and larger numbers through 1988. As many of these events took place in East Berlin in immediate reach of Western journalists, the government tried to apply more covert methods to maintain control compared to the brutal oppression of earlier decades. Human rights groups found increasingly ingenious ways to gain publicity to demand reform. On 7 January 1988, for example, they used the annual Memorial March for Rosa Luxemburg and Karl Liebknecht to display some of the communist intellectuals' own words, making it more difficult to take issue with their messages. Mingling with the regular crowds, they carried banners with slogans such as Luxemburg's 'Freedom is always and exclusively freedom for the one who thinks differently', which led to the incarceration of 150 protesters. The authorities had learned their lessons too and instead of beginning more show trials that would lead to further media attention, they offered the leading dissidents a simple choice: deportation to West Germany or years of imprisonment in the GDR. Most chose to be deported to the FRG, including thirty-eight-year-old Freya Klier and thirty-two-year-old songwriter Stephan Krawczyk who had both become iconic figures in the GDR's civil rights movement. This happened with the support of East Berlin Bishop Gottfried Forck, who had previously carried the emblem of the Sword to Ploughshares movement on his briefcase and opened up many opportunities for young reform leaders to meet in his city. His concern for the protesters in Stasi prison led him to help convince the imprisoned activists to take the deportation offer.

With many of their leaders gone or carrying the whiff of collusion, the movement began to flag a little through 1988. The Stasi noted this with relief, reporting on 16 February that 'in the majority of groups a desolate situation has come about'.[28] But networks had been set up, methods tested and the spirit of reform kindled. More people than ever applied to leave the GDR, with a record 113,000 applications by the end of the year. A stubborn and increasingly ill Honecker responded defiantly in January 1989 with a prognosis that the Berlin Wall would 'still stand in 50 and even in 100 years'.[29] While at this point few seriously expected that the GDR was nearing its end, freedom to travel and the need for political reform became increasingly urgent demands among civil rights activists and started to resonate in the GDR more broadly.

By the time of the local elections on 7 May 1989, the mood was beginning to tilt enough to cause the authorities serious concern, particularly in Berlin. A Stasi report about the 'Reactions of the Population to the Preparations for the Local Election', written eleven days prior to it, reflects the widespread desire for reform. Candidates standing for election faced the public beforehand in 'People's Conversations' (*Volksaussprache*) and this time these conversations took on a decidedly heated character in many regions. The Stasi report states that 'Many citizens, and this is the opinion of those involved in preparing the elections, presented as very critical, partially even demanding. With some force, convincing answers and constructive solutions to the raised questions are demanded of deputies and candidates.'[30] The list of complaints was long, as the Stasi report points out: housing, waiting times for goods and services, lack of replacement parts in industry and agriculture, the state of roads and pavements, street lighting, the lack of consumer goods, price increases and generally 'the nonfulfillment of "election promises" given in previous years'.[31]

Wolfgang Mulinski whose supposedly 'unstable attitude' towards 'work ethic and practice' had been duly noted by the Stasi in 1982 in conjunction with his efforts to join the Liberal Democratic Party of Germany (LDPD) stood as a candidate in the local elections of May 1989. As we have seen, the LDPD had existed since 1945 and was one of a number of bloc parties, alongside the Christian Democratic Union (CDU), the National Democratic Party of Germany and Democratic Farmers' Party of Germany. In contrast to a multi-party democracy, East German voters did not choose between different parties on their ballot paper. Instead there was a single list of candidates of the so-called National Front made up of candidates of these bloc parties together with those from mass organizations and associations such as the FDJ, the Red Cross, the Free German Trade Union Federation or the League of Architects. In theory the goal was to have candidates not of different political persuasions but representing different interest groups such as workers, students and various professions. In practice, the system meant that the list was controlled by the ruling SED party. Towards the end of the 1980s, however, the CDU and Wolfgang's LDPD in particular became more critical and many of their members argued for Gorbachev-style reforms. Wolfgang too saw this as a vehicle for change. Like many East Germans, he wanted reform but the GDR was his home. He didn't want to turn his back on it; he wanted to make it better.

In May 1989, the elections were as undemocratic as ever. Voters still came into the room with their voting registration and their identification document. They were given a ballot paper with the candidates of the National Front in their local area. This paper contained no circles to put a cross in, no boxes to tick, just a list of names. To agree with the list, one simply folded the paper and put it in the ballot box there and then. The only way to express disapproval was to take the paper into the voting booth. In 1986, in the elections for the People's Chamber only one person of the 196 eligible voters in the borough of Wernigerode did so. In the booth, one had to cross out every single name in a neat horizontal line to vote against the list. Crossing out some individual names but not all was still counted as a yes vote. So Wolfgang knew that putting his name on the list for the local elections was not in itself an act of reform, but he hoped it would get him into a position where he could address the concerns of his friends, neighbours and colleagues. Wolfgang too felt the rough wind of change in his 'People's Conversation' in the build-up to the elections. In contrast to previous elections, 'people were very outspoken', he remembered later.[32] 'There was still not enough adequate housing, for example, and people were getting very concerned about the environmental damage that was done in our country. The environment in particular was one of the things people felt most strongly about. These were all genuine concerns and I wanted to help. Becoming a local full-time politician seemed a more constructive way to do something than continuing to grumble in private.'[33]

Opposition activists, particularly in East Berlin, also felt it was time for reform. As the Stasi noted in a report,[34] a group of 160 men and women met at a Protestant community centre in Hohenschönhausen, East Berlin, to discuss 'large-scale monitoring of polling stations'.[35] The plan was for activists to sit in wherever voting was undertaken on 7 May 1989 and watch proceedings very carefully, particularly as votes were counted. They would document the entire process so as to uncover and publicize election fraud. In the small Hohenschönhausen meeting alone five Western journalists were present while Germany's public broadcaster ARD filmed outside.[36] Throughout the 1980s, organized opposition networks had honed their methods: coverage in the Western media was not only the best way to be heard but also valuable protection or at least mitigation against repressive measures from the Stasi. Mielke's agents reported after the election that 'election watch' had indeed been a widespread undertaking:

> *Members of so-called grassroots church groups and applicants for permanent leave were recognized . . . in the polling stations. In relation to the capital such persons were noted in Berlin-Prenzlauer Berg in sixty-four polling stations, in Berlin-Friedrichshain in forty-four polling stations, in Berlin-Mitte in twenty-three polling stations. These persons usually made notes about the election results announced by the electoral officials.*[37]

According to these reports from Berlin, 10 to 20 per cent of the votes cast were votes against the list of candidates of the National Front, which meant that voters went into the booth rather than folding their paper and putting it into the ballot box straight away. The result that Egon Krenz, chairman of the Central Electoral

Commision, read out on television that night was 98.89 per cent approval of the set lists rather than the usual 99.9 per cent. Even the inflated official figures admitted that things were not the same. Indeed, these would be the last election results ever in East Germany with such approval rates.

Throughout 1989, there was a growing sense that things needed to change. Vocal public opposition was still concentrated in East Berlin and most East Germans did not expect or want the state to collapse. But many ordinary people found it increasingly frustrating that the authorities seemed so set in their old ways.

The Last Day of the Republic

East Berlin, 7 October 1989. I was four years old – an excited little girl with unruly, pitch-black hair that resisted every attempt to control it. Wrapping my hands around the handrail of the rotating visitor platform of the Berlin Television Tower, I was straining forward to get as close to the panoramic glass panes as I could. As my feet lifted off the carpet, I went unusually quiet. I gazed down 203 metres at the streets below in amazement, trying to take it all in. The little cars whizzing around Berlin looked marvellous, like my precious collection of Matchbox toys. There were lots of tiny people too and yet more were coming. Delighted with the spectacle of Berlin from above, I turned around and shouted slightly too loudly, 'Papa, come and see! All those people look like little ants!' I pointed downwards eagerly, jumping up and down so I could see better. 'And look! There are police cars everywhere!' At last my words seemed to arrest my father's attention. He'd been buying drinks for me and my pregnant mother from the fancy restaurant in the centre of the observation platform. But those last words made him stop in his tracks. Looking down at the increasingly crowded square at the foot of the Fernsehturm, his face went white. He recognized the armoured vehicles as belonging to Paramilitary People's Police units. Many of the people I was pointing at were protesters. The government clearly expected trouble and was readying itself to respond. 'Katja, come quick, we need to go,' he urged. But I stood rooted to the spot, transfixed by the miniature chaos that was unfolding below. My knuckles turned white with my determination to cling on to the handrail if need be. Just as things became really exciting my father wanted to go. Without listening to my protestations or my mother's questions, he pulled us both along, back into the lift.

On the long journey down, troubling thoughts went through my father's mind: what if the protests escalate? How will the police react? Both questions worried him, but it was best to sit it out at home, outside of the capital. If things were to take a violent turn, at least his young family would be safe. We rushed back to our second-hand white Trabant, which my parents had secured for the extortionate price of 8,000 marks a couple of years earlier to avoid the long waiting times for a new model. The drive home was filled with animated conversation, which I listened to intently from the back seat, my eyebrows furrowed in deep concentration. None of it made any sense but it all seemed very thrilling.

I adored my father, in part because I didn't see him as much as I wanted. He served as an officer in the air force and was often on duty. But when he came home, he would take me on day trips to Leipzig Zoo to feed the elephants or to the vast landscaped gardens of Sanssouci Palace in Potsdam where he would bore me with lectures on Prussian and German history that never seemed to make any sense. That day – 7 October 1989 – was the fortieth anniversary of the GDR, a public holiday. There would be a military parade in Berlin, with foreign dignitaries, including Mikhail Gorbachev himself, in attendance. Like many other families, my parents too were keen to enjoy the unseasonably warm day and relax. Like many families, we did not know that our lives were about to change forever.

As my father rushed us home, he did so with mixed feelings. Like most East Germans, he had no inclination to join the demonstrations in Berlin. Life was fairly comfortable. We lived in a two-bedroom flat in one of the earlier prefabricated housing estates built in the 1960s. Yes, the tiled stoves that served as heating (including for bathwater) could be a nuisance, but carrying coal up from the cellar had become a well-loved father–daughter ritual. I remember filling my own little bucket with enthusiasm before carrying it back up the stairs. The other families in the house also had children my age and I had become fast friends with Romano, the son of the Falk family who lived in the flat below. Summer holidays were spent at the white sandy beaches of the Baltic Sea. In the winter, my father would take us back to his home town of Zella-Mehlis in the Thuringian mountains. Skiing and sledging were still new to me as I was growing up among the wide, flat lands of Brandenburg.

Like most of our neighbours, my father Frank was stationed at the Headquarters of the Air Forces of the National People's Army in Strausberg, 30 kilometres east of Berlin. He was an officer specializing in radio and communications technology and his place of work was just a few minutes' walk from home. Sometimes, he would take me to the base as I was fascinated with all the military equipment and the men and women in uniform. On the whole, Frank enjoyed his job but it was also clear that it was becoming increasingly politicized. When he first joined the NVA officer training in 1981, he was grateful for the opportunity this afforded him. The son of German refugees from the Sudetenland and Pomerania, he gained access to higher education and the chance to climb the career ladder. But it soon became apparent that such opportunities came with political pressure too.

As a second-year recruit in 1982, he was preparing to take part in the annual parade for the Day of the Republic, exactly seven years prior to his hasty retreat from the TV tower in 1989. Expectations were high. The young trainee officers had practised the drills again and again on an airfield before the final two rehearsals took place at night on Berlin's Karl-Marx-Allee where the real parade would be staged. He and his comrades had barely slept and it was impressed upon them that every detail must be perfectly executed. On the night before the event, Frank's group was driven to Berlin for one last practice. As the young men indulged in some nervous banter along the way to calm their nerves, Frank made a fateful mistake. 'If this goes wrong,' he said to no one in particular, 'we may as well grab a bullet and do the honourable thing.' He could tell by his friends' stony faces that he had gone too far. When they arrived in Berlin and the door of the transport vehicle opened, two men in civilian suits were already waiting to arrest him. Frank was immediately taken back to his officer school in Zittau in Saxony where his commanding officer sentenced him to ten days of solitary confinement for 'threatening to commit suicide'. As the young man sat in his cell, which contained nothing but a narrow bed to sleep on, he tried to stay sane by counting out half-hour intervals with tiny tin balls he had made from the piece of foil that had covered his lunch. This harsh punishment was not enough to redeem Frank and he was taken off a career path that included the coding and decoding of sensitive radio signals.

Like many others in his position, Frank was given a stark choice after three years of officer training: become a member of the SED or lose the right to graduate. When he was encouraged to join the party for the first time, it was straight after he had been released from solitary confinement. He could not believe that in the moment of greatest frustration, anger and humiliation, he was asked to join the party that had set up this system. He told the Stasi officers as much. But throwing three years of training away for something many people considered a formality was a different matter. Resigned, he joined and received the red book of the party.

Frank's choice of fiancée also drew the ire of the authorities. My mother Andrea had many relatives in West Germany whom her parents visited regularly. Every time they did, the Stasi officials on the NVA base would take a while to process the information, but around six weeks later, Frank would be ordered into their office. 'Well, comrade,' came the usual opening gambit, 'did you know your future parents-in-law travelled to the Federal Republic to see relatives?' It became a well-worn ritual. Frank would tell them that of course he knew since it had happened weeks ago, and as far as he knew his future in-laws had come back. Andrea only found out years into their marriage that the officers had also tried to encourage her husband to end the relationship in order to remove career obstacles.

In many ways, Frank was a typical example of a well-educated but comparatively unpolitical man who wanted to be able to afford basic commodities, have a fulfilling career and enough money and time to enjoy holidays and family life. This worked for him and many others for some time. But as the authorities' stance hardened in the second half of the 1980s, it began to grate even on those, like Frank, who weren't overtly political.

Fall of the Wall

Rostock, Mecklenburg, 9 November 1989, 7.30 p.m. Roland Schneider, a thirty-three-year-old traffic policeman, was on call. For weeks now, unrest all across the GDR had been getting more and more raucous and he wasn't sure how he felt about that. 'As a civil servant, I was a little concerned what the future might bring,' Roland mused later, 'and I have to say, honestly, I believed in the whole thing. I was raised like that – "socialism will win".'[38] Still, the married father of four had also begun to appreciate why more and more East Germans wanted change. He found that the workers he visited in factories wanted to talk less about traffic and more about reform. The biggest grievances again and again were supply problems and the numbing feeling of not being heard by those in power. When the first demonstrations took place in his home city of Rostock in October 1989, Roland found himself in a strange situation. Looking down on to the street from his window, he heard his fellow Rostockers shout, 'Come down, join in!'[39] Could he? Should he? He was a policeman, after all. It wasn't long until he gave in and joined them – initially still dressed in dark clothing, conscious that he might be recognized.

The dams of change had been broken. All throughout 1989 thousands of East Germans had made their way to the West – either legally, as the authorities granted more and more applications, or through Eastern European countries where Gorbachev's reforms had already brought about change. Many GDR citizens sought refuge in the West German embassies of Warsaw, Budapest, Prague and East Berlin, and when Hungary decided to open its borders to Austria on the night of 10 September, many more availed themselves of this opportunity to travel West. Hungary's Prime Minister Miklós Németh reassured West Germany's Chancellor Kohl that 'deportation of refugees back to the GDR is out of the question. We are opening our border. So long as no military or political power forces us from the outside to change our behaviour, we will keep the border open for GDR citizens.'[40] He knew outside forces were unlikely to materialize this time. Speaking to the Council of Europe a couple of months earlier, on 6 July 1989, Mikhail Gorbachev had clearly stated the Soviet Union's 'respect for the sovereign right of each people to choose their social system at their own discretion'.[41] If Hungary wanted to open the borders to its old partner Austria, it was free to do so and without asking Moscow or Berlin for permission. In September and October, 50,000 GDR citizens travelled to the West this way.

Not everyone wanted to leave their home and begin a new life elsewhere. Many more East Germans were trying to bring about change at home, proving to the government that the problem could not be solved by simply letting go of those who wanted to leave. Where the opposition movement had initially used the slogan 'We want out!', they now began to chant, 'We're staying here!', forming new and bigger political opposition movements within the GDR. For the first time, this happened outside of the umbrella of church opposition. In September, the activist group New Forum was established. Proclaiming its message on many noticeboards across the GDR, its founders announced: 'In our country, the communication between state and society is clearly disturbed . . . it is now important that more people take part in the process of social reform.'[42] This proclamation would eventually be signed by 200,000 people and the movement attracted 10,000 full members. The New Forum provided an opportunity to build links between the 160 or so opposition groups that the Stasi had identified in 1989.[43] Even at this stage, few wanted to abolish the state altogether – political activists called for reform and democratic change. But by the time of the fortieth anniversary of the GDR on 7 October 1989, large-scale demonstrations broke out everywhere across East German cities. While the numbers in Roland Schneider's Rostock were still small at around 600–700 people, in Leipzig, Dresden, Halle and East Berlin itself thousands took to the streets chanting, 'We are the people!', 'Gorby!' and 'No violence!'

Gorbachev, who had come to attend the anniversary parade, warned Erich Honecker that 'Danger awaits those who do not react to the real world,' which became more famous later as 'Life punishes those who come too late.' Honecker, visibly astounded by the lack of support from Moscow, stubbornly responded, 'Forwards ever, backwards never.'[44] The authorities attempted to quell individual gatherings, some brutally with truncheons and dogs, particularly in Berlin. There was no systematic suppression with firearms but the atmosphere remained tense. The Chinese government had fired on protesters in Tiananmen Square in June, killing hundreds, perhaps thousands, of civilians, and a 'Chinese solution' to the threat of an uprising in the GDR seemed still very much on the cards as more and more demonstrators gathered on the streets of East German cities. When the government did not respond with violence, yet more people felt encouraged to join in. On 16 October, 120,000 people took to the streets of Leipzig, demanding democratic change, free elections and freedom of expression. Roland Schneider witnessed a demonstration of 2,000 people in Rostock who were asking for the New Forum to be officially acknowledged. The SED leadership had given orders to deescalate but to do so without the use of firearms. As a result, police units largely concentrated on protecting property and dispersing crowds. This meant that mass gatherings and demonstrations were to become part of the political landscape. The forced democratization of the GDR's political structures had begun and all the SED could do was try to manage it.

With the SED under pressure to show that things were changing, a new leader was needed. Erich Honecker had been incapacitated by health problems for much of the summer of 1989. A gall bladder operation in August was preceded by medical complications and his doctors also began to suspect that the General Secretary was suffering from cancer in his right kidney. Between all the medical procedures and convalescence, Honecker was out of action for nearly three months. On one of his rare public appearances, a visit to the VEB Kombinat Mikroelektronik Erfurt where he was shown the prototype of a 32-bit processor, he seemed entirely detached from what was happening in his country, famously quoting the nineteenth-century socialist August Bebel: 'Neither ox nor ass can stop socialism in its path.'

Five days later, Hungary started to open its borders while Honecker was in hospital recovering from his operation. When he re-emerged at the end of September, emaciated and visibly aged, it was clear to the politburo that its leader was not the right man to stabilize the situation in the GDR. His stubborn refusal to accept criticism or the need to reform was now coupled with a lack of energy and avoidance of conflict. Honecker was spent, his days numbered.

As the seventy-seven-year-old General Secretary entered a plenary session of the politburo at 10.10 a.m. on 17 October, everything seemed normal. He opened the session and asked if anyone had any items for the agenda. Willi Stoph, Chairman of the Council of Ministers, did. Stoph suggested that the first item should be the removal of Honecker from the position of General Secretary and his replacement with Egon Krenz. 'Erich, we can't go on like this. You have to go.' Silence filled the room. Honecker looked ashen. 'Well, I will open the discussion then,' he replied when he had recovered his composure. Three hours later the politburo formally agreed to Honecker's resignation, a unanimous decision that included the General Secretary's own vote. Margot Honecker, who also resigned

from her positions three days later, recalled that her husband con-
fided to her on the evening of his ousting, 'You know, I'm almost
relieved, I couldn't have done it any longer.'[45]

At fifty-two, Egon Krenz, the new General Secretary, seemed
altogether more energetic and willing to accept that the GDR
needed reform. Hated figures like Stasi boss Erich Mielke were
removed from the politburo. In his first televised speech, Krenz
promised a *Wende*, a turning point, coining a term that would
become synonymous with the entire period of change that culminated in the reunification of Germany. But the *Wende* Egon Krenz
outlined did not involve the abolition of the GDR as a state. While
he believed that 'all problems in our society can be solved by political means'[46] and had given the order not to use firearms on the
demonstrators on 13 October without Honecker's approval, it was
also clear that reforms would only go as far as they needed to in
order to quell the immediate anger while preserving SED power.
Krenz was not interested in a complete overhaul of the system. Still,
he initiated the first steps of change. He moved out of the Waldsiedlung settlement to send a signal that he would no longer remove
himself from society in the way his predecessors had. His politburo
passed the draft for a new travel law on 24 October, which was to
allow citizens to apply for travel permits to West Germany without
having to give the usual reasons such as family visits.

But it was too little too late. The draft travel law was only made
public on 6 November and did not specify under what circumstances
applications could be denied. By then mass demonstrations in
almost all cities of the GDR had snowballed, involving people from
all walks of life, even SED members. On 4 November, 500,000
people gathered on Berlin's Alexanderplatz calling for democracy
and freedom to travel. There were politicians too among the twenty
speakers. Günter Schabowski, the former editor of the SED newspaper *Neues Deutschland* who was to become the government's
spokesperson two days later, was there. Markus Wolf, the 'man
without a face', who had headed the Stasi's foreign intelligence
agency until 1986, also made an appearance. Both received some

applause but also boos and whistles. Change was in the air and the political elite was unable to 'climb aboard the revolutionary loco-motive, blow its whistles loudly and bring the speeding vehicle slowly to a stop', as East German historian Stefan Wolle put it.[47]

Five days later, on the evening of 9 November 1989, Rostock policeman Roland Schneider had no idea what exactly was happen-ing in the capital 240 kilometres to the south. So he switched on the TV to watch the news programme *Aktuelle Kamera* at 7.30 p.m. The familiar face of forty-five-year-old presenter Angelika Unterlauf appeared. In her usual formal style, she announced that Günter Schabowski had told the assembled international press earlier that evening that East Germans would be allowed to travel into West Germany, including West Berlin, without obtaining prior permis-sion or travel documents. 'The relevant departments of the People's Police,' she added, 'are ordered to also issue visas for permanent emigration immediately. Permanent emigration is possible via all border checkpoints of the GDR to the FRG and to West Berlin.' While the Central Committee of the SED had intended this change to take effect from 10 o'clock the following morning, Schabowski, who had not been briefed properly, had confirmed to the assembled journalists and people watching the live broadcast on their televi-sions at home that it would take effect 'now, immediately'.

In the Lichtenberg district of Berlin thirty-two-year-old Andreas Falge watched Schabowski's announcement live on his mother's colour TV, a Sharp model from the Intershop. 'What?!' he thought. 'Surely he can't just open the door?'[48] Andreas was excited about the news, but it was a Thursday and he had to be back at the famous Babylon cinema the next day, where he worked as a technician. He decided to go and investigate the matter at the weekend, taking DM100 and a map of West Berlin from his mother's flat before he went home to the Prenzlauer Berg area. There, he turned on his TV to see what the West German broadcaster ZDF had to say on the evening's events but found to his disappointment that they had a football match on. At 10.40 p.m., the news programme finally announced: 'East Berlin has opened the Wall.' The accompanying

footage showed bustling crowds of Berliners at several border crossing points. Now Andreas's curiosity was piqued. He donned his
leather jacket and joined the masses on the streets, walking towards
the Bornholmer Straße crossing with his mother's money and map
in his pocket.

There were people everywhere. 'Have you heard the news?'
everyone seemed to ask. Traffic came to a standstill and trams
couldn't move on their tracks. Andreas was swept along by the inexorable flow towards the Berlin Wall. When he arrived, there was
chaos and nobody seemed to know what was happening. Around
1,000 people had gathered and demanded to pass through under the
new rules announced in Schabowski's press conference.

Again and again Lieutenant Colonel Harald Jäger, who was in
charge of passport control at Bornholmer Straße, called his superiors for instructions. Only when he sounded a silent alarm did they
respond with an order to let individuals through, ideally 'the biggest
troublemakers', and stamp their passports to make them invalid for
return. This was intended to effectively expatriate those who left
earlier than the government had planned. The situation became
increasingly volatile as the guards were vastly outnumbered and
began to lose control. There were no more instructions from the
authorities. The guards had no idea what to do as the atmosphere
became increasingly tense, even 'a little aggressive', as Andreas
recalled. Concerned about a possible escalation and angry with his
superiors shirking their responsibility to make a decision, Harald
Jäger took matters into his own hands. At 11.29 p.m. he decided to
open his border crossing and cease passport checks. The barriers
lifted. For the first time since 1961, East Berliners could freely walk
into West Berlin.

Hundreds of people streamed across the Bösebrücke which
bridged the railway lines that divided East and West Berlin at this
point. Conscious that he would have to return to work the next day,
Andreas jostled his way through to the checkpoint to have his passport stamped. He had no idea that this technically barred him from
re-entering the GDR under existing orders. As he walked across the

bridge and crossed on to the last 30 metres of it, which belonged to the French sector of the city, he saw two West German policemen. Andreas knew they were not allowed into East Berlin. 'At that moment I realized that I really was in the West.'

But where should he go? Even though Andreas was a native Berliner, this part of his city was completely unfamiliar territory. Take the underground train? No, he had no idea how it worked or where it would take him. Call a taxi? The telephone booths were all occupied by excited East Berliners. Maybe he could call one from a nearby bar? But Andreas recalled wryly that he was still somewhat 'sceptical of this wicked capitalism. They might want money to call a taxi.' In the end, he found one waiting on a nearby street and jumped in. When the driver asked him where he was from and he answered, 'Prenzlauer Berg,' the West Berliner gasped, 'But that's in the East! Holy Sh . . .'[49] West Germans were as baffled by the hectic events of the night as their Eastern counterparts. Andreas asked to be taken to the elegant district of Charlottenburg where a friend of his lived in a shared flat. Looking out of the taxi at the dazzling blur of West Berlin's streets and houses flashing by, he thought, 'It looks just like our Berlin, only the shop windows are more colourful. I will never forget their glaring neon lights.' When he arrived in Charlottenburg, the impressions of the night threatened to overwhelm him. It was all too much to take in – as if he had stepped into another world. Relieved to have arrived at his friend's place, he slumped onto a sofa and opened his first bottle of Beck's.[50]

Some 240 kilometres to the north, Roland Schneider also found it hard to comprehend what he had seen on the television. He and his colleagues were responsible for the entire Rostock district, including its border to Schleswig-Holstein in West Germany. What were the police supposed to do? Nobody had told him anything. Did this mean that East Germans approaching the border were allowed to pass? What if he got this wrong?

Schneider met with his colleagues to discuss the situation. Within a couple of hours, a large crowd had gathered at the border post of

Schlutup, demanding to be allowed to cross into West Germany. What to do? The policemen there called the deputy regional leader as their leader, General Major Hader, had 'taken ill'. Eventually, they received orders to 'Open the border'. But what did that mean? Were they not required to check papers any more? If they were, what papers should they check? What if people did not have any papers on them? It was chaos. Traffic jams began to build up into the early hours as the police dithered, unsure what the correct procedure was. Eventually, the cars cleared as morning broke. As Roland put it, 'The diligent people of East Germany had to go to work, naturally.'[51]

All along the inner-German border curious East Germans gathered at the crossing points in their Trabants and Wartburgs, to see what was going on following the bewildering messages they had heard on TV and radio. As 9 November 1989 was a Thursday, and many East Germans were indeed conscious of having to work the next day, the real wave hit the borders over the weekend, when over 4 million visas were issued to GDR citizens travelling to the West. Many wound their car windows down as they passed the border checkpoints, telling the guards, 'Don't worry. We'll come back. We just want to see what it's like.'

Indeed, many East Germans were simply curious about West Germany or wanted to buy particular things now that they could. Later that month, Roland's family too would begin to travel into 'the West'. He remembers that his wife and children went without him at first, because he had to work. His first item from 'over there' was a Mars bar, which he had explicitly requested. Many East Berliners hit West Berlin's famous shopping avenue Kurfürstendamm. The West German government had introduced a 'Welcome Money' scheme in 1970 by which every GDR citizen was entitled to DM30 and later DM100 upon arrival in the FRG. At around 60 pfennigs a piece, many Mars bars could be bought with this. But chaos ensued when 4 million East Germans tried to request their Welcome Money at West German banks over the weekend following the opening of the borders. By 20 November, the number of visitors would swell to

10 million. Many GDR citizens remember fondly what products they bought with this money, from sweets and toys to exotic fruit. Street vendors in border cities and West Berlin were quick to respond and set up their stalls to entice and welcome their new East German customers.

The Road to Reunification

Mellrichstadt, Bavaria, mid-November 1989. Ines Stolpe stood in a small electronics shop and held a Walkman in her hand.[52] She turned it over and over as she wondered whether to buy it or not. It was advertised for DM70, massively overpriced. A few days had passed since the GDR opened its borders to West Germany, and in that time millions of her fellow East Germans had flocked to border towns like Mellrichstadt. Ines too had been curious, but the twenty-two-year-old had her hands full. She was pregnant and she also looked after her first-born, Robert, by herself. Her husband Stefan, a helicopter pilot in the People's Navy, was stationed 640 kilometres to the north in Stralsund, literally at the other end of the country from their Thuringian home. The couple had secured a nice flat in Stralsund with two and a half bedrooms, and Stefan was renovating it even though they were no longer sure whether it was worth moving their young family so far from home. Who knew what would happen in light of the tumultuous political changes that were afoot?

Given their situation, the prospect of joining throngs of people queuing in supermarkets and banks while little Robert squirmed in her arms did not appeal to Ines. But once things had quietened down a bit, curiosity got the better of her. After all, she had never been to West Germany before. She could at least see what it was like. So she made the one-hour journey south and crossed the border into Bavaria. Ines needed West German marks to buy things in Mellrichstadt, but like many East Germans, she felt embarrassed about taking the Welcome Money provided by the banks. She was a kindergarten teacher and had worked for two years before Robert was born. Her husband was a naval officer. The couple had a reasonable income and they worked hard for it too. To Ines, it felt degrading that she found herself queuing in a West German bank for a handout. The fact that she had a stamp in her passport that noted that she had received her DM100 so that she couldn't claim it twice added further insult to injury.

The day did not improve. Somewhere between the bank and the shops Robert's nappy needed changing. Not being able to find a baby-care room, she simply placed her boy on top of a nearby wall and did what needed doing. That taken care of, Ines could finally take a look around the supermarkets and shops of the 6,000-soul border town. She was beginning to feel a little better as the Bavarian shop owners turned out to be incredibly friendly towards her and the other East German visitors. Its proximity to the Iron Curtain had made sleepy little Mellrichstadt a garrison town with two *Bundeswehr* battalions. Its population had felt the tension of the nearby border too and was pleased to welcome people from the other side of it when they could finally come freely. But by the time Ines arrived, the bananas and Walkman she had come for proved difficult to find. The shelves had been emptied by those who had visited earlier and entrepreneurial shop owners were quick to respond to the rising demand by inflating their prices for the stock they had left. Ines felt uncomfortable in the electronics outlet as she handed over the money that wasn't hers to buy a Walkman that wasn't worth its price tag.

On the way home, Ines wondered what the future might hold for her and her young family. She understood that things needed to change. 'Everyone knew that the state didn't work,' she recalled, 'but I was frightened about what this would mean for us. Nobody seemed to know anything. Everything we had banked on and planned for was now uncertain.'[53] It was with such mixed feelings that many GDR citizens approached the *Wende*. There was a sense that this would be a change of historic proportions, which had to be a good thing, given the need for political reform and the economic situation. But it was also disconcerting to many who had built their lives and identities on forty years of East German socialism. What would become of their livelihoods, their families and their personal circumstances? Nobody could tell them.

At the political level things moved along at breakneck speed after the borders were open. Those who had firmly sat in the political saddle for years could no longer be certain of their positions. On 13 November, just four days after the fall of the Berlin Wall, the People's Chamber, the GDR's parliament, convened to discuss the situation in the country. Buoyed by recent events and keen to preserve its own existence, the institution had gained confidence and was keen to show that they could hold to account those responsible for the lack of openness, democracy and reform. Representatives of the other political parties demanded the SED relinquish its constitutional supremacy and allow free elections without set lists of candidates. Long-established politicians such as the Chairman of the Council of Ministers Willi Stoph were put on the spot. Even Stasi boss Erich Mielke, who had himself been a deputy of the People's Chamber for thirty-one years but had never before addressed it, now had to face questions from fellow members.

Once the most feared man in the GDR, Erich Mielke was now nearly eighty-two years old and looked it. Ignoring his notes, he rambled through well-worn political platitudes. It was immediately obvious that he no longer wielded the fear and control that had allowed him to stay in power for so long. When Mielke told parliament, 'We have, comrades, dear deputies, an extraordinarily high degree of contact with all working people,' laughter filled the chamber.[54] Now insecure and defensive, his speech became incoherent as he tried to engage an audience that had lost all respect. A deputy interrupted him to take issue with his repeated use of the word 'comrades', which had clearly been second nature to him since he had joined the youth wing of the Communist Party as a teenager in 1921. 'Not everyone who sits in this chamber is a comrade,' came the much-applauded intervention.[55] Now completely flustered, Mielke stuttered, 'That's just a question of formality. I love – I love everyone, all humans.'⁵⁶ With the raucous laughter that accompanied these ramblings, the spell of the Stasi was broken.

Mielke's own Ministry for State Security now turned against him – 91,000 employees embarrassed by his public showing, worried about how they would be judged. Five days after Mielke's disastrous appearance in the People's Chamber, he was out of his job. His creation, the Ministry for State Security, was renamed the Office of National Security, headed by his former deputy Wolfgang Schwanitz. On 3 December, Mielke was thrown out of the SED and four days later he was arrested. The destruction of documents and evidence that Mielke had ordered since the beginning of November was also brought to a halt when on 4 December people all over the country occupied their local Stasi offices. On 15 January 1990, the headquarters in Berlin-Lichtenberg followed. Most of the data was rescued with the exception of the HVA's – the Stasi's foreign intelligence arm, once led by Markus Wolf – which was allowed to dissolve itself including the destruction of almost all of its files. Erich Mielke and the Stasi were finished.

Many more high-profile figures fell in rapid succession. Willi Stoph, the former Chairman of the Council of Ministers who had asked Erich Honecker to resign, admitted in front of the People's Chamber that he and his council had never fulfilled their constitutional role as the government of the GDR and instead allowed the Central Committee of the politburo of the SED to run the country. He was therefore hardly fit to usher in the required changes. On the same day when Erich Mielke embarrassed himself in front of them, the deputies of the People's Chamber chose a replacement for Stoph from just outside the inner circle of the SED: Hans Modrow. The sixty-one-year-old had been the SED's First Secretary in Dresden since 1973 and had only just become a member of the politburo a few days earlier. Unlike Stoph, Krenz, Mielke and Honecker, Modrow did not reside in the secretive Waldsiedlung north of Berlin. He lived in a three-bedroom flat in central Dresden to which, upon his election, he rushed back briefly to 'say goodbye to my wife for the next few weeks and take the required clothing for Berlin'.⁵⁷ Many

SED deputies of the People's Chamber hoped that Modrow would be seen as an authentic and affable figure, someone who could convince the public that the party and the GDR as a whole were capable of reform.

But there was no saving the SED. Its reputation was already in tatters and new revelations about corruption and misuse of power were being uncovered by an inquiry commission of the People's Chamber. In addition, many of the party's reluctant members saw that their affiliation no longer held any benefits and, quite to the contrary, might soon prove a dark blemish. The party haemorrhaged members on a huge scale. By the beginning of December, it had already lost 600,000 members. By the end of January it would be 900,000. At the same time, it had to give up its 'leading role', enshrined in the constitution. With the SED now just one party among others, its General Secretary Egon Krenz was no longer the de facto leader of the country, a role that now shifted to Modrow's Council of Ministers.

The remaining SED members – still well over a million – also demanded that the party itself be reformed. The old leadership was forced to resign wholesale, including the entire Central Committee, on 3 December 1989. Once-powerful figures such as Erich Honecker, Erich Mielke, Alexander Schalck-Golodkowski and Willi Stoph were expelled from the party. Indeed, some already sat in protective custody at this point. What remained of the party renamed itself the Party of Democratic Socialism (SED-PDS). It would continue to exist until 2007 when it merged with a West German party to form Die Linke (The Left). Relatively unknown up to that point, a forty-one-year-old attorney called Gregor Gysi became its new Chairman. He had been an SED party member for twenty-two years but had also defended many opposition leaders such as Bärbel Bohley, one of the founders of the New Forum who had been imprisoned for her political activity. Gysi's eloquence and rhetorical flourish gained him much media attention as he advocated reform during the demonstration on Alexanderplatz on 4 November and later on television. 'My switch to politics happened by accident but also by design,' he remembered later. 'The party became particularly interesting to me when it stood on the brink.'[58]

The SED-PDS proved difficult to salvage. Having lost its enshrined supremacy over other parties and groups, it now had to work and compete with them. A Round Table was formed as an interim governing committee of sorts, including not just the PDS, but also representatives of all other parties and other political groups like the New Forum. It convened for the first time on 7 December in East Berlin and political worlds collided in its heated discussions. Ulrike Poppe, a founding member of the opposition group Democracy Now and a Round Table participant, recalled later how different the position of groups like hers was compared to the established parties: 'The party representatives had their offices, systems, their advisors behind them while we were still sitting in our kitchens, tearing our hair out.'[59] Nonetheless, the Round Table would meet sixteen times and have a profound influence as it planned and prepared the first free and secret elections in the GDR on 18 March 1990.

The big question for this election was one that had divided the different political groups for a while: should the GDR be reformed and democratized while remaining a separate state or should it be reunited with West Germany? Many of those who had opposed the SED regime were not fundamentally averse to the GDR's economic system. There was much talk of a 'third way' between socialism and capitalism. On 28 November 1989, thirty-one public figures, among them the well-known writers Christa Wolf and Stefan Heym, published an appeal entitled 'For Our Country' to the press. In this they argued for the retention of an independent GDR because the alternative was 'the beginning of a sellout of our material and moral worth and sooner or later the annexation of the German Democratic Republic by the Federal Republic of Germany'.[60] But the public mood was drifting in a different direction. At the Monday demonstrations before the fall of the Berlin Wall, a popular slogan had been 'We are the people!', which was intended to remind the authorities, and notably the People's Police, who they had pledged to serve. But as the mass gatherings continued beyond the fall of the Wall and into the winter, the slogan changed to one directly demanding reunification: 'We are one people!'

Keen to use the window of opportunity afforded by the mood swing in the GDR, West German Chancellor Helmut Kohl felt he had to act quickly to bring about unification. There was scepticism towards such a plan from Moscow, Paris, London and much of Eastern Europe for fear that a united Germany would once again dominate the continent. Initially only US President George H. W. Bush unreservedly backed German reunification. But Kohl knew that the express wish of the German people, indeed their right to self-determination, would be hard to oppose from the outside. Anticipating West German resistance to reunification too, not least in Bonn, he surprised everyone on 28 November 1989 by presenting the *Bundestag* with a ten-point plan for reunification which would merge the two states over the course of a ten-year process. This fait accompli was an ingenious plan. Parliamentarians couldn't help but signal their approval – few wanted to be seen to stand in the way of this historic moment. With West German consent in the bag, Kohl travelled to East Germany on 19 December, going to Dresden where demonstrations had been regular, large and vociferous. The Chancellor was met with a sea of black, red and gold. Banners demanded 'Put Reunification on the Programme!' and quoted 'Germany – United Fatherland' from the East German national anthem which had mostly been played as an instrumental version only for the last twenty years due to this line. Kohl was struggling with a deep political crisis at home, in part caused by ongoing unemployment. He saw a golden opportunity for the 1990 elections and seized it. Reunification couldn't wait ten years. It had to happen sooner.

Many East Germans agreed and supported the idea of a quick reunification process in their first and last free parliamentary election in March 1990. By that point, almost all political parties opted for reunification of some description, but they differed on the timescale for it. A coalition of parties called Alliance for Germany, which included the Christian Democratic Union, Democratic Awakening and the German Social Union, gained nearly half of the votes cast, with a high turnout of 93.4 per cent. They had advocated the quickest path to reunification under the slogan 'Never again Socialism'. This would entail:

- joining West Germany on the basis of its existing constitution rather than drafting a new common framework
- the introduction of the West German Deutsche Mark as a common currency with an exchange rate of 1:1 for savings accounts
- the introduction of a market economy with unlimited access for Western investors to East German markets and assets.

The newly formed East German SPD (called SDP before January 1990) only gained 22 per cent with its demands for a social market economy and a somewhat more cautious approach to reunification. The former ruling party, now PDS, only received 16.4 per cent of votes. Such a clear result was taken as a mandate for reunification and for one that involved East Germany joining the existing system in the West rather than creating a new Germany out of the two parts.

While the months of arguing, protesting and decision-making were exciting for many who had craved transparent politics, they also brought much social, financial and psychological insecurity. Since her brief excursion to Bavaria, Ines Stolpe had joined her husband Stefan in Stralsund, moving into the newly renovated flat that had once been intended as a long-term home for the young family while Stefan was stationed there. Now their future was uncertain. West Germany had far fewer childcare opportunities. Would reunification mean that Ines would not be able to return to work as a kindergarten teacher until Robert and her unborn child both went to school? What was going to happen to the armed forces of the GDR who employed her husband? How long would it be before East German officers would lose their posts with few skills that would be needed in a privatized job market? Would they stay up in

Stralsund, hundreds of kilometres from home? Ines's second child, a baby girl, was born in May 1990. Ines was relieved to be able to start another year of maternity leave, but then what? 'Nobody knew what was going to happen,'[61] she recalled. A kindergarten teacher and an officer, both young parents were employed by the state. They had envisioned long fulfilling careers. Now they anxiously tried to predict an uncertain future.

The Stolpes and many other East Germans struggled to keep up with the tumultuous political changes following the elections. Once a Grand Coalition of Alliance for Germany, Social Democrats and Liberals had been formed under the leadership of Lothar de Maizière of the East German CDU, things moved very quickly notwithstanding the huge tasks that lay ahead. Over the four decades of its existence, the GDR had built up entirely different political, economic and societal structures from those of the FRG. Yet, Wolfgang Schäuble, the West German Minister of the Interior who led the reunification negotiations with the East, declared that change would have to come from the GDR only. 'This is not the unification of two equal states,' he insisted. 'There is a constitution, and there is a Federal Republic of Germany. Let us start with the assumption that you have been excluded from both for forty years. Now you are entitled to take part.'[62] The direction of the negotiations was not up for debate, the question was only how quickly the measures could and should be implemented.

A major step on the road to reunification was the monetary union of the two states, effective from 1 July 1990. Long queues formed at the banks as people converted savings of up to 6,000 East German marks at an exchange rate of 1:1. The *Treuhandanstalt* (Trust Agency) or *Treuhand* for short, which had been founded by parliament shortly before to oversee the privatization process of the state economy, now really kicked into gear selling 'people's property' such as state-run factories and other public assets into private hands. The *Treuhand*'s lack of expertise, oversight and personnel led to chaos and corruption and the process was seen by many East Germans as an undignified 'bargain-basement' sellout of their country. Many workers who had been proud of their trade and earned good money in their jobs now found themselves preparing machinery and vehicles for West German companies who bought them cheaply (often for the symbolic value of DM1) and took them away. Others were asked to dismantle their own factories and workplaces wholesale, effectively working to make themselves redundant. The feeling of helplessness many experienced as their country was dismantled would stay with them for decades to come.

On 23 August 1990, the People's Chamber formally voted to merge the GDR into the FRG and a week later, on 31 August, the final reunification treaty was signed between the two states. It set 3 October 1990 as the date on which the states would become one and stipulated that it should be a public holiday henceforth – German Unity Day. Over eight weeks of negotiations, the two sides had hastily tried to find solutions for fundamental differences between the two countries, be that economically and politically or socially. Sensitive issues such as abortion and women in the armed forces had caused heated debate. While solutions were found for some issues, others were deferred. On 12 September, the complicated negotiations between the two Germanies and the victors of the Second World War, the so-called Two Plus Four negotiations, came to a successful conclusion in the signing of a treaty in Moscow. It granted the reunified country full sovereignty, allowed it to be a full member of NATO and ordered the removal of foreign troops from its soil. By the end of September, all preparations for the reunification of the two post-war Germanies were complete. Even the main political parties, with the exception of the PDS, merged with their West German counterparts. The road to reunification had reached its end.

Anticipated with a mixture of jubilation and anticipation, the day of German reunification was heralded by a number of official and unofficial celebrations. The People's Chamber ceremoniously dissolved itself, the German embassies in East Berlin and Bonn were closed and there was an official event in front of the disused

Reichstag building in West Berlin. Many people waved banners and flags welcoming what they saw as a long-overdue reunion. A few protested one last time against the loss of their state.

At midnight on 3 October 1990, the German Democratic Republic ceased to exist.

Epilogue: Unity

'We have achieved what Germany has strived for since the times of our forebears: unity.'[1] When Kaiser Wilhelm I spoke those words to the first all-German parliament on 21 March 1871, the country had only just been unified from a patchwork of kingdoms and principalities. While most Germans embraced national unity, this did not mean that they were ready to forget everything that had come before. Economic, cultural and social traditions that had evolved in different regions were not erased by political unification overnight.

Like unification in 1871, reunification nearly 120 years later should be understood as a waymarker on Germany's quest for unity rather than its happy ending. Former West German Chancellor Willy Brandt's prophecy that 'what belongs together will grow together' will take time and empathy to unfold. It is tempting to see 3 October 1990 as the restoration of Germany's status quo. But this interpretation equates 'West German' with 'normal'. Many assumed that it was just a question of time until former GDR citizens would shed the habits impressed on them by an alien socialist system and become fellow Germans once more.

Yet East Germans have not been asked to return to something they were once part of but to blend into a West German state that had evolved without them after the Second World War. While there are common cultural, linguistic and social roots, what had grown from them since 1949 had diverged significantly in East and West. It is telling that many East Germans tend not to use the word 'reunification', but instead speak of a *Wende* or *Wendezeit*, an era of transformation. While West German lives continued as before, for East Germans 3 October 1990 triggered a wave of change whose force, direction and pace were uncontrollable. It was sink or swim.

There has always been a quiet hope that lingering differences in lifestyles, expectations and attitudes would naturally fade as the first generation of East Germans born and raised after reunification play their part in society. And yet the old fault lines are not disintegrating. Take a map showing patterns of almost anything in Germany and more often than not the old East–West fault lines will appear: from voting, vaccines acceptance and obesity to language use, attitudes towards Russia and wine consumption. Like an afterimage that will not fade, the GDR's imprint on Germany refuses to dissipate.

In the grand scheme of things the four decades of German division during the Cold War may not seem a lot, but in 1990, they amounted to a third of the country's existence. In that time East Germans and West Germans found different ways to build back from the horrors of Nazism and genocide. Both their systems were direct responses to these catastrophes, born out of the same idea: 'never again' must such evil emanate from German soil. And for a long time both co-existed as different visions of how this was best achieved. Accepting this and trying to place the GDR into the context of Germany's tumultuous twentieth-century history is not the same as endorsing the brutality of the Berlin Wall or the oppressive apparatus of the Stasi. It does involve accepting that East and West Germans lived very different realities in the formative post-war decades, and that these are all part of the national story.

One of the biggest obstacles to German unity post-1990 has been the economic imbalance between East and West. When the GDR's nationalized economy was sold out and privatized, many West German observers felt that the resulting unemployment and economic deprivation could be overcome through targeted investment. A 'solidarity surcharge' of 5.5 per cent of the tax for higher incomes was introduced in 1991 to pay for the costs of reunification and upgrades in infrastructure in the former East. But better roads and phone lines were not much solace to those who lost their jobs. By 2005, one fifth of all East Germans were unemployed. High as they are, such figures still mask the true extent of professional upheaval. While temporary employment schemes were quickly rolled out, they asked a proud and well-skilled workforce to take on temporary labour such as cleaning, maintenance of public spaces or, worst of all, the disheartening task of dismantling factories so they could be sold.

In the post-1990 world, many GDR jobs simply no longer existed. Within the first twenty months of reunification alone, 4,000 companies were closed down and only a quarter of employees of state-run enterprises kept their jobs. Retraining programmes were rolled out to help. Some of them were undoubtedly useful, particularly where they introduced office workers to computer technology, an area where the GDR had lagged behind. But many East Germans were asked to relearn jobs they had been doing for decades. Many teachers, for instance, were sent back to university, even if they had been in the job for years.

To most East Germans, reunification was a time of immense economic upheaval; one that brought new chances alongside uncertainty. Many West Germans argued that it was to be expected that the transition would be economically painful in the short term – a natural consequence of the inferiority of socialism. East Germans who point to the economic insecurity they have been suffering since 1990 are still being rebuked for their 'moaning' and told to 'move on'. While it is possible to argue over the economic successes and failures of the reunification process itself, the drastic impact on East German lives and lifestyles is undeniable. Some gained and some lost out in this process, but every single East German was touched by it in some way.

The social policies of the GDR have also left deep marks that could not be eradicated by reunification in 1990. One of the greatest social challenges of reunification was that the role of women had developed in fundamentally different ways. In 1989, the GDR had the highest rate of female employment in the world with nearly all women in jobs. In the FRG only half of women worked, the majority in part-time employment.[2] It had become entirely normal for East German women to have a career and children with little compromise. Childcare from birth had been readily available and practically free. Running from 6 a.m. to 6 p.m., it was designed to cover regular working hours, allowing both parents to work full time. While the West German system had come a long way since the 1950s, childcare was still considered a personal choice requiring private funding and involvement from parents as well as often only being available for parts of a working day. In the first two years after the fall of the Berlin Wall, half of all available places for children under three years old were scrapped in East Germany in an attempt to scale down the extremely expensive socialist welfare state. The downward trend continued until 2007 when the offering reached its nadir and there were only places for 40 per cent of this age group. Many East German mothers suddenly found it difficult to square motherhood and career opportunities, and they were baffled when they had to justify why they even wanted both. Many felt that they were judged to be bad mothers if they tried to make this work. As East German women tended to have their first child at the average age of twenty-three, six years earlier than Western mothers, there were other demographic side effects of GDR policies. The last generation of children who were born before 1990 grew up with much younger parents compared to their peers in the West. In this and many other ways, the GDR's social policies had left a legacy that far outlasted its own existence.

The shift to a multi-party democracy has also been challenging for some East Germans. At the general election in 2021, over a quarter of them didn't vote at all while nearly 16 per cent voted for the far-right party Alternative für Deutschland and 7 per cent for the far-left Die Linke. Taken together, this suggests that almost half of East Germans seem to have turned their backs on mainstream parties. Such disaffection with centrist politics is often met with derision rather than dialogue. In 2021, the Federal Commissioner for the Affairs of the Eastern States, Marco Wanderwitz, claimed that some East Germans had 'still not arrived in our democracy even after 30 years'.[3] Coming from the man tasked to improve the situation in the former GDR regions, such words reveal an astonishing degree of defeatism. Instead of inviting dialogue to find out why some East

Germans feel the political system isn't working for them, it is assumed that the existing political system and parties on offer are beyond criticism or reform and that some East Germans just fail to understand it. Yet the first free election in 1990 suggests otherwise. It drew nearly all GDR citizens into the polling stations and the vast majority voted for mainstream democratic parties. East Germans had once chosen parliamentary democracy over dictatorship. The disillusionment of many of them today is not an indication that they are lost to democracy but rather that they feel the current system doesn't work for them.

Another aspect of the unification process that worries many West Germans is East Germans' refusal to forget the GDR. 'The country my mother left behind was a country she believed in; a country we kept alive till her last breath; a country that never existed in that form,' mused the protagonist Alex Kerner at the end of the 2003 film *Good Bye Lenin!* The tragicomedy cleverly unpacks the difficulties faced by many East Germans in coming to terms with the disappearance of the country they were born in. Alex's mother Christiane genuinely believes in the state and its ideology when she falls into a coma in October 1989, shortly before the fall of the Berlin Wall. When she wakes up eight months later, her doctors warn that she is still very weak, and emotional upheaval might cause a fatal heart attack. Alex decides to try to shelter her from the changes unravelling outside her bedroom by pretending the GDR is still as it had been. While the fictional premise of the film is exaggerated, there were indeed many East Germans who genuinely believed in the GDR's socialist ideology and found it hard to accept that the entire system had ceased to exist on 3 October 1990. But Western fears of widespread *Ostalgie*, as nostalgia for East Germany has been dubbed, are unfounded. While electoral support for the SED's successor parties has always been higher in the eastern states, it tends to remain a minority choice. Bodo Ramelow, the Minister President of Thuringia, remains the only member of Die Linke elected into a major political office so far. There is little evidence that the majority of East Germans long for a return to GDR socialism.

As a catch-all term, *Ostalgie* is also often used to describe fond memories East Germans might have of their lives before 1990. There are indeed many indications that former GDR citizens enjoy reminiscing about the past. Restored Trabants are surging in popularity and can fetch up to €10,000. Some GDR brands have been revived and find customers mainly among those who knew the original. Vita Cola, a result of the second five-year plan in the late 1950s that sought to emulate Western consumer products, was relaunched in 1994 and is now the best-selling German cola brand. Many East Germans will insist on dusting off their old Frank Schöbel LPs for Christmas each year. His *Weihnachten in Familie* album first came out in 1985 and was relaunched in CD format in 1994. Such lingering fondness for East German products and memories is troubling to many West Germans who see it as rose-tinted nostalgia glorifying a dictatorial regime. Yet unlike Christiane in *Good Bye Lenin!*, most East Germans are well aware that the GDR has gone for good and have no desire to bring it back. To them, the sounds, sights, tastes and smells of life in the GDR bring back personal memories. The sickly taste of the bright-green peppermint liqueur consumed in secret behind the sports hall during a school disco. The sharp smell of Wofasept, a ubiquitous disinfectant used in public buildings across the GDR. Or the distinctive sound of the Trabant's two-stroke engine that accompanied summer journeys to the Baltic Sea. For the most part *Ostalgie* is no more than harmless indulgence in fond memories. When Angela Merkel asked the *Bundeswehr* to play Nina Hagen's 'Du hast den Farbfilm vergessen' for her retirement ceremony in 2021, it was hardly out of a desire to bring back the GDR. The tears in her eyes were tears of emotion as she remembered her life before and after the Berlin Wall.

There is an opportunity in the fact that the first generation of East and West Germans born after the fall of the Berlin Wall is beginning to grow into these patterns as well as shape new ones. They might be able to chip away at Germany's obsession with *Vergangenheitsbewältigung*, the process of 'overcoming' its own history. This concept has too often prevented the country from accepting continuities where it only wants to see clean breaks. It has made it tempting to see 1990 as a watershed moment that erased the GDR from the national narrative for good. Yet reunification is no more the end of history than the unification was in 1871. German unity cannot be 'achieved' in a single event. Rather the East German approach of the *Wende* as the beginning of a dynamic process seems more constructive. It allows a fluid, open and changeable interpretation of a country that no longer exists, that is no longer an enemy to be overcome. It is time to take the German Democratic Republic for what it is – a part of German history, beyond the Wall.

Notes

Preface

1. Merkel, Speech on German Unity Day, 3 October 2021.   **2.** Quoted in Bollmann, p. 95.   **3.** Ibid., p. 96.   **4.** Merkel, Speech on German Unity Day, 3 October 2021.   **5.** Ibid.   **6.** Ibid.   **7.** https://www.bpb.de/themen/deutsche-einheit/lange-wege-der-deutschen-einheit/501149/buerger-zweiter-klasse/   **8.** Merkel, Speech on German Unity Day, 3 October 2021.

Chapter 1: Trapped between Hitler and Stalin (1918–1945)

1. Account from interviews Jöris gave to the Swiss historian Andreas Petersen. In: *Die Moskauer*, p. 40.   **2.** Interview with the author.   **3.** 'Was sahen 58 Deutsche Arbeiter in Rußland?'   **4.** Leonhard, *Die Revolution*, p. 20.   **5.** Mussijenko and Vatlin, S. 472–5.   **6.** Operativer Befehl No. 00439 des Volkskommissars für innere Angelegenheiten der Union der Sozialistischen Sowjet-Republiken.   **7.** Hitler, *Mein Kampf*, p. 751.   **8.** Birt, p. 611.   **9.** Ibid., p. 613.   **10.** Schlögel, p. 637.   **11.** Petersen, pp. 13–15.   **12.** Factual information from Weber.   **13.** Gerbilskya's memories of her husband, quoted in Pastor, p. 37.   **14.** Müller, *Menschenfalle Moskau*, p. 13.   **15.** Quoted in Georgi Dimitrov diaries in Dimitroff, p. 149.   **16.** Quoted in Petersen, p. 82.   **17.** Kerneck.   **18.** Leonhard. *Die Revolution*, p. 37f.   **19.** Ibid., p. 57.   **20.** Ibid.   **21.** Kerneck.   **22.** Damerius, p. 72.   **23.** Hager, p. 79.   **24.** Vorschlag Walter Ulbrichts, Doc. 3.   **25.** Quoted in Knopp, p. 27.   **26.** See Frank, p. 142.   **27.** Ibid., p. 143.   **28.** Quoted in Knopp, p. 31.   **29.** See Frank, p. 160.   **30.** Quoted in Knopp, p. 32.   **31.** Quoted in Decker, p. 31.   **32.** Entry 'Fritz Erpenbeck' in Müller-Enbergs, *Wer war wer in der DDR?*   **33.** Interview with the author, July 2021.   **34.** Laufer, p. 151.   **35.** Ibid.   **36.** Initially, there had been a third man, Wilhelm Florin, but he died in July 1944 of natural causes.   **37.** LeMO: Biografie Ackermann.   **38.** Quoted in Petersen, p. 153.

Chapter 2: Risen from Ruins (1945–1949)

1. Dorothea Günther. Zeitzeugen Eintrag. **2.** Halder, p. 335. **3.** Anonymous, p. 84. **4.** Interview with the author. **5.** Ibid. **6.** Ibid. **7.** Ibid. **8.** Ibid. **9.** Kardorff, p. 266. **10.** Namensliste der KPD Einsatzgruppe. **11.** Leonhard, *Die Revolution*, p. 404. **12.** Morré, *Hinter den Kulissen*, p. 166. **13.** Frank, p. 185. **14.** Michelmann, p. 110. **15.** Frank, p. 185. **16.** Loth, p. 62. **17.** Leonhard, *Die Revolution*, p. 440. **18.** Otto Müllereisert's notes. **19.** Jähner, p. 31. **20.** Erika Reinicke's recollections. **21.** Interview with the author. **22.** Leonhard, *Die Revolution*, p. 429. **23.** Ibid., p. 438. **24.** Ibid., p. 439. **25.** Herrnstadt, p. 7. **26.** This line originally stemmed from Stalin's Order No. 55 given on 23 February 1942. **27.** Quoted in Knopp, p. 35. **28.** Bericht des Nationalkomitees Freies Deutschland in Greifswald, 3.5.1945. **29.** Quoted in Knopp, p. 35. **30.** Morré, 'Sowjetische Speziallager', p. 610. **31.** Bahr and Ensikat, p. 20. **32.** Helmut Breuninger's notes. **33.** Gröttrup, p. 159. **34.** Quoted in Müller-Güldemeister. **35.** Ibid. **36.** Anonymous, p. 99f. **37.** Quoted in Mählert, p. 37. **38.** Ibid., p. 34 **39.** Ibid., p. 38. **40.** Interview with the author. **41.** Both quotes from the minutes taken at Stalin's meeting with Ulbricht, Pieck and Grotewohl on 18 December 1948. **42.** Suckut, p. 161.

Chapter 3: Birth Pangs (1949–1952)

1. Pieck, p. 303. **2.** Quoted in Knopp, p. 39. **3.** Quoted in Judt, *DDR-Geschichte in Dokumenten*, p. 77. **4.** Frank, p. 217. **5.** Quoted in Frank, p. 216 **6.** Quoted in Knopp, p. 41. **7.** Pieck, 'Die gegenwärtige Lage'. **8.** Schroeder, p. 51. **9.** Ulbricht, Schreiben, 1 December 1950. **10.** A phrase used by historian Wilfried Loth and others who argue that Stalin never wanted the GDR to be a Soviet satellite state. **11.** Entry 'Leo Bauer' in Müller-Enbergs, *Wer war wer in der DDR?* **12.** Mählert, p. 57. **13.** Fulbrook, *The Divided Nation*, p. 190. **14.** Leonhard, *Meine Geschichte*, p. 132. **15.** Quoted in Lorenzen, p. 62. **16.** Ibid., p. 63. **17.** Modrow, p. 56. **18.** Lorenzen, p. 61. **19.** Honecker, p. 38. **20.** Quoted in Mählert, p. 59. **21.** Ibid. **22.** Müller, *Die DDR war immer dabei*, p. 38. **23.** Erler, 'Vom MGB zum MfS/SfS', p. 42. **24.** Recording of Rosenberg's interrogation by the Stasi. **25.** Quoted in Rasch and Dedio, p. 71. **26.** Kurt Müller's letter to Otto Grotewohl. **27.** Handwritten biography by Erich Mielke, 15 March 1951. **28.** Quoted in Rasch and Dedio, p. 64. **29.** Fulbrook, *Anatomy*, p. 26. **30.** Reflections by Carl Klußmann's grandson Uwe Klußmann. In: Iken, p. 223ff. **31.** Interview with the author. **32.** Ernst Wicht's recollections. **33.** Ibid.

34. Judt, *DDR-Geschichte in Dokumenten*, p. 116.   35. Schroeder, p. 28.   36. Ibid., p. 29.   37. Information for the politburo, July 1959.   38. Anneliese Fleischer's recollections in *Aktion Ungeziefer*.   39. A former East German policeman interviewed for *Aktion Ungeziefer* put on record that he still believed it 'targeted the right people'.   40. Loth, pp. 175–84.   41. Soviet Draft of a German Peace Treaty – First 'Stalin Note' (10 March 1952).   42. Ibid.   43. Quoted in Loth, p. 180.   44. Soviet Draft of a German Peace Treaty – First 'Stalin Note' (10 March 1952).   45. Loth, p.180.   46. ZK [CentralCommittee] Meeting, 26/27 October 1950.   47. Schroeder, p. 50.   48. Khrushchev, p. 100f.   49. Mählert, p. 62f.   50. Schroeder, p. 50f.

Chapter 4: Building Socialism (1953–1961)

1. Heinz Just's recollections.   2. Interview with the author.   3. Hertle, 'Der Weg in die Krise'.   4. Ulbricht's speech at the SED conference in July 1950.   5. Mählert, p. 65.   6. Knopp, p. 48.   7. Hubert Marusch's recollections.   8. Ibid.   9. See also Frank, p. 244.   10. Ibid., p. 247.   11. Ibid., p. 242.   12. Gerlinde Böhnisch-Metzmacher's and Christa Schleevoigt's testimonies.   13. Werkentin, p. 56.   14. Mählert, p. 68.   15. Gerhard Rudat's private CV, 5 January 1983.   16. Georgy Malenkov's words on 2 June 1953, quoted in Wettig, p. 168.   17. Knopp, p .52.   18. Ibid., p. 53.   19. Mählert, p. 63.   20. Karl-Eduard von Schnitzler's commentary on 17 June 1953.   21. Figures from Schroeder, p. 64.   22. Interview with the author.   23. Fulbrook, *Anatomy*, p. 186.   24. Frank, p. 278.   25. Loest, p. 213f.   26. Mählert, p. 79.   27. Frank, p. 249f.   28. Knopp, p. 60.   29. Loest, p. 214.   30. Interview with the author.   31. Quoted in Müller-Enbergs, *Der Fall*, p. 244.   32. Frank, p. 250.   33. Andrei Gromyko, later Soviet Foreign Minister, remembered Beria saying this and repeated the claim on several occasions.   34. Interview with the author.   35. Ostermann, p. 61.   36. Koop, p. 94.   37. Schroeder, p. 67.   38. Interview with the author.   39. Müller-Enbergs. In: Judt, *DDR-Geschichte in Dokumenten*, p. 433.   40. *Neue Berliner Illustrierte*, Nr. 10/1956, S. 3.   41. Frank, p. 250.   42. Ibid., p. 257.   43. Mählert, p. 85.   44. Schroeder, p. 73.   45. Interview with the author.   46. Schroeder, p. 76.   47. From 311 marks a month in 1950 to 555 marks in 1960. See table showing income of the GDR population 1950–1988. In Segert and Zierke, p. 191.   48. Christine Nagel's recollections.   49. Table showing female employment rates in Segert and Zierke, p. 214.   50. Ickler, p. 245.   51. Interview with Weber-Koch.   52. Hagen Koch's recollections.   53. *Der Spiegel*, 22 July 1953.   54. Ten Commandments for the New Socialist Person.   55. Mählert, p. 91f.   56. Roesler, p. 23.   57. See also Frank, p. 293ff.   58. Stuhler, p. 87f.   59. Ibid.

Chapter 5: Brick by Brick (1961–1965)

1. Kitchen, p. 340. 2. Gerda Langosch. Zeitzeugen Eintrag. 3. Honecker, p. 205. 4. Quoted in Koop, p. 94. 5. Ibid., p. 96. 6. Extracts from 'Mission Statement' of the Secretariat of the FDJ Central Council of 13 August 1961. 7. Mählert and Stephan, p. 139. 8. Kitchen, p. 341. 9. Willy Brandt's speech, 16 August 1963. 10. PdVP-Rapport No. 234, 23/8/1961. 11. *Neues Deutschland*, 1 September 1961, p. 8. 12. See also MacGregor, p. 76f. 13. Bainbridge. 14. Based on Jutta Kuhfeld's account. 15. See 'Urlauberschiff in Not'. 16. Margit Jatzlau's recollections. 17. Rolf Bayer's account. 18. Hinz-Wessels. 19. Schroeder, p. 88. 20. Siegfried Umbreit's recollections. 21. MDR, 'Puppen und Teddys'. 22. Figures: ibid. 23. Quoted in Stuhler, p. 99. 24. Modrow, p. 90f. 25. Quoted in Frank, p. 352. 26. *Süddeutsche Zeitung*, 17 July 1963. 27. 'Carl Zeiss Jena blockt EDV-Entwicklung ab. 19. Januar 1962.' 28. Roesler, p. 27. 29. Herrmann, p. 45. 30. Ibid, p. 43. 31. Interview with the author. 32. Ausstattung der Haushalte, p. 291. 33. Figure 2: Household car ownership (Great Britain), p. 4. 34. The term used by the Soviets and other socialist states for astronauts. 35. See, for example, press coverage of Yuri Gagarin and Valentina Tereshkova visiting the GDR on 19 October 1963. 36. Interview with her son by the author. 37. Figures from Fulbrook, *The People's State*, p. 128. 38. Stuhler, p. 100. 39. Ibid., p. 103. 40. Ibid. 41. Ibid. 42. *Neues Deutschland*, 21 September 1963, p. 3. 43. Ibid., p. 2. 44. Ibid., p. 3. 45. Wolle, *Aufbruch*, p. 198. 46. Ibid., p. 199. 47. Beschluss des Politbüros des ZK der SED über 'Probleme, die sich aus der Einschätzung des Deutschlandtreffens ergeben'. 48. Wolle, *Aufbruch*, p. 219. 49. Fulbrook, *The People's State*, p. 151. 50. *Neues Deutschland*, 23 December 1961, p. 1. 51. Ibid. 52. Quoted in Wolle, *Aufbruch*, p. 220. 53. Ibid., p. 221. 54. Ibid., p. 222.

Chapter 6: The Other Germany (1965–1971)

1. Ulbricht's interpreter, Werner Eberlein, who was also known as 'Khrushchev's German Voice' as he frequently dubbed the Soviet leader on television, expertly transferring the emotional sing-song Russian into German, retold this episode many years later with the benefit of hindsight (Eberlein's account in Lorenzen, p. 98). 2. Quoted in Stuhler, p. 105. 3. Fulbrook, *The People's State*, p. 131. 4. According to his waiter Lothar Herzog. See Herzog, p. 28. 5. Quoted in Lorenzen, p. 53. 6. Quoted in Stuhler, p. 76. 7. Mählert, p. 106. 8. Fulbrook, *The People's State*, p. 131. 9. Quoted in Aehnlich. 10. Fulbrook, *The People's State*,

p. 131. **11.** Quoted in Aehnlich. **12.** Quoted in Schroeder, p. 107. **13.** See also Wilke, 'Die SED und der Prager Frühling 1968'. **14.** Quoted in Rasch and Dedio, p. 110. **15.** Gieseke, p. 76. **16.** Ibid., p. 77. **17.** From Hermann Matern's contribution at the 2nd Conference of the District Delegation of the Ministry for State Security, December 1962. **18.** Quoted in Gieselke, p. 81. **19.** Figures from Rasch and Dedio, p. 105. **20.** Quoted in ibid., p. 111. **21.** Ibid., p. 112. **22.** Quoted in ibid., p. 119. **23.** Interview with the author. **24.** Walther, p. 229. **25.** Mählert, p. 110. **26.** Fulbrook, *The People's State*, p. 216. **27.** Lenhardt and Stock, p. 115. **28.** Soziologischer Almanach; Sozialerhebungen des Deutschen Studentenwerks. **29.** Figures on consumer items from Wolle, *Aufbruch*, p. 183ff. **30.** See also ibid., p. 187. **31.** Mählert, p. 11. **32.** Ulbricht, *Eine unvergeßliche Reise*, pp. 5–6. **33.** Ibid., p. 33. **34.** *Neues Deutschland*, 25 February 1965, p. 1. **35.** See also Frank, p. 375ff. **36.** Ulbricht, *Eine unvergeßliche Reise*, p. 6. **37.** Honecker, p. 226. **38.** *Neues Deutschland*, 9 November 1968, p. 2. **39.** UNICEF Study. **40.** Quoted in protocol published in Przybylski. **41.** Quoted in Frank, p. 386. **42.** Ibid. **43.** Ibid. **44.** Orlow, p. 546. **45.** Ibid. **46.** Eberlein, p. 355. **47.** Ibid.

Chapter 7: *Planned Miracles (1971–1975)*

1. Bassistov, p. 222. **2.** Modrow, p. 125. **3.** Quoted in protocol published in Przybylski. **4.** Interview with the author. **5.** *Neues Deutschland*, 4 May 1971, p. 1. **6.** Modrow, p. 125. **7.** Ulbricht, *Mein Leben*, p. 25. **8.** Ibid., p. 14. **9.** Ibid., p. 15. **10.** Ibid., p. 25. **11.** Quoted in Frank, p. 431. **12.** Ibid., p. 432. **13.** Ibid., p. 433. **14.** Quoted in Schroeder, p. 101. **15.** Herzog, p. 103ff. **16.** Quoted in Kuppe, p. 448. **17.** Mählert, p. 121. **18.** Roesler, p. 35. **19.** Interview with the author. **20.** Quoted in Wolle, *Die heile Welt*, p. 44. **21.** See, for example, the letter sent by the Academy of Sciences to its employees. In Menzel, p. 161. **22.** Angela Merkel quoted in Bollmann, p. 49. **23.** Uwe Schmieder's account. **24.** Manfred Rexin's account. **25.** Interview with the author. **26.** Ibid. **27.** Ina Merkel's account. **28.** Interview with the author. **29.** Frank, p. 446. **30.** *Freie Welt*, 25/1974, p. 8. **31.** Laszewski, p. 122. **32.** Interview with Wiebke Reed in *Superillu*, 22 August 2007. **33.** Ernsting, p. 130. **34.** *Volksstimme*, 17 August 1972. **35.** Interview with the author. **36.** Hampel. **37.** Ibid. **38.** Francke. **39.** Quoted in Gieseke, p. 220. **40.** Gieseke, p. 221. **41.** Quoted in Mitteregger, p. 36. **42.** Protocol of 45th session of the National Defence Council of the GDR on 3rd May 1974. **43.** Schalck-Golodkowski, p. 207f. **44.** Ibid., p. 208. **45.** Judt, 'Häftlinge für Bananen', p. 417. **46.** Ibid., p. 426. **47.** Ibid., p. 439. **48.** Wolle, *Die heile Welt*, p. 195. **49.** Ibid., p. 197. **50.** Quoted in Knopp, p. 221. **51.** Ibid.

Chapter 8: Friends and Enemies (1976–1981)

1. Funeral of Pastor Oskar Brüsewitz in Rippicha (Zeitz). **2.** Report about the self-immolation of Pastor Oskar Brüsewitz in Zeitz. **3.** Oskar Brüsewitz's letter to the Sisters and Brothers of the Church Community of Zeitz. **4.** Message to the Parish, 21 August 1976. **5.** Funeral of Pastor Oskar Brüsewitz in Rippicha (Zeitz). **6.** *Neues Deutschland*, 21 August 1976, p. 2. **7.** Ibid., 31 August 1976, p. 2. **8.** Reactions to the self-immolation of Pastor Oskar Brüsewitz on 18 August 1976 in Zeitz. **9.** Ibid. **10.** Bollmann, p. 5. **11.** Ibid., p. 52. **12.** Report about Wolf Biermann's Performance in St Nicholas Church in Prenzlau on 11 September 1976. **13.** Biermann. In: *Der Spiegel*, 19 September 1976. **14.** Axel Wladimiroff's recollections. **15.** Quoted in Wolle, *Die heile Welt*, p. 200. **16.** Ibid. **17.** Axel Wladimiroff's recollections. **18.** Herzog, p. 121. **19.** Ibid. **20.** Interview 1 with Siegfried Kaulfuß. **21.** Interview 2 with Siegfried Kaulfuß. **22.** MDR, 'Kaffee gegen Waffen'. **23.** Jorge Norguera's recollections. **24.** Ibid. **25.** For more on workers from Mozambique in the GDR see Van der Heyden et al. **26.** Interview and notes shared with the author. **27.** Ulrich Steinhauer's Stasi file. **28.** Quoted in Ahrends. **29.** Ibid. **30.** Interview and notes shared with the author. **31.** Interview with the author. **32.** Ibid. **33.** Interview and notes shared with the author. **34.** Thoralf Johansson's recollections. **35.** *Neues Deutschland*, 19 February 1978. **36.** Quoted in Wolle, *Die heile Welt*, p. 258. **37.** Ibid. **38.** Ibid. **39.** Sourcing of new military recruits. **40.** Figures from Bald, p. 11. **41.** Figures from Gebauer et al., pp. 300, 301. **42.** Erika Krüger's account. **43.** Figures from Wolle, *Die heile Welt*, p. 76. **44.** Quoted in Rasch and Dedio, p. 142. **45.** Erich Mielke's presentation at the central conference on 3 April 1981.

Chapter 9: Existential Carefreeness (1981–1986)

1. Honecker, pp. 363–4. **2.** Eberlein, p. 388. **3.** Figures from Friedrich-Ebert-Stiftung, 'Die Energiepolitik der DDR', p. 10. **4.** Ibid., p. 26. **5.** Hertle, *Der Fall der Mauer*, p. 60. **6.** Transcript of the meeting between Comrade L. I. Brezhnev and Comrade E. Honecker at Crimea on 3 August 1981. **7.** Quoted in Lorenzen, p. 149. **8.** Quoted in Mählert, p. 136. **9.** Ibid., p. 137. **10.** Klaus Deubel's recollections. **11.** Stoph, p. 11. **12.** Mittag, loc. 2449. **13.** Ibid. **14.** Nendel, loc. 721. **15.** Ibid. **16.** Roloff in Nendel, loc. 721. **17.** Schöne, p. 181. **18.** Werner Krolikowski's note about the domestic situation in the GDR of 30 March 1983. **19.** Ibid. **20.** Interview with the author. **21.** Brückner, p. 47.

22. Schalck-Golodkowski, p. 289.   **23.** Ibid., p. 284.   **24.** Ibid., p. 285.   **25.** Ibid., p. 289.   **26.** See *Der Spiegel*'s sympathetic report 'Schlicht verschlafen' from 24 April 1983.   **27.** Schalck-Golodkowski, p. 292.   **28.** Ibid., p. 294.   **29.** Ibid.   **30.** Ibid., p. 295.   **31.** Roesler, p. 54.   **32.** Quoted in original footage in Schönfelder.   **33.** Markham, *New York Times*.   **34.** Wolle, *Die heile Welt*, p. 134.   **35.** Engelberg, loc. 1263.   **36.** Quoted in *Washington Post*, 12 March 1985.   **37.** Quoted in *Neues Deutschland*, 13 March 1985.   **38.** Transcript of a phone conversation between Erich Honecker and Helmut Kohl, 19 December 1983.   **39.** Ibid.   **40.** Ibid.   **41.** Ibid.   **42.** Transcript of a meeting between Honecker and Chernenko in Moscow, 17 August 1984.   **43.** Ibid., p. 46f.   **44.** Ibid., p. 47.   **45.** Ibid., p. 69.   **46.** Ibid., p. 72.   **47.** Lorenzen, p. 173.   **48.** Krenz, *Herbst '89*, p. 117.   **49.** Thatcher, p. 461.   **50.** Schabowski, p. 214.   **51.** Kotschemassow, p. 137.   **52.** Both quoted in Wilke, 'Der Honecker-Besuch'.   **53.** Interview with the author.   **54.** Judt, *DDR-Geschichte in Dokumenten*, p. 158.   **55.** Figures from DDR Museum Berlin.   **56.** Ibid.   **57.** See Bollmann, p. 80.   **58.** Ibid., p. 81.   **59.** Quoted in Bollmann, p. 84.   **60.** See Bollmann, pp. 77–84.   **61.** Quoted in Bollmann, p. 94.   **62.** Ibid., p. 96.   **63.** Ibid., p. 97.   **64.** Figures from Würz.   **65.** Quoted in Stuhler, p. 169.   **66.** File provided to the author.

Chapter 10: Everything Takes its Socialist Course (1987–1990)

1. Peter Claussen's recollections in Zeitzeugenportal.   **2.** Interview with Peter Claussen in The Local, 6 November 2009.   **3.** Peter Claussen's recollections in Zeitzeugenportal.   **4.** Ibid.   **5.** Walter, Spiegel Online, 26 August 2007.   **6.** *Neues Deutschland*, 28 August 1987, p. 3.   **7.** Ibid.   **8.** Ibid.   **9.** Krenz, *Wir und die Russen*, p. 68.   **10.** Stasi Report. Reaktion der Bevölkerung auf das SED-SPD-Grundsatzpapier.   **11.** Krenz, *Wir und die Russen*, pp. 67–8.   **12.** Ibid.   **13.** Ibid.   **14.** Ibid.   **15.** *Neues Deutschland*, 10 April 1987, p. 3.   **16.** Speech was printed in *Neues Deutschland*, 28 October 1987.   **17.** Quoted in Lorenzen, p. 182.   **18.** Katarina Witt's account of Calgary 1988.   **19.** Ibid.   **20.** Interview with the author.   **21.** Ibid.   **22.** Quoted in Mählert, p. 152.   **23.** Ibid.   **24.** Ibid.   **25.** Stasi Report. Information an die SED-Führung über eine Petition für mehr Menschenrechte.   **26.** Ibid.   **27.** Quoted in Wolle, *Die heile Welt*, p. 297.   **28.** Ibid., p. 302.   **29.** Bundesregierung, Archiv.   **30.** Stasi Report. Reaktion der Bevölkerung auf Vorbereitung der Kommunalwahl   Bericht O/216.   **31.** Ibid.   **32.** Interview with the author.   **33.** Ibid.   **34.** Stasi Report. Gegen die Kommunalwahlen (7. Mai) gerichtete, feindliche Aktivitäten.   **35.** Ibid.   **36.** Ibid.   **37.** Quoted in Wolle, *Die heile Welt*, p. 307.   **38.** Schneider, p. 7.   **39.** Ibid.   **40.** Quoted in Schroeder, p. 135.   **41.** Address given by Mikhail

Notes

Gorbachev to the Council of Europe (6 July 1989). **42.** Dokument 'Aufbruch 89 – Neues Forum'. **43.** Schöne, p. 219. **44.** Both quoted in Schroeder, p. 136. **45.** Lorenzen, p. 209. **46.** Mählert, p. 165. **47.** Wolle, *Die heile Welt*, p. 326. **48.** Andreas Falge's account. **49.** Ibid. **50.** Ibid. **51.** Schneider, p. 7. **52.** Names changed for her and her family members. Interview with the author. **53.** Interview with the author. **54.** Erich Mielke's speech in the *Volkskammer*, 13 November 1989. **55.** Ibid. **56.** Ibid. **57.** Modrow, p. 327. **58.** Interview with the author. **59.** Ulrike Poppe's recollections on 'Achievements and Problems of the Round Table'. **60.** Aktion Aufruf. 'Für unser Land'. **61.** Interview with the author. **62.** Quoted in Mählert, p. 179f.

Epilogue: Unity

1. Reichstag protocol of its first session on 21 March 1871. **2.** Wippermann, p. 10. **3.** Quoted in Steppat.

Bibliography

All quotes from sources originally in the German language were translated by the author.

Individual documents

Address given by Mikhail Gorbachev to the Council of Europe (6 July 1989). In: Council of Europe – Parliamentary Assembly. Official Report. Forty-first ordinary session. 8–12 May and 3–7 July. Volume I. Sittings 1 to 9. 1990. Strasbourg: Council of Europe. 'Speech by Mikhail Gorbachev', pp. 197–205.

Aktion Aufruf. 'Für unser Land'. BArch, TonY 16/123.

Andreas Falge's account. 'How the Fall of the Berlin Wall on 9 November 1989 felt'. In: https://www.berlin.de/tourismus/insidertipps/5055005-2339440-wie-sich-der-mauerfall-am-9-november-198.html (last accessed 30 July 2022)

Ausstattung der Haushalte mit langlebigen technischen Konsumgütern. In: *Statistisches Jahrbuch der Deutschen Demokratischen Republik*. Zeitschriftenband (1990), pp. 291–6.

Axel Wladimiroff's recollections on 'The Coffee Crisis'. In: Stiftung Haus der Geschichte der Bundesrepublik Deutschland. Zeitzeugenportal. 2012. https://www.zeitzeugen-portal.de/themen/wirtschaft-mangel-und-ueberfluss/videos/SEhWQ4EXpOQ (last accessed 9 February 2022)

Bassistov, Yuri. 'Die DDR – ein Blick aus Wünsdorf'. In: Biographische Skizzen/Zeitzeugenberichte, *Jahrbuch für Historische Kommunismusforschung*, 1994, pp. 214–24.

Bericht des Nationalkomitees Freies Deutschland in Greifswald, 3.5.1945. Museum der Hansestadt Greifswald.

Beschluss des Politbüros des ZK der SED über 'Probleme, die sich aus der Einschätzung des Deutschlandtreffens ergeben'. In: SAPMO-BArch, DY 24/6030.

Biermann, Wolf. 'Es gibt ein Leben vor dem Tod'. *Der Spiegel*, 19 September 1976.

'Carl Zeiss Jena blockt EDV-Entwicklung ab. 19. Januar 1962.' Extract in: Judt, *DDR-Geschichte in Dokumenten*.

Christine Nagel's recollections on 'Happiness in 36 Square Metres'. In: Stiftung

Haus der Geschichte der Bundesrepublik Deutschland. Zeitzeugenportal. 2013. https://www.zeitzeugen-portal.de/zeitraeume/epochen/1949-1961/die-aera-ulbricht/g6BqL2qeclI (last accessed 2 August 2021)

Dokument 'Aufbruch 89 – Neues Forum'. Stiftung Haus der Geschichte, EB-Nr. 1990/6/104, Foto: Axel Thünker. In: https://www.hdg.de/lemo/bestand/objekt/dokument-aufbruch-89.html (last accessed 2 July 2022)

Dorothea Günther. Zeitzeugen Eintrag: Das Kriegsende in Potsdam 1945, Berlin, June 2010. In: https://www.dhm.de/lemo/zeitzeugen/dorothea-g%C3%BCnther-das-kriegsende-in-potsdam-1945 (last accessed 6 June 2021)

Erich Mielke's presentation at the central conference on 3 April 1981 about problems and tasks in relation to the further qualification and perfection of the political-operative work and its leadership regarding the solution to the question 'Who is who?'. BStU, MfS, BdL/Dok. 7385, BL. 7.

Erich Mielke's speech in the *Volkskammer*, 13 November 1989. Protokoll der 11. Tagung der Volkskammer der DDR. In: Chronik der Mauer. https://www.chronik-der-mauer.de/material/180401/rede-von-stasi-minister-erich-mielke-in-der-ddr-volkskammer-13-november-1989 (last accessed 11 November 2022)

Erika Krüger's account. 'Früher dachte ich: Gott sei Dank, du lebst bei Erich in der DDR'. In: *Republik der Werktätigen. Alltag in den Betrieben der DDR*, pp. 113–23. Bild und Heimat. 2020.

Erika Reinicke's recollections. In: Iken et al., p. 33.

Ernst Wicht's recollections on 'Peace Ore'. In: Hertle, *Damals in der DDR*, pp. 40–45.

Figure 2: Household car ownership (Great Britain). In: Leibling, David. *Car ownership in Great Britain*. Royal Automobile Club Foundation for Motoring. 2008.

Freie Welt, 25/1974, 3 June 1974.

Funeral of Pastor Oskar Brüsewitz in Rippicha (Zeitz). BStU, MfS, ZAIG 2617, Bl. 10–15.

Gerda Langosch. Zeitzeugen-Eintrag: Erinnerungen an den 13. August 1961, Berlin, 2000. In: https://www.hdg.de/lemo/zeitzeugen/gerda-langosch-erinnerungen-an-den-13-august-1961.html (last accessed 15 August 2021)

Gerhard Rudat's private CV, 5 January 1983. Document held by his family.

Gerlinde Böhnisch-Metzmacher's and Christa Schleevoigt's testimonies. In: Der 17. Juni 1953 in Jena. Skizzen eines Aufstandes. Projekt „Zeitzeugenwerkstatt" of the Geschichtswerkstatt Jena (2014).

Hagen Koch's recollections on 'Motivations to Join the Guards Regiment of the Stasi'. In: Stiftung Haus der Geschichte der Bundesrepublik Deutschland. Zeitzeugenportal. 2011. https://www.zeitzeugen-portal.de/zeitraeume/epochen/1949-1961/die-aera-ulbricht/B-A2C6DH9Ck (last accessed 2 August 2021)

Handwritten biography by Erich Mielke, 15 March 1951. In: Staatsanwaltschaft II Berlin, Az. 2/24 Js 245/90, Bd. 19, Bl. 45–54.

Heinz Just's recollections on 'Backbreaking Work at the Milling Machine'. In: Stiftung Haus der Geschichte der Bundesrepublik Deutschland. Zeitzeugenportal. 2013. https://www.zeitzeugen-portal.de/themen/wirtschaft-mangel-und-ueberfluss/videos/qHbEnYot2lY (last accessed 26 July 2021)

Helmut Breuninger's notes. Wie wir am 22.10.1946 nach der Sowjetunion kamen. Persönliche Aufzeichnung von Dr. Helmut Breuninger. In: http://www.karlist.net/spez/Wie-wir-in-die-UdSSR-kamen-1946.pdf (last accessed 30 October 2022)

Hermann Matern's contribution at the 2nd Conference of the District Delegation of the Ministry for State Security, December 1962. In: Bundesarchiv, SAPMO, DY 30 A 2/12/128, p.17f.

Hubert Marusch's recollections on the 'Fateful Year of 1953'. In: University of Leipzig. AG Zeitzeugen. 2014. https://research.uni-leipzig.de/fernstud/Zeitzeugen/zz1060.htm (last accessed 26 July 2021)

Ina Merkel's account of the 10th World Youth Festival. In: https://www.bpb.de/mediathek/380/hinterher-war-alles-beim-alten#:~:text=Die%20Kulturwissen-schaftlerin%20Ina%20Merkel%20ist%C3%BCrzte,eher%20tristen%20real%2Dsozialistischen%20Alltag (last accessed 8 January 2022)

Information for the politburo, July 1959. In: SAPMO-BArch, DY 30/IV 2/2029 (Büro Apel)/34, o. Bl.

Interview 1 with Siegfried Kaulfuß. In: *Die DDR-Kaffee-Offensive – Bückware ade*, an MDR Production first broadcast on 20 October 2015.

Interview 2 with Siegfried Kaulfuß. In: Kaffeebohnen mit Geschichte. https://www.daklakcoffee.de/ (last accessed 12 Feburary 2022)

Interview with Peter Claussen by Kristen Allen. The Local, 6 November 2009. In: https://www.thelocal.de/20091106/23073/ (last accessed13 June 2022)

Interview with Weber-Koch. Stasi-Unterlagen-Archiv. Kreisdienststelle Zerbst. Hagen Koch. 27 January 1960.

Jorge Norguera's recollections on 'Cubans in the GDR'. 2021. In: https://www.youtube.com/watch?v=E6Zv5USAMU8 (last accessed 20 Februrary 2022)

Jutta Kuhfeld's account. In: https://urlauberschiff-fritzheckert.de/geschichte/reisebericht.html (last accessed 18 August 2021)

Karl-Eduard von Schnitzler's commentary on 17 June 1953. In: Schroeder, p.169f.

Katarina Witt's account of Calgary 1988. In: https://www.katarina-witt.de/de/eiskunstlauf/olympiasiegerin-1988.html (last accessed 27 September 2022)

Klaus Deubel's recollections on 'Rationalising Away' and 'Inefficient Economic System'. In: Stiftung Haus der Geschichte der Bundesrepublik Deutschland. Zeitzeugenportal. 2014. https://www.zeitzeugen-portal.de/personen/zeitzeuge/klaus_deubel (last accessed 15 May 2022)

Kurt Müller's letter to Otto Grotewohl. 'Ein historisches Dokument aus dem

Jahre 1956. Brief an den DDR-Ministerpraesidenten Otto Grotewohl'. In: *Aus Politik und Zeitgeschichte*. 9 March1990.

Manfred Rexin's account of the 10th World Youth Festival. In: https://www.bpb. de/mediathek/383/das-erlebnis-einer-ddr-die-nicht-so-muffig-war (last accessed 7 January 2022)

Margit Jatzlau's recollections on 'Stuffed Trabant'. In: Stiftung Haus der Geschichte der Bundesrepublik Deutschland. Zeitzeugenportal. 2013. https://www. zeitzeugen-portal.de/videos/bKnL3NuOWVc (last accessed 18 August 2021)

Markham, James. 'East Germany finally embraces Luther'. *New York Times*. 8 May 1983.

Merkel, Angela. Speech on German Unity Day. Rede von Bundeskanzlerin Merkel anlässlich des Festakts zum Tag der Deutschen Einheit am 3. Oktober 2021 in Halle/Saale. In: https://www.bundesregierung.de/breg-de/suche/rede-von-bundeskanzlerin-merkel-anlaesslich-des-festakts-zum-tag-der-deutschen-einheit-am-3-oktober-2021-in-halle-saale-1964938 (last accessed 10 July 2022)

Message to the Parish, 21 August 1976, Church Leadership of the Protestant Church of the Church Province of Saxony. In: https://www.ekmd.de/asset/_nwdGs1YRnmDq66_q_WVRA/pm-bruesewitz-wort-an-gemeinden-1976-09-08-2006.pdf (last accessed 25 September 2022)

Minutes taken at Stalin's meeting with Ulbricht, Pieck and Grotewohl on 18 December 1948. In: Laufer, Jochen and Kynin, Georgij (Eds). *Die UdSSR und die deutsche Frage 1941–1949. Dokumente aus russischen Archiven, Band 4*. Duncker & Humblot. 2012, p. 209ff.

'Mission Statement' of the Secretariat of the FDJ Central Council of 13 August 1961. In: Bundesarchiv. SAPMO, DY 24/3753-I.

Namensliste der KPD Einsatzgruppe. BArch, NY 4036/517.

Neue Berliner Illustrierte, Nr. 10/1956.

Neues Deutschland, 10 April 1987, p. 3; reprinted in 'SED und KPD zu Gorbatschows "Revolution"' ['SED and DKP (German Communist Party) on Gorbachev's "Revolution"'], Deutschland Archiv 20, no. 6 (1987), pp. 655–7. Translation: Allison Brown.

Operativer Befehl No. 00439 des Volkskommissars für innere Angelegenheiten der Union der Sozialistischen Sowjet-Republiken. Transcribed from a photocopy from the FSB Archives in St Petersburg by the Krasnoyarsk 'MEMORIAL' Society. In https://memorial.krsk.ru/deu/Dokument/Dok/370725.htm (last accessed 29 May 2021)

Oskar Brüsewitz's letter to the Sisters and Brothers of the Church Community of Zeitz. BStU, MfS, BV Halle, AP, Nr. 2950/76, Bl. 61–3.

Otto Müllereisert's notes. In: Iken et al., p. 22.

PdVP-Rapport No. 234, 23/8/1961. In: PHS, PdVP-Rapporte, Archiv-No. 8037, Bl. 8.

Peter Claussen's recollections. In: Stiftung Haus der Geschichte der Bundesrepublik Deutschland. Zeitzeugenportal. 2015. https://www.zeitzeugen-portal.de/themen/kultur-kunst-und-propaganda/videos/qKRWdWIqYzw and https://www.zeitzeugen-portal.de/themen/kultur-kunst-und-propaganda/videos/Da8nplfBBkM (last accessed 13 June 2022)

Pieck, Wilhelm. 'Die gegenwärtige Lage und die Aufgabe der Sozialistischen Einheitspartei Deutschlands'. 24 July 1950. Extract in: Judt, p. 487.

Pieck, Wilhelm. 'An der Wende der deutschen Geschichte'. In: *Reden und Aufsätze*. Bd. II. 1954, p. 295–303.

Press coverage of Yuri Gagarin and Valentina Tereshkova visiting the GDR on 19 October 1963. In: https://www.mdr.de/zeitreise/video-204670_zc-9291bc85_zs-6c7954ac.html (last accessed 22 August 2021)

Protocol of 45th session of the National Defence Council of the GDR on 3 May 1974. In: BA, DVW 1/39503, Bl. 34.

Reactions to the self-immolation of Pastor Oskar Brüsewitz on 18 August 1976 in Zeitz. BStU, MfS, ZAIG, Nr. 2617, Bl. 17–28.

Recording of Rosenberg's interrogation by the Stasi. BStU, MfS, ZAIG, Tb 274.

Reichstag protocol of its first session on 21 March 1871. In: http://www.reichstagsprotokolle.de/Blatt3_k1_bsb00018324_00030.html (last accessed 31 July 2022)

Report about the self-immolation of Pastor Oskar Brüsewitz in Zeitz. BStU, MfS, BV Halle, AP, Nr. 2950/76, Bd. 3, Bl. 40–48.

Report about Wolf Biermann's Performance in St Nicholas Church in Prenzlau on 11 September 1976. BStU, MfS, AOP, Nr. 11806/85, Bd. 18, Bl. 121–4.

Rolf Bayer's account on 'Possibilities for GDR citizens to travel abroad'. Arbeitsgruppe Zeitzeugen der Seniorenakademie. University of Leipzig. In: https://research.uni-leipzig.de/fernstud/Zeitzeugen/zz177.htm (last accessed 18 August 2021)

Siegfried Umbreit's recollections on 'Testing Toys in the GDR'. In: Stiftung Haus der Geschichte der Bundesrepublik Deutschland. Zeitzeugenportal. 2015. https://www.zeitzeugen-portal.de/personen/zeitzeuge/siegfried_umbreit/videos/KgOf7hGEIeU (last accessed 18 August 2021)

Sourcing of new military recruits, Ministry for National Education/Main Division Extended Schools. SAPMO-BArch, ZPA, IV 2/2039/201, Bl. 1.

Soviet Draft of a German Peace Treaty – First 'Stalin Note' (March 10, 1952). In: 'Note from the Soviet Foreign Ministry to the American Embassy, Enclosing a Draft for a German Peace Treaty, March 10, 1952'; reprinted in *Documents on Germany, 1944–1959: Background Documents on Germany, 1944–1959, and a Chronology of*

Political Developments affecting Berlin, 1945–1956, pp. 85–7. Washington, DC: General Printing Office. 1959.

Stalin, Joseph. Order No. 55, Moscow, February 23, 1942. In: http://www.ibiblio.org/pha/policy/1942/420223a.html (last accessed 14 July 2021)

Stasi Report. Gegen die Kommunalwahlen (7. Mai) gerichtete, feindliche Aktivitäten. BStU, MfS, ZAIG 3763, Bl. 9–13 (11. Expl.).

Stasi Report. Information an die SED-Führung über eine Petition für mehr Menschenrechte. BStU, MfS, ZAIG, Nr. 2557, Bl. 1–6.

Stasi Report. Reaktion der Bevölkerung auf das SED-SPD-Grundsatzpapier. BStU, MfS, ZAIG, Nr. 4230, Bl. 1–9.

Stoph, Willi, *Direktive des X. Parteitages der SED zum Fünfjahrplan für die Entwicklung der Volkswirtschaft der DDR in den Jahren 1981 bis 1985*. Dietz Verlag. 1981.

Table showing female employment rates. In Segert and Zierke, p. 214.

Table showing income of the GDR population 1950–1988. In: Segert and Zierke, p. 191.

Ten Commandments for the New Socialist Person. 30 July 1958. Issued by the Central Committee of the SED. Section Agitation and Propaganda. Bundesarchiv 183-57163-0001.

Thoralf Johansson's recollections on 'Defence Education in the GDR'. In: Stiftung Haus der Geschichte der Bundesrepublik Deutschland. Zeitzeugenportal. 2013. https://www.zeitzeugen-portal.de/personen/zeitzeuge/thoralf_johansson/videos/tr4mrfp_7TE (last accessed 8 March 2022)

Transcript of a meeting between Honecker and Chernenko in Moscow, 17 August 1984. SAPMO-BArch, DY 30/2380, Doc 104.

Transcript of a phone conversation between Erich Honecker and Helmut Kohl, 19 December 1983. SAPMO-BArch, DY 30, SED Doc 41664.

Transcript of the meeting between Comrade L. I. Brezhnev and Comrade E. Honecker at Crimea on 3 August 1981. SAPMO-BArch, ZPA, J IV 2/2/A-2419.

Ulbricht, Walter. Schreiben vom 1 Dezember 1950 an alle Mitglieder und Kandidaten der SED. Extract in: Judt, p. 478.

Ulbricht's speech at the SED conference in July 1950. Report in TV news programme *Der Augenzeuge* 34/1950. DEFA.

Ulrich Steinhauer's Stasi file. BStU, MfS, AOP 3507/91, Bd. 3, Bl. 212–13.

Ulrike Poppe's recollections on 'Achievements and Problems of the Round Table'. In: Stiftung Haus der Geschichte der Bundesrepublik Deutschland. Zeitzeugenportal. 2013. https://www.zeitzeugen-portal.de/personen/zeitzeuge/ulrike_poppe/videos/lnrFrMFecQw (last accessed 6 July 2022)

'Urlauberschiff in Not'. In: Archiv-Leipziger Volkszeitung, Ressort Magazin, Sektion L/ Leipziger Volkszeitung-Stadtausgabe/Stadtausgabe.

Uwe Schmieder's account of the 10th World Youth Festival. In: https://www.bpb.de/geschichte/deutsche-geschichte/weltfestspiele-73/65333/wie-ein-rausch-und-die-flachtrommel-mit-dabei (last accessed 7 January 2022)

Volksstimme, 17 August 1972.

Vorschlag Walter Ulbrichts zu den Änderungen der Politik der KPD-Politik nach dem Stalin-Hitler Pakt. Russian State Archives for Social and Political History. 495/10a/317,100-102. In: Gleb, Albert, Document 457.

'Was sahen 58 deutsche Arbeiter in Rußland? Bericht der deutschen Arbeiter-Delegation über ihren Aufenthalt in Rußland vom 14. Juli bis zum 28'. Neuer Deutscher Verlag. 1925.

Werner Krolikowski's note about the domestic situation in the GDR of 30 March 1983. In: Przybylski.

Willy Brandt's speech, 16 August 1963. Bundeskanzler-Willy-Brandt-Stiftung Berlin. In: https://www.willy-brandt-biografie.de/wp-content/uploads/2017/08/Rede_Brandt_Mauerbau_1961.pdf (last accessed 15 August 2021)

ZK [Central Committee] Meeting, 26/27 October 1950. In: Central Party Archive IV 2/1/45, Bl. 247, 44, 175.

Articles and other media

Aehnlich, Kathrin. 'Der Leipziger Beataufstand'. MDR. 2016. In: https://www.mdr.de/zeitreise/stoebern/damals/renft220_page-0_zc-6615e895.html (last accessed 25 August 2021)

Aktion Ungeziefer – Vertrieben in der DDR by Sven Stephan. 2020.

Ahrends, Martin et al. 'Todesopfer. Ulrich Steinhauer'. In: Chronik der Mauer. https://www.chronik-der-mauer.de/todesopfer/171329/steinhauer-ulrich?n#footnote1-2 (last accessed 21 July 2022)

Bainbridge, John. 'Die Mauer. The Early Days of the Berlin Wall'. In: *The New Yorker*. 27 October 1962.

Bald, Detlef. 'Sozialgeschichte der Rekrutierung des deutschen Offizierskorps von Reichsgründung bis zur Gegenwart'. In: Sozialwissenschaftliches Institut der Bundeswehr. Berichte. Heft 3. 1977.

Birt, Raymond. 'Personality and Foreign Policy: The Case of Stalin'. In: *Political Psychology*. Vol. 14, No. 4 (December 1993), pp. 607–25.

Der Spiegel. 'Schlicht verschlafen'. In: *Der Spiegel*. 17/1983, 24 April 1983. https://www.spiegel.de/politik/schlicht-verschlafen-a-600eb300-0002-0001-0000-000014021175 (last accessed 27 September 2022)

Bundesregierung, Archiv. 'Honecker: Die Mauer besteht auch noch in 50 und

auch in 100 Jahren'. In: https://www.bundesregierung.de/breg-de/service/
archiv/alt-inhalte/honecker-die-mauer-besteht-auch-noch-in-50-und-auch-in-
100-jahren-905890#:~:text=18.,in%20100%20Jahren%20noch%20bestehen%
E2%80%9C (last accessed 11 November 2022)

Erler, Peter. 'Vom MGB zum MfS/SfS. Die Übernahme sowjetischer Haftorte
und die Entwicklung des Gefängniswesens der DDR-Staatssicherheit in der
ersten Hälfte der 1950er Jahre in Ostberlin. Eine chronologische Übersicht'. In:
Zeitschrift des Forschungsverbundes. 33/2013, pp. 36–56.

Erler, Peter. 'Einsatzplanung der Moskauer KPD-Kader im Frühjahr 1945. Zur
Entstehungsgeschichte der Gruppen „Ackermann", „Sobottka" und „Ulbricht"'.
In: *Zeitschrift des Forschungsverbundes.* 35/2014, pp. 116–27.

Francke, Victor. 'Kanzler-Spion Guillaume Der Tag, der die Bonner Republik
erschütterte'. In: Bonner Rundschau. 23 April 2014. https://www.rundschau-
online.de/region/bonn/kanzler-spion-guillaume-der-tag--der-die-bonner-republik-
erschuetterte-2729772?cb=1664106096562& (last accessed 25 September 2022)

Friedrich-Ebert-Stiftung. 'Die Energiepolitik der DDR: Mängelverwaltung zwischen
Kernkraft und Braunkohle'. Verlag Neue Gesellschaft GmbH Bonn, pp. 5–63.

Gebauer, Ronald, Remy, Dietmar and Salheiser, Axel. 'Die Nationale Volksarmee
(NVA)—Eine Arbeiter- Und Angestelltenarmee? Empirische Befunde Zur
Rekrutierung von Offizieren in Der DDR'. In: *Historische Sozialforschung.* 32,
no. 3 (121) (2007), pp. 299–318.

Hampel, Torsten. 'Die Endlosband'. *Der Tagesspiegel.* 3 January 2009.

Herrmann, Daniel. 'Halle-Neustadt. Späte Besinnung auf die Moderne'. In:
http://www.kulturblock.de/downloads/Halle-Neustadt.pdf (last accessed 7
November 2022)

Hertle, Hans-Hermann. 'Der Weg in die Krise: Zur Vorgeschichte des Volksauf-
standes vom 17. Juni 1953'. In: Bundeszentrale für politische Bildung. https://
www.bpb.de/geschichte/deutsche-geschichte/der-aufstand-des-17-juni-1953/
154325/der-weg-in-die-krise (last accessed 26 July 2021)

Hinz-Wessels, Annette. 'Tourismus'. In: Lebendiges Museum Online, Stiftung Haus
der Geschichte der Bundesrepublik Deutschland. http://www.hdg.de/lemo/
kapitel/geteiltes-deutschland-modernisierung/bundesrepublik-im-wandel/tour-
ismus.html (last accessed 18 August 2021)

Ickler, Günter. 'Erwerbsbeteiligung im Wandel. Entwicklung des Arbeitskräfte-
angebots seit 1950'. In: *Statistische Monatshefte Rheinland-Pfalz Erwerbstätigkeit.*
04/2007, pp. 242–7.

Judt, Matthias. 'Häftlinge für Bananen? Der Freikauf politischer Gefangener aus
der DDR und das "Honecker-Konto"'. In: *Vierteljahrschrift Für Sozial- Und
Wirtschaftsgeschichte.* 94(4), pp. 417–39.

Kerneck, Barbara. 'Traumschule des Sozialismus'. *Die Tageszeitung*. 6 January 1997, p. 15.

Kuppe, Johannes. 'Die Imponderabilien eines Machtwechsels in Diktaturen'. In: Timmermann, Heiner. *Die DDR zwischen Mauerbau und Mauerfall*, pp. 445–9. Lit Verlag. 2012.

Laufer, Jochen. 'Stalins Friedensziele und die Kontinuität der sowjetischen Deutschlandpolitik 1941–1953. Stalin und die Deutschen. Neue Beiträge der Forschung'. In: *Schriftenreihe der Vierteljahrshefte für Zeitgeschichte Sondernummer*, pp. 131–58.
Oldenbourg Wissenschaftsverlag. 2006.

LeMO. Stiftung Haus der Geschichte der Bundesrepublik Deutschland. Various biographies and articles as indicated in notes. https://www.dhm.de/lemo/

Michelmann, Jeannette. 'Die Aktivisten der ersten Stunde. Die Antifa 1945 in der sowjetischen Besatzungszone zwischen Besatzungsmacht und Exil-KPD'. Friedrich-Schiller-University of Jena. In: https://d-nb.info/964631822/34 (last accessed 18 June 2021)

MDR. 'Kaffee gegen Waffen' (06 August 2014). In: https://www.mdr.de/geschichte/ddr/wirtschaft/kaffee-gegen-waffen-aethiopien-100.html (last accessed 25 September 2022)

MDR. 'Puppen und Teddys aus Sonneberg' (27 February 2020). In: https://www.mdr.de/zeitreise/ddr-spielzeug-aus-sonneberg-100.html (last accessed 18 August 2021)

Morré, Jörg. 'Sowjetische Speziallager in Deutschland'. In: Kaminsky, Anna (Ed.): *Orte des Erinnerns. Gedenkzeichen, Gedenkstätten und Museen zur Diktatur in SBZ und DDR*, pp. 610–14. Third ed., Ch. Links Verlag. 2016.

Müller-Güldemeister, Katharina. 'Papa baute Raketen für Stalin: Deutsche Techniker in der Sowjetunion'. In: https://www.suedkurier.de/ueberregional/wissenschaft/Papa-baute-Raketen-fuer-Stalin-Deutsche-Techniker-in-der-Sowjetunion;art1350069,9650454 (30 October 2022)

Niemetz, Daniel. ' "Junkerland in Bauernhand" – Bodenreform in der Sowjetzone'. In: MDR Zeitreise (3 September 2020). https://www.mdr.de/zeitreise/schwerpunkte/1945/bodenreform-fuenfundvierzig-sbz-sachsen-anhalt-thueringen100.html (last accessed 14 July 2021)

Orlow, Dietrich. 'The GDR's Failed Search for a National Identity, 1945–1989'. In: *German Studies Review*. Vol. 29, No. 3 (2006), pp. 537–58.

Ostermann, Christian F.. ' "Keeping the Pot Simmering": The United States and the East German Uprising of 1953'. In: *German Studies Review*. Vol. 19, No. 1 (1996), pp. 61–89.

Reed, Wiebke. 'Wiebke Reed spricht über US-Rocker Dean Reed'. In: *Superillu*

(22 August 2007). https://www.superillu.de/magazin/stars/wiebke-reed/wiebke-reed-ueber-dean-reed-85 (last accessed 9 November 2022)

Schneider, Roland. 'Die friedliche Stimmung stand manchmal auf der Kippe'. In: Rahming, Dörte. *1989 – Die Wende in Rostock – Zeitzeugen erzählen*, pp. 6–9. Wartberg Verlag. 2019.

Schönfelder, Jan. 'Nationale Neubesinnung in der DDR' (4 May 2017). In: https://www.mdr.de/nachrichten/thueringen/kultur/zeitgeschehen/wartburg-refjahr-lutherjahr-ddr-100.html (last accessed 28 May 2022)

Segert, Astrid and Zierke, Irene. 'Gesellschaft der DDR: Klassen – Schichten – Kollektive'. In: Judt, Matthias (Ed.). *DDR-Geschichte in Dokumenten*, pp. 165–224.

Steppat, Timo. F.A.Z. 'Podcast für Deutschland. Ostbeauftragter über AfD-Wähler: "Nach 30 Jahren nicht in der Demokratie angekommen"'. In: *Frankfurter Allgemeine Zeitung*. 28 May 2021. https://www.faz.net/podcasts/f-a-z-podcast-fuer-deutschland/ostbeauftragter-ueber-afd-waehler-nach-30-jahren-nicht-in-der-demokratie-angekommen-17363632.html (last accessed 11 November 2022)

Soziologischer Almanach. Sozialerhebungen des Deutschen Studentenwerks, 1979. In: Geißler, Rainer. Bildungsexpansion und Bildungschancen. Bundeszentrale für politische Bildung. https://www.bpb.de/shop/zeitschriften/izpb/198031/bildungsexpansion-und-bildungschancen/ (last accessed 22 November 2022)

Suckut, Siegfried. 'Die Entscheidung zur Gründung der DDR. Die Protokolle des SED-Parteivorstandes am 4. und 9. October 1949'. In: *Vierteljahreshefte für Zeitgeschichte*. 1/1991.

UNICEF Study. Hohe Wirtschaftskraft Garantiert Keine Bildungsgerechtigkeit. 30 October 2018. In: https://www.unicef.de/informieren/aktuelles/presse/2018/ungleiche-bildungschancen-kinder-in-industrielaendern/177516 (last accessed 26 September 2021)

Walter, Franz. Spiegel Online. 26 August 2007. In: https://www.spiegel.de/geschichte/das-sed-spd-papier-a-947080.html (last accessed 14 June 2022)

Walther, Peter. 'Bilding und Wissenschaft'. In: Judt, Matthias (Ed.). *DDR-Geschichte in Dokumenten*, pp. 225–42.

Werkentin, Falco. 'Die strafrechtliche "Bewältigung" des 17. Juni 1953 in der DDR'. In: Friedrich-Ebert-Stiftung. 'Der 17. Juni 1953, der Anfang vom Ende des Sowjetischen Imperiums'. Büro Leipzig. 1993, pp. 55–61.

Wettig, Gerhard. 'Vorgeschichte und Gründung des Warschauer Paktes'. In: *Militärgeschichtliche Zeitschrift*. 64/2005, pp. 151–76.

Wilke, Manfred. 'Der Honecker-Besuch in Bonn 1987'. In: Deutschland Archiv. Bundeszentrale für politische Bildung. 25 July 2012. https://www.bpb.de/themen/deutschlandarchiv/139631/der-honecker-besuch-in-bonn-1987/ (last accessed 3 June 2022)

Wilke, Manfred. 'Die SED und der Prager Frühling 1968. Politik gegen Selbst-bestimmung und Freiheit'. In: *Die Politische Meinung*, Konrad-Adenauer-Stiftung. 456. 08/2008, pp. 45–51.

Wippermann, Carsten. '25 Jahre Deutsche Einheit. Gleichstellung und Geschlech-tergerechtigkeit in Ostdeutschland und Westdeutschland'. Bundesministerium für Familie, Senioren, Frauen und Jugend. 2015.

Würz, Markus. 'Ausreise'. In: Lebendiges Museum Online, Stiftung Haus der Geschichte der Bundesrepublik Deutschland.

http://www.hdg.de/lemo/kapitel/geteiltes-deutschland-krisenmanagement/niedergang-der-ddr/ausreise.html (last accessed 7 July 2022)

Books

Anonymous. *A Woman in Berlin*. Virago. 2002.

Bahr, Egon and Ensikat, Peter. *Gedächtnislücken zwei Deutsche erinnern sich*. Aufbau Verlag. 2012.

Bollmann, Ralph. *Angela Merkel. Die Kanzlerin und ihre Zeit*. C. H. Beck. 2015.

Boveri, Margret. *Tage des Überlebens: Berlin 1945*. Wjs Verlag. 2004.

Brückner, Bernd. *An Honeckers Seite. Der Leibwächter des ersten Mannes*. Das Neue Berlin. 2014.

Damarius, Helmut. *Unter falscher Anschuldigung: 18 Jahre in Taiga und Steppe*. Aufbau. 1990.

Decker, Gunnar. *1965: Der Kurze Sommer der DDR*. Carl Hanser Verlag. 2015.

Dimitroff, Georgi. *Tagebücher 1933–1943*. Aufbau Verlag. 2000.

Eberlein, Werner. *Geboren am 9. November. Erinnerungen*. Das Neue Berlin. 2002.

Engelberg, Ernst. *Bismarck: Sturm über Europa. Biographie*. Siedler Verlag. 2014.

Ernsting, Stefan. *Der Rote Elvis. Dean Reed – Cowboy – Rockstar – Sozialist*. Fuego. 2014.

Gröttrup, Irmgard. *The Rocket Wife*. Andre Deutsch. 1959.

Frank, Mario. *Walter Ulbricht: Eine Deutsche Biografie*. Verlag Wolf Jobst Siedler GmbH. 2001.

Fulbrook, Mary. *Anatomy of a Dictatorship. Inside the GDR, 1949–1989*. Oxford University Press. 1995.

Fulbrook, Mary. *The Divided Nation: A History of Germany, 1918–90*. Oxford University Press. 1993.

Fulbrook, Mary. *The People's State. East German Society from Hitler to Honecker*. Yale University Press. 2008.

Gieseke, Jens. *Die Stasi. 1945–1990*. Pantheon Verlag. 2011.

Gleb, Albert. *Deutschland, Russland, Komintern – Dokumente (1918–1943). Nach der Archivrevolution: Neuerschlossene Quellen zu der Geschichte der KPD und den deutsch-russischen Beziehungen.* De Gruyter Oldenbourg. 2015.

Hager, Kurt. *Erinnerungen.* Faber & Faber. 1996.

Halder, Fritz. *Kriegstagebuch. Tägliche Aufzeichnungen des Chefs des Generalstabes des Heeres 1939–1942, Bd. 2: Von der geplanten Landung in England bis zum Beginn des Ostfeldzuges.* Kohlhammer. 1963.

Herrnstadt, Rudolf. *Über 'die Russen' und über uns. Diskussion über ein brennendes Thema*, pp. 3–12. Gesellschaft für Deutsch-Sowjetische Freundschaft. 1949.

Hertle, Hans-Hermann. *Damals in der DDR.* Goldmann. 2006.

Hertle, Hans-Hermann. *Der Fall der Mauer. Die unbeabsichtigte Selbstauflösung des SED-Staates.* VS Verlag für Sozialwissenschaften. 2013.

Hitler, Adolf. *Mein Kampf.* Eher Verlag/Zentralverlag der NSDAP. 1943 reprint.

Hoffmann, Dierk. *Otto Grotewohl (1894–1964): Eine politische Biographie.* Oldenbourg Verlag. 2009.

Honecker, Erich. *Aus Meinem Leben.* Dietz Verlag. 1987.

Hortzschansky, Günter and Wimmer, Walter. *Ernst Thälmann. Eine Biographie.* Frankfurt am Main Verlag. 1979.

Iken, Katja, Klußmann, Uwe and Schurr, Eva-Maria (Eds). *Als Deutschland sich neu erfand. Die Nachkriegszeit 1945–1949.* Penguin Verlag. 2019.

Jähner, Harald. *Wolfszeit: Deutschland und die Deutschen 1945–1955.* Rowohlt Taschenbuch Verlag. 2020.

Jöris, Erwin. *Mein Leben als Verfolgter unter Stalin und Hitler.* Selbstverlag. 2004.

Judt, Matthias (Ed.). *DDR-Geschichte in Dokumenten.* Bundeszentrale fur politische Bildung. 1998.

Kardorff, Ursula von. *Berliner Aufzeichnungen Aus den Jahren 1942–1945.* Deutscher Taschenbuch Verlag. 1992.

Kotschemassow, Wjatscheslaw. *Meine letzte Mission, Fakten, Erinnerungen, Überlegungen.* Dietz Verlag. 1994.

Khrushchev, Nikita. *Khrushchev Remembers: The Glasnost Tapes.* Little, Brown & Co. 1990.

Kitchen, Martin. *A History of Modern Germany. 1800 to the Present.* Wiley-Blackwell. 2012.

Knopp, Guido. *Goodbye DDR.* Bertelsmann. 2005.

Koop, Volker. *Armee oder Freizeitclub? Die Kampfgruppen der Arbeiterklasse in der DDR.* Bouvier. 1997.

Krenz, Egon. *Herbst '89.* Edition Ost im Verlag Das Neue Berlin. 2014.

Krenz, Egon. *Wir und die Russen: Die Beziehungen zwischen Berlin und Moskau im Herbst '89.* Das Neue Berlin. 2019.

Laszewski, Chuck. *Rock'n' Roll Radical: The Life & Mysterious Death of Dean Reed.* Bookhouse Fulfillment. 2005.

Lenhardt, Gero and Stock, Manfred. *Bildung, Bürger, Arbeitskraft. Schulentwicklung und Sozialstruktur in der BRD und der DDR.* Suhrkamp. 1997.

Leonhard, Wolfgang. *Die Revolution Entlässt Ihre Kinder.* Kiepenheuer & Witsch. 2019.

Leonhard, Wolfgang. *Meine Geschichte der DDR.* Rowohlt. 2007.

Lippmann, Heinz. *Honecker: Porträt eines Nachfolgers.* Verlag Wissenschaft und Politik. 1971.

Lorenzen, Jan. *Erich Honecker. Eine Biographie.* Rowohlt. 2001.

Loest, Erich. *Durch die Erde ein Riß. Ein Lebenslauf.* Hoffmann Und Campe. 1981.

Loth, Wilfried. *Die Sowjetunion und die deutsche Frage: Studien zur sowjetischen Deutschlandpolitik von Stalin bis Chruschtschow.* Vandenhoeck & Ruprecht. 2007.

MacGregor, Iain. *Checkpoint Charlie: The Cold War, the Berlin Wall and the Most Dangerous Place on Earth.* Constable. 2019.

Mählert, Ulrich. *Kleine Geschichte der DDR.* C. H. Beck. 2010.

Mählert, Ulrich and Stephan, Gerd-Rüdiger. *Blaue Hemden Rote Fahnen. Die Geschichte der Freien Deutschen Jugend.* Leske + Brudrich. 1996.

Menzel, Rebecca. *Jeans in der DDR. Vom tieferen Sinn einer Freizeithose.* Ch. Links. 2004.

Michels, Eckard. *Guillaume, der Spion: Eine deutsch-deutsche Karriere.* Ch. Links. 2013.

Mittag, Günter. *Um jeden Preis: Im Spannungsfeld zweier Systeme.* Das Neue Berlin. 2015.

Mitteregger, Dennis. *Die konstruierte Nation und ihre Manifestierung im Fußball: Die Verbindung von Nationsvorstellung und Fußball bei der Weltmeisterschaft 1974. Ein Vergleich zwischen der Deutschen Demokratischen Republik und der Bundesrepublik Deutschland.* Diplomica Verlag. 2011.

Modrow, Hans. *Ich wollte ein neues Deutschland.* Econ Tb. 1999.

Morré, Jörg. *Hinter den Kulissen des Nationalkomitees: Das Institut 99 in Moskau und die Deutschlandpolitik der UdSSR 1943–1946.* Oldenbourg Verlag. 2010.

Müller, Michael Ludwig. *Die DDR war immer dabei: SED, Stasi & Co. und ihr Einfluss auf die Bundesrepublik.* Olzog. 2010.

Müller, Reinhard. *Menschenfalle Moskau. Exil und stalinistische Verfolgung.* Hamburger Edition. 2001.

Müller-Enbergs, Helmut. *Der Fall Rudolf Herrnstadt. Tauwetterpolitik vor dem 17. Juni.* LinksDruck Verlag. 1991.

Müller-Enbergs, Helmut (Ed.). *Wer war wer in der DDR? Ein Lexikon ostdeutscher Biographien.* CH Links Verlag. 2010.

Mussijenko, Natalija and Vatlin, Alexander. *Schule der Träume: Die Karl-Liebknecht-Schule in Moskau (1924–1938) – Reformpädagogik im Exil.* Klinkhardt, Julius. 2005.

Bibliography

Nendel, Karl. *General der Mikroelektronik: Autobiographie*. Edition Berolina. 2017.

Pastor, Werner. *Willi Budich. Eine biografische Skizze. Ein unbeugsamer Revolutionär aus Cottbus*. Druckerei Lausitzer Rundschau. 1988

Petersen, Andreas. *Die Moskauer: Wie das Stalintrauma die DDR praegte*. S. Fischer. 2019.

Przybylski, Peter. *Tatort Politbüro. Die Akte Honecker*. Rowohlt. 1991.

Rasch, Birgit and Dedio, Gunnar. *Ich. Erich Mielke. Psychogramm des DDR-Geheimdienstchefs*. Sutton Geschichte. 2015.

Roesler, Jörg. *Aufholen ohne Einzuholen. Ostdeutschlands rastloser Wettlauf 1965–2015*. Edition Berolina. 2016.

Schabowski, Günter. *Der Absturz*. Rowohlt Repertoire. 2019.

Schalck-Golodkowski, Alexander. *Deutsch-deutsche Erinnerungen*. Rowohlt. 2000.

Schlögel, Karl. *Terror und Traum: Moskau 1937*. Hanser Verlag. 2008.

Schöne, Jens. *Die DDR. Eine Geschichte des 'Arbeiter- und Bauernstaates'*. Berlin Story Verlag. 2020.

Schroeder, Klaus. *Die DDR: Geschichte und Strukturen*. Reclam. 2019.

Stuhler, Ed. *Margot Honecker. Eine Biographie*. Ueberreuter. 2003.

Thatcher, Margaret. *The Downing Street Years*. HarperCollins. 1993.

Ulbricht, Lotte. *Eine unvergeßliche Reise*. Verlag für die Frau. 1965.

Ulbricht, Lotte. *Mein Leben*. Heyne. 2003.

Van der Heyden, Ulrich, Semmler, Wolfgang and Straßburg, Ralf (Eds). *Mosambikanische Vertragsarbeiter in der DDR-Wirtschaft. Hintergründe, Verlauf, Folgen*. Lit Verlag. 2014.

Weber, Hermann (Ed.). *Deutsche Kommunisten: Biographisches Handbuch 1918 bis 1945*. Karl Dietz Verlag. 2008.

Wilke, Manfred (Ed.). *Anatomie der Parteizentrale – Die KPD/SED auf dem Weg zur Macht*. Akademie Verlag. 2014.

Wolle, Stefan. *Aufbruch nach Utopia. Alltag und Herrschaft in der DDR 1961–1971*. Bundeszentrale für politische Bildung. 2011.

Wolle, Stefan. *Die heile Welt der Diktatur. Alltag und Herrschaft in der DDR 1971–1989*. Bundeszentrale für politische Bildung. 1998.

Acknowledgements

Writing *Beyond the Wall* was intense. There was hardly a minute of the day (or night) when my mind was not drawn to the peculiar vanished country I was researching. People around me coped remarkably well with the fact that I was not only thinking about East Germany around the clock but also talking about it nearly as much. Their willingness to engage, inform, challenge, encourage and support has kept me tethered to the present during my explorations into the past. I would like to start by thanking my incredible editor Casiana Ionita, whose enthusiasm and dedication to the project have been phenomenal. Assistant Editor Edd Kirke and Publicity Manager Corina Romonti completed the dream team at Penguin. My agent Toby Mundy believed in the idea from the start and asked all the right questions. Historians such as Christian Ostermann and Sergey Radchenko gave up their time to share their research with me.

The people who populated the German Democratic Republic became the heart of the book. I would like to thank them for sharing their stories with me; from Inge Schmidt, the accountant who kept track of currencies new and old during the Berlin Blockade, to Erich Kuhfeld and his hair-raising adventures as a plumber onboard a cruise ship. I laughed, cried, marvelled, pondered and listened as they trusted me with their life stories. I would like to thank my family and friends. Their infinite patience, generosity and encouragement has made all the difference. Mutti gave up her weekend to drive me to coffee with Egon Krenz. Papa sneaked into the *Waldsiedlung* with me where we spent the day matching houses to the politicians who once lived there. Nora bought me a Döner in Lichtenberg when I needed one after a difficult visit to the Stasi headquarters. Harry the cat formed a purring loaf on my keyboard when he knew I should take a break. I would like to thank my Twitter followers and all those who come to my talks, read my articles and listen to my podcasts. I am humbled by the amount of people who choose to engage with my work and have found their challenges and praise intensely rewarding. There are many more people I would like to thank for making me think, pause, explain, eat, sleep and reflect. You know who you are and how grateful I am. With my mind still firmly stuck in East German history, it makes me quietly happy that this book is the result of a collective effort.

Index

health sector: emigration of doctors/
nurses, 125, 162, 171, 385–6; in Soviet
Union, 15; spending on, 124; typhus,
50, 52, 59, 65

Helgoland, island of, 101

Helsinki Accords (August 1975), 291–2,
386

Hentschel, Ilse, 52, 124

Herrnstadt, Rudolf, 55–7, 58, 120, 122,
132, 140, 163, 169

Herzog, Lothar, 252–3, 297

Heym, Stefan, 411

Hillers, Marta, 42–3, 69

Hindenburg, Paul von, 11

Hitler, Adolf, 10, 11, 41, 58, 75, 197;
failure of German left to unite
against, 64; *Mein Kampf*, 18; SA
thugs, 14–15; suicide of (30 April
1945), 47

Hitler Youth, 99, 100

Ho Chi Minh, 15, 296

Holliday, Jake, 145

the Holocaust, 118

Honecker, Erich: background of, 96–7,
274–5, 348; and Bavarian loan
(1983/4), 344, 357; becomes First
Secretary (June 1971), 248, 250,
253–4; and the Berlin Wall, 174, 175;
and campaign against Häber, 356–7;
captivity at hands of the Nazis, 96,
97–8, 111, 286, 293; character of, 253;
clashes with Moscow over policy on
FRG, 355–7, 358–9; criticism of in
late-1980s, 383–4; crusade against
'moral decay' of GDR's youth,
211–14, 221, 267; cultural
conservatism of, 201, 210, 212; and
elite life at Vilm, 252–3; and events
of October 1989, 399, 400–1; and fall
of Ulbricht, 241–5, 247–52, 353; as
FDJ's founder/leader, 94, 95–6,
99–100, 102, 201, 210, 256; five-year

plan (1971), 253–9; friendship with
Brezhnev, 210, 212, 215, 241, 244, 250,
328–30; and GDR's Prussian legacy,
351; Gorbachev opposes meeting
with Kohl, 358–9; growing power
circle around, 214–15; Haus
Hubertusstock (hunting residence),
345; 'Honecker Account,' 279, 281;
house on Majakowskiring, 163;
increasing ill-health of, 390, 400; and
inner-German thaw (1970s), 275–6,
322–5, 327, 331–2, 352–3, 355–6; at
International Lenin School, 97; and
Helmut Kohl, 352, 353–6, 357, 359–60;
and 'Luther Year' (1983), 348–9;
material desires as key for, 256–9;
and militarization of society, 314,
318–19; at opening of Fernsehturm,
226; personal life, 98, 210–11, 326;
policy of active detachment from
USSR (1978), 378, 383; and popular
musicians, 265, 267, 268; promise
over living standards (1971), 255, 280,
320, 321, 325, 365; pushes for
industrial modernization, 336–7;
relationship with Gorbachev, 358–9,
377–8, 383, 399; removed as General
Secretary (17 October 1989), 400–1;
removes phrase 'German nation'
from constitution (1974), 254–5;
returns economy to Soviet bloc,
254–5, 274; reverts title back to
General Secretary, 291; ruthless
sidelining of Ulbricht, 249–52, 262;
as Saarlander, 274–5, 348, 360; and
SED-SPD joint paper (1987), 374–5;
seeks to satisfy material desires of
populace, 255, 279, 280, 325, 327, 334,
336–7; selling of prisoners to FRG,
277–9, 282, 387; and Soviet objection
to inter-German dialogue, 331–2, 352–3,
355–6, 358–9; spoken voice of, 96, 253;